'With this book, Healy et al. have launched a giant into the relatively empty space of literature that exists on effective mentoring of geography teachers. The passionate theme that courses through the chapters is of the importance of subject specificity (geography) in approaches to mentoring to ensure that beginning teachers are inducted, not only into generic principles of teaching and learning, but into those which lead to exceptional teachers of geography. The book contextualises the broader picture of contemporary geography education in which mentors find themselves, which addresses the knotty issue of how that could inform approaches to mentoring and highlights the opportunities effective geography mentoring can offer not just the mentee, but importantly and often forgotten, the mentor. Included throughout are strategies, tasks and discussion questions to support readers, particularly geography mentors, to reflect and apply the principles to their own practice. This is a must-read for every geography teacher educator from novices to experts and will be sure to give rise to critical reflection of mentoring practice and productive discussions of ways in which mentoring of beginning teachers can continue to improve.'

Elizabeth Butler, Lead Geography Consultant, Harris Federation

'There has been a welcome knowledge-turn in our schools and with it an increased awareness of the differences between subject disciplines. However, until now, there has been little thought given to the considerations that are needed when mentoring people who are becoming teachers of those distinct subject disciplines. *Mentoring Geography Teachers in the Secondary School* changes that. This book takes a rigorously academic, whilst still practical, look at how we can support people in becoming teachers who are teachers of geography first and foremost. All aspects of the mentor's role is given comprehensive consideration, from the day-to-day such as observing lessons and holding mentoring conversations, to the bigger picture of what sort of geography education these teachers will be providing. I have no doubt that this book will be a valuable guide for anyone who is taking on the role of mentor or those who have been mentoring for some time but without the subject-specific guidance necessary to truly support the next generation of geography teachers entering the profession.'

Mark Enser, Head of Geography and Research Lead and author of
Powerful Geography: Curriculum with Purpose in Practice

'As the political landscape rightly shifts to focus increasingly on the role of mentoring, this book makes a timely and important contribution. It is well grounded in the existing research literature and yet asks the questions of the moment. Bringing together authors who are at the forefront of supporting mentors and mentees, the book firstly develops critical stances around what it means to be a mentor within geography education, bringing questions of disciplinary knowledge and identity to the fore. The book then explores a variety of lived perspectives on the theory and practice of mentors, offering readers ways to consider their own practices. It then supports mentors to draw on research in offering ways to develop geography teachers through processes which develop mentors, mentees and students. In this way the book manages to be both practical and ambitious, enabling all involved in geography education to have agency in a highly dynamic world.'

Dr Mark Hardman, Associate Professor, Centre for Teachers and
Teaching Research, UCL Institute of Education, UK

'*Mentoring Geography Teachers in the Secondary School* is an innovative and insightful must-read. Ideal for new and experienced ITE and ECT mentors, the book encapsulates all aspects required to fully excel in the role of the geography mentor, including lesson observations, subject knowledge, and well-being for both the beginning teacher and mentor. The book is divided into three sections: mentoring in geography education, perspectives and experiences in geography mentoring, and being a geography mentor, taking the reader on a journey of excellence in the realm of geography mentoring. The chapters are deeply rooted in research and pedagogy, posing a variety of typologies and frameworks for success for the reader to interpret how they wish. The book is guaranteed to leave the reader feeling inspired and upskilled in the role of the geography mentor to help shape a new wave of well-rounded and impactful beginning geography teachers.'

Simran Jouhal, Senior Teacher responsible for New and Beginning Teachers and former Head of Geography, The Archer Academy, North London, UK

'The implementation of the Early Career Framework, which articulates increased expectations for school-based subject mentors, means that *Mentoring Geography Teachers in the Secondary School* is both much needed and timely. It provides a comprehensive exploration of what it means to be a geography mentor in a secondary school, which is grounded in both personal experiences and the wider policy landscape. While the authors draw extensively on the research literature and write in an authoritative tone, the chapters are, without exception, highly accessible for busy teachers. Discussion questions, suggestions for further reading and practical tasks punctuate the chapters, combining theory with practice and encouraging readers to take their thinking further. Whether you intend on dipping in or reading cover to cover, this book is an essential text for all those involved in the mentoring of geography teachers in secondary schools.'

Dr Rebecca Kitchen, CPD, Curriculum and Marketing Manager, Geographical Association

'Questioning what "identity" can encompass for teachers and mentors is a theme that runs throughout. This resonated with me since being not just a teacher or a mentor, but also a learner, is key to my identity. This collection of provocative, thoughtful and example-based insights reminds mentors that we will always be learners and that it is through community and collaboration where we can get the best out of early career teachers in our care. I found reading this a cause for deep introspection and somewhat unsettling, and to quote Palombo and Daly in Chapter 14, "indeed it should be". This book is also timely and relevant, not fearing to weave in current affairs and controversial issues. John Morgan's chapter is particularly punchy and necessarily so. After all, tackling contemporary issues is one thing that Geography does best, right?'

Kit Rackley, freelance educator and Associate ITE Tutor and former geography school teacher and mentor based at the University of East Anglia, UK

'This is a book every geography mentor and anyone involved in their training should read. It recognises the complexity and challenges of the role of mentor and is ambitiously wide-ranging in its scope and scale, from the global context to the detailed planning of lessons. The book draws on an impressive range of literature and theoretical thinking and also gives voice to the experiences and views of mentors, tutors and, illuminatingly, of mentees. Throughout the book there is an emphasis on the need for geography mentors to be concerned with what is being taught, how and why. There are practical examples of how a focus on geography can be used to support lesson planning, classroom observation, post-lesson discussion and marking pupils' work. Mentors are encouraged to challenge assumptions and to consider the implications of different ways of conceptualising the important mentor/mentee relationship. The questions for discussion, suggestions for further reading and a range of tasks provide excellent support for professional development helping both mentors and mentees to learn from the process of mentoring.'

Margaret Roberts MBE, former Senior Lecturer in Geography Education, University of Sheffield, UK

'Mentors and the work of mentoring form a vital part of Initial Teacher Education and ongoing teacher professional development. This book provides a comprehensive and rich consideration of mentoring teachers in the context of secondary school geography, bringing together perspectives from both school and university settings. This is a valuable and timely contribution which will be essential reading for both mentors and mentees within and beyond secondary school geography.'

Dr Elizabeth Rushton, Lecturer in Geography Education, King's College London, UK

'This edited volume addresses the complexities of mentoring beginning teachers through the lenses of policy, theory, research and practice, at a range of scales. Acknowledging the pivotal role of subject identity and knowledge(s) in mentoring geography teachers, many of the chapters are also uniquely geographical in orientation. This book is a godsend to geography teacher mentors the world over, given its strong theoretical and empirical underpinnings, and applicability to a range of contexts.'

Dr Tricia Seow, Senior Lecturer, National Institute of Education, Nanyang Technological University, Singapore

'As the role of mentoring in schools seemingly comes to the fore, this is a timely publication. This book will serve as a much-needed addition to the literature – particularly given its consideration of mentoring through a uniquely geographical lens. Reading as a teacher and PGCE mentor, this book provided me with plenty of food for thought through its combination of theoretical underpinnings, discussion of empirical findings and links to implications for classroom practice. With an unashamed focus on mentoring teachers to be the very best *geography* teacher possible, this is a must-read for experienced and new mentors alike.'

Kate Stockings, Head of Geography, Hampstead School

'This excellent and very timely publication offers a detailed analysis of the role of the subject-specialist mentor in schools and very effectively highlights and examines the complex context within which ITE operates. The text helps teachers recognise and adapt to the enhanced profile that mentoring now attracts and offers a thorough grounding in its character, role, challenge and value. It is written in a very personal and engaging style, carefully and thoughtfully guiding the reader to examine and critically reflect upon the pivotal role that the geography mentor undertakes.'

Justin Woolliscroft, former PGCE Programme Director and Lecturer in Education (Geography), University of Hull, UK

MENTORING GEOGRAPHY TEACHERS IN THE SECONDARY SCHOOL

Mentoring Geography Teachers in the Secondary School supports both new and experienced mentors in developing their knowledge and skills in mentoring in geography education. Within the book, chapter authors critically consider how mentoring has been conceptualised and represented in policy and academic debate, as well as examining how mentoring in geography education has been experienced and perceived in practice.

Chapters in the book explore a range of perspectives, experiences and aspects of mentoring geography teachers, including:

- Critical engagement with educational policy and practice
- Perspectives from beginning geography teachers
- Mentoring as a professional development opportunity
- The value of engaging with the geography education community in teacher education
- How mentoring meetings and conversations can support beginning geography teachers in their growth and development

This book is a vital source of support and inspiration for all those involved in developing the next generation of geography teachers. The themes of *justice, agency and voice* – raised and engaged with implicitly and explicitly throughout this edited collection – are of critical importance to mentors, beginning teachers and geography education more broadly in developing and enacting a progressive vision of mentoring.

Grace Healy is Curriculum Director at David Ross Education Trust.

Lauren Hammond is Lecturer in Geography Education at UCL Institute of Education.

Steve Puttick is Associate Professor of Teacher Education at the University of Oxford.

Nicola Walshe is Professor of Education and Head of Department of Curriculum, Pedagogy and Assessment and Professor of Education at UCL Institution of Education.

MENTORING TRAINEE AND EARLY CAREER TEACHERS

Series edited by: Susan Capel, Trevor Wright, Julia Lawrence and Sarah Younie

The **Mentoring Trainee and Early Career Teachers** series are subject-specific, practical books designed to reinforce and develop mentors' understanding of the different aspects of their role, as well as exploring issues that mentees encounter in the course of learning to teach. The books have two main foci: first, challenging mentors to reflect critically on theory, research and evidence, on their own knowledge, their approaches to mentoring and how they work with beginning teachers in order to move their practice forward; and second, supporting mentors to effectively facilitate the development of beginning teachers. Although the basic structure of all the subject books is similar, each book is different to reflect the needs of mentors in relation to the unique nature of each subject or age phase. Elements of appropriate theory introduce each topic or issue, with emphasis placed on the practical application of material. The chapter authors in each book have been engaged with mentoring over a long period of time and share research, evidence and their experience.

We hope that this series of books supports you in developing into an effective, reflective mentor as you support the development of the next generation of teachers.

For more information about this series, please visit: www.routledge.com/Mentoring-Trainee-and-Early-Career-Teachers/book-series/MTECT

Titles in the series

Mentoring Science Teachers in the Secondary School
Edited by Saima Salehjee

Mentoring Teachers in the Primary School
Edited by Kristy Howells and Julia Lawrence, with Judith Roden

Mentoring Geography Teachers in the Secondary School
Edited by Grace Healy, Lauren Hammond, Steve Puttick and Nicola Walshe

Mentoring Teachers in Scotland
Edited by Jane Essex, Sandra Eady, Margaret McColl and Kay Livingston

MENTORING GEOGRAPHY TEACHERS IN THE SECONDARY SCHOOL

A Practical Guide

Edited by Grace Healy, Lauren Hammond, Steve Puttick and Nicola Walshe

LONDON AND NEW YORK

Credit line: © Getty Images

First published 2022
by Routledge
2 Park Square, Milton Park, Abingdon, Oxon OX14 4RN

and by Routledge
605 Third Avenue, New York, NY 10158

Routledge is an imprint of the Taylor & Francis Group, an informa business

© 2022 selection and editorial matter, Grace Healy, Lauren Hammond, Steve Puttick and Nicola Walshe; individual chapters, the contributors

The right of Grace Healy, Lauren Hammond, Steve Puttick and Nicola Walshe to be identified as the authors of the editorial material, and of the authors for their individual chapters, has been asserted in accordance with sections 77 and 78 of the Copyright, Designs and Patents Act 1988.

All rights reserved. No part of this book may be reprinted or reproduced or utilised in any form or by any electronic, mechanical, or other means, now known or hereafter invented, including photocopying and recording, or in any information storage or retrieval system, without permission in writing from the publishers.

Trademark notice: Product or corporate names may be trademarks or registered trademarks, and are used only for identification and explanation without intent to infringe.

British Library Cataloguing-in-Publication Data
A catalogue record for this book is available from the British Library

Library of Congress Cataloging-in-Publication Data
A catalog record has been requested for this book

ISBN: 978-0-367-74321-5 (hbk)
ISBN: 978-0-367-74322-2 (pbk)
ISBN: 978-1-003-15712-0 (ebk)

DOI: 10.4324/9781003157120

Typeset in Interstate
by Newgen Publishing UK

To those who have mentored us – both formally and informally – thank you for your time, patience, guidance and kindness.

CONTENTS

List of illustrations	xiii
List of tasks	xv
Foreword	xvii
Acknowledgements	xx
List of contributors	xxi
An introduction to the series: Mentoring Trainee and Early Career Teachers	xxvi

1 **Introduction: mentoring matters in and for geography education**   1
  Nicola Walshe, Grace Healy, Steve Puttick and Lauren Hammond

SECTION 1   MENTORING IN GEOGRAPHY EDUCATION   11

2 **Navigating the policy landscape: conceptualising subject-specialist mentoring within and beyond policy**   13
  Grace Healy and Nicola Walshe

3 **Mentoring as a spatial practice**   31
  Clare Brooks

4 **What sort of mentoring for what sort of geography education?**   42
  John Morgan

SECTION 2   PERSPECTIVES AND EXPERIENCES IN GEOGRAPHY MENTORING   57

5 **Working with the complexity of professional practice and development**   59
  Phil Wood and Aimee Quickfall

6 **Mentoring as a professional development opportunity**   75
  Richard Bustin

7 Mentoring that makes a difference: perspectives from beginning geography teachers 88
Gemma Collins

8 Mentoring within the geography subject community 102
Alan Kinder

9 Supporting the development of geography mentors – the potential of professional learning at Masters level 119
Ann Childs

SECTION 3 BEING A GEOGRAPHY MENTOR 135

10 Mentoring meetings and conversations supporting beginning teachers in their development as geography teachers 137
Emma Rawlings Smith

11 Planning in geography education: a conversation between university-based tutors and school-based mentors in Initial Teacher Education 156
Faizaan Ahmed, Lauren Hammond, Sara-Anne Nichols, Steve Puttick and Amy Searle

12 Geography lesson observations at the interface between research and practice 173
Steve Puttick

13 Geography and geography education scholarship as a mechanism for developing and sustaining mentors' and beginning teachers' subject knowledge and curriculum thinking 187
Grace Healy

14 Educative mentoring: a key to professional learning for geography teachers and mentors 208
Maria Palombo and Caroline Daly

15 Well-being: theory and practice for beginning geography teachers 224
Emma Clarke, Aimee Quickfall and Shaun Thompson

SECTION 4 CONCLUSION 241

16 Mentoring matters: contributing to a more just tomorrow in geography education 243
Lauren Hammond, Steve Puttick, Nicola Walshe and Grace Healy

Index 252

ILLUSTRATIONS

Boxes

2.1	The Carter review of Initial Teacher Training	18
2.2	National Standards for school-based initial teacher training (ITT) mentors	19
2.3	The Early Career Framework	20
2.4	Ofsted's Initial Teacher Education Inspection Framework	22
5.1	Case study one – Olivia plans a field trip	61
5.2	Case study two – Sami and workload	63
5.3	Case study three – Pat, mentor and being mentored	70
9.1	The aims of the Masters in Teacher Education	125
10.1	Reflecting on learning through enquiry (after Roberts, 2003, and Rawlings Smith, 2020)	150

Figures

2.1	Timeline illustrating key policies which influence mentors of beginning teachers in England 2015 to 2020. Policies above the timeline are explored in detail within the chapter text	17
3.1	Model of ITE practice (source: Brooks, 2021a, p. 204)	37
5.1	A 'possible model' of pedagogic literacy – it is a framework for discussion and reflection, NOT a complete tick-box list to be 'achieved' (source: Cajkler and Wood, 2016, p. 514)	70
8.1	Dimensions of a teacher's professional knowledge (source: BERA, 2014, p. 10)	103
10.1	Positive learning dispositions (adapted from Claxton, 2006, p. 6)	138
10.2	Balancing support and challenge for beginning teachers (adapted from Martin, 1996)	139
10.3	Mentors involvement in the learning cycle	140
10.4	Gibbs' (1988, pp. 53–54) cyclical model of reflection	142
10.5	Framework for learning and reflecting through enquiry (after Roberts, 2003, p. 44)	150
11.1	Critical questions underpinning curriculum-making in geography (informed by the GeoCapabilities approach) (source: Hammond, 2021b)	162

12.1	Possible power/knowledge relations around lesson observations (presented as illustrative possibilities, not organised around rows/columns)	174
14.1	Underpinning principles and characteristics of educative mentoring	209
14.2	An example of a year 8 response to an exam-style question, at the end of a unit on rivers	219
15.1	Research findings using the 'see-saw'	228
15.2	Photographs depicting ITE trainee well-being	229

Tables

2.1	Mentoring and coaching approaches integrated within ECF programmes	21
8.1	A selection of opportunities for mentors and mentees to engage with the geography subject community	108
8.2	Readings and professional development opportunities in relation to mentors in geography education from the GA	110
10.1	Developing reflective practice	143
10.2	From directive to non-directive approaches to lesson feedback	145
10.3	Thinking environment components (adapted from Kline, 1999, p. 35)	147
10.4	Dialogic repertoire for beginning teachers	149
12.1	Aspects of lesson observation pro formas	182
13.1	Shulman's (1986) categorisation of 'content knowledge in teaching' (p. 9)	189
13.2	Three futures for subject knowledge adapted from Young and Muller, 2010 (source: Mitchell, 2017, p. 68)	190
13.3	Subject knowledge development for beginning geography teachers	193
13.4	What types of insights can geography education scholarship provide?	199
14.1	Expansive-restrictive learning environments for teachers (source: Hodkinson, 2009, p. 165)	211

TASKS

5.1	Mentor reflection: expectations of mentor relationships	60
5.2	Reflections on complexity	66
5.3	Change and review	68
6.1	Lesson study	77
6.2	Mentor reflection: leadership opportunities from mentoring	78
6.3	Mentor reflection: subject-specific feedback	81
7.1	Involving your beginning teacher in planning geographical fieldwork	91
7.2	Developing communication in the observation and feedback process	97
8.1	Mentor reflection: conceptualising the subject discipline	104
8.2	Mentor reflection: existing contacts with the wider geography subject community	105
8.3	Mentor reflection: developing subject expertise through the subject community	111
8.4	Mentor reflection: exploring opportunities to engage with the geography subject community	113
9.1	Mentoring reflection: what beliefs do beginning geography teachers have?	127
9.2	Mentor reflection: the balance between generic and subject-specific guidance for beginning geography teachers	130
9.3	Mentor reflection: your own self-study/investigation	131
10.1	Mentor reflection: support and challenge	140
10.2	Mentor reflection: what would you do in this scenario?	145
10.3	Mentor reflection: instructional coaching	146
10.4	Mentor reflection: active listening	147
11.1	Exploring lesson plan pro formas	161
11.2	Co-planning with your beginning teacher	165
11.3	Developing critical awareness of curriculum artefacts	167
12.1	Mentor reflection: experiences of observed lessons	174
12.2	Focussing on 'the geography' in lesson observation feedback	181
12.3	Constructing lesson observation pro formas	183
13.1	Mentor reflection: reflecting on content knowledge for geography teaching	189

13.2	Mentor reflection: reflecting on how geography teachers can remain engaged as geographers	195
13.3	Supporting the development of beginning teachers: how is place characterised and represented in school geography?	196
14.1	Enquiring into teaching about 'development': an educative mentoring approach	215
14.2	Observing a lesson: using the classroom as a site of enquiry	218
15.1	Mentor reflection activity: promoting individual resilience	226
15.2	Mentor reflection activity: preparing for fieldtrips and undertaking fieldwork	230
15.3	Mentor reflection activity: developing relationships	231

FOREWORD

If you are picking up this book as a new geography mentor, then you have stumbled on a rich and rare resource. It is rich in the many intellectual and practical resources through which the authors discuss subject mentoring. It is rare in the aspiration that is embodied in the authors' and editors' adoption of the second person 'you' to whom they address their remarks – a convention that I am inspired to follow. The editors have striven to produce something that is not a distanced commentary, not addressed academic to academic, nor even trainer to trainer. It is, rather, a direct reaching out to experienced geography teachers to think very deeply both about their geography education practice and about their geography mentoring practice, and to draw on rich wells of thought and experience in tightly connecting the two.

It has been a rare privilege for me to read all the chapters in draft. Inevitably, I read it through relevant parts of my own experience – especially leading the initial teacher education of history teachers at the University of Cambridge, a responsibility which, for me, was synonymous with leading and learning from teams of committed and inspirational mentors. This underlines the book's striking similarity with and striking difference from my own experience.

The striking similarity is the central importance of the subject in defining the mentoring role and practice. Generic training of mentors will never do. We can speak of such things as listening, dialogue and reflection in all mentoring roles, but what the mentor listens *to* is a trainee's geographical decision-making, a trainee's geographical assumptions and a trainee's knowledge refracted through numerous small classroom moves, planned and unplanned, all of which have a profound bearing on micro-curricular choices. What the mentor co-constructs in dialogue concerns geography – its spatial and cultural axes, its epistemology, its distinctive ways of seeing, knowing and interpreting the world, and the careful judgement of the new geography teacher about how these intersect with children's prior geographical knowing. What the mentor reflects on is how their own geographical practice is challenged, and the vast reaches of new geographical knowledge and experience that the trainee brings. For school geography, like school history, sees trainees and novice geography teachers arrive with such diverse subject knowledge that mentoring every single beginning teacher is always a fresh education in new geographical scholarship, in new geographical lenses and, often, in whole new territories of content.

The striking difference is exactly the above, all over again. Subjects are structured in distinctive ways, address distinctive questions and are constructed over time through many overlapping stories of disciplinary traditions. The amount and type of issues that are open and up for trainee decision-making – whether choice of example, emphasis of delivery or trajectory of lesson sequence – are quite different even between geography and history, and certainly between geography and modern languages or mathematics. When I listen to expert geography mentors and their leaders and researchers, I feel that strange disorientation of the parallel universe – profound resonances, but equally profound differences: 'no, in my subject the emphasis on this, the significance of that, the way of framing the other, these would all be different'.

Writing now, in England, in 2021, your subject expertise as a geography mentor has never been more important. As many authors in this volume note, we are entering a new and uncertain phase in the development of teachers where, despite policy rhetoric about the importance of subjects and despite a welcome focus on curriculum and subjects by Ofsted, the collective regeneration and renewal of subject-curricular expertise is newly fragile. This is because in new content frameworks advanced for initial teacher education and for early career teachers, the subject dimension feels like a sub-set, like something fitting into and exemplifying broader frameworks concerning such matters as cognitive science of memory. This is dangerous because it fails to foreground two things: (i) the fact that the thing being taught is primary, and (ii) the fact that the thing being taught is not a given.

What is taught to pupils never can be a given in a field such as geography. Rather, all practice is curricular practice. The smallest dilemmas of your trainee will have a micro- or macro-curricular dimension. What geography? Why? Why this bit now? What effect might doing this bit *next* to this bit have? And how will pupils' prior geographies affect their reception? And how can I know? What ethical-intellectual responsibilities do I have in emphasising, choosing or problematising this or that aspect of content, right now? What geographical question is explicit or implicit in the trajectory of how I have planned this lesson sequence? Should it be more or less explicit? What balances of certainty and uncertainty are acceptable? What simplifications are acceptable? How should I challenge the impoverished or unscholarly representation of geography in this textbook or that examination specification? What is the best site for that challenge – my own or local curricular practice? New research? Discussion with geography teachers in contrasting settings?

And as you plan your weekly mentor meetings by drawing on the careful guidance in this volume, or as you set your mentee readings from geographical scholarship to bring into each discussion, you will be serving an even higher good than nurturing this, particular, new geography teacher. You will be playing your part in renewing geography itself, as a school subject and as vital, ongoing, specialist practice that all of society needs in order to shape new questions and new accounts of the world.

Teacher development has to be curriculum development. Curriculum development cannot happen without teacher development. In fact, curriculum development is profoundly social and relational in all its phases. It speaks to all the sources of knowledge production that feed into the discipline(s) and its school-mediated versions. All pupils in future will need inspirational, emancipatory and challenging geography and the only way that can happen is if teachers take collective responsibility for its renewal – sharing, comparing and challenging one another's curricular work and holding it up for scrutiny in the light of new scholarship, wider culture and teachers' own, persistent enquiry into their own practice.

As a geography mentor in a school setting, you are not preparing trainees, like apprentices, just to enact a craft (although elements of that, of course, do figure). Rather, you are preparing them to enter a vibrant intellectual community. You are preparing them to assume responsibility for keeping it vibrant through their own future mentoring, management, leadership and curriculum design. This book will help you to conceptualise the practical and intellectual complexities of this challenge, and so to navigate manageable pathways through them.

Christine Counsell

ACKNOWLEDGEMENTS

The editors share their sincere gratitude with the chapter authors who contributed their time and expertise to this book.

We are also very grateful to the following individuals, groups and organisations for granting permission to reproduce material in the following chapters:

Chapter 3. Taylor & Francis Group for the figure from: *Initial Teacher Education at Scale*, Clare Brooks. Copyright (2021) Routledge. Reproduced by permission of Taylor & Francis Group.

Chapter 5. Taylor & Francis Group for the figure from Cajkler, W., and Wood, P., 2016. Lesson study and pedagogic literacy in initial teacher education: Challenging reductive models. *British Journal of Educational Studies, 64*(4),503–521.

Chapter 8. British Educational Research Association, for the figure from: BERA, 2014. *Research and the Teaching Profession: Building the capacity for a self-improving education system.* London: BERA. Copyright BERA.

Chapter 13. David Mitchell, for the table from: Mitchell, D., 2017. Geography curriculum making in changing times. (PhD thesis). University College London.

Chapter 14. Taylor & Francis Group for the table from: *Changing Teacher Professionalism*, by Heather Hodkinson. Edited by S. Gewirtz, P. Mahony, I. Hextall and A. Cribb. Copyright (2009) by Routledge.

CONTRIBUTORS

Faizaan Ahmed is a geography teacher and Head of Research at Oaks Park High School, a secondary comprehensive in London. Faizaan has held several positions, including Head of Geography, Head of Initial Teacher Training, and Lead Mentor at the UCL Institute of Education Geography PGCE course. Faizaan's academic expertise lies in educational philosophy and theory and he has recently completed a Masters in Philosophy of Education at UCL. Faizaan's current interests are focussed on investigating the challenges presented by school attainment data.

Clare Brooks is Professor of Education and Pro-Director, Education at UCL Institute of Education in London. Her background is in geography education: as a former geography teacher in East London, then as a geography educator developing both initial and continuing teacher education programmes at UCL Institute of Education. Her research has been in the area of geography teacher subject identity and subject expertise and more recently on high-quality teacher education at scale. Until recently she was Co-Chair of the International Geographical Union Commission for Geography Education, and editor of their book series, and Chair for the UK-based Geography Education Research Collective.

Richard Bustin is Head of Geography at Lancing College, UK, having previously worked as a geography teacher and Deputy Headmaster. He regularly works with beginning teachers, both as a mentor and visiting lecturer to PGCE courses. He has published widely; his doctorate on GeoCapabilities became the focus of his book: *Geography Education's Potential and the Capabilities Approach: GeoCapabilities and Schools*, which won the publisher's award from the Geographical Association in 2020. He presents regularly to teachers on a number of topics, including leading the geography 'KnowHow' webinar series for Key Stage 3 teachers, and is on the Editorial Board of *Teaching Geography* journal.

Ann Childs completed her PhD in chemistry at Birmingham University in 1982 and then trained to be a science teacher at Oxford University. She taught for 11 years in Oxfordshire and in Sierra Leone for Voluntary Services Overseas (VSO). During her work as a teacher in Oxfordshire she mentored beginning science teachers on the Oxford Internship Scheme. She took up her current post as an Associate Professor in Science Education in 1997 where she now teaches on the PGCE and is director of the Masters in Teacher Education. Her key research interests are in the professional development of science teachers.

Emma Clarke has taught in mainstream primary schools for almost 18 years and now teaches on a primary PGCE course. Her interests include research methodologies, approaches to managing behaviour, and challenging behaviour in primary schools. Her PhD thesis considered the tensions experienced by teaching assistants in mainstream primary schools when managing behaviour. She has presented her research nationally and internationally, as well as publishing in both books and peer-reviewed journals.

Gemma Collins is a Senior Lecturer in Geography Education at the University of Birmingham, UK. A former secondary-school teacher, ITE mentor and head of department, Gemma is now a teacher educator, working with student teachers completing the Postgraduate Diploma in Education, and supervising teacher-researchers completing the MA Teaching Studies. As well as a research interest in threshold concepts in geography and geography education, Gemma's current research focusses on the transition between school and academic geography, and the role that initial teacher education plays in strengthening that transition. As part of this research, she works closely with the School of Geography, Earth and Environmental Sciences at the University of Birmingham, helping to connect local schools with academic researchers.

Christine Counsell is an education consultant and Director of *Opening Worlds*, a primary curriculum company. She led the secondary PGCE programme for history at the University of Cambridge for 19 years, a course which she describes as 'school-led at the subject level'. Christine has been a Director of Education of a multi-academy trust where she founded a new SCITT with a strong emphasis on subject-specificity. Alongside her current curriculum and teacher development work, she serves on the boards of David Ross Education Trust, Ark Curriculum Plus and Now Teach.

Caroline Daly is Professor of Teacher Education and Director of the Centre for Teachers and Teaching Research at the UCL Institute of Education, where she teaches and researches in teacher education and professional learning for early career teachers. She taught in secondary schools before teaching on the PGCE programme at the Institute of Education and leading the Master of Teaching programme. In recent years, Caroline has led teacher education development projects with a number of universities in England and Wales. Her research has investigated the role of digital technologies in professional learning, mentor learning and school factors that affect teacher development. Caroline is a Fellow of the International Professional Development Association

Lauren Hammond is Lecturer in Geography Education at UCL Institute of Education (IOE), where she co-leads the secondary geography PGCE, convenes an undergraduate module for students in UCL's geography department 'geography education', and supervises students at Masters and Doctoral level. At the IOE, Lauren has also worked in mentoring and partnership across Initial Teacher Education programmes, and retains a research interest in mentoring. Lauren is committed to researching with, and for, young people and her research straddles the fields of children's geographies, children's rights, geography and education. Lauren is SFHEA (Senior Fellow of the Higher Education Academy) and FRGS (Fellow of the Royal Geographical Society). Prior to working in academia, Lauren was a secondary-school geography teacher in the UK and Singapore.

Grace Healy is the Curriculum Director at David Ross Education Trust. As part of this role, she leads the Trust's curriculum and teacher development work and a curriculum team

List of contributors   xxiii

of Trust-wide subject leaders. She is also the Director of a newly designated Teaching School Hub. In her previous role, she led the geography subject community across a trust of 13 primary and secondary schools and contributed to the leadership of a SCITT. She is currently undertaking a PhD at UCL Institute of Education. Grace is a corresponding editorial board member of *Teaching Geography*, chair of the Geographical Association's Teacher Education Phase Committee, and Honorary Secretary (Education) for the Royal Geographical Society (RGS). She is Treasurer for the Geography Education Research Collective (GEReCo) and the RGS's Geography and Education Research Group. She also serves on British Educational Research Association's Publication Committee and on the editorial boards of *The Curriculum Journal* and the *London Review of Education*.

Alan Kinder is a former geography teacher, field studies officer and teacher educator and now leads the professional association for teachers of geography, the Geographical Association (GA). As GA Chief Executive, Alan's work lies at the intersection of policy, practice and research. It involves advocating geography education across the sector and with the government and its agencies, representing the views of teachers of geography and developing the GA's national and international work to support high-quality geography in schools.

John Morgan taught geography in schools and colleges in London before leading the Secondary Geography PGCE course at the University of Bristol. He worked at the Institute of Education (London) and Futurelab before taking up his current role as Professor of Education at the University of Auckland, where he is Head of the School of Critical Studies in Education. His most recent books are *Teaching Secondary Geography as if the Planet Matters* (Routledge, 2012) and *Culture and the Political Economy of Schooling: What's left for Education?* (Routledge, 2018).

Sara-Anne Nichols is a geography teacher at Didcot Girls' School, South Oxfordshire, where she is currently also Second in Charge of Geography, responsible for Key Stage 3. Sara-Anne recently completed an MA in Teaching Studies at the University of Birmingham; the aim of her research was to investigate and interrupt the forgetting curve and improve student confidence. Sara-Anne's academic interests include metacognition techniques and interleaving Key Stage 4 assessments; she has also published an article through the Geographical Association on creative transition activities. Sara-Anne has a range of mentoring experience, from NQT to PGCE, whilst working alongside Oxfordshire Teaching Schools Alliance and the University of Oxford.

Maria Palombo has been a Senior Teaching Fellow since 2016 at UCL Institute of Education and currently works on the Geography Teach First and SCITT Geography programmes. Prior to this, she was a Head of Geography and Assistant Headteacher in an 11-18 inner-city school in London. Maria's current interests are in mentoring in geography ITE, which has led to her conducting a national survey of geography mentors, and contributing to articles in *Teaching Geography* and workshops at the Geographical Association Annual Conference.

Steve Puttick is Associate Professor of Teacher Education at the University of Oxford, Fellow of St Anne's College and subject lead for Geography PGCE. He is a qualified geography teacher and was previously the head of department at a comprehensive secondary school in Oxfordshire, and Head of Programmes at Bishop Grosseteste University,

Lincoln. Steve serves on the editorial board of the journal *Geography*, and is Chair of the Geography Education Research Collective (GEReCo with UK IGU-CGE).

Aimee Quickfall is Head of Programmes for Primary and Early Years Initial Teacher Education at Bishop Grosseteste University. She was a primary and early-years teacher for 15 years and loves helping others to achieve their dream of being a life-changing teacher; her trainees are some of the loveliest people on Earth. Aimee's current research interests are the experiences of teachers who are also mothers, well-being and workload for teachers and teacher trainees, and the experiences of students on her programmes. Her most frequently used methodologies/methods are narrative and feminist approaches, life-history interviews and discourse analysis.

Emma Rawlings Smith is a Lecturer and PGR Lead in the School of Educational Sciences at Bangor University and she spends her time focussing on research in teacher education. Emma previously worked at the University of Leicester as PGCE Geography Lead and School-Centred Initial Teacher Training Academic Lead. In 2009, she gained Chartered Geographer accreditation from the Royal Geographical Society (with IBG) and is now an assessor for Chartered Geographers and the Geographical Association's Enhanced Professional Award. She leads the NASBTT Networks Live sessions for secondary geography, providing valuable insight and learning for PGCE students and Early Career Teachers. Emma is a member of the *Teaching Geography* Editorial Board and the Geography Education Research Collective (GEReCo). Her research focusses on mentoring, reflective practice, professional learning and place pedagogy, and she is an advocate of participatory action research, lesson study and Q methodology.

Amy Searle is a geography teacher and the whole-school Curriculum Coordinator: Research and Development Lead at Burford School in Oxfordshire. She is in her eighth year of teaching and has experience of being an NQT and PGCE mentor, working closely with the University of Oxford. Amy has a passion for teaching and learning and has used this energy to successfully complete an MA in Teaching Studies at the University of Birmingham. Her research explored the effect of skills-based retrieval practice on student confidence in GCSE Geography. Amy peer-reviews articles written by sixth-form and undergraduate geographers for *Routes: The Journal for Student Geographers*.

Shaun Thompson is a Senior Lecturer at Bishop Grosseteste University. He teaches across primary Initial Teacher Education programmes, leading on mathematics and special educational needs. Shaun gained a wealth of experience teaching and leading in schools, before moving into higher education. His research interests are around mathematical problem-solving and strategies to support autistic pupils. He is also involved in international comparative research exploring the well-being of trainee teachers and considering strategies to support and develop trainees' well-being. He has presented his work both nationally and internationally and has contributed to a variety of publications.

Nicola Walshe is Head of the Department of Curriculum, Pedagogy and Assessment and Professor of Education at the UCL Institute of Education. Previously she gained a PhD in Glaciology and taught and worked as Head of Geography in three secondary schools in the UK before going on firstly to teach and lead the Geography PGCE course at Cambridge University, and then to become Head of the School of Education and Social Care at Anglia Ruskin University. Nicola is Secretary of the Geography Education

Research Collective (GEReCo) and co-convenor of the Environmental and Sustainability Education Research (ESER) network in the European Educational Research Association (EERA). Her research is predominantly in the field of geography education, with a particular focus on high-quality teacher education practices in environmental and sustainability education and utilising technology for teacher development. Recently, she has been exploring pedagogies at the intersection of nature, the arts and well-being; her AHRC-funded project, Eco-Capabilities, examines the processes by which creative, nature-based practice supports the well-being of primary-school children.

Phil Wood is Professor of Educational Change at Bishop Grosseteste University, Lincoln, where he is head of the PhD programme. His main research interests centre on the development of learning organisations as a source of change, understood through the lenses of complexity theories and process philosophy.

AN INTRODUCTION TO THE SERIES
Mentoring Trainee and Early Career Teachers

Mentoring is a very important and exciting role. What could be better than supporting the development of the next generation of subject teachers? A mentor is almost certainly an effective teacher, but this doesn't automatically guarantee that he or she will be a good mentor, despite similarities in the two roles. This series of practical workbooks covers primary mentoring and most subjects in the secondary curriculum. They are designed specifically to reinforce mentors' understanding of different aspects of their role, for mentors to learn about and reflect on their role, to provide support for mentors in aspects of their development and to enable them to analyse their success in supporting the development of beginning subject teachers (defined as trainee and early career teachers). This book has two main foci: first, the focus is on challenging mentors to reflect critically on theory, research and evidence, on their own knowledge, how they work with beginning teachers, how they work with more experienced teachers and on their approaches to mentoring in order to move their practice forward. Second, the focus is on supporting mentors to effectively facilitate the development of beginning teachers. Thus, some of the practical activities in the books are designed to encourage reflection, whilst others ask mentors to undertake activities with beginning teachers.

This book can be used alongside generic and subject books designed for student and early career teachers. These books include Capel, Leask and Younie's (2019) *Learning to Teach in the Secondary School: A Companion to School Experience*, which deals with aspects of teaching and learning applicable to all subjects, and Cremin and Burnett's (2018) *Learning to Teach in the Primary School*. Further, the generic books are complemented by three series: Learning to Teach [subject] in the Secondary School: A Companion to School Experience; A Practical Guide to Teaching [subject] in the Secondary School; and Learning to Teach in the Primary School. These books are designed for student teachers on different types of initial teacher education programmes (and indeed a beginning teacher with whom you are working may have used or is currently using them). However, these books are proving equally useful to tutors and mentors in their work with student teachers, in relation both to the knowledge, skills and understanding the student teacher is developing and to some tasks that mentors might find it useful to support a beginning teacher to do. They are also supported by a book designed for early career teachers, *Surviving and Thriving in the Secondary School: The NQT's Essential Companion* (Capel et al., 2019) as well as *Starting to Teach in the Secondary School: A Companion for the Newly Qualified Teacher* (Capel et al., 2004). These titles cover material not generally needed by student teachers on an initial teacher education course, but which is needed by early career teachers in their school work and early career.

The information in this book should link with the information in the generic text and relevant subject book in the three series in a number of ways. For example, mentors might want to refer a beginning teacher to read about specific knowledge, understanding and skills they are focussing on developing, or to undertake tasks in the book, either alone or with their support, then discuss the tasks. It is recommended that you have copies of these books available so that you can cross- reference when needed.

In turn, the books complement a range of resources on which mentors can draw (including other mentors of beginning teachers in the same or other subjects or age phases, other teachers and a range of other resources including books, research articles and websites).

The positive feedback on Learning to Teach and the related books above, particularly the way they have supported the learning of student teachers in their development into effective, reflective teachers, encouraged us to retain the main features of that book in this series. Like teaching, mentoring should be research- and evidence-informed. Thus, this series of books introduces theory, research and professional evidence-based advice and guidance to support mentors as they develop their mentoring to support beginning teachers' development. The main focus is the practical application of material. Elements of appropriate theory introduce each topic or issue, and recent research into mentoring and/or teaching and learning is integral to the presentation. Tasks are provided to help mentors identify key features of the topic or issue and reflect on and/or apply them to their own practice of mentoring beginning teachers. Although the basic structure of all the subject books is similar, each book is different to reflect the needs of mentors in relation to the unique nature of each subject.

The chapter authors in the books have been engaged with mentoring over a long period of time and are aiming to share research/evidence and their experience. We, as series editors, are pleased to extend the work in initial teacher education to the work of mentors of beginning teachers. We hope that this series of books supports you in developing into an effective, reflective mentor as you support the development of the next generation of subject teachers.

Finally, we would like to remember Trevor Wright and thank him for his contribution as an editor of the series.

Susan Capel, Julia Lawrence, Trevor Wright and Sarah Younie

1 Introduction

Mentoring matters in and for geography education

Nicola Walshe, Grace Healy, Steve Puttick and Lauren Hammond

Introduction

Mentoring is a significant part of how teachers are educated. It is hard to overstate how much it *matters* in and for geography education. Mentoring matters to the development of the next generation of those working in geography education – including student teachers, early career teachers, established teachers and heads of department, as well as those working in Initial Teacher Education (ITE) and researching in the field. Mentoring also matters to the recruitment and retention of geography teachers; to the professional development of those who mentor; to the future of geography education; and ultimately to ensuring that the children and young people who are taught engage with the best possible geographical education.

Mentoring has been conceptualised in many different ways, leading Colley (2003) to claim that as a practice, mentoring is 'ill-defined, poorly conceptualized and weakly theorized' (p. 13). Yet Kemmis et al. (2014) suggest that this is not 'so much about a lack of theories, but rather a plurality of theories' (p. 154). Indeed, various models and approaches to mentoring have been discussed (e.g. Maynard and Furlong, 1995; Langdon and Ward, 2015; Hobson, 2016; Lofthouse, 2018), and whilst the policy and spatial context shape the practice of mentoring (Brooks, 2022; Healy and Walshe, 2022), different views of mentoring, such as 'mentoring as supervision, mentoring as supporting and mentoring as collaborative self-development' (Kemmis et al., 2014, p. 162), often coexist within countries and contexts. There is also general agreement that mentoring is distinct from coaching due to the significance placed on mentors being experienced in, and knowledgeable about, the role the mentee is undertaking to enable them to set targets with, assess and support the mentee (Lofthouse, 2019).

Three influential models of mentoring are: the apprenticeship model (learning to teach under supervised practice), the competency model (learning to teach through attention to predefined competencies) and the reflective practitioner model (learning to teach where reflection on practice is at the heart of the learning process) (Maynard and Furlong, 1995). Maynard and Furlong (1995) argue that each model is partial and inadequate for contributing to a beginning teacher's development by itself, but that by drawing together the different models, this allows for 'a view of mentoring' (p. 78) that provides scope for mentors to be responsive to beginning teachers. Throughout the book, chapter authors draw upon, implicitly and explicitly, various models and approaches to mentoring, and illustrate how these can manifest themselves in respect to certain aspects of mentoring, or in relation to the particular stages of beginning teachers' development. Whilst models different from those set out by Maynard and Furlong (1995) might be used, the principle of critically drawing upon these models and approaches to shape and reflect upon your mentoring practices can support and inform your mentoring of beginning geography teachers.

Within this book, chapter authors from a range of school and university-based contexts, predominantly (but not exclusively) geography educators in England, engage with a range of these different approaches to mentoring, exploring the importance of knowledge, experience and the desire to support beginning teachers' and other colleagues' professional development through mentoring. In the book, chapter authors often draw upon the richness of their own geographical context through critical engagement with policy, theory, practice, research and experience (and the relationships between them). If you are reading this book from beyond the same spatial-temporal contexts, we hope these arguments and analyses also support you to critically reflect upon your own expertise, experience and context: what similarities do you notice across these contexts? What unique external conditions are shaping your mentoring?

When we think of 'who' is being mentored, there is a wide range of terminology that is used in practice, literature and policy; for example, novices, interns, trainee teachers, student teachers, learner teachers, beginning teachers, newly qualified teachers (NQTs) and early career teachers (ECTs). In this book, chapter authors use *beginning teachers* as an all-encompassing term when discussing the mentoring of geography teachers. However, where authors refer to research, theory and experiences that apply to a particular stage of teacher education, this is reflected in the use of trainee and student teachers for mentoring within ITE, and ECTs for mentoring within the first two years after that. The language and meaning ascribed to mentors matter too, with chapter authors in this book referring to mentors, school-based mentors and teacher educators, and also addressing mentors directly as the reader.

In this introductory chapter, we set out the context and significance of mentoring in geography education before examining the roles of theory and practice in mentoring in geography education. Following this, we present an overview of the three sections of *Mentoring Geography Teachers in the Secondary School* – section one: Mentoring in geography education; section two: Perspectives and experiences in geography mentoring; and section three: Being a geography mentor. In doing so, we begin to set out the importance of the academic and policy case for the value of mentoring in geography education, alongside the embodied and personal nature of mentoring.

Introducing the case for subject mentoring

Whilst the significance of school-based mentoring is increasingly internationally recognised in education policy (e.g. England; Carter Review, 2015; DfE, 2016, Darling-Hammond, 2017), there has been limited attention to the role and importance of subjects in school-based mentoring (Hammond et al., 2019). Using the English context as an example, we now introduce the case for subject mentoring. If you are reading from outside of the English context (or indeed after a few years past the book's publication in England), we encourage you to reflect on the specifics of your context. In England, whilst the Early Career Framework (ECF: DfE, 2019) provides a focus on the mentoring and development of early career teachers, it can be seen to neglect the significance of subject-specific support (Rowe, 2019). However, within the geography education and geography teacher education communities, it is important to recognise, and celebrate, that a strong argument has been made for the importance of geography to teaching and teachers (Brooks, 2017; Lambert, 2015; 2018; Healy et al., 2020).

Through drawing on the discipline of geography, their education as a geography teacher, communities of practice of which they are a part of, and subject associations and learned societies (Kinder, 2022), mentors can support less-experienced colleagues, and also continue to develop their knowledge and practice as teachers of geography. Brooks' (2016, p. 12) narrative research with geography teachers found that geography was a fundamental element of what she conceptualised as a 'professional compass', which enabled the teachers to navigate the institutions and policy contexts that they worked within, and to make informed decisions about their teaching and careers more broadly. Here, we echo Brooks' (2017) suggestion that the notion of a meaningful professional compass is helpful not only for teaching geography, but also for mentoring in geography education.

Whilst this book makes a case for subject-specific mentoring and turning to geography education discourse, chapter authors also engage with research and debate situated within and at the boundaries of the disciplines of geography and education more broadly. For example, Morgan (2022) engages with the work of David Harvey throughout his chapter as he explores the question: *What sort of mentoring for what sort of geography education?*, whilst Palombo and Daly (2022) begin their chapter by outlining the principles and characteristics of educative mentoring, before then applying this approach in geography education. The nature of the discipline and school subject of geography also means there can be value in looking to discourse from other subject-specialist communities, because of the curricula overlap and interplay that exist with other subject areas. For example, alongside drawing on literature exploring the knowledge base of teacher educators, Childs (2022) brings our attention to science education discourse that provides rich examples of mentors developing their practice.

In all routes into teaching, mentoring is critical to beginning teachers' experience and development as mentors are the teachers' primary point of contact and support during their school placements. However, as teacher education in England has become increasingly fragmented and there has been an increase in school-led provision (DfE, 2017; Whiting et al., 2018; Biddulph and Kinder, 2020), the role and influence of subject mentoring have expanded. The remit of mentors is also increasing in England through the introduction of the Early Career Framework (ECF); the DfE (2019) sets out that the ECF will 'underpin an entitlement to training and support for early career teachers' (p. 5). These changes in both policy and teacher education landscapes mean that it is of the utmost importance that mentors are supported and developed in their subject mentoring. In examining this further, we now move on to critically consider the importance of both theory and practice in mentoring and mentor development.

The role of theory and practice in mentoring and mentor development

In arguing for the value and significance of partnerships between schools and HEIs (higher education institutes) in (initial) teacher education, Brooks and McIntyre (2020, n.p.) assert that educating is:

a professional, thoughtful and intellectual endeavour that should draw on research as well as practical experience and that educators should use research as a matter of course to underpin, challenge and illuminate their practice.

We hope this book provides opportunities for you, as a mentor, to reflect on your own practice through theoretically informed and research-engaged analyses. One example of the use of theory to illuminate practice is through Palombo et al.'s (2020) use of Bernstein's (2000, p. 168) conceptualisation of 'reservoirs' of knowledge and 'repertoires' of practice to consider what strong subject mentoring in geography looks like. Palombo et al. (2020) argue that mentors should support mentees to draw upon the reservoir that is geographical knowledge to inform, critically reflect upon and expand their repertoire of practice. This is an ambitious and challenging vision for mentoring: as a mentor you can enable mentees to benefit from the research and teaching of others within the wider geography education community. This kind of mentoring seeks the longer-term development of beginning geography teachers' professional agency beyond the limits of their own experience (Healy, 2021). The influence of mentors also has the potential to extend beyond the formal period of mentoring. As a mentor, you have an opportunity to cultivate an ethos that enables geography teachers to understand the importance of reflecting and learning throughout their career in ways that will sustain and nourish their subject expertise (Brooks, 2016).

Throughout this book we want to highlight learning opportunities for you as a mentor to 'deepen and enrich your professional knowledge and research-engagement' (Burn and Mutton, 2018, p. 61) which also enables you to support mentees' induction into the wider conversations within the field of geographical education (Brooks, 2018). As you mentor you can help beginning teachers develop 'an informed understanding of the theoretical and research-based principles that underpin current practices' (Burn and Mutton, 2018, p. 60), which provides them with the capacity to interrogate their own practice and adapt to the different school contexts they might find themselves teaching within throughout their professional career.

Introducing *Mentoring Geography Teachers in the Secondary School*

Mentoring Geography Teachers in the Secondary School comprises 14 substantive chapters organised into three key sections. Across each section of the book, chapter authors conclude their chapters with points for discussion. These discussion points either draw upon specific points or more holistically connect aspects of the chapter together to leave you with questions to frame your thinking and reflection after reading the chapter. Within the second and third sections of the book, you will find tasks that link directly to the text they are positioned by. Tasks have been constructed carefully by chapter authors to provide opportunities for you to reflect on your own knowledge and practice in mentoring geography teachers, supporting you to invest in your own professional development as a mentor and helping you continue to expand – while also critically reflecting on – the ways in which you mentor beginning geography teachers.

Within the first section, **Mentoring in geography education**, authors draw on research and policy to examine what it means to be a mentor in geography education. In the first chapter,

Grace Healy and Nicola Walshe examine how mentors can critically engage with policy to navigate the professional landscape. Exploring the complex relationships between mentors as policy subjects and actors through four policy documents in England, they argue for an approach towards mentoring that is critically engaged with the wider educational policy landscape. The theme of policy landscape is continued in Clare Brooks' chapter, which examines mentoring as a spatial practice. She argues that the localised settings in which teacher education takes place are influenced by a range of scales, from individual experiences, immediate contextual influences, national policies and international debates. Drawing on a model of influences of ITE as a spatial practice, Clare explores what spatial knowledges are needed for the effective mentoring of beginning teachers and outlines implications for mentors. In the final chapter of Section one, John Morgan poses the question *what sort of mentors are needed for what sort of geography education?*, arguing that to *persevere with geography* is necessary to address what he describes as the triple crisis faced by geography teachers; the environment, economy and social division. Setting out a typology of mentoring approaches, John argues that to find ways to represent how the world works, geography educators need sustained engagement with theory which, in turn, should be nurtured by the mentor.

The second section critically explores **Perspectives and experiences in geography mentoring,** drawing upon the voices of mentors, beginning teachers and those from the wider subject community. Phil Wood and Aimee Quickfall begin this section by examining the use of mentoring as a core process through which professionals can support each other to develop their practice. They highlight the epistemic and practice-based environment in which mentoring occurs, critically exploring the assumptions we make about what it means to be a teacher, and the process of practice development. To consider these questions, Phil and Aimee employ the lens of *critical processual complexity*, and, through the use of the pedagogic black box and pedagogic literacy, they show how a flexible and critical approach to mentoring might be established. In the following chapter, Richard Bustin examines mentoring as a professional development opportunity, suggesting that it can bring a range of advantages, including increased professional competency, opportunities for reflective practice, collaborative learning, leadership and personal benefits for mentors. Richard argues that by engaging in geography education scholarship, particularly around ideas of curriculum thinking, mentors can increase their own understanding of these complex issues, improving their own professional development, and guiding the beginning teachers they mentor. Moving towards a focus on mentees, in the third chapter in this section Gemma Collins foregrounds the voices of seven beginning teachers of geography as they reflect on their experiences of being mentored. Reflecting on how mentors helped them to successfully negotiate the liminal space and troublesome moments in learning to teach geography, Gemma explores what beginning teachers valued as making a difference to them, considering both tasks and targets that mentors set, and also reflecting on how successful mentor/mentee relationships might foster trust and facilitate continuous professional dialogue, reflection and critical engagement for both mentor and mentee. In the next chapter, Alan Kinder returns to the importance of geography, inviting readers to consider the extent to which high-quality geography teaching and mentoring is founded on sustained engagement with the wider subject-specialist community. In particular, Alan explores the ways in which the subject community intersects with the practice of mentoring, considering the potential of the subject community to influence the professional identity, understanding of purpose and professional practice of mentor and mentee. In the final chapter of Section 2, Ann Childs illustrates one approach to professional development for mentors through a rich description of a part-time Masters programme. Beginning by setting out key challenges identified in the literature around the expertise and education of school-based geography mentors, she describes approaches to teacher educator learning. Ann then presents the structure, rationale and theoretical underpinning of this Masters in Teacher Education, drawing on the experiences of running this programme to suggest a number of tasks that mentors might undertake to focus on subject-specific development of beginning teachers and mentors' own development as teacher educators.

Within the final section, **Being a geography mentor**, authors explicitly and critically consider the ways in which mentors can support beginning teachers in their development as geography teachers. In the first chapter of this section, Emma Rawlings Smith focuses on the role of mentor meetings and conversations for supporting beginning teachers. Beginning by considering the qualities effective mentors bring to formal mentor-mentee meetings, and why these are key to successful teacher growth and development, she then sets out a number of practical strategies and frameworks which can be used to support beginning geography teachers in their professional development. In the following chapter, school-based mentors Faizaan Ahmed, Sara-Anne Nichols and Amy Searle write alongside university-based tutors Lauren Hammond and Steve Puttick to examine the theory and practice of planning in geography education before engaging in a dialogic conversation to critically consider their experiences of, and perspectives on, planning with beginning teachers. Their reflection highlights the complexities and challenges of the mentor's role in supporting beginning teachers to think critically about their planning, and the value of partnership between schools and universities in developing well-informed and empowered beginning geography teachers. In the next chapter, Steve Puttick considers lesson observations at the interface between research and practice, suggesting that observing lessons and giving written feedback are fundamental aspects of mentoring which offer exciting opportunities for intellectually stimulating, enriching dialogue through which beginning teachers and mentors can be challenged and grow in their professional practice. Drawing on theoretical insights and research which give increasing attention to the written accounts and their potential for contributing to critical and expansive dialogue about the subject, he applies a situated and tentative approach towards knowledge which has implications for the ways in which we might engage with lesson observations and feedback. Steve then makes practical suggestions for increasing the ways in which mentors might support beginning teachers to become increasingly empowered to critically engage with and use a wide range of evidence in their professional growth. Within the next chapter, Grace Healy explores the ways in which geography and geography education scholarship can act as a mechanism for developing and sustaining mentors' and beginning teachers' subject knowledge and curriculum thinking. She argues that geography and geography education scholarship can (and should) play a significant role in nourishing the professional practice of teachers and informing their professional decision-making. Seen in this way, mentoring provides an important opportunity for teachers to be inducted into the repertoire of experience and theories that exist within geography education. Notions of shared dialogue are also important to the notion of *educative mentoring* which Maria Palombo and Caroline Daly's chapter argues is key to professional learning for geography teachers and mentors. Maria and Caroline's chapter begins with an exploration of the principles of educative mentoring and co-construction of knowledge within a professional learning community, before going on to consider three tasks that can be undertaken by a mentor and beginning geography teacher through an educative mentoring lens. In doing so, they suggest ways in which geography mentors can take an educative mentoring approach in collaborative planning, observation and post-lesson dialogue, and collaborative marking. In the final chapter of this section, Emma Clarke, Aimee Quickfall and Shaun Thompson consider the well-being of beginning teachers, drawing on their research on supporting beginning teachers. They combine research, theory and practical examples to show how relationships are a particularly important mediating factor in the well-being of beginning teachers. Drawing on the concept of the dynamic flux of well-being, Emma, Aimee and Shaun examine the balance between the challenges beginning teachers' (and mentors') experience and the resources they have to support them, considering how positive relationships can mitigate some of the challenges they experience, as well as how to develop the resources that both beginning teachers and mentors can draw on to facilitate their well-being.

Within the concluding chapter of the book, we reflect on themes emerging across, and provoked by, the critical contributions made by all of these chapter authors to argue for an ambitious vision for mentoring in geography education that contributes towards a more just tomorrow in geography education. In particular, we highlight themes of justice, agency and voice through which we discuss how and why mentoring matters in and for geography education. Our hope is that through this book you will be supported, challenged and stretched in ways that empower you to critically reflect on – and then enact – mentoring that makes valuable contributions in ways you might not even anticipate to tomorrow's teachers and young people.

References

Bernstein, B., 2000. *Pedagogy, Symbolic Control and Identity: Theory, Research, Critique*. London: Rowman & Littlefield.
Biddulph, M., and Kinder, A., 2020. Training and retaining geography specialists for schools in England. *Geography*, 105(2), 101–107.
Brooks, C., 2016. *Teacher Subject Identity in Professional Practice: Teaching with a Professional Compass*. London: Routledge.
Brooks, C., 2017. Pedagogy and identity in initial teacher education: Developing a professional compass, *Geography*, 102(1), 44–50.
Brooks, C., 2018. Insights on the field of geography education from a review of master's level practitioner research. *International Research in Geographical and Environmental Education*, 27(1), 5–23.
Brooks, C., and McIntyre, J., 2020. Better together: Why teacher education needs universities as well as schools. Available at: https://ioelondonblog.wordpress.com/2020/02/05/better-together-why-teacher-education-needs-universities-as-well-as-schools/ [accessed 20 September 2020].
Brooks, C., 2022. Mentoring as a spatial practice. In G. Healy, L. Hammond, S. Puttick and N. Walshe (eds), *Mentoring Geography Teachers in the Secondary School*. Abingdon: Routledge, 31–41.

Burn, K., and Mutton, T., 2018. Constructing the curriculum of (initial) teacher education; When should new teachers be encouraged to ask critical questions? *Impact*, 4. 59-61.

Carter, A. 2015. *The Carter Review of Initial Teacher Training (ITT)*. London: Department for Education.

Childs, A., 2022. Supporting the development of geography mentors – the potential of professional learning at Masters level. In G. Healy, L. Hammond, S. Puttick and N. Walshe (eds), *Mentoring Geography Teachers in the Secondary School*. Abingdon: Routledge, 119-134.

Colley, H., 2003. *Mentoring for Social Inclusion: A Critical Approach to Nurturing Mentor Relationships*. Abingdon: Routledge.

Darling-Hammond, L., 2017. Teacher education around the world: what can we learn from international practice? *European Journal of Teacher Education*, 40(3), 291-309.

Department for Education [DfE]. 2016. *National Standards for School-Based Initial Teacher Training (ITT) Mentors*. London: Department for Education.

Department for Education [DfE]. 2017. Initial Teacher Training (ITT) census for the academic year 2017-2018 England. Available at: https://assets.publishing.service.gov.uk/government/uploads/system/uploads/attachment_data/file/663141/SFR68_2017_Text.pdf [accessed 18 October 2020].

Department for Education [DfE]. 2019. *Early Career Framework*. London: Department for Education.

Hammond, L., Mitchell, D., and Palombo, M., 2019. Mentors in geography education: an under-used and under-represented community? *Teaching Geography*, 44(1), 6.

Healy, G., 2021. Insights from professional discourse on GIS: A case for recognising geography teachers' repertoire of experience. In N. Walshe and G Healy (eds), *Geography Education in the Digital World: Linking Theory and Practice*. London: Routledge, 89-101.

Healy, G., and Walshe, N., 2022. Navigating the policy landscape: conceptualising subject-specialist mentoring within and beyond policy. In G. Healy, L. Hammond, S. Puttick and N. Walshe (eds), *Mentoring Geography Teachers in the Secondary School*. Abingdon: Routledge, 13-30.

Healy, G., Walshe, N., and Dunphy, A., 2020. How is geography rendered visible as an object of concern in written lesson observation feedback? *The Curriculum Journal*, 31(1), 7-26.

Hobson, A. J., 2016. Judgementoring and how to avert it: Introducing ONSIDE Mentoring for beginning teachers. *International Journal of Mentoring and Coaching in Education*, 5(2), 87-110.

Kemmis, S., Heikkinen, H., Fransson, G., Aspfors, J., and Edwards-Groves, C., 2014. Mentoring of new teachers as a contested practice: supervision, support and collaborative self-development. *Teaching and Teacher Education*, 43, 154-164.

Kinder, A., 2022. Mentoring within the geography subject community. In G. Healy, L. Hammond, S. Puttick and N. Walshe (eds), *Mentoring Geography Teachers in the Secondary School*. Abingdon: Routledge, 102-118.

Lambert, D., 2015. Research in geography education. In G. Butt (ed), *Masterclass in Geography Education: Transforming Teaching and Learning*. London: Bloomsbury, 15-30.

Lambert, D., 2018. Teaching as a research-engaged profession: Uncovering a blind spot and revealing new possibilities. *London Review of Education*, 16(3), 357-370.

Langdon, F., and Ward, L., 2015. Educative mentoring: A way forward. *International Journal of Mentoring and Coaching in Education*, 4(4), 240-254

Lofthouse, R. M., 2018. Re-imagining mentoring as a dynamic hub in the transformation of initial teacher education: The role of mentors and teacher educators. *International Journal of Mentoring and Coaching in Education*, 7(3), 248-260.

Lofthouse, R. M., 2019. Using mentoring and coaching to focus on the curriculum in action. Available at: www.bera.ac.uk/blog/using-mentoring-and-coaching-to-focus-on-the-curriculum-in-action [accessed 3 October 2020].

Maynard, T., and Furlong, J., 1995. Learning to teach and models of mentoring. In T. Kerry and A. Shelton-Mayes (eds), *Issues in Mentoring*. London: Routledge, 10-14.

Morgan, J., 2017. Persevering with geography. *Documents d'Anàlisi Geogràphica*, 63(3), 529-544.

Morgan, J., 2022. What sort of mentoring for what sort of geography education? In G. Healy, L. Hammond, S. Puttick and N. Walshe (eds), *Mentoring Geography Teachers in the Secondary School*. Abingdon: Routledge, 42-56.

Mutton, T., Burn, K., and Hagger. H., 2010. Making sense of learning to teach: Learners in context. *Research Papers in Education*, 25(1), 73-91.

Palombo, M., and Daly, C., 2022. Educative mentoring: A key to professional learning for geography teachers and mentors. In G. Healy, L. Hammond, S. Puttick and N. Walshe (eds), *Mentoring Geography Teachers in the Secondary School*. Abingdon: Routledge, 208-223.

Palombo, M.. Hammond, L., and Mitchell, D., 2020. The findings of the survey of mentoring in geography education. *Teaching Geography*, 45(1), 9-11.

Rowe, J., 2019. 5 reasons why plans for NQTs might make things worse. *Times Education Supplement*. Available at: www.tes.com/news/5-reasons-why-plans-nqts-might-make-things-worse [accessed 20 September 2020].

Whiting, C., Whitty, G., Menter, I., Black, P., Hordern, J., Parfitt, A., Reynolds, K., and Sorensen, N. 2018. Diversity and complexity: Becoming a teacher in England in 2015-2016. *Review of Education*. 6(1), 69-96.

SECTION 1
Mentoring in geography education

2 Navigating the policy landscape
Conceptualising subject-specialist mentoring within and beyond policy

Grace Healy and Nicola Walshe

Introduction

As a mentor, you play a significant role in teacher professional development – a role that is increasingly being recognised in Initial Teacher Education (ITE)[1] and beyond (Lofthouse, 2018). As of the last two decades, trainee teachers generally now spend more time in schools[2] and this has led to greater attention internationally to both the role of mentors and mentoring with policy and guidance documents in ITE and beyond (Darling-Hammond, 2017).

Ball (1993a) suggests that 'policy "matters: it is important, not the least because it consists of texts which are (sometimes) acted on"' (Beilharz, 1987, p. 394). Drawing upon Ball and Bowe's (1992) characterisation of teachers' engagement with curriculum policy, we feel that mentors should be empowered to interpret policy in ways that are 'proactive, critical and self-assured' (what Barthes (1976) terms *writerly*), rather than in ways that are 'reactive, passive and unquestioning' (what Barthes (1976) terms *readerly*) (Ball and Bowe, 1992, p. 112). Within this chapter, we will explore a range of policy texts in order to provide space for you, as a mentor, to reflect on policy enactment, which we define as 'the grassroots interpretation and recreation of policy *in situ*' (Ball, 1993b, p. 120). To do this we first explore some pertinent aspects of policy enactment and key shifts in policy in relation to ITE and teacher professional development more broadly, and mentoring specifically. We then introduce an account of how mentoring is conceptualised through the lens of four policies that were published in England between 2015 and 2020, demonstrating how the role of the mentor has not always been recognised in policy in its full complexity.[3] Finally, we highlight how, as a mentor, you might embrace this complexity through critically engaging with policy (in ways which are *writerly*), so as to understand and be more intentional in how you navigate and become a policy actor (rather than policy subject) within the professional landscape you are mentoring beginning geography teachers within.

Policy enactment within school and ITE contexts

In order to actively take account of the educational policy that is influencing your mentoring, we need to first consider the relationship between policy and practice. Ball et al. (2012) highlight there has been much attention on researching policy implementation as a means of evaluating the effectiveness of policies, rather than consideration of how the policy is enacted

DOI: 10.4324/9781003157120-3

in practice per se. However, Ball et al. (2012) propose that a focus on policy enactment is important as it allows for attention to those who 'work to fabricate and forge practices.... in light of their situated realities' (p. 142). In the professional landscape as a mentor working within your school and/or an ITE partnership, you might well have seen the 'negotiation, contestation or struggle between different groups who may lie outside the formal machinery of official policy making' (Ozga, 2000, p. 113) as policy is enacted. This might involve compromise between directors of ITE and SCITT (School-Centred Initial Teacher Training), school leaders who are involved in partnership agreements, and those leading and supporting both mentors and beginning teachers.

Ball et al. (2012) argue that policy-making often assumes the *best possible* environments; this is pertinent given their findings also illustrate that contextual factors, such as the finances and the profile of staff, play a role in policy enactment as constraints, pressures and enablers. Policy enactment within schools and across ITE providers means that, as a mentor, you will have been both subject to and an actor of such policies, and as such have no doubt encountered them as constraints, pressures or enablers at some point. When engaging with how policy is reshaping the ITE partnerships you are involved with, you will see first-hand where assumptions about what is achievable within *best possible* environments are mediated by the realities of the contexts you are part of.

Further to this consideration of the environment, Braun et al. (2010) argue that policy enactment can be dependent on the confidence of a school to withstand 'the demands of a performative, audit society', such that if a school has a comparatively privileged positioning among school hierarchies, this 'mediates [its] relationship with bodies such as the local authority and Ofsted' (p. 557). We would extend this point and suggest that this does not just shape policy enactment for schools but also applies to schools and universities that lead ITE partnerships.

Mentors and mentoring within the ITE and beginning teachers' professional development policy context

The role of mentors and mentoring is increasingly recognised in policies, professional qualifications and inspection frameworks in relation to ITE, teacher professional development and leadership. Within ITE partnerships and schools, such policies are rendered visible in a wide range of artefacts: for example, partnership agreements and mentoring handbooks. In a single chapter, we cannot provide a critical analysis of all this policy to date, so in this section we will set out some of the recent and significant shifts in the policy in relation to ITE and beginning teachers' professional development. This will serve to contextualise what you know from your own experience and lead to an account focussing on key policies from the context of England 2015–2020, which will allow you to reflect more deeply on the ways that policy might contextualise and conceptualise mentorship and, thereby, shape your mentoring practice.

Drawing on McIntyre's (2018) critical analysis of teacher education policy in England, Scotland and Wales,[4] we can see even within three countries from the UK there is divergence in how ITE is conceived and reshaped through national reviews that have taken place in the last decade (DfE (2015) in England; Donaldson (2011) in Scotland; Furlong (2015) in Wales). The shared commitment to reforming ITE as a driver for improving teacher quality is common across England, Scotland and Wales, and across international contexts (Darling-Hammond and Lieberman, 2012; McIntyre, 2018; Menter, 2019). Pertinent to our focus on mentoring *geography* teachers and this book's concern for subject specificity, and illustrative of the (recent) discourse around subject within ITE more broadly, all reviews included a focus on subject knowledge. Significantly, the diversification of routes and qualifications in England has been notably different from the approach in Scotland and Wales, perhaps indicative of the pendulum swing towards 'school-led' policy of teacher preparation in England (Mutton et al., 2017; McIntyre, 2018) which mirrors the emphasis placed on school-based mentoring internationally (Darling-Hammond, 2017).

Since the 1980s, the role of school-based mentoring has been recognised both in England and internationally (Hobson and Malderez, 2013); this is argued to be the result of a number of factors, such as the introduction of school-based routes into teaching, to support the retention of newly and recently qualified teachers, or as a retention strategy for teachers who might become mentors (Hobson et al., 2009). However, the shift in England towards partnerships within ITE between HEIs and schools has more recently led to an emphasis on the expertise and professional development of school-based mentors (Murray and Mutton, 2016). As a mentor, you are likely to hold responsibility for both supporting the development of beginning teachers and contributing to assessment against national standards (Hobson and Malderez, 2013). The introduction of this dual role for mentors of both developing and assessing beginning geography teachers has been argued to have imposed a judgemental approach to mentoring (Hobson and Malderez, 2013). Hobson and Malderez (2013) take *judgementoring* to mean:

> a one to one relationship between a relatively inexperienced teacher (the mentee) and a relatively experienced one (the mentor) in which the latter, in revealing too readily and/or too often her/his own judgements on or evaluations of the mentee's planning and teaching (e.g. through "comments", "feedback", advice, praise, or criticism), compromises the mentoring relationship and its potential benefits.
>
> (p. 90)

In practice we know that mentors can adopt various 'supportive roles', which include those of:

> *educator* (which involves, e.g. listening, coaching and creating appropriate opportunities for the mentee's professional learning), *model* (inspiring, demonstrating and making visible aspects of being a teacher), *acculturator* (helping the mentee into full membership of the particular professional culture), *sponsor* ("opening doors" and introducing the mentee to the "right people"), and *provider of psychological support* (providing the mentee with a safe place to release emotions or "let off steam") (Malderez and Bodoczky, 1999; Malderez and Wedell, 2007).
>
> (Hobson and Malderez, 2013, p. 90)

Even when mentors actively take different approaches to their mentoring, they can find that their mentees' awareness of the dual role influences their mentoring relationship. In practice, Puttick's (2018) research on the positionalities of beginning teachers within subject departments highlights that trainee geography teachers can be cautious about being self-critical and asking questions that could indicate they do not hold strong subject knowledge. This echoed Sirna et al.'s (2008) conclusions that trainee teachers 'sacrificed asking questions... because they feared that it might make them seem incompetent or otherwise negatively affect their evaluation' (p. 296). In our own research, we have questioned whether the evaluative role mentors hold might lead to mentors focussing on evidencing secure subject knowledge rather than 'supporting critical engagement with the substance of geography being taught' (Healy et al., 2020, pp. 18-19). As such, it is important to consider the impact of the dual role you have as a mentor on both your mentorship and the subsequent development of your mentee; for example, through actively considering how and to what extent this potentially *judgemental* aspect influences your (combined) practice.

Focussing on mentoring for newly qualified teachers, Langdon et al. (2019) have argued that research is needed to 'prevent policymaking that addresses induction and mentoring as discrete entities that are developed and managed separately from attention to school cultures' (Langdon et al., 2019, p. 262). As a mentor and someone who also experienced the processes of induction and mentoring within your own teaching career, you might want to reflect on the extent to which you have perceived this is an issue. Brooks (2022) argues that both ITE and mentoring can be viewed as a spatial practice which is shaped by factors at other scales; for example, 'schools are beholden to national and regional accountability regimes and governance structures, which, in turn, are often influenced by global trends and the prevalence of policy borrowing or policy lending' (p. 35). Further, Langdon et al. (2019) have also emphasised that situated realities matter for mentoring beyond ITE, placing attention on how beginning teachers' professional learning is situated within the whole school community that they are part of. This, therefore, highlights the importance of the perceptions of both mentoring and professional learning within the whole school community, especially from those in leadership positions. Moving beyond policy enactment within a school, Lofthouse (2018) highlights that joined-up thinking in relation to mentoring can only be realised if there is 'system-wide enactment of professional development policies' (p. 252), which can be hindered by the complexity of the professional landscape for ITE and continued professional development.

Based on re-analysis of data from the 'Becoming a Teacher' study (2003-2009) and the 'Modes of Mentoring and Coaching' study (2010-2012), which included interviews with beginner teachers and mentors in both primary and secondary schools, Hobson and Malderez (2013) argue that national policy-makers in England have neglected to give sufficient status to the mentoring role, failed to ensure that both trainee and newly qualified teachers can access subject-specialist support, and also failed to promote an 'understanding of what mentoring ought to entail or what mentors should be seeking to achieve' (p. 100). Such policy failings mean that it is then less likely that the 'conditions for effective mentoring' (Hobson et al., 2009, p. 214) are met. Through the account set out in the next section we will illustrate the ways in which policy has developed since these findings were reported.

This initial section has begun to explore the relationship between policy development and enactment, highlighting the significance of context in realisation of those policies, at partnership, school and even departmental level. It has also called attention to some of the tensions created when policy is enacted within school contexts through the example of the dual role of mentors as developers and assessors of beginning teachers. We now move to exemplifying how mentoring can be conceptualised, through a short account.

An account of how mentoring is conceptualised in policy: through the lens of four key policies in England 2015-2020

In this section, we will illustrate the ways in which the role of mentoring can be conceptualised within policy documentation, and subsequently shapes mentoring practice, through an account set in the context of England 2015-2020. This account of policy is situated with a particular timespan and geographical context; however, as an illustrative example it will allow us to exemplify the ways in which policy might influence practice, thereby allowing for a more considered discussion as to how mentors might benefit from a clearer understanding of the relationship between policy and practice. We will consider four policies[5] which relate to the mentoring of beginning teachers in England 2015-2020: the Carter review of Initial Teacher Training (ITT) (DfE, 2015); the National Standards for school-based Initial Teacher Training Mentors (DfE, 2016); the Early Career Framework (DfE, 2019b); and the Ofsted Initial Teacher Education Inspection Framework (Ofsted, 2020). These policies, summarised in Boxes 2.1 to 2.4, are illustrated alongside key policies which influenced and informed mentoring in England 2015-2020 in Figure 2.1.

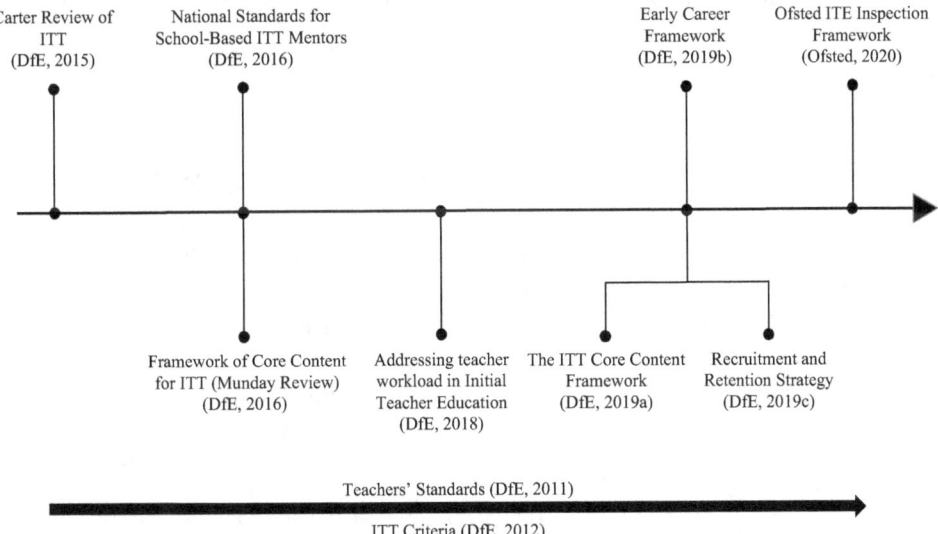

Figure 2.1 Timeline illustrating key policies which influence mentors of beginning teachers in England 2015 to 2020. Policies above the timeline are explored in detail within the chapter text.

Grace Healy and Nicola Walshe

The Carter review of Initial Teacher Training (ITT)

> **Box 2.1 The Carter review of Initial Teacher Training**
>
> The Carter review of Initial Teacher Training (ITT) (DfE, 2015) was commissioned by the Secretary of State for Education with the aim of identifying those elements of high-quality ITT, across phases and subject disciplines, which are central to equipping trainee teachers with the required skills and knowledge to become outstanding teachers. Led by Sir Andrew Carter OBE, an Advisory Group which comprised leaders from two Higher Education Institutions (HEIs) and three multi-academy trusts (MATs) worked to define effective ITT practice, assess the extent to which the system currently delivers effective ITT, and then recommend where and how improvements could be made.
>
> Within the Carter review there are perhaps not surprisingly a significant number of references to mentoring or mentors. For example, within the recommendations it states:
>
> 'Partnerships should ensure all trainees experience effective mentoring by:
>
> i. selecting and recruiting mentors who are excellent teachers, who are able to explain outstanding practice (as well as demonstrate it)
> ii. providing rigorous training for mentors that goes beyond briefing about the structure and nature of the course, and focusses on how teachers learn and the skills of effective mentoring
> iii. considering whether they are resourcing mentoring appropriately – the resource allocated to mentoring should reflect the importance of the role.'
>
> (Recommendation 11: DfE, 2015, p. 12)

The Carter review saw a shift in discourse towards recognition of the value of the mentor, for example:

> XXXI. There is evidence to suggest that high quality mentoring is critically important for ITT (Hobson and others, 2009). Effective mentoring has wider benefits, providing professional development opportunities for mentors and building the capacity of the school as a whole. Effective mentors are outstanding teachers and subject experts, who are also skilled in explaining their own practice. We have found that the best programmes also give careful thought as to how to train and recognise mentors effectively.
>
> (DfE, 2015, p. 12)

Within this context, the Carter review (DfE, 2015) begins explicitly to introduce the notion of *expert* through the idea of *best*: 'ITT should also provide an environment for new teachers to learn from our best teachers' (pp. 3-4). This is further extended to describe best practice as being 'where school-based trainers are also actively engaged with research and evidence-based teaching (Sahlberg and others, 2014), where mentors, for example, actively demonstrate engagement with research' (DfE, 2015, p. 28). However, at the same time there is a warning that mentoring across England is 'not as good as it should be' (Hobson and

Malderez, 2013) and a concern that the 'qualities of effective mentors' (DfE, 2015, p. 12) need to be better understood.

Whilst its focus on mentoring can be seen as significant, the Carter review has been criticised, for example by Mutton et al. (2017, p. 15), as a manifestation of the 'practicum turn', represented by the 'drive for increased opportunities for school experience during initial teacher preparation' (Conroy et al., 2013, p. 558). While Mutton et al. (2017) argue that the Carter review explicitly assumes that school-based mentors are critical in trainee teacher development, there is also an underlying assumption that schools are working collaboratively with a university partner. While close collaborative partnership between university and school is widely held to have the potential to bring 'research-based understandings of teaching and learning into dialogue with the professional understandings of experienced classroom teachers' (Burn and Mutton, 2013, p. 3), there is, however, very little acknowledgement within the Carter review that such collaborative, research-driven partnerships are potentially now less common in England (Mutton et al., 2017). Further, there is a lack of recognition of concerns raised, for example by the Geographical Association, about the variability of time spent on subject-specific input in geography ITE programmes (e.g. fewer than 30 hours in one SCITT through to over 200 hours in one HE-led partnership [Tapsfield et al., 2015]), and the greater burden for mentors to provide subject-specific input where there is limited time spent on subject-specific input.

Within the Carter review, subject knowledge development and subject-specific pedagogy were highlighted as being significant for trainee teachers, with an early comment that the review had identified gaps 'in areas such as subject knowledge development, subject-specific pedagogy, behaviour management, assessment and special educational needs and disabilities (SEND)' (DfE, 2015, p. 6). As such, while this review does not privilege subject knowledge over pedagogy, it does set a challenge to ITE providers to engage more meaningfully with subject specificity for both trainees and mentors. In relation to this, Mutton et al. (2017) argue that the inclusion of subject-specific pedagogy as a separate element within the Carter review represents a clear rejection of the view advanced by many neoliberal critics of teacher education that secure subject knowledge is essentially all that teachers require (e.g. Lawlor, 1990). Of further note is Mutton et al.'s (2017) comment that in terms of subject knowledge development, the Carter review 'sees the answer lying in the establishment of stronger subject communities, with trainees having access to subject experts, and highlights the important role that subject associations can play' (p. 20). Within the Carter review (DfE, 2015, p. 41), being a member of 'subject mentor networks' and accessing 'resources from subject associations' is shared as a characteristic of effective mentoring.

National Standards for school-based initial teacher training (ITT) mentors

> **Box 2.2 National Standards for school-based initial teacher training (ITT) mentors**
>
> A key recommendation of the Carter review was for a set of non-statutory standards to be developed to help bring greater coherence and consistency to the school-based mentoring arrangements for trainee teachers; this became The National Standards

for school-based Initial Teacher Training (ITT) Mentors (DfE, 2016). Developed by the Teaching Schools Council, the aims of the National Standards for school-based ITT mentors were threefold: 'to foster greater consistency in the practice of mentors', thereby leading 'to an improved and more coherent experience for trainees'; 'to raise the profile of mentoring and provide a framework for the professional development of current and aspiring mentors'; and 'to contribute towards the building of a culture of coaching and mentoring in schools' (DfE, 2016, p. 3).

Within the National Standards, mentorship is very clearly conceptualised with a focus on trainee assessment but also the importance of engagement with and understanding of subject expertise:

> A mentor should understand the course structure and the requirement of trainees to meet the Teachers' Standards. They should prioritise meetings and discussions with a trainee, monitor performance, and help develop their teaching practice and effective classroom management strategies. A mentor should also keep their subject knowledge up-to-date and have the awareness to signpost trainees to other expertise and knowledge, for example subject associations.
>
> (DfE, 2016. p. 8)

The National Standards provide a gatekeeper view of mentoring that assumes, implicitly, an expert/novice model in which knowledge is transmitted from the expert teacher to 'inculcate the novice teacher into the specific school context' (Murtagh and Dawes, 2020, p. 3). This is in contradiction to an alternative, dialogic model which favours a collaborative process of mutual knowledge generation and stimulates concurrent professional learning for mentor and mentee (see Palombo and Daly, 2022, for detailed consideration of an educative mentoring approach). However, this less hierarchical model is more difficult to enact within a 'heavily standardised and accountable educational system that assumes a technical, performative version of professional practice' (Ball et al., 2012; Polesel et al., 2014) (Murtagh and Dawes, 2020, p. 33). Further to this, Kinder (2022) argues that merely signposting is not enough and advocates mentors actively engaging with the geography subject community in order to model how teachers can achieve greater agency.

Whilst the National Standards appear to offer recognition for the role of mentors (Lofthouse, 2018), Peiser et al. (2018) argue that the National Standards are an oversimplification of the complexity of the mentoring role; yet the complexity of the role has been recognised for decades (e.g. McIntyre and Hagger, 1993; Vonk, 1993; Furlong and Maynard, 1995). Further to this, the non-statutory nature of the National Standards might limit the impact of this policy in practice.

The Early Career Framework

Box 2.3 The Early Career Framework

Released alongside the ITT Core Content Framework, the Early Career Framework (ECF) set out early career teachers' entitlement to professional development and 'a fully-funded, two-year package of structured training and support for early career teachers linked to the best available research evidence' (DfE, 2019, p. 4). At the point of writing the ECF had not yet been nationally rolled out (due September 2021) and was being piloted; the ECF is expected to include funded time for mentors to support early career teachers, as well as fully funded mentor training (DfE, 2019b).

While mentors are not referenced explicitly within the ECF, the ECF core induction pilot programme suppliers (of which there are four who have each developed their own core induction programme based on the ECF: Ambition Institute, Education Development Trust, Teach First and UCL Early Career Teacher Consortium) appear to conceptualise mentoring in different ways, as indicated in the mentor support materials, and with mentor support also varying across ECF provider. For example, Ambition Institute's handbook for mentors states: 'Your role as a mentor encompasses everything you do to support your NQT. Instructional coaching is a central and critical aspect of this role – one that can make a big difference to your teacher's practice' (Ambition Institute, 2020, p. 1). Ambition Institute, Education Development Trust and Teach First set out the role of mentor through the framework of instructional coaching; this approach is described in Table 2.1. Conversely, the UCL Early Career Consortium (2020) recommends two complementary mentoring approaches: Hobson's (2016) ONSIDE mentoring

Table 2.1 Mentoring and coaching approaches integrated within ECF programmes

Mentoring or coaching approach	Description provided within ECF provider materials
Educative mentoring	'Educative mentoring is based on a vision of teachers as learners and the classroom as a site of inquiry, and on collaborative principles that involve building knowledge together about teaching and learning. The development of alternative beliefs and viewpoints is facilitated alongside collecting and assessing high-quality evidence that is professionally relevant to the novice teacher.' (UCL Early Career Consortium, 2020, p. 35)
ONSIDE mentoring	'ONSIDE mentoring aims to be: • offline – separated from line-management and non-hierarchical • non-evaluative – and non-judgemental • supportive – of mentees' psychological needs and well-being • individualised – tailored to the specific and changing needs of the mentee • developmental – and growth oriented through appropriate challenge • empowering – progressively non-directive to support autonomy and agency The seventh imperative of ONSIDE mentoring is that, as the mnemonic implies, mentors are first and foremost on the side of – allies, champions and advocates for – their mentees.' (UCL Early Career Consortium, 2020, pp. 35-36)
Instructional coaching	Instructional coaching emphasises the role of mentor as expert as, for example, it 'focusses on feedback which is led and directed by the "coach" through the identification of precise actions and the use of directed and specific probing questions.... The mentor leads these interactions, adopting the role of the expert in the interaction.' (Teach First, 2020, p. 7).

model and educative mentoring as described in Table 2.1. Within these approaches, mentors and their relationships with their mentees are conceptualised in different ways.

There has already been attention given to the perceived neglect of subject-specific support within the ECF. For example, Healy et al. (2020) suggest that there needs to be more attention to how mentors can develop practices that place the subject curriculum at the heart of their work and highlight the concern raised by Rowe (2019) that the ECF neglects subject-specific development. This builds on a wider body of research and advocacy across a variety of disciplines which calls for greater consideration of subject-specific support across mentoring (e.g. Pinnick, 2020) and professional learning more broadly (Institute of Physics, 2021).

Ofsted's Initial Teacher Education Inspection Framework

> **Box 2.4 Ofsted's Initial Teacher Education Inspection Framework**
>
> The final policy document of relevance for note is the Ofsted Initial Teacher Education (ITE) Inspection Framework (Ofsted, 2020); this is significant as the ways that Ofsted interpret previous policy documentation can shape practice as a result of associated assessment and accountability. Within the Ofsted ITE Framework (2020) there is a stronger emphasis on subject; for example, 'Inspectors will use meetings with mentors to consider how the training and support they provide for trainees is part of a subject- and phase-specific curriculum that is purposefully integrated (where applicable) across the centre- and placement-based settings' (Ofsted, 2020, pp. 25–26). Further, Ofsted itself notes the need to create
>
> > 'opportunities for subject leaders and other subject trainers (and, in secondary, subject mentors) to renew and strengthen the subject dimensions of training. This might happen through collaboration in sourcing, producing or adapting high-quality subject resources or through giving trainers opportunities to consider quality in subject practice or subject curriculums.'
> >
> > (Ofsted, 2020, p. 47)

At the time of writing this chapter, the Ofsted Initial Teacher Education Framework has not yet been fully enacted due to the CV-19 pandemic, and there is limited published literature available. As a result, here we focus on responses available from within the geography education community. Kinder (2022) highlights the impact of changes to the Ofsted inspection framework for ITE in England from 2020, noting it places 'increased weight on teachers acquiring and applying robust disciplinary and specialist pedagogical knowledge to their practice (Kinder and Owens, 2019)' and suggests this 'need for such knowledge in teaching, and about the effects on teaching and training quality when it is absent or insufficient' (p. 105) has been increasingly evident in school inspection reports. The Geographical Association (GA) response to the consultation on the framework highlights the challenges of this subject specificity, for example 'the contributions expected from subject mentors as "expert colleagues"' in the context of a lack of mentor time and training, and the 'highly uneven' (GA, 2020, p. 3) spatial distribution of geography-specific mentors. However, Healy

(2020) and Kinder (2022) do suggest that despite these challenges, high-quality subject mentoring has ultimately been achievable in some partnerships; as such, as mentors, there is value in reflecting on the extent to which time and mentor training is enabling or constraining your mentoring. Further, it could be useful for you to consider how you might take account of the ways in which beginning teachers' earlier experiences of mentoring, for example within their ITE experience, might influence the ways in which they respond to your mentoring.

Embracing the complexity of mentoring: within and beyond the lens of policy

In this section, we will draw together the account by illustrating how the conceptualisation of mentors in policy can appear incongruent with the complexity of what has been explored about the role through research and practice. In particular, we will first problematise the notion of mentors as experts through consideration of professional identity and development and then address mentor subject expertise and context through consideration of developed and extended mentoring.

Moving beyond the notion of mentors as experts through consideration of professional identity and development

The notion of expert appears to be frequently used within policy in relation to the mentoring of beginning teachers. However, Burn's (2007) research with school-based mentors indicates there is a greater complexity between having subject expertise and being able to use this within a mentoring role, as:

> analysis of the mentors' input revealed that those most able to provide the student teachers with relevant, contextualised suggestions for practice, based on their own well developed PCK [pedagogical content knowledge], seemed reluctant and occasionally even unable to do so.
>
> (p. 458)

Through a subject-specific lens, Burn (2007) questions the narrative of mentors as purely experts, and this research indicates that the professional identity of mentors is forged through mentoring, which leads to 'an identity which depends not merely on *existing* knowledge, but on the capacity to generate *new* professional knowledge; an identity which includes a role as learner, not merely one as an 'expert' teacher' (p. 460).

Whilst the professional learning of mentors is recognised within policy documents, Burn (2007) argues it is also necessary to consider the professional identity and development of mentors as both teachers and learners. For mentors to model their own professional development as both a teacher and learner complements an approach to ITE and mentoring that enables beginning teachers to understand the value of, and be well placed to, sustain their own professional learning throughout their careers (Burn, 2016; Brooks, 2017; Lofthouse, 2018). This approach also acknowledges that whilst beginning teachers can be enabled to gain 'some mastery over a body of professional knowledge', it is just as important that this includes awareness of the 'ways in which that knowledge base can and needs to be extended'

(Fordham, 2016, p. 148); this means accepting that there are aspects of teaching where mentors cannot be experts.

With the focus on mentors' professional identity and development, Brooks (2017) argues that subject expertise matters and that this in turn determines what can be achieved through subject-specialist mentoring for beginning teachers. In particular, this requires mentors 'to have a clear pedagogical approach to their mentoring (as they would their teaching) and that approach needs to be underpinned by a philosophical understanding of what it is that they want to achieve' which requires a 'robust sense of the discipline of geography' (Brooks, 2017, p. 49); this highlights the importance of acknowledging the ongoing role of subject-specific mentoring development.

Valuing mentor subject expertise and context through consideration of developed and extended mentoring

The extent to which the individual expertise and context of the mentor is valued and drawn upon in mentoring varies across policy documents within the account above. However, like McIntyre and Hagger (1993), we feel it is important to recognise that mentors might often be working beyond minimal expectations for mentoring; McIntyre and Hagger (1993) explore the ways in which mentoring roles might be developed or extended. This captures how as a mentor you can enable beginning geography teachers to benefit from your expertise and context. This might relate to the subject-specialist expertise you have as you mentor individual beginning geography teachers, but also might be captured through the wider contributions you have to mentoring beginning geography teachers across your ITE partnership. This, for example, is recognised within Ofsted's (2020) ITE framework where the role of mentors should be to 'renew and strengthen the subject dimensions of training' (p. 47) across all ITE routes. In particular, Healy (2020, n.p.) argues that in such cases it has potential 'both to strengthen the professional learning of beginning teachers and provide enriching subject-specific opportunities for their experienced mentoring teachers to more fully be engaged with the entire course and through doing so, be more active in shaping new teachers' knowledge of their subject community's history'.

Tapsfield proposed a partnership model for training beginning teacher mentors whereby 'every geography "mentor" should contribute to at least one "taught" session for the session for the group of students, either based in the HEI or in their school' (TEWG, 1993, p. 2). While this may not be possible within larger partnerships with significant numbers of mentors, this extended mentoring approach is not all that different from the kind of ownership and engagement by mentors that is being encouraged through Ofsted's (2020) ITE inspection framework. Here, you might want to reflect on whether policy appears to be revealing or concealing the ways in which as mentor you can be actively enabled to use your subject expertise within your mentoring. The concern around the extent to which mentor expertise is valued is also raised by Brooks (2022), who highlights the danger of a prescriptive, framework-driven policy of encouraging a reductionist approach to mentoring which does not value mentor expertise and experience and, as a result, is less effective in broadening the 'horizon, repertoire and experience of new and early career teachers' (p. 36). Taking full advantage of a mentor's context is something that responds to Langdon et al.'s (2019) calls to ensure both induction and mentoring are situated within the whole school community; whilst awareness of the value of drawing on your context can come from you as a mentor, it is necessary to acknowledge that this is dependent on school culture (Langdon et al., 2019) and whether national policy is enabling the 'conditions for effective mentoring' (Hobson et al., 2009, p. 214) to be met.

Conclusion

We hope this chapter has helped you see how, through taking on the role of policy actor, you can critically engage with the educational policy landscape that underpins your mentoring practice. This starts from having awareness of the kinds of policy documents that exist, their purpose, and how they might conceptualise mentoring. In some cases, we illuminate that the way the role of mentoring, especially subject-specialist mentoring, is captured in policy is limited and does not fully engage with existing theory and research in relation to mentoring beginning teachers. As subject-specialist mentoring is not fully appreciated within policy, there is a lack of investment in the hidden and more complex aspects of the role that contribute to beginning geography teachers' development.

In this chapter, we have focussed on how the role of mentors and mentoring is conceptualised in policy; however, there is also value in understanding how beginning teachers are being conceptualised in policy. For example, there has been concern as to whether beginning teachers have been treated 'as apprentices, not as future members of a profession' (Young, 2020, p. 22), and there is also a need to acknowledge the value placed on subject-specific professional development within the wider educational context. There is continued advocacy in this area; for example, the Institute of Physics' (2021) *Subject Matters* report includes the recommendation that governments should 'establish an entitlement for teachers which ensures that at least half of their professional learning is subject-specific', and includes explicit reference to the need to drive 'a sector-wide culture change that improves the perception of the value and importance of subject-specific professional learning' (p. 6). This emphasises that whilst in the geography-education community the importance of subject expertise (Brooks, 2016) and subject-specific professional learning is well established (Kinder, 2022), this is not fully recognised in policy; this can, therefore, have a substantial impact on all geography teachers' access to subject-specific professional development throughout their careers.

For discussion

1. Consider the recent policy documentation in your specific (spatial and temporal) context; how does this conceptualise mentoring, particularly with reference to subject-specificity of mentor support? To what extent does this shape your practice as a mentor?
2. Reflect on how you might respond to the release of new policy documentation or frameworks as a mentor of beginning teachers in the future; what questions might you ask to draw out implications for your practice?
3. If you are mentoring trainees, consider the mechanisms that the ITE partnership provides for you to contribute your expertise to the ITE programme. In what ways does this support your development as a mentor?

Notes

1. In this chapter, we have chosen to use Initial Teacher Education (ITE) to refer to pre-service teacher education; however, we also defer to the terminology used within the policy documents under discussion throughout this chapter and so will use Initial Teacher Training (ITT) where this term is used in the documents we are drawing upon.
2. Within England and Wales, the DfE's (1992) circular on Initial Teacher Training [ITT] set the minimum requirement of 24 weeks (120 days) for time spent in school.
3. For those working outside of England, we would encourage you to review the policies specific to your own context alongside this chapter.
4. McIntyre (2018) does not include Northern Ireland in the analysis; this might be because the last policy review of teacher education in Northern Ireland was in 2005 (Osler, 2005) and, therefore, does not provide us insight into how teacher education has been reshaped in the last decade. The Department for Education (n.d.) in Northern Ireland is 'currently engaging with educational stakeholders to develop, for consultation, its vision for teacher professional learning through to 2025'.
5. It should be noted that there were other policies which reference mentors during this time, for example the ITT Core Content Framework (DfE, 2019a).

Further reading and resources

1. Mutton, T., Burn, K., and Menter, I., 2017. Deconstructing the Carter review: Competing conceptions of quality in England's 'school-led' system of initial teacher education. *Journal of Education Policy*, 32(1), 14-33.

This open access article in the *Journal of Education Policy* provides an exemplification of policy analysis. Mutton et al. (2017) focus on the Carter review, but this illustration of policy critique could inform how you might critically engage with future policy that affects your professional landscape and mentoring.

2. Tapsfield, A., 2020. Training new teachers: A shift in emphasis? *Teaching Geography*, 6(3), 114-117.

This *Teaching Geography* article provides an insight into developments in ITE across the last decade and explores the prospective impact of the ITT Core Content Framework and the ECF.

References

Ambition Institute, 2020. Mentor handbook: Coaching guidance. Available at: www.early-career-framework.education.gov.uk/ambition/wp-content/uploads/sites/3/2020/08/Ambition-EarlyCareerTeachers_2020_MentorHandbook_Guidebook_FULL_DEV.pdf [accessed 30 December 2020].

Ball, S. J., 1993a. What is policy? Texts, trajectories and toolboxes. *The Australian Journal of Education Studies*, 13(2), 10-17.

Ball, S. J., 1993b. Education policy, power relations and teachers' work. *British Journal of Educational Studies*, 41(2), 106-121

Ball, S. J., and Bowe, R., 1992. Subject departments and the 'implementation' of National Curriculum policy: an overview of the issues. *Journal of Curriculum Studies*, 24(2), 97-115.

Ball, S. J., Maguire, M., and Braun, A., 2012. *How Schools do Policy: Policy Enactments in Secondary Schools*. Abingdon: Routledge.

Barthes, R., 1976. *The Pleasure of the Text*. Trans. Richard Miller. London: Cape.

Braun, A., Maguire, M., and Ball, S. J., 2010. Policy enactments in the UK secondary school: examining policy, practice and school positioning. *Journal of Education Policy*, 25(4), 547-560.

Brooks, C., 2016. *Teacher subject Identity in Professional Practice: Teaching with a Professional Compass*. Abingdon: Routledge.
Brooks, C., 2017. Pedagogy and identity in initial teacher education: Developing a professional compass, *Geography*, 102(1), 44–50.
Brooks, C., 2022. Mentoring as a spatial practice. In G. Healy, L. Hammond, S. Puttick and N. Walshe (eds), *Mentoring Geography Teachers in the Secondary School*. Abingdon: Routledge, 31–41.
Burn, K., 2007. Professional knowledge and identity in a contested discipline: Challenges for student teachers and teacher educators. *Oxford Review of Education*, 33(4), 445–467.
Burn, K., 2016. Sustaining the unresolving tensions within history education and teacher education. In C. Counsell, K. Burn and A. Chapman (eds), *Masterclass in History Education*. London: Bloomsbury Publishing, 223–242.
Burn, K., and Mutton. T., 2013. *Review of Research-Informed Clinical Practice in Teacher Education*, Paper Submitted to the BERA-RSA Inquiry. London: BERA/RSA.
Conroy, J., Hulme, M., and Menter. I., 2013. Developing a 'clinical model' for teacher education. *Journal of Education for Teaching*, 39(5), 557–573.
Darling-Hammond, L., 2017. Teacher education around the world: What can we learn from international practice? *European Journal of Teacher Education*, 40(3), 291–309.
Darling-Hammond, L., and Lieberman, A., 2012. Teacher education around the world. What can we learn from international practice? In L. Darling-Hammond and A. Lieberman (eds), *Teacher Education around the World: Changing Policies and Practices*. London: Routledge, 151–69
Department for Education [DfE], 1992. *Initial Teacher Training (Secondary Phase)*. London: HMSO.
Department for Education [DfE], 2015. *Carter Review of Initial Teacher Training*. London: DfE. Available at: https://assets.publishing.service.gov.uk/government/uploads/system/uploads/attachment_data/file/399957/Carter_Review.pdf [accessed 30 December 2020].
Department for Education [DfE], 2016. *National Standards for School-Based Initial Teacher Training (ITT) Mentors*. London: DfE. Available at: https://assets.publishing.service.gov.uk/government/uploads/system/uploads/attachment_data/file/536891/Mentor_standards_report_Final.pdf [accessed 30 December 2020].
Department for Education [DfE]. 2018. *Addressing Teacher Workload in Initial Teacher Education (ITE): Advice for ITE Providers*. London: Department for Education.
Department for Education [DfE], 2019a. *ITT Core Content Framework*. London: DfE. Available at: https://assets.publishing.service.gov.uk/government/uploads/system/uploads/attachment_data/file/919166/ITT_core_content_framework_.pdf [accessed 30 December 2020].
Department for Education [DfE], 2019b. *Early Career Framework*. London: DfE. Available at: https://assets.publishing.service.gov.uk/government/uploads/system/uploads/attachment_data/file/913646/Early-Career_Framework.pdf [accessed 30 December 2020].
Department for Education, n.d. An overview of teacher education review. Available at: www.education-ni.gov.uk/articles/overview-teacher-education-review [accessed 19 February 2021].
Department for Education [DfE], 2019c. *Teacher Recruitment and Retention Strategy*. London: DfE. Available at: https://assets.publishing.service.gov.uk/government/uploads/system/uploads/attachment_data/file/786856/DFE_Teacher_Retention_Strategy_Report.pdf [accessed 27 February 2021].
Donaldson, G., 2011. *Teaching Scotland's Future: Report of a Review of Teacher Education in Scotland*. Edinburgh: Scottish Government.

Fordham. M., 2016. Realising and extending Stenhouse's vision of teacher research: The case of English history teachers. *British Educational Research Journal*, 42(1), 135-150.

Furlong, J., 2015. *Teaching Tomorrow's Teachers: Options for the Future of Initial Teacher Education in Wales*. Cardiff: Welsh Government.

Furlong, J., and Maynard, T., 1995. *Mentoring Student Teachers: The Growth of Professional Knowledge*. Routledge, London.

Geographical Association. 2020. Ofsted ITE Framework Consultation 2020 – GA response (March 2020). Available at: www.geography.org.uk/write/MediaUploads/Advocacy%20Files/Ofsted_ITE_framework_consultation_2020_GAresponse_18.3.2020_(1).pdf [accessed 17 January 2021].

Healy, G., 2020. What does effective professional learning – for teachers and school leaders – look like in the 21st century? *Education Exchange*. Available at: https://theeducation.exchange/what-does-effective-professional-learning-for-teachers-and-school-leaders-look-like-in-the-21st-century/ [accessed 17 January 2021].

Healy, G., Walshe, N., and Dunphy, A., 2020. How is geography rendered visible as an object of concern in written lesson observation feedback? *The Curriculum Journal*, 31(1), 7-26.

Hobson, A. J., 2016. Judgementoring and how to avert it: Introducing ONSIDE Mentoring for beginning teachers. *International Journal of Mentoring and Coaching in Education*, 5(2), 87-110.

Hobson, A. J., and Malderez, A., 2013. Judgementoring and other threats to realizing the potential of school-based mentoring in teacher education. *International Journal of Mentoring and Coaching in Education*, 2(2), 89-108.

Hobson, A. J., Ashby, P., Malderez, A., and Tomlinson, P. D., 2009. Mentoring beginning teachers: What we know and what we don't. *Teaching and Teacher Education*, 25(1), 207-216.

Institute of Physics, 2021. *Subjects Matter A Report from the Institute of Physics*. London: Institute of Physics.

Kinder, A., 2022. Mentoring within the geography subject community. In G. Healy, L. Hammond, S. Puttick and N. Walshe (eds), *Mentoring Geography Teachers in the Secondary School*. Abingdon: Routledge, 102-118.

Langdon, F., Daly, C., Milton, E., Jones, K., and Palmer, M., 2019. Challenges for principled induction and mentoring of new teachers: Lessons from New Zealand and Wales. *London Review of Education*, 17(2), 249-265.

Lawlor, S., 1990. *Teachers Mistaught: Training in Theories or Education in Subjects?* London: Centre for Policy Studies.

Lofthouse, R. M., 2018. Re-imagining mentoring as a dynamic hub in the transformation of initial teacher education: The role of mentors and teacher educators. *International Journal of Mentoring and Coaching in Education*, 7(3), 248-260.

Menter, I., 2019. The interaction of global and national influences. In T. Tatto and I. Menter (eds), *Knowledge, Policy and Practice in Learning to Teach: A Cross-National Study*. London: Bloomsbury, 268-279.

McIntyre, D., and Hagger, H. 1993. Teachers' expertise and models of mentoring. In D. McIntyre, H. Hagger and M. Wilkin (eds), *Mentoring: Perspectives on School-based Teacher Education*. Abingdon: Routledge, 86-103.

McIntyre, J., 2018. Restructuring teacher education in the UK: Insights into the future. In A. R. Simões, M. Lourenço and N. Costa. (eds.), *Teacher Education Policy and Practice: Challenges and Opportunities for the Future*. Abingdon: Routledge, 143-160.

Murray, J., and Mutton, T., 2016. Teacher education in England: Change in abundance, continuities in question. In Teacher Education Group (ed), *Teacher Education in Times of Change*. Bristol: Policy Press, 57-74.

Murtagh, L., and Dawes, L., 2020. National Standards for school-based mentors: The potential to recognise the "Cinderella" role of mentoring? *International Journal of Mentoring and Coaching in Education*, 10(1), 31–45.

Mutton, T., Burn, K., and Menter, I., 2017. Deconstructing the Carter review: Competing conceptions of quality in England's 'school-led' system of initial teacher education. *Journal of Education Policy*, 32(1), 14-33.

Office for Standards in Education, Children's Services and Skills [Ofsted], 2020. *Initial Teacher Education Framework and Handbook*. Manchester: Ofsted. Available at: https://assets.publishing.service.gov.uk/government/uploads/system/uploads/attachment_data/file/895321/Initial_teacher_education_framework_and_handbook.pdf [accessed 30 December 2020].

Osler, D., 2005. Policy review of teacher education in Northern Ireland. Available at: www.education-ni.gov.uk/sites/default/files/publications/de/osler-report.pdf [accessed 19 February 2021].

Ozga, J., 2000. *Policy Research in Educational Settings: Contested Terrain*. Buckingham: Open University.

Palombo, M., and Daly, C., 2022. Educative mentoring: A key to professional learning for geography teachers and mentors. In G. Healy, L. Hammond, S. Puttick and N. Walshe (eds), *Mentoring Geography Teachers in the Secondary School*. Abingdon: Routledge, 208-223.

Peiser, G., Ambrose, J., Burke, B., and Davenport, J. 2018. The role of the mentor in professional knowledge development across four professions. *International Journal of Mentoring and Coaching in Education*, 7(1), 2-18.

Pinnick, S., 2020. Mentoring secondary English trainee teachers: a case study. *English in Education*, 54(3), 251-264.

Polesel, P., Rice, S., and Dulfer, N. 2014. The impact of high-stakes testing on curriculum and pedagogy: A teacher perspective from Australia. *Journal of Education Policy*, 29(5), 640-657.

Puttick, S., 2018. Student teachers' positionalities as knowers in school subject departments. *British Educational Research Journal*, 44(1), 25-42.

Rowe, J., 2019. 5 reasons why plans for NQTs might make things worse. Available at: www.tes.com/news/5-reasons-why-plans-nqts-might-make-things-worse [accessed 20 January 2021].

Sahlberg, P., Broadfoot, P., Coolahan, J., Furlong, J., and Kirk, G. 2014. Aspiring to Excellence, final report of the International Review Panel on the Structure of Initial Teacher Education in Northern Ireland. Available at: https://dera.ioe.ac.uk/20454/1/aspiring-to-excellence-review-panel-final-report.pdf [accessed 29 December 2020].

Sirna, K., Tinning, R., and Rossi, T., 2008. The social tasks of learning to become a physical education teacher: Considering the HPE subject department as a community of practice. *Sport, Education and Society*, 13(3), 285-300.

Tapsfield, A., 2020. Training new teachers: A shift in emphasis? *Teaching Geography*, 6(3), 114-117.

Tapsfield, A., Roberts, M., and Kinder, A., 2015. *Geography Initial Teacher Education and Teacher Supply in England. A National Research Report by the Geographical Association*. Sheffield: Geographical Association.

Teacher Education Working Group [TEWG], 1993. *Report on the Conference on Geography in Initial Teacher Education: issues and challenges for ITE in geography*. Sheffield: Geographical Association.

Teach First, 2020. Early Career Framework: Mentor handbook. Available at: www.early-career-framework.education.gov.uk/teachfirst/wp-content/uploads/sites/4/2020/10/Early-Career-Framework-Programme-Mentor-Handbook-PDF.pdf [accessed 30 December 2020].

UCL Early Career Teacher Consortium, 2020. Early career professional development programme: Programme handbook. Available at: www.early-career-framework.education.gov.uk/ucl/wp-content/uploads/sites/5/2020/12/Programme-Handbook-Updated.pdf [accessed 17 January 2021].

Vonk, J. H. C., 1993. Mentoring beginning teachers: Mentor knowledge and skills. *Mentoring Partnership in Teacher Education*, 1(1), 31–41.

Young. M., 2020. From powerful knowledge to the powers of knowledge. In C. Sealy (ed), *The ResearchED Guide to The Curriculum*. Woodbridge: John Catt, 13–17.

3 Mentoring as a spatial practice

Clare Brooks

Introduction

Many years ago, back when I was a geography mentor, I recall a student teacher asking my advice about a large group of students who had not completed their homework, and how he should handle it. In our discussion, he talked about his relationship with the pupils, which he had thought was very positive, and how he was now concerned that the lack of homework was a sign that the relationships had deteriorated, and he did not know why. The homework in question was a survey of family-related occupations, to be used in subsequent lessons to explore categorisations and data trends related to industry and industrial change. The pupils who had not completed their homework were typically those who did not have families with a track record of formal work; their lack of homework completion more likely tied up with complex reasons to do with their circumstances and experiences, than with their relationship with the student teacher. The student teacher, a young middle-class geography graduate not from the local area, had not considered that this might be the case in our school, which had a comprehensive intake which included large numbers of white working class children, and children from a diverse range of (often refugee) backgrounds. Our conversation also considered how the teacher's conception of a *good teacher* as one who connects the classroom learning with the experiences of their pupils might develop in relation to this experience: what was the homework for? What did completing it mean for the classroom dynamic as well as for the pupils' learning to progress in this module? We discussed the implications for the overall learning of the unit, and the conceptual leaps that some of the pupils would need to make in order to fully grasp the content of the module, particularly if they had no direct experience of family members in formal work. We talked about how in a different school, with different groups of pupils, other modifications might need to be made. We both drew upon our spatial and geographical understanding in what turned into a rich mentoring conversation.

Why see mentoring through a spatial lens?

Whilst most geography teachers and geography educators have excellent spatial awareness and use it often in their teaching, perhaps they less frequently use their geographical understanding to think about the practice of teaching, and indeed mentoring. This is a shame, because teaching is no doubt a spatial practice: a practice that occurs within space and is, in

DOI: 10.4324/9781003157120-4

many ways, beholden to spatial variations. Indeed, as this chapter will argue, teaching and mentoring can be enhanced through using a spatial lens. For example, through using a spatial lens we can see that both teaching and mentoring varies:

- in relation to its location (for example how mentoring someone in a rural school might differ from that in an urban school, which in turn may vary from other urban schools);
- in relation to relative space (through understanding how individual mentoring practices are scaled and relate to individuals (the body), the school, its affiliates, wider community and neighbours, local and national education policies and international trends);
- in relation to representational space (how *good* teaching is understood variously within the scales highlighted above).

An emphasis on the spatial is particularly important for mentoring as it takes place in a variety of settings, not just in different places but also in different schools with different departments and different classrooms, each of which has a particular locational footprint. Individual settings do not exist in isolation but are situated within national policy contexts and global debates. They have their own networks and internal structures. In addition, they affect individuals at a local scale: through their personal experience of both being mentored and of mentoring.

The example offered at the beginning of this chapter indicates how such a spatial perspective can influence even individual acts of mentoring. Understanding what may seem like a simple problem, the lack of homework completed, tapped into a range of spatial factors including: the location of the school, its catchment community and the characteristics of the neighbourhood; expectations of the school around homework learning and the relationship between homework tasks and being ready to learn; the ability to connect local experiences with local and national trends (both in the topic being covered and around education); and conceptions of the practices of *good* teachers and how they behave.

Adopting a spatial perspective means seeing mentoring as a spatial practice which recognises that the act of mentoring produces and reproduces space through the messages it communicates about education, its role in society and what it means to be a good teacher (both in this location and more generally). These messages occur in both epistemological and ontological space through sites of practice and dominant discourses that we are all exposed to about what it means to be a teacher and to undertake teaching.

The arguments and perspectives outlined in this chapter stem from the outcomes of a two-year research project into high-quality, large-scale initial teacher education (ITE) programmes located in five universities in Australia, Canada, England, New Zealand and USA (see Brooks, 2021a). The research set out to focus on the practices of ITE or pre-service teacher training and preparation, but, in doing so, it became clear that to understand practices it is important to understand the contexts in which those practices sit. However, the application of spatial theory takes us to a deeper level of understanding beyond context. Through seeing teacher education, and by extension mentoring, through a spatial lens, we can fully appreciate the complexity of the practice. Moreover, such a perspective can also suggest innovative ways in which mentoring can support beginning teachers through a more explicit spatial focus. In this chapter I will outline the key ideas pertinent to mentoring and offer some examples of how these ideas can enhance mentoring practices.

Mentoring and the production of space

Lefebvre (1991) argues that space matters: spatial practice mediates between production and reproduction, revealing both the conceptual and the representational, and in doing so perpetuates the flow of capital. Lefebvre acknowledges that education is not directly controlled by capital but is needed (and provided by governments) to support the flow of capital. Therefore, education, conceptualised as the flow of social, cultural and intellectual capital, can perpetuate uneven development, as more affluent communities have access to higher-quality education and disadvantaged communities are left with less-qualified teachers (Allen and Sims, 2018). Geographers have used these ideas to understand geographies of education (see e.g., Katz, 2008); put in practical terms, the concerns of mentoring in one school, in one location will be as spatially and socially relevant as the concerns of mentoring in another: even though the teachers involved and the challenges they face will be quite different. However, the spatial context will influence how the *problems* for teaching are defined and how the practice of mentoring needs to adapt accordingly. Seeing mentoring as a spatial practice recognises that mentoring is influenced by several factors, including the socio-economic and academic background and intersectional identities and relationships of both the mentor and the mentee, the needs of the communities they serve and the priorities and policies of the schools, organisations of schools, governments and regulatory bodies where they work.

Adopting a Marxist analysis, Lefebvre (1991) and Harvey (2004) contend that space, how it is experienced, conceptualised and enacted, is key in how activities and inequalities (or to use Smith's (2010) phrase 'uneven development') get produced, evolve and are sustained. Lefebvre draws upon a conceptual triad to support his critical examination of space. The three fundamental pillars of this triad he calls the spatial practice, representations of space and representational space (Lefebvre, 1991). The pillars are not intended to be viewed separately but as a relationship between the lived and conceived space. David Harvey has connected his own thinking around space to that of Lefebvre, by exploring how practices move between these spaces, noting the distinction between actual space (as location), relative space (in how spaces relate to each other) and representational space (how ideas are represented spatially). Through critically exploring and seeking to understand the complexities of these spatial practices, Harvey argues we will be in a position to transform them (for further explorations of how these ideas can be useful for geography education see Hammond, 2020).

There are many similarities between Harvey's and Lefebvre's conceptions of space (Harvey, 2001), and taken together they provide a useful framework for looking at spatial influences on mentoring, which I outline below.

Location within space

Teaching in some locations will emphasise different things than in others. These locations have features in themselves such as local population characteristics which can affect the practice of teaching, and mentoring needs to respond accordingly. The differences between these locations are underpinned by a complex web of geographical/socio-economic factors: changing population demographics, economic developments, cultural traditions and changing social dynamics. Such features are dynamic and so factors that influence teaching will continue to change as the cities morph, their regions change and their populations change through time. No doubt the differential ways in which communities have been affected by the COVID-19 pandemic will also influence not just the cities where schools and universities are based (such as the decentralisation of city workers and the resultant impact on suburbs), but also the teaching and mentoring practices that happen within them.

Location, however, does not just set the spatial context for practice, but also is key in the temporal context. Schools and communities have long-standing reputations and what Kemmis et al. (2014) have called practice traditions which can be location-specific and can be enduring. Schools are complex places which can have enduring practice traditions but are also dynamic and have changing needs. A beginning teacher, as well as coming to terms with learning to teach, also needs to become aware of these particular features. As a mentor, you need to be attuned to both the enduring practice traditions and the changing needs of a dynamic community: you need to be able to make those needs explicit, and consider how they will affect teaching and how beginning teachers need to respond.

This perspective adds a new dimension to mentoring: placing mentors as important gatekeepers to the mystifying world of schools. They should be able to explain what may seem to be idiosyncratic behaviour or policies, and also why schools in a seemingly similar community can have very different expectations of staff and students, and how teaching and learning are played out to other schools in similar locations. The temptation may be to use external rationales: that a certain behaviour may be a response to this policy, research or trend. However, the interpretation of those external rationales will depend on the specific context of the school, and the mentor can seek to make that explicit.

To use a simple example, a geography teacher working in a coastal town in England explained to me how the location of the school played a role in many of the initiatives of the school: a focus on coastal processes and tourism in the geography curriculum were obvious examples. What was less obvious was the attention paid to literacy and numeracy: influences that were closely aligned with a fairly new *tradition* in the school of needing to emphasise academic skills over the vocational emphasis which had previously led to low expectations of the pupils. The mentor explained that this seemed counter-intuitive to many beginning teachers, who wanted to prepare the pupils for (mainly seasonal tourism) work available in the area. The experience of the school leaders, however, indicated that these older practice traditions, endemic though they were, needed to change.

Relative space

Mentoring normally happens between the mentor and the mentee: in that sense it occurs at the scale of the individuals involved. However, it also takes place within a department and a school (or a university) which is in itself a scaled entity that has its own policies and networks and is nested within national and regional policies, and global influences.

Whilst the local context is important, mentoring is influenced by what happens at a number of other scales. The smallest spatial scale is that of the individual. How mentoring is experienced by individuals is particularly significant for those individuals. As schools change so mentoring needs to take into account how this might change the mentoring relationship and emphasis. Much mentor training focusses on this important one-to-one relationship and in how mentors can maximise the impact of their interactions with mentees.

A spatial lens also highlights that there are other scales that will affect practices. Teaching and schools are beholden to national and regional accountability regimes and governance structures, which, in turn, are often influenced by global trends and the prevalence of policy borrowing or policy lending. This also has an impact on teacher education (for pre-service and early career teachers). Mayer (2017) has argued that the Global Education Reform Movement (as termed by Sahlberg, 2010) has resulted in a limited range of policies which have dominated national teacher-education policies. Advisory reports provided for governments often survey the policy context of other nations/regions in order to make recommendations for future teacher-education policy directions. For example, Ingvarson (2014) and Igvarson et al. (2019) specifically advise that increasing the role of Teacher Standards is an international benchmark of quality. However, a common problem with policy borrowing is that it fails to take into account the locational complexity and the influential practice traditions outlined in the section above.

Therefore if we see mentoring as situated within these relative spaces, it can help mentors to move beyond feedback specifically oriented to a beginning teacher's behaviour and enable them to move into a more educative relationship, which sees that behaviour nested within a range of policies, trends and initiatives. For example, if a mentoring conversation focusses on how a beginning teacher has tried a strategy related to climate-change education, this conversation can be enhanced if the mentor is able to talk about developments in climate-change education as well as in climate change. Understanding how climate-change education has grown and developed, the move away from *shock and awe* pedagogy, the importance of developing a robust understanding of the science of climate change, is important and requires the mentor to understand and be able to explain how the educational understanding of teaching about climate change has changed and continues to change and not least in how climate change fits into national curriculum. This may initially sound daunting, but most mentors, as more experienced subject experts, will be familiar with these debates and recent changes. The emphasis here is that mentors can contextualise behaviours and trends within the bigger picture of how these have developed both nationally and internationally. For further exploration of educative mentoring, see Palombo and Daly (2022).

These scaled perspectives will affect mentoring not just in relation to what goes on in schools but also about expectations of the mentors themselves. For example, in 2020, the UK Department for Education (DfE) introduced (for England) the Initial Teacher Training Core Content Framework (DfE, 2019a), along with the Early Career Framework (DfE, 2019b), which prescriptively defines both the curriculum and pedagogy of mentoring programmes for early career teachers. Both are based on a narrow and limited range of research and a focus on teacher behaviours over knowledge and understanding. The policy rhetoric around this framework is about raising standards and providing a baseline of entitlement, but Mills (2020) has argued that it demonstrates a fundamental lack of respect for teachers. In practice, these initiatives seek to influence the mentoring process and the capacity for mentors to draw upon their own expertise in how they adapt their work. As some mentors enable, and in some cases even welcome, such approaches they diminish their ability to self-determine how mentoring contributes to teacher professionalism. A scaled perspective on mentoring should encourage mentors to move beyond these frameworks and to bring into mentoring their own expertise and experience to support the development of beginning teachers, as well as to use mentoring as an opportunity to broaden the horizon, repertoire and experience of beginning teachers.

Representational space

Mentoring is all about improving teaching and so is dominated by images or conceptions of how teaching and teachers should be. All teachers practise within this representational space, and are used to discourses around quality, standards and agendas for improvement.

Discourses about quality and what makes a good teacher dominate both the public and private spaces of education. In that sense, teacher education can be seen as a representational space: representing images of what education is for, what is a *good* teacher and what teachers are expected to do. Mentoring is the point in time when many of these messages are communicated: through feedback, target-setting and reflections on practice. Sometimes these are aligned with progress towards meeting the Teacher Standards. Biesta (2019) argues for a turn away from the current emphasis on outcome and attainment, which he describes as the age of measurement, towards realigning with the challenging and complex questions about educational purpose. Biesta argues that focussing on educational purpose should be at the centre of teacher education from the outset, as teaching is a moral endeavour - one where the educational purpose is embedded in every action and decision, and that teacher education should foreground these challenges and questions for teachers to use as part of their understanding of their role and responsibilities. This perspective refocusses the mentoring activity as not just being focussed on meeting the Teacher Standards in England (Department for Education, 2012), but incorporating wider discussions about quality in teaching and what we understand that to be and why.

Quite simply, this can mean using mentoring conversations to move beyond discussions of the practical and what can be done in relation to one scenario or another: and to enable the mentee to critically question their conceptions and understanding of being a "good" teacher. The dominance of what Lortie (1975, p. 61) called the 'apprenticeship of observation' (based on our own experience as a pupil) influences our images of what it means to be a teacher, and therefore what 'feels right' when you are learning to teach. These conceptions are strong and resilient, but beginning teachers are also influenced by public trends and debates around high-quality education and what it looks like. Beginning teachers need to be vigilant in their own thinking and how these ideas are affecting their interpretation of their own practice.

This is a challenge for mentors as the representational space of being a teacher, and of education, is shot through with competing notions of what it means to be a *good* teacher. Connell (2009) has argued that new discourses of the good teacher focus on the auditability of teachers' work that can demonstrate impact within a narrow set of indicators. Mentors need to be aware that the discourses of standards, quality indicators and quality assurance are paramount in defining what it means to teach and that these discourses will influence what beginning teachers believe they are striving for.

The model of ITE practice

These three spatial perspectives offer a way of thinking about mentoring as a spatial practice which can help mentors rethink their mentoring. Mentoring can be enhanced by thinking about the relative and representational spaces that affect both the practice of mentors and their mentees. I offer here a model of ITE practice (see Brooks 2021a) that was initially designed to reflect teacher education as a whole, but can also be used to support mentors to reflect on their work as teacher educators.

The model of ITE practice (see Figure 3.1) highlights three spatial knowledges which are pertinent to teacher education and mentoring. The layout of the model illustrates how these three spatial knowledges are related and interconnected through teacher education practice: in that sense they also relate to the practice of mentoring. These relationships are bidirectional: spatial influences will affect practices and pedagogy and, in turn, these may shape ways of knowing about teacher education. The framework is designed as a way of laying these elements out, showing how they intersect and interrelate. The model has been developed through my study of large-scale, high-quality initial teacher education programmes in five international contexts.

Each knowledge is related to the specific location of the practice and how it is situated within the relevant relative and representational spaces of ITE. The spatial knowledges are therefore contingent upon the location of the practice, the degree of control and influence that mentors can exert and the dominant representations of being a *good teacher* in this context.

Situated knowledge

Teachers and mentors have an in-depth knowledge of education in both a broad and a localised sense: they draw upon a detailed understanding of the catchment area of the school, its unique features and key issues/priorities. This understanding is situated within national and global discourses: for example, what are the specific demands of teachers in

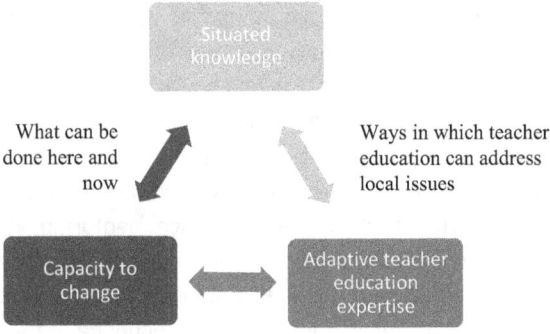

Figure 3.1 Model of ITE practice.
Source: Brooks, 2021a, p. 204.
Reproduced by permission of Taylor & Francis Group from: Initial Teacher Education at Scale, Clare Brooks, Copyright (2021) Routledge.

this local area? This knowledge needs to be mindful of the scale of the individual: how do these debates/issues affect pupils, students and teachers? The localised knowledge is highly situational: it includes educational debates and issues that matter at a range of scales, but specifically how they affect the local context, the school community and neighbourhood, and affiliations (such as within a Multi-Academy Trust (MAT) or Teaching School Hubs). The knowledge is dynamic and will be affected by trends in education as well as more local concerns that affect the school.

Adaptive teacher education expertise

Mentoring navigates complex accountability structures and multiple stakeholders across schools and teacher education providers (such as universities) and situates them within teachers' practice, particularly in relation to pedagogy and practice. To do this requires teacher education expertise stemming from a range of sources, including theories of professional learning, the experience of working with beginning teachers in a range of contexts and knowledges of learning and teaching from other fields, knowledge and experience of the school and from research. This specialist mentoring expertise is grown from, but distinct to, the experience of teaching, and has to be highly adaptive to local and dynamic contexts. This knowledge base enables mentors to make informed decisions about how to structure, teach and assess their mentoring. It will also inform mentoring conversations as mentors encourage beginning teachers to think about a range of aspects of their practice.

Capacity to change

The ability to make the decisions outlined above is often limited and constrained by context such as school governance systems, local funding or accountability arrangements or practice traditions around partnership. Universities and schools are necessarily designed for other activities (such as research, teaching and education of students or pupils), and so their systems may not be optimum for mentoring. Therefore, any adaptations need to be adjusted with these constraints (and opportunities) in mind. This might influence, for instance, how often mentors can meet with mentees, how lessons are observed and discussed and how mentors can influence the practice of mentees and how they teach.

The three factors identified are spatially situated, interdependent and contingent upon each other. For example, in a place where there is a strong situated knowledge, like the dominant and shared discourse around the need for more equity in education in New Zealand (Cochran-Smith et al., 2016), this discourse will influence mentoring, which is itself contingent upon the degree of autonomy and agency afforded to mentors. The situated knowledge may not directly change practice itself but will be highly influential, as it will drive not only what changes are needed (for example, in response to a change in the local curriculum or school policies), but also how mentoring can respond to such changes. As a mentor, therefore, you should develop an understanding of the challenges that both mentors and beginning teachers face, and pertinent infrastructural factors such as local governance (school autonomy or oversight) which can influence how mentoring partnerships are negotiated.

Similarly, a limited capacity for change, for example, in a highly regulated context with a prescriptive curriculum, will likely restrict opportunities for innovation or adaptations due to a change in circumstances. Capacity to change may be outside the scope of the mentors, or indeed the school or teacher education partnership to which they belong. It may be controlled externally by professional associations or government bodies. It is,, however, also scaled, contingent on individual institutions through the autonomy and agency afforded to individual teacher educators or programme leaders.

Central to the maintenance of high-quality mentoring is the adaptive expertise of mentors themselves, which will also vary across different locations and roles (particularly between university, schools and other partners). It is necessary in both leaders and individual mentors. Approaches which are too fixed or dogmatic are unlikely to respond to a changing local context. Mentors themselves may fail to recognise this expertise, or to appreciate that its adaptive nature is key when responding to dynamic definitions of quality.

Conclusion: using the model of ITE practice for mentoring

The three spatial knowledges therefore are interrelated. As change occurs in one area of the model such as in the local context, or through new regulations, or new research, so other areas of the model need to adapt. In some ways this illustrates the complexity of the mentoring role: having to continually assess and position mentoring practice within this knowledge landscape. It can also be helpful. When mentors are faced with a tricky mentoring situation, such as the one outlined at the start of this chapter, where a student teacher presents a problem or issue that they need to resolve, mentors can use the spatial knowledges as a way of thinking through different ways to help:

- What is particular about this (social and spatial) context that might be affecting this situation?
- How might looking at this situation from a different scale affect our understanding of it?
- In what ways are we conceptualising good teaching, a good lesson or good learning in this scenario, and how is that affecting our expectations?

This approach requires you, as a mentor, to reflect on your mentoring practice in a number of ways: the influence of policy, the influence of the school community and practices, and the expectations of the mentoring activity, as well as considering the capacity and development of yourself and the mentee involved. The model offers a way of conceptualising or informing mentoring. By extension, it suggests that mentors have a range of specific actions you can take to improve the quality of your mentoring, through:

- ensuring that you are fully conversant in the situated scaled knowledges around education, teacher education and mentoring practices pertinent to your context;
- considering the capacity to change afforded to you and the extent to which you are enabled or constrained to undertake high-quality mentor practices; and
- ensuring that your mentoring expertise is suitably adaptive and responsive to changing situations.

For discussion

- In what ways have you used, or could you use, your local situated knowledge to add to the mentoring conversation?
- What are the limits and opportunities to your mentoring, and how can you be more adaptive in your mentoring practice to work around those limits and with those opportunities?
- Consider having a conversation with your mentees about their images of a 'good teacher' and how that is specific to your department, school and location, and how it might vary from the images of a 'good teacher' held by other members of the school community.

Further reading and resources

1. Harvey, D., 2004. *Space as a key word*. Paper presented at the Marx and Philosophy Conference, Institute of Education, London. Available at: http://frontdeskapparatus.com/files/harvey2004.pdf.

To find out more about the ideas around space articulated here, David Harvey's 2004 essay is a good introduction. The essay explores the ideas about relative and representational space, where they have come from and their relevance. It also includes some personal examples that help to explore the themes.

2. Brooks, C., 2021b. Research capacity in initial teacher education: trends in joining the 'village'. *Teaching Education*, 32(1), 7-26. doi:10.1080/10476210.2020.1862077.

If you are interested in how this approach to mentoring relates to research, then some comparative examples are given in Brooks, 2021b. Research is an important dimension in the content of teacher education, but is often not featured as part of the mentoring conversation. This paper helps to explain why and could be a useful starting point for talking to beginning teachers about how they view research and what it contributes to their understanding.

References

Allen, R., and Sims, S., 2018. Do pupils from low-income families get low-quality teachers? Indirect evidence from English schools. *Oxford Review of Education*, 44(4), 441-458.

Biesta, G., 2019. Reclaiming teaching for teacher education: Towards a spiral curriculum. *Beijing International Review of Education*, 1(2-3), 259-272.

Brooks, C., 2021a. *Initial Teacher Education at Scale: Quality Conundrums*. London: Routledge.

Brooks, C., 2021b. Research capacity in initial teacher education: Trends in joining the 'village'. *Teaching Education*, 32(1), 7-26. doi:10.1080/10476210.2020.1862077.

Cochran-Smith, M., Ell, F., Grudnoff, L., Haigh, M., Hill, M., and Ludlow, L., 2016. Initial teacher education: What does it take to put equity at the center? *Teaching and Teacher Education*, 57, 67-78.

Connell, R., 2009. Good teachers on dangerous ground: Towards a new view of teacher quality and professionalism. *Critical Studies in Education*, 50(3), 213-229.

Department for Education [DfE], 2012. *Teachers' Standards*. London: DfE. Available at: https://assets.publishing.service.gov.uk/government/uploads/system/uploads/attachment_data/file/665520/Teachers__Standards.pdf [accessed 12 March 2021].

Department for Education [DfE], 2019a. ITT Core Content Framework. London: DfE. Available at: https://assets.publishing.service.gov.uk/government/uploads/system/uploads/attachment_data/file/919166/ITT_core_content_framework_.pdf [accessed 12 March 2021].

Department for Education [DfE], 2019b. Early Career Framework. London: DfE. Available at: https://assets.publishing.service.gov.uk/government/uploads/system/uploads/attachment_data/file/913646/Early-Career_Framework.pdf [accessed 12 March 2021].

Hammond, L. E., 2020. *An Investigation into Children's Geographies and their Value to Geography Education in Schools*. London: UCL (University College London). Available at: https://discovery.ucl.ac.uk/id/eprint/10090131/1/Lauren%20Hammond.FINAL%20THESIS.pdf.

Harvey, D., 2001. *Spaces of Capital: Towards a Critical Geography*. Abingdon: Routledge.

Harvey, D., 2004. Space as a key word. Paper presented at the Marx and Philosophy Conference, Institute of Education, London. http://frontdeskapparatus.com/files/harvey2004.pdf.

Ingvarson, L., 2019. Teaching standards and the promotion of quality teaching. *European Journal of Education*, 54(3), 337-355.

Ingvarson, L., Reid, K., Buckley, S., Kleinhenz, E., Masters, G., and Rowley, G., 2014. *Best Practice Teacher Education Programs and Australia's Own Programs*. Canberra: Department of Education.

Katz, C., 2008. Cultural Geographies lecture: Childhood as spectacle: relays of anxiety and the reconfiguration of the child. *Cultural Geographies*, 15(1), 5-17.

Kemmis, S., Wilkinson, J., Edwards-Groves, C., Hardy, I., Grootenboer, P., and Bristol, L., 2014. *Changing Practices, Changing Education*. London: Springer Science and Business Media.

Lefebvre, H., 1991. *The Production of Space*. Trans. D. Nicholson-Smith. (Vol. 142). Oxford: Blackwell.

Lortie, D. C., 1975. *Schoolteacher*. Chicago: University of Chicago Press.

Mayer, D., 2017. Professionalizing teacher education. In *Oxford Research Encyclopedia of Education* (Vol. 1). Oxford: Oxford University Press.

Mills, M., 2020. *Inaugural Lecture: Teachers and Teaching: the politics of respect*. London: UCL Institute of Education.

Palombo, M., and Daly, C., 2022. Educative mentoring: A key to professional learning for geography teachers and mentors. In G. Healy, L. Hammond, S. Puttick and N. Walshe (eds), *Mentoring Geography Teachers in the Secondary School*. Abingdon: Routledge, 208-223.

Sahlberg, P., 2010. Educational change in Finland. In A. Hargreaves, A. Lieberman, M. Fullan and D. Hopkins (eds), *Second International Handbook of Educational Change*. Dordrecht: Springer, 323-348.

Smith, N., 2010. *Uneven Development: Nature, Capital, and the Production of Space*. Georgia: University of Georgia Press.

4 What sort of mentoring for what sort of geography education?

John Morgan

Introduction

The question in my title – what sort of mentoring for what sort of geography education? – is a deliberate reference to earlier contributions by David Harvey (1974) and John Huckle (1987). Both Harvey and Huckle were insisting that geographers take seriously the social and political purposes that underpin geographical education in its widest sense. They were pointing out the importance of challenging the pretensions of geographers to think about their work as a series of technical procedures and problem-solving. Decades later, when we face challenges of ecological catastrophe, economic crisis and social conflict, critical geography educators should resist any initiative that serves to *take the heat* out of a world which is, in the words of Naomi Klein (2017), *On Fire*.

We have been here before; as long ago as 1973, in an article in the TES (Times Educational Supplement) entitled *Geography is Bunk*, Merriam (1973) warned geography teachers that:

> The truth of the matter is that the relevant questions concerning the environment today and man's relation to it are not being asked by a geography which inherits assumptions of nineteenth-century natural philosophy, assumptions which have been successfully challenged in other fields and which can be challenged in geography by secondary school students…. The relevant questions are more unsettling than any asked by today's geography and they concern the values by which human decisions that affect our spatial existence are made…. Too often geography has raised a smokescreen of fact which has obscured significance. To mention in passing that bulk foodstuffs can be produced on a larger scale, more cheaply than in Western Europe, is to conceal the nature and practice of the economic control of underdeveloped countries by the developed countries and the philosophy behind development itself.
>
> (p. 6)

It might be tempting to dismiss this statement as coming from a bygone age, and that Merriam's warning to put its house in order was heeded by geography teachers as the various humanistic, radical, feminist and cultural turns transported geography as an academic discipline to the intellectual cutting edge in the 1990s and beyond.

However, almost half a century after it appeared, Merriam's (1973) comment still makes us sit up. In part, that is because the year – 1973 – was such a momentous one. Historians often use 1973 as shorthand to denote the end of the long post-war boom in advanced economies. To paraphrase Levinson (2016): as economic growth exploded, people could feel their lives improving almost by the day. New homes, cars and consumer goods were within reach for average families and government social programmes and accords between capital and labour created an unprecedented sense of personal financial security. People who had imagined they would be sharecroppers in the Alabama cotton belt or day labourers in the Mezzogiorno found opportunities of which they could never have dreamed.

After 1973 the world changed dramatically. The warmth of prosperity gave way to cold insecurity – the *Ice Age* as novelist Margaret Drabble dubbed it in 1977 – trade wars, exchange rate worries and competition for foreign investment meant that the middle classes felt insecure, and blue-collar workers felt they were slipping down the economic ladder. The age of anxiety replaced an age of boundless optimism (see Reid-Henry, 2019).

Merriam's (1973) article was drawing attention to the cracks that were beginning to appear. He appears to say that geography was complacent about its political neutrality, its methods and its philosophy. As taught and studied in schools, geography was unable to provide realistic maps with which to understand a changing world. Despite the very real changes in what it means to teach geography since that time, it is possible to argue that school geography and the institutional arrangements that have supported teachers and their work in classrooms have dramatically failed to grasp the severity and scale of the crises that, today, have reached breaking point. As I will argue in the next section, the triple crisis of environment, economy and racism must take centre stage in any discussion of education for a just and ecologically sustainable world. Any discussion of effective mentoring requires an answer to the question, *what sort of mentoring for what sort of geography education?*

A world in crisis?

History seems to throw up some years that dramatically change the axis on which the world spins. Thus, we can think of 1945, 1967, 1979, 1989, 2001, 2008, and now 2020. The world faces three distinct crises – of environment, economy and culture – that will shape the lives of the generation of children growing into adulthood. These are things that geography educators should have seen coming, were probably aware of, but which were consigned to the 'too hard' basket. Here, I use *geography teachers* as a sub-set of a wider set of *geography educators*, which includes those who train teachers, research geography in schools and contribute to wider discussions of the theory and practice of teaching geography. The first is the strong sense that we are living in the Anthropocene, an epoch in which it is increasingly apparent that human activity is changing the operations of Earth's physical systems. The second is the economic crisis that has been developing as the decade of growth unleashed by forces of globalisation came to an end, and which has been most clear in the aftermath of the global financial crisis of 2008, and the 'corona crunch' associated with the global pandemic. The third is related to the growing recognition of the iniquities and systemic violence of racial capitalism, whereby the costs of uneven economic growth are experienced by *surplus populations*. For decades, geography educators have tended to avoid the *difficult* issue of race and racism, but, with the emergence of *Black Lives Matter* and moves to decolonise the curriculum, that is no longer possible (see Puttick and Murrey, 2020). In the remainder of this section, I will attempt to substantiate that claim.

The environmental crisis has been on the horizon for at least the last 60 years, with the publication of Rachel Carson's (1962) *Silent Spring*, the rise of *ecology* as a science, and the cultural impact of the moon landings and the image of the Earth from space. This new consciousness gave rise to environmental education. It seems obvious that this was the stuff of geography, but geographers were quite reluctant to embrace this at first, not least because it seemed to threaten the subject's place in the school curriculum. Environmental studies was a subject for pupils deemed 'non-academic', whilst geography was for those deemed 'academic'. There were attempts to introduce problem-solving and issues-based enquiries, but the new geography introduced into schools was composed of 'mind-bending exercises in statistics largely irrelevant to the urgent problems confronting the environment we live in' (Wheeler, 1975, p. 22). The emergence of sustainability as a policy goal was a spur to take the environment seriously, but the models geography educators adopted were largely education about and education through the environment (Pepper, 1984). Less developed were approaches that argued the case for education for the environment, based on socially critical or political education. This was a lost opportunity, but it was based on the assumption that there was a separation between *people* and *environment* or *society* and *nature*. Geographers may be keen to claim the Anthropocene, as a natural addition to the curriculum, but what that actually means in practice is unclear (Bonneuil and Fressoz, 2016).

It is increasingly clear that the *corona crash* is a crisis of political economy (Blakeley, 2021). The global lockdowns of 2020 (which are still ongoing at the time of writing in early 2021) are a classic case of what happens when capital stops flowing. Profits are interrupted, and workers, who already have few savings to sustain them for any length of time, face a loss of income. In this instance, nation-states moved quickly to support the economy: effective printing money to allow firms to keep workers on their books. The economic model was already in crisis following the global economic shock of 2008, with governments maintaining interest rates at or near zero in order to encourage investment. In the case of Britain this was a part of a long-standing problem of how to ensure the conditions for accumulation, and there was a growing sense that the neoliberal model was on the way out, with an important critical literature on what would come next (e.g. Gamble, 2019). At its best this work pointed to the need for a radical rethink of political priorities and the nature of a just transition to a sustainable economy (e.g. Raworth, 2017; Pettifor, 2019). There is an urgent need to ensure that these insights are incorporated into a reformed geographical education. Benko and Scott (2004) state that the task of a modern economic geography is to 'elucidate ways in which geography influences the economic performance of capitalism' (p. 47), but geography education has steadfastly avoided any attempt to engage with the field of political economy and its discussion.

The depth of geography's problems with dealing with any political challenge can be seen when it comes to race and racism. The Black Lives Matter movement has prompted a rapid process of learning, but the subject as taught in schools is taught through a 'white racial frame' (Feagin, 2013). Despite the fact that as early as 1977 a Green Paper on education stated that 'the curriculum appropriate to our imperial past cannot meet the requirements of modern Britain' (DES, 1977, p. 41), race and racism have yet to become an 'essential and continuing theme running throughout a rigorous geographical education' (Bonnett and Nayak, 2003). The reasons for this have yet to be fully explored (Morgan and Lambert, in preparation), but we can note that, even in the 1980s, a time when debates about racism and education gained visibility, the Geographical Association's (GA) response was to remove the political aspects of these issues (Gill, 1982; Walford, 1985). Rawling's (2001) acclaimed study of the changing place of geography as a school subject in national curriculum policy does not refer to these debates; Butt's (2020) otherwise exhaustive treatment of the literature of geographical education research makes no reference to the issue, and successive editions of the GA's *Handbook for Secondary Geography* (Jones, 2017) are likewise silent. The result is that now there is talk of white ignorance and white supremacy, there are calls to *decolonise the geography curriculum* and for the introduction of *black geographies*.

Whilst it would be easy to get defensive about these things, that, I think, is the wrong response. It assumes that teachers are in control of their work, when in fact what and how they teach is – in part – shaped by external forces. As John Huckle (1985) reminded us:

> Contrary to the beliefs of many geography teachers, changes in the nature of schooling, curriculum content, and methodology are not… simply a response to the growth of knowledge or the changing preoccupations of geographers and educationalists.
>
> (p. 294)

Huckle went on to suggest that the challenges to education in the 1980s provided opportunities for geographers to argue for a genuine polytechnic education, one that would provide students with a practical and theoretical understanding of work and the economy, and a critical grasp of the social relations under which these take place (for an overview of the arguments around curricular socialism in post-war schooling, see Morgan, 2020). Instead, geography educators got excited about enquiry learning, assessment for learning, geographic literacy, thinking skills, technology, and GIS (geographical information systems), personalisation and so on. These were all things that dovetailed more or less neatly with the modernising agenda of the educational state. They all diverted attention away from what should – from a critical perspective – be core to geography teaching: how to represent and understand what Harvey (2016) calls *The Ways of the World*. Again, there are good reasons for this; if ever there was a *Golden Age* for school geography, it is long past. The response to the economic crises of the 1970s and 1980s was for governments to reassert control over teachers' work, orient schooling to the *needs of industry*, and nationalise the curriculum.

Geography educators were relatively acquiescent in this process. The main subject organisation – the Geographical Association – took the line that any geography in the curriculum was better than none at all. It made the case for geography (Bailey and Binns, 1986) but removed from that case much of the baggage of progressive education (Jones, 1983). The result is that many of the promising moves towards a reconceptualised geography education that were afoot in the 1980s, often encouraged and supported by sympathetic geographers working in higher education, were short-lived (see Lee, 1983; and, on the journal *Contemporary Issues in Geography and Education*, Norcup, 2015).

A typology of mentors for geography teachers

In the light of these challenges, there is an urgent need for mentors to engage colleagues in sustained conversations about the theory and practice of geography education. Inevitably, definitions and ideas about mentoring will reflect models of the 'good teacher' that currently exist within schools, and it is possible to suggest a typology of approaches to *actually existing mentoring*. I have been developing this *typology* over a number of years, as something of an occasional hobby, starting from the assumption that – contrary to what some may claim (e.g. Coe et al., 2014) – there can never be complete agreement as to what it means to be a *good teacher* (see Moore, 2000). I identify here five ways of thinking about the work of teachers, making some brief comments about styles of mentoring.

Evidence-based learning

Perhaps the dominant approach to mentoring draws upon the imperative – much supported by policy-makers – for teachers to make use of insights from educational effectiveness research to improve practice and raise educational attainment. The focus is on *evidence-based* research – or *what works* – and responds to the demands of policymakers to guarantee teacher quality. The ur-text for this is John Hattie's (2008) *Visible Learning*. The book assumes that the most important variable in explaining differences in student performance is the teacher. The idea that mentors should work alongside teachers to implement those pedagogical processes that have demonstrable effects on student learning is a beguiling and attractive prospect. There are a number of problems with this. First, in the absence of an agreed and 'evidenced' body of knowledge about what constitutes 'effective geography teaching', there is a danger of falling back into generic approaches in which the *science of learning* is applied to geography lessons. Without careful thought, mentoring can become a highly structured and technical practice, with a focus on *demonstrable* results. At worst, it is an approach which ignores questions about the fundamental purpose of education.

Reflective knowledge

Almost diametrically opposite to this is mentoring which assumes that teaching is so deeply complex and contextual that any attempt to describe and understand the variegated ecosystems of actual classrooms will inevitably fail. Rather than seek to apply *proven* insights from the *learning sciences*, a reflective approach to mentoring seeks to place the teacher at the centre of a discussion about what happens in geography classrooms, and use these insights to experiment with changes and make adjustments to pedagogy. In this instance, the skill of the mentor is to enable such reflection by drawing on his or her own experiences and to provide timely and pin-pointed insights that allow the teacher to see their practice in new ways. As with evidence-based mentoring, there is a danger that geographical knowledge can end up being side-lined, with an undue attention to the *latest fashion* in pedagogy (e.g. dual-coding).

Teachers as activists

An alternative approach to mentoring is to adopt an *activist* perspective. This draws upon a long-established tradition of *progressive* and *radical* teaching which insists that schools and teachers operate at the cutting-edge of social change. The idea of teachers as bringing about social improvement grew in importance with the expansion of education in the post-war period under the auspices of the welfare state, which promised, in principle at least, a fairer, more just society. However, in the 1970s, with the collapse of social democracy and the growth of new social movements around race, gender and environment, many critics argued that schools were effectively a means of reproducing an unequal society. Knowledge in schools, it was suggested, reflected the interests of powerful groups in society and a hidden curriculum ensured that schools were places where the social hierarchy was maintained.

Though radical geography has been a marginal tradition in school geography, the continued crises of economy, environment and inequality promise a renewal of the tradition of *dissident geographies* (Blunt and Wills, 2000), and the rise of activist mentors who seek – by any means necessary – to deconstruct and alter the social relations of the geography classroom, develop a Freire-inspired (1969) *Pedagogy of the Oppressed*, and teach from the standpoint of the least advantaged. The activist mentor, in short, seeks to persuade geography teachers to become transformative intellectuals.

The knowledge-focussed mentor

A key feature of educational development over the past three decades has been the growth of the idea that being a good teacher is less about having secure grasp of large stocks of subject knowledge which should be transmitted to students and more about being a skilled facilitator of learning. This argument is predicated on the notion that knowledge is more and more available and accessible, and the role of the teacher is to help students to *learn how to learn*. In response, there are moves to *bring knowledge back* in (Young, 2008). Michael Young's argument is that many teachers are suspicious of teaching knowledge for its own sake, worrying that it is a form of imposition or conservativism, and may alienate some children.

The networked teacher mentor

Some commentators argue that society is on the cusp of a tumultuous quantitative and qualitative shift driven by technological changes that will transform the nature of teachers' professional work (e.g. Susskind and Susskind, 2015). Social media is changing the ways in which teachers communicate, access research, share knowledge, present themselves, build *communities of practice* and co-operate (and perhaps compete). New teacher identities will inevitably shape ideas and practices of mentoring. For example, the rise of new platforms for sharing ideas and examples of resources and teaching plans may allow for greater access to geographical resources. There may arise new affinity groups with interest in specific aspects of geography education. These examples are undoubtedly positive, though to date there has been little discussion of the ways in which *platform capitalism* is re-shaping geography teachers' work (though see Walshe and Healy, 2021).

Mentors – part of the solution or part of the problem?

In practice, of course, any individual mentor will be operating with a mix of these different approaches, responding flexibly to the situation in which they operate. Mentoring in its pure state is clearly a desirable thing. However, in an educational system that has been transformed (deformed?) to accommodate managerialism and accountability, it is important to ask questions about the politics of mentoring: mentors are, after all, likely to be appointed and/or sponsored by school managers and leaders and the *language* that surrounds their work may reflect this. Thus, in various chapters in this volume, we learn that mentors will *empower* teachers to critically engage with evidence in their personal growth. They will provide nourishment and induction into a repertoire of techniques, offer practical robust advice for planning lessons, and enable professional support opportunities for learning and professional development. This is intended as a mutually reciprocal relationship as mentor and mentees support each other to develop their practice and *cross thresholds*.

Obviously, this is a demanding role, and mentors are likely to be experienced practitioners who model high-quality teaching and professionalism. This means that they can induct teachers into learning communities, enabling innovation and creativity. In practical terms, mentors observe lessons, provide feedback, ask questions, and instigate dialogue in order to set appropriate development targets. Overall, successful mentoring will encourage teachers' self-efficacy and produce autonomous, self-sufficient, reflective and creative planners.

On one level, it is hard to argue with any of this. But the language of mentoring reads as if it is taken straight from the manual of how to construct a neoliberal subject (Dardot and Laval, 2017). It risks being highly individualised, evaluative, performative, and relies on the type of affective labour which blurs the boundaries between the personal and the professional. When mentoring becomes part of being a professional, as opposed to being something that springs from the common ground of shared interest and purpose, it is important to check whether the relationship is enabling or constraining. Here, it is helpful to remember geographer Andy Merrifield's critique of professionalism:

> Professionals are everywhere. Little gets done nowadays without a professional 'expert' offering their specially acquired knowledge: downscaling and evaluating, measuring and advising, scheming and sorting out life for millions of people the world over. It's as if everybody needs to get in on the act, to brand their whole personality as a compliant 'professional', to advance their career, to live a happy life. It's like we are told there are only two types of people: professionals (including wannabe professionals) and losers.
> (Merrifield, 2017, p. xi)

Without wanting to get into a heated discussion about exactly what we mean by *professional* (Hoyle and John's 1995 book remains a helpful guide to these arguments), I think Merrifield's (2017) plea for the amateur, someone who looks to find pleasure in doing what they love, is worth geography teachers' consideration. After all, professional educators are everywhere these days, and has it made much difference? Is there a danger that geography mentors will take on the role of instructors who effectively decide what teachers must learn, what they must read, how they must present themselves? These may be annoying questions but they raise fundamental issues about who has the power to define the parameters of our work as educators, and in what terms we should talk about it. This is the real issue: we have all worked in institutions where we attend training sessions run by professionals who are armed with the ring-bound manual and *talk us through* what is needed to improve. How many of us have sat there, politely, whilst in private fearing that these people never read books, and show little sign of interest in the most inspiring and impressive subjects?

Interestingly, Merrifield (2017) talks about David Harvey as a geographer who, whilst eschewing professionalism, has maintained a committed, scholarly and deeply humane approach. For Merrifield, Harvey displayed the qualities of a true mentor, which were: 'Intellectual amateurism'; 'a *sensibility* to de-professionalise reality; and a *political* allegiance to ordinary folk' (p. 12).

The thread that runs through Harvey's work, from *Explanation in Geography* in 1969 to the present, is that he has insisted on the importance of theory in representing the world. *Explanation in Geography* was an attempt to impose a theoretical framework on a discipline that was tending towards anarchy. Harvey (1969, p. 486) insists that 'by our theories shall they know us'. The theory Harvey had in mind here was informed by positivism, but his famous volte face to Marxism, announced a few years' later in *Social Justice and the City*, continued that quest. In his 2016 book *The Ways of the World* – composed of papers and chapters written from 1973 to 2010 – Harvey talks of his work as being concerned to produce some *cognitive* maps that provide the basis for making sense of the ways that the world works. The cognitive maps provide 'pegs' and 'handholds' with which to survey the current state of the world and 'perhaps hint at how we might take an exit from the predicament we face' (2016, p. 8). Harvey (2016) rarely speaks of learning, but at this point he says:

> Learning... means extending and deepening the cognitive maps we carry in our heads. These maps are never complete and in any case are rapidly changing, these days at faster and faster rates. but perhaps they provide a foundation for a critical understanding of the ways of the complicated geography in which we live and have our being.
>
> (p. 8)

Geography mentors face the future

In order to face the challenges of the future, we need geography mentors who are able to help others 'persevere with their geography' (Morgan, 2017, p. 532). Against the short-termism of contemporary school improvement and effectiveness paradigms, such mentors will model what it means to see geography as a central element of a humanistic and critical education. The phrase 'persevering with geography' comes from the late scholar Stuart Hall (2008, p. 12), who started his career teaching geography in Brixton in the late 1950s. Hall's was a model of what it means to keep grappling with understanding the changing meaning of the social and cultural landscape (Morgan, 2017). Applied to geography, this means a commitment to developing frameworks that can help us to understand what David Harvey (2016) calls 'the ways of the world'. In order to do this, we require theory.

Again, despite the undoubted changes that have taken place in geography education over the past few decades, much geography teaching in schools remains unaware of the intellectual origins of concepts and fails to offer a unified set of frameworks through which students can be helped to understand how geographies are made and re-made (see Lambert and Morgan, 2010, for an extended discussion of this point). As Derek Gregory, addressing geography teachers, wrote in 1983, there is a need for theoretical effort, because the world in which we live is an opaque one. Theory is needed so as to avoid presenting the subject as an assemblage of random examples, case studies or illustrative sketches, but as a connected whole.

This type of theorising is hard work. It does not yield immediate lessons for working with 9C on a Monday morning. But its purpose is to help us, as adults – as educators – to develop cognitive maps that, at some point, and however imperfectly, we can share with students. Where can this begin? I will finish with two examples.

The obvious place is with a geographical model. On page 2 of Harvey's (2017) *Marx, Capital and the Madness of Economic Reason*, there is a diagram of a staple of geography textbooks – the hydrological cycle. Harvey uses this diagram, with its flows and stores as water moves through the landscape at different rates and in different forms before being circled back to the atmosphere, as a visual aid to describing and explaining the flow of capital. This, of course, is a classic pedagogical tool. Reading and re-reading Harvey's account, and working through the analogy, can help teachers and student teachers to grasp a fundamental process shaping our geographies – the circulation of capital.

This idea, that we live in a world dominated by one economic system – capitalism, and the claim that capital is the key process that shapes our landscapes – invariably raises all sorts of questions, especially around the non-economic processes that shape the places and localities in which people live. In a sense, the claim that capital shapes the landscape is like claiming that water shapes the landscape; it is a theoretical proposition that requires examination. Harvey (2010) addresses this in chapter 6 of his book *The Enigma of Capital (and the crisis of capitalism)*. The chapter is called 'The geography of it all', and develops a co-evolutionary model of how capital changes, based on the idea that there are seven 'activity spheres' (Harvey, 2010, p. 121). These are:

- Technologies and organisational forms
- Social relations
- Institutional and administrative arrangements
- Labour and production processes
- Relations to nature
- Social reproduction
- Mental conceptions of the world

Whilst at first these can seem quite abstract, with some close reading and discussion teachers are able to describe places and regions they know well in terms of these seven activity spheres. In chapter 6 of *Enigma*, Harvey seeks to show how these are all interrelated: change one of these and others change. He shows how these result in distinctive places.

Thus, Harvey describes one place where the population is relatively homogeneous, and reasonably affluent. The built environment is laid out so as to facilitate the consumption of goods and services. Local employment is dominated by services, and whatever production that takes place is geared towards servicing the needs of this suburban population. The tax base is stable; social relations are relatively harmonious, apart from the occasional high-profile crime and marital breakdown. There is a strong image of individualism, though the shared collective value is home-ownership. Commuting distances are quite long, but high levels of consumption compensate for this inconvenience.

For Harvey this is an example of a place where the seven activity spheres listed above are roughly harmonised. The flows of capital into, through and out of this place are relatively stable and are facilitated by the organisation of these activity spheres. He goes on to compare this with another locality, not far away, a former steel and metal-making area, which has suffered from deindustrialisation and plant closure. The blue-collar population was once stable but is now facing challenges. The housing stock is deteriorating, those who can move away and the tax base is declining. Social problems are rife, and the gender regime has changed as family breakdown increases, and women are the primary breadwinners. The low property values attract low-income groups and relations between the old and new populations are tense, occasionally erupting in racial violence. Here, for Harvey, a change in the productive base has set in train shifts in all seven activity spheres and these are out of balance, with it being difficult to see how they can be made to balance.

The important thing about the examples here is that they illustrate the process of adopting a theoretical framework. A further example is found in Harvey's chapter 6. Once again, Harvey uses a standard pedagogic tool to illustrate an aspect of capital's operation. He asks readers to think of a satellite image taken from space of the weather systems swirling across the planet. At first all this motion within weather systems appears chaotic and unpredictable but observation and analysis reveal patterns within the chaos, and long-term changes in climatic signals can also be detected. The economic geographer is faced with a similar problem of finding distinctive patterns and long-term signals of change within the seeming chaos of economic activity:

> A synoptic map of economic activity in the 1980s, for example, would have depicted a series of highs building and swirling around the Pacific edge of much of east and south-east Asia as well as down the west coast of USA and throughout Bavaria and Tuscany. It would have depicted most of Latin America stagnant but prone to violent political and economic upheavals, and a series of deep depressions passing across the Ohio Valley and Pennsylvania, the British industrial heartlands as well as across the Ruhr Valley of Germany. The big difference to the study weather and climate, however, is that whereas the laws of fluid dynamics can be presumed to be constant over time, the laws of capital accumulation are constantly evolving as human behaviours adapt reflexively to new circumstances.
>
> (Harvey, 2010, p. 154)

It is important to note that Harvey (2016) is not claiming to tell the whole story about *The Ways of the World*. It is best to see theories as *takes* on the world, which, for geographers, are a response to patterns and events, and which are refined and modified in the light of changes to that world. Harvey's work has been strongly critiqued, not least from feminist geographers who question his insistence on capital as the primary force shaping social landscapes and the totalising and omnipotent 'male gaze' his approach entails (see the essays in Castree and Gregory, 2006). For his part, Harvey has insisted that to analyse capital is not the same as analysing capitalism, which makes use of and links to a wider set of social formations such as patriarchy or racism. The point is that understanding and explaining the world – surely the goal of geographers and geography education – require continual theory-building and refinement.

I have focused on David Harvey's work since, over the course of my career as a geography educator, his work has been a constant resource for helping me think and teach. I always learn something from re-reading his work that makes me a 'better' geography teacher, that makes me want to persevere with my geography (see for instance, Harvey's (2020) analysis of the coronavirus). Of course, there is more to life than David Harvey, but the point is that as geography educators we should grapple with the arguments and ideas that shape our field.

Thinking theoretically – and then developing ways to teach and communicate in ways that move from the concrete to the abstract, or vice versa – is hard intellectual work; it is going to require a new generation of geography educators who are prepared to take on the *cyberanthropes* of school improvement planners and engage them in a debate about what the 'value' represents in 'contextual value-added'. It is going to require teacher educators to demand that new teachers focus on the theoretical basis of the geography they teach. This is the type of mentoring we need for a worthwhile geography education.

Conclusion

Writing this chapter has prompted me to think about what exactly we want from professional discussions about geography teaching. School geography has contributed to the story we have been telling ourselves that economic growth is the most direct path to prosperity, that the good life implies material affluence and that a judicious mix of technology and governance can solve most of our social and environmental problems (see Inglis, 1985; Gilbert, 1984; Huckle, 1988). Even if as geography educators we have our personal doubts about the plausibility of this story, the wider ideology of *educational fundamentalism* which holds that education is the source of social and human capital has dragged us along (see Morgan, 2019, chapter 8, for a discussion). The COVID-19 pandemic is a radical reassertion of history against this complacent narrative. It is a painful and sobering reminder that humans and nature are inextricably linked. There are powerful voices that urge us all to *bounce back* and resume the neoliberal *normal*, even as it is increasingly hard to know how the ways of the world will be changed as a consequence of the *break*. The drive to ensure examination grades and university entrance is smooth is a classic instance of the *bounce back* narrative, but what I have argued in this chapter is that there is a wider set of aims and purposes for geography teachers. It is to address the question posed at the start of this chapter: *what sort of geography education for what sort of society?*

For discussion

- As a mentor, what are the most important challenges you face in working with geography teachers?
- Has the COVID-19 pandemic made you think differently about your work as a mentor? If so, in what ways? If not, why not?
- How do you respond to geographer Andy Merrifield's criticisms of *professionalism*? What does it mean to be a professional geographer in today's world?

Further reading and resources

1. Harvey, D., 2010. The Enigma of Capital (and the crises of capitalism). London: Profile Books.

Read chapter 5 ('Capital evolves') and chapter 6 ('The geography of it all'). Harvey's style is to write relatively short sharp sentences, which are packed with concepts. These two chapters set out the basis for a theory of capital, and show how geography matters. What do you learn from them that can sharpen the theoretical focus of your geography teaching?

2. Merrifield. A., 2017. *The Amateur*. London: Verso.

Merrifield is passionate in his belief that capitalism has constructed institutions that are designed to safeguard powerful interests and dampen down human freedom and creativity. His solution to this is to resist attempts to tell us what to think and do, and think for ourselves. What are the implications of this analysis for geography teachers?

References

Bailey, P., and Binns, A., 1986. *A Case for Geography*. Sheffield: Geographical Association.
Benko, G., and Scott, A., 2004. Economic geography: tradition and turbulence. In G. Benko and U. Strohmeyer (eds), *Human Geography: A History for the 21st Century*. London: Arnold, 47–63.
Blunt, A., and Wills, J., 2000. *Dissident Geographies: An Introduction to Radical Ideas and Practice*. London: Prentice Hall.
Bonnett, A., and Nayak, A., 2003. Cultural geographies of racialization – the territory of race. In K. Anderson, M, Domosh, S. Pile and N. Thrift (eds), *Handbook of Cultural Geography*. London: Sage.
Bonneuil, C., and Fressoz, J.-B., 2016. *The Shock of the Anthropocene: The Earth, History, and Us*. London: Verso.
Blakeley, G., 2021. *The Corona Crash: How the Pandemic Will Change Capitalism*. London: Verso.
Butt, G., 2020. *Geography Education Research in the UK: Retrospect and Prospect*. Singapore: Springer.
Carson, R., 1962. *Silent Spring*. Boston, MA: Houghton Mifflin.
Castree, N., and Gregory, D. (eds), 2006. *David Harvey: A Critical Reader*. Oxford: Basil Blackwell.
Coe, R., Aloisi, C., Higgins, S., and Elliott-Major, L., 2014. *What Makes Great Teaching? Review of the Underpinning Research*. London: Sutton Trust.
Dardot, P., and Laval, C., 2017. *The New Way of the World: On Neoliberal Society*. London: Verso.
DES, 1977. *Education in Schools: A Consultative Document*. London: HMSO.
Feagin, J., 2013. *The White Racial Frame: Centuries of Racial Framing and Counter-Framing*. London: Routledge.
Freire, P., 1969. *Pedagogy of the Oppressed*. London: Penguin.

Gamble, A., 2019. Why is neo-liberalism so resilient? *Critical Sociology*, 45(7-8), 483-94.

Gilbert, R., 1984. *The Impotent Image: Reflections of Ideology in the Secondary Social Studies Curriculum*. Brighton: The Falmer Press.

Gill, D., 1982. *Assessment in a Multicultural Society, Schools Council Report: Geography*. London: Commission for Racial Equality.

Gregory, D., 1983. Ideology and human geography. In ACDG (eds), *Racist Society, Geography Curriculum*. London: ACDG.

Hall, S., 2008. An interview with Stuart Hall, December 2007. By Colin MacCabe. *Critical Quarterly*, 50(1-2), 12-42.

Harvey, D., 1969. *Explanation in Geography*. London: Edward Arnold.

Harvey, D., 1972. The role of theory. In N. Graves (ed), *New Movements in the Study and Teaching of Geography*. Melbourne: Cheshire Publishing, 29-41.

Harvey, D., 1974. What kind of geography for what kind of public policy? *Transactions of the Institute of British Geographers*, 63, 18-24.

Harvey, D., 2010. *The Enigma of Capital (and the crises of capitalism)*. London: Profile.

Harvey, D., 2016. *The Ways of the World*. London: Profile.

Harvey, D., 2017. *Marx, Capital and the Madness of Economic Reason*. London: Profile.

Harvey, D., 2020. Anti-Capitalist politics in the time of COVID-19. Available at: http://davidharvey.org/2020/03/anti-capitalist-politics-in-the-time-of-covid-19/.

Hattie, J., 2008. *Visible Learning*. London: Routledge.

Hoyle, E., and John, P., 1995. *Professional Knowledge and Professional Practice*. London: Cassell.

Huckle, J., 1985. Schooling and geography. In R.J. Johnston (ed), *The Future of Geography*. London: Methuen.

Huckle, J., 1987. 'What *sort* of geography for what *sort* of school curriculum?' *Area*, 19(3), 261-265.

Huckle, J., 1988. *What We Consume: The Teachers' Handbook*. Godalming: WWF-UK / Richmond Press.

Inglis, F., 1985. *The Management of Ignorance; A Political Theory of the Curriculum*. Oxford: Basil Blackwell.

Jones, K., 1983. *Beyond Progressive Education*. London: Methuen.

Jones, M., 2017. *Handbook of Secondary Geography*. Sheffield: Geographical Association.

Klein, N., 2017. *On Fire: The Burning Case for a Green New Deal*. New York: Simon and Schuster.

Lambert, D., and Morgan, J., 2010. *Teaching Geography 11-18: A Conceptual Approach: A Conceptual Approach*. London: McGraw-Hill Education.

Lee, R., 1983. Teaching geography: The dialectic of structure and agency. *Journal of Geography*, 82(3), 102-109.

Levinson, M., 2016. *An Extraordinary Time: The End of the Post-War Boom and the Return of the Ordinary Economy*. London: Random House.

Merriam, T., 1973. Geography is bunk. *Times Educational Supplement* (6 October).

Merrifield, A., 2017. *The Amateur: The Pleasures of Doing what you Love*. London: Verso.

Moore, A., 2000. *The Good Teacher*. London: Routledge.

Morgan, J., 2017. Persevering with geography. *Documents D'Analisi Geografica*, 63(3), 529-544.

Morgan, J., 2019. *Culture and the Political Economy of Schooling: What's Left for Education?* London: Routledge.

Morgan, J., 2020. The prospects for knowledge socialism in one country. In M. Peters, T. Belsley, P. Jandric and Xudong Zhu (eds), *Knowledge Socialism: The Rise of Peer Production, Collegiality, Collaboration, and Collective Intelligence*. Singapore: Springer, 235-252.

Morgan, J., and Lambert, D., in preparation. *Race, Racism and Geography Teaching*.

Norcup, J., 2015. Awkward geographies? An historical and cultural geography of the journal Contemporary Issues in Geography and Education (CIGE) (1983-1991). PhD thesis. Available at: https://core.ac.uk/download/pdf/293049187.pdf.

Pepper, D., 1984. *The Roots of Modern Environmentalism*. London: Croom Helm.

Pettifor, A., 2019. *The Case for the Green New Deal*. London: Verso.

Puttick, S., and Murrey, A., 2020. Confronting the deadening silence on race in education in England: Learning from anti-racist, decolonial and black geographies. *Geography*, 103(3), 126-134.

Rawling, E., 2001. *Changing the Subject*. Sheffield: Geographical Association.

Raworth, K., 2017. *Doughnut Economics*. London: Random House.

Reid-Henry, S., 2019. *Empire of Democracy: The Remaking of the West since the Cold War, 1971-2017*. London: John Murray.

Susskind, R., and Susskind, D., 2015. *The Future of the Professions*. Oxford: Oxford University Press.

Walford, R. (ed), 1985. *Geographical Education for a Multicultural Society*. Sheffield: Geographical Association.

Walshe, N., and Healy, G., (eds), 2021. *Geography Education in the Digital World: Linking Theory and Practice*. London: Routledge.

Wheeler, K., 1975. The genesis of environmental education. In G. Martin and K. Wheeler (eds), *Insights into Environmental Education*. St. Albans: Hart-Davis Educational.

Young, M., 2008. *Bringing Knowledge back in: From the New Sociology of Education to Social Realism*. London: Routledge.

SECTION 2
Perspectives and experiences in geography mentoring

5 Working with the complexity of professional practice and development

Phil Wood and Aimee Quickfall

Introduction

It has long been recognised that the quality of teaching within an education system is one of the most important factors in ensuring a high quality experience for children (Hattie, 2003; Darling-Hammond et al., 2005), although what constitutes *quality* is disputed (Flores, 2019). The countries with the highest-performing school systems have succeeded in making teaching one of the pre-eminent professions, respected throughout society and attractive to the highest achievers. They have focussed attention on the effective recruitment, selection and initial training of teachers, so that all those who begin a career in the classroom are well equipped to do so (DfE, 2011, referencing Barber et al., 2007). Subsequent to the initial education of teachers, continued professional development is also crucial to continued engagement and growth of professionals. This has resulted in the evolution of a range of approaches to teacher professional development over time, from external training courses, through internal training to the use of practitioner research and engagement with academic research. These have all been part of teacher development ecosystems as schools try to develop informed and extensive support, especially for teachers in the early part of their career.

Since 2010, there has been an increasing focus on the development of beginning teachers, perhaps in response to high attrition rates among recently qualified teachers (RQTs). Statistics published by the Department for Education (DfE) show that more than one in six (15.3 per cent) of the teachers who qualified in 2017 dropped out after just one year of teaching (DfE, 2019). In reaction to these negative trends the DfE has developed an Early Career Framework (DfE, 2020) for Early Career Teachers (ECTs) to ensure they retain the momentum in developing their expertise, the foundation of which has been laid in their period of initial teacher education (ITE). From September 2021, the NQT (newly qualified teacher) title was replaced by ECT, who will receive 'development support and training over two years instead of one, underpinned by the early career framework' (DfE, 2021, p. 3). Support includes training development materials and funding for mentor time.

The stress which has been put on different developmental activities has shifted over time and has often reflected political *innovations*. Such developments include the introduction of the National Strategies and the creation of research schools which now act as *clearing houses* for engagement with a narrow range of educational research evidence

DOI: 10.4324/9781003157120-7

from organisations such as the Education Endowment Foundation. The use of randomised controlled trials has led to 'channelling the focus of innovation and development to tightly structured interventions and generating a series of narrowing effects' (Burnett and Coldwell, 2020, p. 1). Whilst various fads have come and gone, the role of mentoring has been relatively consistent over a long period of time. It continues to be a powerful activity for orienting and enculturating those early in their career to give them a positive start as well as helping individuals to develop and hone their practice with the help of a more knowledgeable other. In this chapter we offer a new way for you to understand mentoring, by emphasising its process, and add to this the use of a framework for developing dialogues about your pedagogic practice, namely pedagogic literacy. We also draw upon case studies from our experiences of working with mentors and beginning teachers. Case-study teachers have been given pseudonyms and have consented to their stories being told in this chapter.

> **Task 5.1 Mentor reflection: expectations of mentor relationships**
>
> What are your expectations of mentoring?
> What expectations are there of the role, and what is beyond the remit of a mentor?
> What are your expectations of a mentee?
> What are the likely areas for development beginning teachers might wish to focus on in a mentoring relationship?

Basic features of mentoring approaches

A basic model of mentoring activity was outlined by Kram (1985), who split the process into four steps as the relationship begins, matures and eventually reaches some form of conclusion: initiation, cultivation, separation and redefinition. To begin with, there is a stage of *initiation*. In this phase the mentee begins by reflecting on both their strengths and possible areas for development before considering possible goals to frame the mentoring activity to come. They begin to work with a more experienced individual who often has a lot of professional and social capital within the organisational context of the mentorship. The initiation stage involves discussion and reflection to find common ground and the establishment of a relationship which can be more or less formal in character. Having gone through this relationship- and focus-building phase, the mentor and mentee move into a *cultivation* phase where the relationship begins to develop through conversations, rounds of questioning and the use of feedback. Over the course of this phase the intention is to build self-efficacy within the mentee, particularly through negotiation and a continued move towards the goals set out at the beginning of the process. As the mentee develops their independence and the depth of their skills and knowledge, the relationship moves into the third phase of *separation*. This can be a positive separation where the goals set by the mentee have broadly been met and they feel more confident or more experienced. However, the separation can also be negative if the relationship has become fraught for some reason, or if the mentee is not showing the growth hoped for. Beyond the separation phase comes the phase of *redefinition*.

Here, separation is complete but, where the relationship has been positive, may lead to peer co-working on new ideas or issues. Kram's model is a useful framework for beginning to think about the ways in which your mentoring relationship might grow and eventually conclude, as it includes the idea of time frames in this development (Penikett et al., 2019, p., 407) . It is essentially a linear model with a start, a middle and an end, albeit the cultivation phase may have several cycles of development, dependent on the focus of the aims chosen at the beginning of the relationship.

Mentoring can serve many different aims but two main reasons for entering into a mentoring relationship are career development and psychosocial development (Chanchlani et al., 2018). Career development might focus on elements of classroom practice or even subject knowledge. Geography degrees often lead to specialism and cannot hope to cover all aspects of such a vast multi-disciplinary field. As a result, it is plausible that a beginning teacher might be responsible for teaching glacial geomorphology and basic Quaternary science with no experience of that element of the subject at any level within their own education. Therefore, an element of a mentoring relationship might focus on developing a good level of subject knowledge so that the mentee can feel confident in teaching Key Stage 3, General Certificate of Secondary Education (14-16-year-olds) or Advanced-level (16-19-year-olds) students. In the case of classroom practice, most beginning teachers may have little experience of leading fieldwork, even within the confines of the school grounds where the health and safety issues may be minimal; they probably will not have experience of filling in the risk-assessment forms developed by the school of which they are now a part. The use of mentoring can therefore help ECTs develop their context-specific practice more efficiently and with less anxiety than if they had been left to enculturate themselves. The following case study is drawn from our own experiences of mentoring beginning teachers; this one is about Olivia (pseudonym), and gives an example of how this mentoring support may occur.

Box 5.1 Case study one – Olivia plans a field trip

Olivia was in her second year of qualified teaching when she was tasked with planning a coastal environments field trip for the Year 10 students at her school, with particular focus on updating some dated materials following new fieldwork questions published by the examination board, which led to a need to create some new activities. This put her in a challenging situation, because her formal period of NQT mentoring had finished after a year (based on the pre-2021 NQT regulations) and she was now regarded within the department as a confident and experienced member of the team. In fact, chances were that she would have her own beginning teacher mentee from September, due to retirements and promotions in the Geography department. Complicating things further, Olivia had worked as a teaching assistant in her current school for many years before qualifying to teach through a school-based training programme – so other members of staff really saw her as 'part of the furniture' and a very safe pair of hands in terms of school policies and procedures.

> Asking for advice and support with this planning was really tough for Olivia. First she had to think carefully about who to approach. The head of department had made reference a few times to Olivia's prior knowledge and understanding of school processes – 'oh but you have been doing all that for years, Olivia'. Her mentor now had two other beginning teachers to support (one on their ITE school placement, the other recently employed by the school). She put off doing the planning for as long as she could, but this just increased the anxiety that she was getting behind on her work and could be missing a vital element of the task. In the end, Olivia had an informal chat with the school visits coordinator, who showed her the risk-assessment system and gave her some pointers. Armed with this information, Olivia felt confident enough to approach her head of department to 'check' what she had done so far, to start a discussion on how to go about updating resources for the fieldwork and, most importantly, to ask if she could have a coach for future situations like this.
>
> Olivia's request was met with the familiar response: 'you know the ropes better than I do, Olivia!'

Mentoring might alternatively focus on psychosocial aspects of development. The mentor may act as a role model for the mentee, for example by discussing organisational politics and how to navigate them or by using classroom observation to understand how to develop presence in the classroom, especially when trying to develop behaviour management. For beginning teachers, the use of role modelling may help them in the early months as they will employ a form of *imitate the successful* heuristic (basically a rule of thumb) (Hertwig et al., 2012) while they build their own confidence. However, where this happens it will be important to help them move on to develop their own approaches and practices so that they continue to develop rather than merely continuing to imitate the practice of others. Taking the example of leading fieldwork again, to imitate a more experienced mentor might help build confidence and familiarisation with the subject matter and geographical context. The field trip might make use of a local nature reserve unknown to the mentee. To begin by observing the mentor leading a group before then leading elements and then a whole trip themselves will almost certainly involve an imitation of the mentor's style. But there needs to be reflection and a move towards the mentee considering how they wish to develop their practice in an authentic manner, relying on their own teaching and behaviour-management style.

Another psychosocial focus that a mentoring relationship might consider is issues of social acceptance. Joining a new school community can be both confusing and daunting, and having a more experienced individual who is able to introduce you to the right people and to help you navigate the unwritten rules of the organisation and the daily life within it is useful. Meeting and reflecting on how school life works and how to immerse yourself in the complexities and life of the staff room or school meetings can be very helpful and can again save both time and anxiety in making the transition into feeling like any other member of staff as well as opening up discussions about workload and wider well-being issues.

Where issues begin to emerge, either in the classroom or in the wider navigation of the school, the final psychosocial focus, counselling might help. Here, the mentor acts to talk through issues that the mentee might be having and offers directions in which they might go to solve the problems they are facing. This can be a crucial aspect of a mentoring process, especially for beginning teachers who may feel unprepared, vulnerable and unsure of their place within the wider life of the school, and who might, quite naturally, struggle with aspects of their classroom practice and work-life balance. In the following case study, we describe a teacher whom one of the authors knew through their ITE programme – Sami (pseudonym) – and kept in touch with during their early career.

Box 5.2 Case study two – Sami and workload

Sami had been teaching for five years when workload started to be more than just a manageable challenge. He had devoted evenings and weekends to lesson preparation, planning and assessment through his teacher education and into his early career, always planning his social life around his school workload and sometimes prioritising marking over family events and nights out with friends.

Five years into his career, Sami had a partner and a toddler, with another baby on the way. Workload had now become untenable, with Sami getting to school at 7am to try and catch up on marking, missing lunch and often staying late so that he didn't have to take work home as well. His sleep was disrupted, and about to get even worse, sharing night feeding duties with his partner.

Sami's relationship with his NQT mentor had remained strong, and had become more of a coaching situation, with Sami and his mentor working alongside each other, talking through problems as equally knowledgeable professionals and sharing experiences to help them solve issues. Sami's mentor sympathised completely with his workload crisis – she was experiencing a similar one herself – but their coaching relationship was now just reinforcing the idea that working long hours and weekends was normal, and having a family and being a teacher were not easily compatible. It wasn't until Sami's mentor found him one evening, crying alone in the staffroom, that they both started to take the situation seriously and took their concerns over work/life balance, marking expectations and the long-hours culture of the department to the senior leadership team.

Clearly, the relationship between Sami and his mentor had evolved over time, and did not have the same parameters that it did when Sami was a beginning teacher, when his mentor would have stepped in quickly to resolve a workload issue as part of the basic support and target package.

The discussion above is obviously a simple overview of the mentoring relationship and has only tried to tease out some of the core roles of what mentoring activity might include. However, some important underlying characteristics are apparent. Firstly, the mentoring process here seems quite linear, with goals being set at the start of the mentoring period, and then steps being taken to meet those goals. The relationship may be more open than this, but the focus is on developing practice and well-being through dialogue and support (see Clarke et al., 2022). In addition, there is no particular medium or framework for thinking about teaching practice, or for structuring the process of mentoring itself. The Early Career Framework (ECF) might support teachers in their first two years of teaching, but it is a narrow, perhaps too narrow, framework for considering practice, and by definition will generally be seen as inapplicable for older teachers who are seeking mentoring. Finally, there is an implicit notion in this model that beginning teachers need a degree of support in the early stages of their careers, but after a while, and with the care and support of a more experienced colleague, they too become the *final product*, a few years into their career. The ECF suggests that teachers, having followed online materials over two years, are ready and have become mature practitioners. Indeed, the new Ofsted criteria (Ofsted, 2019), whilst moving away from individual judgements, promotes the idea that expertise is expected from the beginning of a teaching career. This idea, despite being diluted in the most recent framework (Ofsted, 2019), has been theorised as at risk of undermining 'what is reasonable and possible in the pursuit of an unattainable perfection that in too many cases demoralises rather than motivates' (Richards, 2015, p. 237). In the next section we suggest a very different way of understanding the mentoring process, and the way teachers might think about their developing practice using aspects of process philosophy and complexity theory to recast mentoring as an activity.

Processual complexity

> No man ever steps in the same river twice, for it's not the same river and he's not the same man.
>
> Heraclitus

Heraclitus is often identified as the father of process philosophy in Western Europe. The quote above emphasises the dynamic, flowing nature of reality, the basis for a process ontology. In this ontology, the universe is seen as primarily constituted of processes rather than substances. As Rescher (2000, p. 5) argues, 'The fundamental "stuff" of the world is not material substance, but volatile flux'. We can translate this insight to the social world by stressing social processes as continually at the centre of human activity and society. In addition, it emphasises human existence as a process of becoming, that rather than identifying us as static entities, human *beings*, we can be characterised as human *becomings*. We are never static in time, we do not have an early period in our lives where we change, followed by a period of stasis once we are adults. Instead, our interaction with the world and our exposure to constantly new experiences means that we are ourselves constantly in a state of flux. As we will see below, this can have a profound impact on how we think about processes such as mentoring and how teachers understand their own development as professionals.

Process philosophy (Whitehead, 1929/1967) provides a simple yet profound insight, that education is made up of a huge number of processes, all of which are to a greater or lesser extent interconnected. For example, if we consider for a moment a geography textbook, a huge range of processes, from the education of the author, to their engagement with a computer, reference sources, paper, electricity, etc. to the printing and even the reading of the text by students, are all flowing forward and intertwining and diverging to give the textbook, and the context for learning at that specific time. These processes interact in different and often non-linear ways, and as such the processes involved can also be characterised as complex in nature. As a consequence of this complex nature, the learning which takes place, as well as the development of teachers as a form of professional learning, will be complex and emergent in nature. In other words, within educational contexts, it is almost impossible for us to identify single processes and argue that they individually lead to given cause-and-effect patterns. As a result of this, it is problematic to suggest easy or single solutions to complex educational and pedagogic issues.

Complex systems are not random or chaotic, they have identifiable patterns (Johnson, 2007; Mitchell, 2009). They can be generally predictable whilst not allowing for detailed prediction of the future. This is best exemplified by the difficulty we have in accurately predicting weather more than three or four days ahead of the present, whilst being able to describe general, expected conditions at different points during a year. In complex systems, we can say generally what might occur using evidence and past patterns of experience, but we cannot examine and predict the detail very far into the future.

Another crucial characteristic of complex systems is our inability to consciously know all that is going on within that system at any point in time (Richardson and Tait, 2010). We have the best impression of the system through the processes and elements closest to us, those elements we are directly interacting with. But as the system becomes more remote from us, our ability to sense and interact rapidly decays to nothing. Hence, if we accept that processes are fundamental to the reality and flow of the ever-changing and evolving world around us, we can only hope to gain insight and understanding of those processes closest to us and of which we might be a part.

To give a simple, but relevant, example of this argument, we can use a teacher's activity during a lesson. The lesson is composed of a multitude of processes, from reading, discussion, thinking, listening or writing, to the creation of resources, the planning of the lesson by the teacher and the behaviour of the students. Any of these processes themselves can be broken down into further processes. For example, behaviour is an emerging set of apparent processes such as sulking, smiling, shouting or crying, the result of interactions within the brain which are emergent through iterative connections to social and emotional interactions with others. In turn, these behavioural characteristics, which may well change themselves from minute to minute or even second to second, will create new processes in terms of peer and adult response. The complex multitude of processes interact with each other in emergent patterns that the teacher is able to interact with, and, as they themselves go through longer-term processes of professional development, may be able to understand and progressively react more proactively to positively impact on student behaviour (Bronfenbrenner, 1979; Merçon-Vargas et al., 2020).

Because of the sheer complexity of the interacting processes in the classroom, the teacher will only be able to interact with those in their immediate vicinity. The teacher can talk with a student who is struggling to understand river meandering, and explicitly work with them to aid their understanding. But they are not able to understand and interact with a student at the same time who is on the other side of the room; indeed they will not be able to claim any real insight as to the cognitive processes that student is engaged with at that distance. And in both cases, the teacher will have to interact with the child as well as the learning; the student they are helping might feel anxious about not understanding the subject content, the student across the room might be bored and considering disrupting the work of others.

Whilst this insight into a complex processual reality might seem almost random, it is not. As stated above, complex systems have patterns and classrooms likewise tend to be quite stable, with students experiencing their work in a generally predictable way. We merely have to accept that we cannot claim to *know* what is happening across the system at any given point in time and what we do know we only have partial knowledge and understanding of. For example, see the arguments in Puttick (2022) about the ways in which tentative and situated understandings limit the kind of certainty with which we might make claims in the context of lesson observations. As teachers become more experienced, they begin to understand the patterns and processes involved in the continual emergence of learning in classrooms, and in part they become confident in admitting that they do not have an omnipotent insight. As one geography teacher commented to one of us after a lesson study observation, he had always believed that he knew exactly how his students were interacting and how much they were learning. Having engaged with lesson study,[1] with observation of just three students and the use of interviews with them after the lesson to reflect on what and how they had learned, he admitted that he was confident that they had learned what he wanted them to, but the processes they had followed to achieve this were unexpectedly diverse, and he still only had a partial level of understanding of how they had managed it. For beginning teachers, the temptation is to blame themselves for lacking an overview of this immense complexity, rather than questioning a system that expects it.

> **Task 5.2 Reflections on complexity**
>
> Think about mentoring experiences you have had – either as mentor or mentee, in education or outside of it. Have you ever set or been set targets that reduce a complex situation to simple cause and effect, with an expectation that a quick change will provide a lasting solution? As a mentor, do you encourage your mentee to consider the complexity of practice?

A process model for practice development and mentoring in geography

What does a complex processual approach offer us when we begin to consider mentoring? Perhaps mentoring needs to be cast as an activity which is taking place within the complex flow of a multitude of processes which intertwine and diverge at different times and in different contexts. Experience and expertise are partly couched in recognising and acting within the patterns such processes create. To foster the emergence of new practice, or to enable greater confidence in organisational cultures, the mentoring pair will focus on a small number of foci to make their work manageable and understandable, but in reality there will never be a clear cut-off between the processes they are focusing on and others which impinge on the issues they have chosen to explore.

Because complexity suggests that detailed predictions cannot be made very far into the future, a processual approach to mentoring suggests that there is little point in setting goals at the beginning of the process, other than to suggest broad areas in which it might be useful to work. Instead, we argue that we need to remember that at the core of a mentoring relationship is the desire to learn. Whitehead (1929/1967), in his processual philosophy of education, sees learning as a cyclic process consisting of three stages (see also Allen and Evans, 2006). The first stage is that of *Romance*, a stage where the excitement of finding out has primacy, that subject matter is chosen that 'holds within itself unexplored connexions with possibilities half-disclosed by glimpses and half-concealed by the wealth of material' (p. 17). This means that within the mentoring relationship, the mentee brings areas of keen interest, areas they have a desire to explore. Hence, it is not a deficit model focussing merely on righting perceived weaknesses, but an approach which enthuses the mentee into developing practice or helping them make sense of their school in ways that they find interesting and which will help them develop their expertise. As such, mentoring might focus on areas which are already strong but which can be explored further as well as areas of perceived weakness.

Having identified an area of curiosity, the next stage is that of *Precision*. Here, the processes or issues identified in the Romance stage are explored in detail and are expanded on. Here, Whitehead emphasises that 'in the stage of precise progress we acquire other facts in a systematic order, which thereby form both a disclosure and an analysis of the general subject-matter of the romance' (p. 19). This is a process of detailed exploration and development based on a variety of evidence and information to allow for considered action and critical learning.

The final stage in Whitehead's model is that of *Generalisation*, which is synthetic in nature. How can we embed and understand our new insights not only in their own right but in relation to our wider understanding of the world, or in this case education? It is an attempt to create an ever-greater holistic understanding where the different aspects of teacher work are explicitly seen as elements of a single network of processes.

Whitehead's processual model of learning offers a way of giving coherence to the mentoring process by dispensing with the false certainty of goals whilst giving shape to an emerging narrative and areas for exploration. In addition, it allows both the mentor and the mentee to experience learning, perhaps with different foci, as well as contextualising that new learning in wider, holistic systems. This then suggests that all mentoring is to a greater or lesser degree a peer-driven activity. Seeing the process of mentoring as complex and processual might help to mitigate some of the damage that deadlines, performativity and accountability do to teachers at all stages of their career (see Perryman and Calvert, 2020, for more on this topic).

> **Task 5.3 Change and review**
>
> It may be helpful to think about your previous experiences of being mentored yourself.
>
> - How useful is it to set targets at the beginning of the mentoring period?
> - Do your needs as a mentee stay the same? How are changes in needs usually communicated?
> - How easy has it been to review targets if your needs/context have changed since they were set?

A process-driven mentoring approach is therefore characterised by a rhythmic learning exploration, which fosters emergent narratives over time. This being the case, as a mentor, you need to be aware of the complexity of the processes which make up the educational landscape of which you are a part and be open about this with your mentee, that the expectation of knowing everything all the time, whilst ignoring the social, emotional needs and secrets of the other people in the room, is just not possible. This complexity also suggests that any notion that a set of goals can be set and met in a linear, reductive sense is a mirage. Instead, a Whiteheadean approach to the learning present in mentoring suggests the need for ongoing mentoring throughout a career (Whitehead, 1929/1967). The current national focus of mentoring beginning teachers in England is unhelpful, as this suggests that, with some help over a limited number of years, teachers reach an optimal point from which they can then carry on ad infinitum. Whilst aspects of the ECF are suggestive of this reductive, simplistic model, instead a process approach would suggest that all teachers should continue learning through evolving mentoring pairs and groups throughout their career.

To help develop the coherence in learning explorations at the core of a processual mentoring approach, it might be useful to offer suggested avenues for reflection and dialogue. In our view, the ECF runs the risk of missing an opportunity to be a positive support for mentoring that enables open discussion of practices. It can be interpreted as offering a narrow perspective on what it means to be a teacher, and a mentor. As Lofthouse points out:

> Mentoring needs to be situated in a professional educational landscape in which new teachers and mentors challenge professional working practices that are restrictive, too often performative and sometimes even punitive.
>
> (Lofthouse, 2019)

Any framework that sets out the roles of mentors and beginning teachers needs to support this practice of challenge and critique. In addition, it is all too easily applied as a ticklist which encourages participants to demonstrate competence in instrumental ways. Here, we offer an alternative which is inherently complexly processual in nature.

Cajkler and Wood (2016) developed a model of pedagogic literacy based on their research into lesson study in initial teacher education (Cajkler et al., 2013). Their work starts from the premise that the rise of professional standards has had the impact of narrowing the work of teachers and has led to ever-rising levels of performativity. They reflect on their use of lesson study in initial teacher education and argue that there is evidence, albeit small-scale, that

> Using lesson study in ITE provided participants with a structured collaborative opportunity for exploration of the complexity of the classroom, not compromising the need to meet the teaching standards but leading to a more rounded understanding of what it means to be a teacher.
>
> (Cajkler and Wood, 2016, p. 511)

Seeing the pedagogic process as 'rational, creative, and intuitive, but fundamentally… complex, defying simplistic "business capital" prescriptions' (p. 513), they develop a more holistic view of individuals' emerging practice and reflexivity, pedagogic literacy. This term is defined as:

> the complex of skills, knowledge, attitudes and values that enable teachers to use their reading of the classroom to reflect-in-action and to make learner-responsive decisions that support learning in all its complexity (cognitive, social and emotional).
>
> (Cajkler and Wood, 2016, p. 513)

They have developed a model of pedagogic literacy (Figure 5.1) which is composed of a number of dimensions which all go to make up elements of teacher work and the wider pedagogic thinking and practice of teachers. Engagement with this diagram needs care! They refer to it as an emergent view. In other words, the model is a vehicle for dialogue and reflection. It can only ever serve this purpose as the processes involved in teaching are so varied, by nature and by number, and emerge and change over time so much that any attempt to capture pedagogy in its entirety is not possible. This is why they problematise standards, as they are only ever a reductive, politically preferred tick-list. Here, the dimensions are offered as no more than a touchstone for discussion and exploration, and the examples in each dimension are just that, examples, which can be debated and added to by any teacher using the model. In addition, it might become pertinent to add extra dimensions; indeed, in subsequent presentations to the publication of the 2016 paper, Cajkler has added further complexity to the model. But crucial here is the admission that the model of pedagogic literacy is a partial view of ever changing, converging and diverging complex processes which go to make up the work of teachers. For this reason it should have currency for all in the profession whatever their stage of development and expertise. But this can only be the case where it is used to open up creativity, dialogue and professional exploration. This is why it can act as a positive navigational aid when exploring new practice or psychosocial issues through Whiteheadean learning cycles (Whitehead, 1929/1967).

This model can also remain relevant at all points during a career, and hence offers coherence in a complex processual mentoring model which emerges and changes over the course of whole careers. And it is this insight that is crucial in understanding perhaps one of the more important insights we gain from assuming a processual model of mentoring. In the following case study, we share Pat's (pseudonym) experience of being mentored later in her career, as experienced by one of the authors, who worked with her.

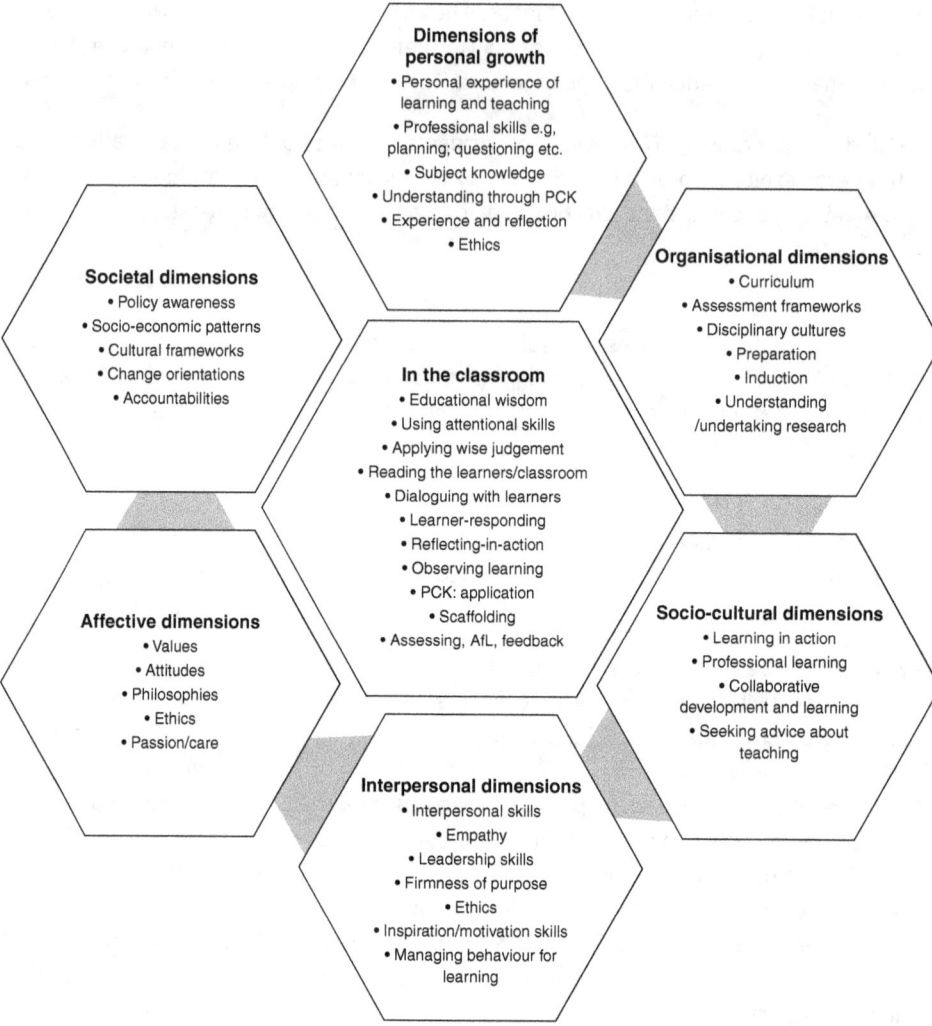

Figure 5.1 A 'possible model' of pedagogic literacy – it is a framework for discussion and reflection, NOT a complete tick-box list to be 'achieved'.
Source: Cajkler and Wood, 2016, p. 514.
Reproduced by permission of Taylor & Francis Group from: Cajkler, W., and Wood, P., 2016. Lesson study and pedagogic literacy in initial teacher education: Challenging reductive models. *British Journal of Educational Studies*, 64(4), 503–521. Taylor & Francis Ltd, www.tandfonline.com.

Box 5.3 Case study three – Pat, mentor and being mentored

Pat had been teaching for 25 years when she was offered the chance to be involved in mentoring – this time, as the mentee. Pat had been head of department for years, and had mentored many student and early career Geography teachers. She felt one of her greatest achievements in teaching was mentoring and supporting another member of the department from promising NQT to now leading Geography, with Pat taking a step back and working part-time with a view to retirement in a few years time.

Pat was open to the idea of mentoring, but as one of the most experienced teachers in not just the department, but the whole school, she was sceptical about the nature of the process and what it might entail – she certainly was not interested in being given targets to improve based on snapshot observations, book scrutiny, or her most recent set of GCSE results. Pat was paired with a younger member of the team, with a commitment to meet once a month and no expectation of targets being set at the outset.

Pat reported after a year that the mentoring process had given her a new enthusiasm for her role, even after many years of teaching. The process began with conversations about what Pat really wanted to have a go at: perhaps something new, something she had never had a chance to pursue, a project or area of her work that she would like to review. There was no expectation that Pat would have areas for development or weaknesses; the process focussed on her passions and what could be done to nurture and encourage those interests. Pat was given time to concentrate on her previously unexplored love of philosophical inquiry with children, and how this could be used in the geography department to develop complex ideas through discussion. She felt supported, enthused and valued, at a time when there was a risk of her fading into the background and all her expertise and passion being lost. Together with her mentor, they explored this focus over a number of cycles, driving her passion and deepening her critical practice.

She is now working with three other teachers from other subject areas to see how they might begin to adopt a similar approach, working as a team of peers to extend their understanding and practice.

Conclusion

In this chapter we have considered the epistemic and practice-based environment in which mentoring occurs. We have challenged the assumptions we make as mentors, and as professionals – what does it mean to be a teacher, what would a 'finished' teacher look like?

To consider these questions we reflected upon the role of the teacher. We discussed pedagogic literacy as a useful model to show how a flexible, critical approach to mentoring might work in practice. We used case studies from our own experience to think about the real-life experiences of mentors and mentees in geography departments, and how these experiences could be improved.

In summary, all teachers, regardless of their experience, or number of years 'served', can gain positively from ongoing mentoring dialogues. Political fixation with attempting to reach 'expert' level early in a career is suggestive of 'having arrived', of *being* the finished article. But, when we are thinking about teacher development, we are talking about a continuously emergent process of *becoming* over an entire career.

For discussion

We have set out our ideas for a different approach to mentoring beginning geography teachers. Reflect on your experiences as a mentor and mentee during your career, particularly with regard to the pedagogic literacy model:

- Complex systems can never be captured completely, as we have discussed; based on your experience, what is missing from this model?
- Which aspects would you highlight as most important to your own development as an early career teacher and mentor?

Note

1. A process in which teachers work together to target an area for development in their students' learning, using discussion and reflection to refine practice (see Cajkler et al., 2013; Wood et al., 2020).

Further reading and resources

1. Allen, G., and Evans, M. D., 2006. *A Different Three Rs for Education: Reason, Relationality, Rhythm*. Amsterdam: Rodopi.

This book sets out an alternative approach to education using the process philosophy of Alfred North Whitehead as its foundation. It offers a view of formal education much at odds with current English policy and thinking about pedagogy.

2. Cajkler, W., and Wood, P., 2016. Lesson study and pedagogic literacy in initial teacher education: Challenging reductive models. *British Journal of Educational Studies*, 64(4), 503-521.

This paper outlines the evidence on which the model of pedagogic literacy was based, before going on to make the case for pedagogic literacy as a concept and framework for developing teacher work.

3. Whitehead, A. N., 1929/1967. *The Aims of Education and Other Essays*. New York: The Free Press.

The original book containing Alfred North Whitehead's philosophy of education based on his process philosophy and cyclic model of learning.

References

Allen, G., and Evans, M. D., 2006. *A Different Three Rs for Education: Reason, Relationality, Rhythm*. Amsterdam: Rodopi.

Barber, M., Mourshed, M., and Whelan, F., 2007. Improving education in the Gulf. *The McKinsey Quarterly*, 3947, 101-116.

Bronfenbrenner, U., 1979. *The Ecology of Human Development: Experiments by Nature and Design*. Cambridge, MA: Harvard University Press.

Burnett, C., and Coldwell, M., 2020. Randomised controlled trials and the interventionisation of education. *Oxford Review of Education*. DOI: 10.1080/03054985.2020.1856060.

Cajkler, W., and Wood, P., 2016. Lesson study and pedagogic literacy in initial teacher education: Challenging reductive models, *British Journal of Educational Studies*, 64(4), 503-521.

Cajkler, W., Wood, P., Norton, J., and Pedder, D., 2013. Lesson study: Towards a collaborative approach to learning in Initial Teacher Education? *Cambridge Journal of Education*, 43(4), 537–554.

Chanchlani, S., Chang, D., Ong, J. S., and Anwar, A., 2018. The value of peer mentoring for the psychosocial wellbeing of junior doctors: A randomised controlled study. *Medical Journal of Australia*, 209, 401–405. https://doi.org/10.5694/mja17.01106.

Clarke, E., Quickfall, A., and Thompson, S., 2022. Well-being: Theory and practice for beginning geography teachers. In G. Healy, L. Hammond, S. Puttick and N. Walshe (eds), *Mentoring Geography Teachers in the Secondary School*. Abingdon: Routledge, 224–240.

Darling-Hammond, L., Holtzmann, J. D., Gatlin, S., and Heiling, V. J., 2005. Does teacher preparation matter? Evidence about teacher certification, Teach for America, and teacher effectiveness. *Education Policy Analysis Archives*, 13(42), 1–51.

Department for Education, 2011. *Training our Next Generation of Outstanding Teachers: An Improvement Strategy for Discussion*. London: DfE.

Department for Education, 2019. *School Workforce in England: November 2018*. London: DfE.

Department for Education, 2020. Early career framework reforms. Available at: www.gov.uk/government/collections/early-career-framework-reforms [accessed 2 January 2021].

Department for Education, 2021. Early career framework reforms: overview (policy paper). Available at: www.gov.uk/government/publications/early-career-framework-reforms-overview/early-career-framework-reforms-overview [accessed 2 January 2021].

Flores, M.A., 2019. Unpacking teacher quality: Key issues for early career teachers. In A. Sullivan, B. Johnson and M. Simons (eds), *Attracting and Keeping the Best Teachers. Professional Learning and Development in Schools and Higher Education*, vol. 16. Singapore: Springer. https://doi.org/10.1007/978-981-13-8621-3_2.

Hattie, J. 2003. Teachers make a difference: What is the research evidence? Paper presented at Australian Council for Educational Research Conference, Melbourne, October. http://research.acer.edu.au/research_conference_2003/4 [accessed 23 February 2021].

Hertwig, R., Hoffrage, U., and ABC Research Group, 2012. *Simple Heuristics in a Social World*. Oxford: Oxford University Press.

Hudson, P., 2013. Mentoring as professional development: 'Growth for both' mentor and mentee. *Professional Development in Education*, 39(5), 771–783.

Johnson, N., 2007. *Simply Complexity: A Clear Guide to Complexity Theory*. Oxford: Oneworld Publications.

Kram, K. E., 1985. *Mentoring at Work: Developmental Relationships in Organizational Life*. Glenview, IL: Scott Foresman.

Lofthouse, R., 2019. *Teacher Mentoring; Rising to the Challenge of the Early Career Framework*. Leeds Beckett Carnegie Education Blog. Available at: www.leedsbeckett.ac.uk/blogs/carnegie-education/2019/02/teacher-mentoring-rising-to-the-challenge-of-the-early-career-framework/ [accessed 4 May 2021].

Merçon-Vargas, E. A., Lima, R. F. F., Rosa, E. M., and Tudge, J., 2020. Processing proximal processes: What Bronfenbrenner meant, what he didn't mean, and what he should have meant. *Journal of Family Theory and Review*, 12, 321–334. https://doi.org/10.1111/jftr.12373.

Mitchell, M., 2009. *Complexity: A Guided Tour*. Oxford: Oxford University Press.

Ofsted, 2019. *Education Inspection Framework*. London: Ofsted.

Penikett, J., Daly, C., and Milton, E., 2019. A study of mentors in Wales 'coming to closure'. *Professional Development in Education*, 45(3), 405–417.

Perryman, J., and Calvert, G., 2020. What motivates people to teach and why do they leave? Accountabilty, performativity and teacher retention. *British Journal of Educational Studies*, 68(1), 3–23. DOI: 10.1080/00071005.2019.1589417.

Puttick, S., 2022. Lesson observations at the interface between research and practice. In G. Healy, L. Hammond, S. Puttick and N. Walshe (eds), *Mentoring Geography Teachers in the Secondary School*. Abingdon: Routledge, 173–186.

Rescher, N., 2000. *Process Philosophy: A Survey of Basic Issues.* Pittsburgh: University of Pittsburgh Press.

Richards, C., 2015. More outstanding nonsense: A critique of Ofsted criteria. *Forum*, 57(2), 233-238.

Richardson, K. A., and Tait, A., 2010. The death of the expert? *E:CO*, 12(2), 87-97.

Whitehead, A. N., 1929/1967. *The Aims of Education and Other Essays.* New York: The Free Press.

Wood, P., Larssen, D. L. S., Helgevold, N., and Cajkler, W., 2020. *Lesson Study in Initial Teacher Education: Principles and Practices.* Bingley: Emerald Publishing.

6 Mentoring as a professional development opportunity

Richard Bustin

Introduction

The opportunity to mentor a beginning teacher into the profession has been described as a 'cost-effective form of professional development' (Hudson, 2013, p. 771) for you, your department and wider school. This chapter sets out to discuss this in relation to mentoring in geography education. In the first section of this chapter, I outline the many benefits that mentoring in geography education in secondary schools can bring, based on the framework from Huling (2001) discussed in relation to geography education by Tapsfield (2019). The second section of this chapter discusses a theme emerging from recent debates: the role played by the subject of geography in developing beginning teachers which links to the work of Brooks (2016) on teacher professional identities. An important thread running through this chapter is the argument that you can maximise the professional development benefits of mentoring by reflecting on your own stance on geographical knowledge, pedagogy, skills and values.

The professional benefits of being a mentor in geography education.

Whilst the majority of literature on mentoring focusses on how mentors can support their mentees (e.g. Mena et al., 2017; Gholam, 2018), an increasing literature focusses on the benefits that mentoring can bring to you as a mentor (e.g. Holloway, 2001; Tonna et al., 2017). Huling (2001) identifies a series of benefits: increased professional competency, opportunities for more reflective practice, opportunities for collaboration, increased leadership and personal psychological benefits of career renewal. This set of ideas frame the discussion in the first part of this chapter, which I relate to the work of Tapsfield (2019) in discussion of geography education mentoring.

Professional competency

The first professional development opportunity from mentoring identified by Huling (2001, p. 2) is 'professional competency'; as Huling (2001) argues, when mentoring, your teaching ability improves. When being observed by a beginning teacher on a regular basis, it is natural that you will want to ensure the lessons you are producing are the best they can be, so that you are seen to be modelling the sort of teacher knowledge and behaviour that you want your beginning teacher to emulate. Discussion between you and your beginning teacher can then unpick the various elements of the lesson which, in turn, can enable a deeper, more critical reflection of practice. Most discussion about what this looks like refers to general teacher activities, such as questioning skills and behaviour management (e.g. Clinard and Ariav, 1998) but in her work on mentoring geography beginning teachers, Tapsfield (2019) identified subject-specific competencies, arguing a good mentor needs to 'be a good geographer… they should have a clear understanding of what constitutes high-quality, challenging geography teaching that brings about effective learning' (p. 3). It is this focus on geography that ensures your professional competencies include subject specialism, a contention returned to later in the chapter.

Reflective practice

Professional competencies can be improved through 'reflective practice' (Huling, 2001, p. 2): thinking critically about your own beliefs and values in teaching and how this manifests itself in the classroom, and in professional practice. This critical reflectivity forms a part of your own professional identity as a geography teacher. Mentoring can provide an opportunity for you to reflect on new ideas as well as providing validation of what you believe to be important in education (Ganser, 1997). As Tapsfield (2019) explains, a good mentor is 'committed to their own ongoing learning' (p. 3).

A potential opportunity for critical reflectivity comes through another of Huling's (2001) key professional development opportunities, *collaboration*. The most significant collaboration is between mentor and beginning teacher. A collaborative relationship between mentor and beginning teacher means moving away from a *tick-box* mentality whereby the mentor simply checks and ticks off various teaching standards (DfE, 2011) as the beginning teacher meets them, towards a much more personal approach, building and developing bonds to nurture the talents of a new teacher. As such, this 'requires mentors to be open to learn from their mentees in reciprocal arrangements where both learn from each other' (Hudson, 2013, p. 772). A study in 2005 (Lopez-Real and Kwan) reported that 70% of 259 mentors surveyed indicated that working as a mentor increased their own professional development through the process of self-reflection and collaboration. It is through collaboration that an *educative mentoring* approach can be taken (Feiman-Nemser, 2001; Palombo and Daly, 2022). This approach draws on Dewey's (1938) notion of educative *experiences* which are those interactions that promote growth and development in individuals. Educative mentoring

> rests on an explicit vision of good teaching and an understanding of teacher learning. Mentors who share this orientation attend to teachers' present concerns… without losing sight of long term goals.
>
> (Feiman-Nemser, 2001, p. 18)

In research into the ideas and experiences of mentoring in geography education, Palombo et al. (2020) surveyed 87 mentors and concluded 'that drawing on the discipline of geography and the notion of "educative mentoring"… could support mentors and mentees and improve mentors' professional development' (p. 9).

Collaboration

Developing reflective practice as a form of professional development can be achieved in collaboration not only with a beginning teacher but with other teachers too. As Wood and Rawlings Smith (2017) explain, 'one way in which teacher development can be encouraged is through the creation of professional learning communities within and across schools whereby teachers are given the opportunity to share experiences and develop their own practice' (p. 91). One mechanism to enable this can come in the form of lesson study (Cajkler et al., 2013), discussed in relation to geography education by Wood and Rawlings Smith (2017). This is a process by which a team of teachers work together to identify a particular challenge that students face in the classroom. The teachers then identify the reasons behind the challenge, and possible solutions. A *research lesson* is then taught to the students which is observed and reflected on by the group. The lesson is then refined and re-taught. This process can lead to a 'sustained positive impact on classroom practice and curriculum development' (Wood and Rawlings Smith, 2017, p. 94), and enable teachers to build a collaborative form of professional development.

Task 6.1 Lesson study

Identify an area of common misconception or challenge that your students face in a lesson, such as challenging content or a difficult skill to master. Work with your beginning teacher and wider department to conduct a *lesson study* following the guidance from Wood and Rawlings Smith (2017); you could involve your geography class in the process. Reflect on the benefits that collaboration brings to improve not only the student experience, but also the development of the beginning teacher and your own practice.

Mentoring can also lead to wider professional collaborations which can enable further professional development opportunities. An example of these could be between you and the wider geography subject community, such as a local university or subject association (see Kinder, 2022). Through these, you could reflect on the national standards required for qualified teacher status within your own teaching (for example, in England the Teachers' Standards; DfE, 2011), or become part of a wider geography teaching community of practice beyond the immediate school department. On many routes into teaching, there is a tangible link to a university department. As Hudson (2013) identifies, 'recognitions for mentors from their universities can include: university library access privileges; awards for outstanding mentors nominated by their mentees; free attendance to particular university seminars; and other professional acknowledgements' (p. 781). For example, UCL Institute of Education (IOE) runs Master's degree modules on effective mentoring (UCL IOE, n.d.) as part of postgraduate study programmes. Many Initial Teacher Education (ITE) programmes offer the chance for mentors to be involved in shaping the ITE course (Ofsted, 2020; see Healy and Walshe, 2022) and work on various projects in collaboration with the university. Being actively involved with the education and geography departments at a local university not only provides you with opportunities for your own professional development but also is a source of ideas to stimulate further discussion with the beginning teachers you work with.

Leadership

As a result of critical reflection on practice, often in collaboration with other teachers, opportunities for leadership and career enhancement for you as a mentor can arise. As Huling (2001) explains, 'it is not uncommon for mentors to move into leadership positions as a result of their success as mentors, and it is often the case that they are more effective in these new positions because of the training and insights they received as mentors' (p. 3). These insights can include enhanced communication, the ability to have challenging and critical conversations with colleagues, and increased professional status that comes with being a mentor (Hudson, 2013). With many schools now taking on more of a leading role in the development of new teachers (Geographical Association, 2018), teachers with the skills developed in and through mentoring are also valuable assets in leadership roles.

Task 6.2 Mentor reflection: leadership opportunities from mentoring

Reflect on your time as a mentor. List the range of skills that you have gained as a result of your time mentoring, and consider how these could be transferable across other leadership roles in your school.

Personal and whole-school benefits

Career development opportunities are one example of many benefits that working as a mentor can bring to you and the school where you work. It also enables you to re-focus your energy back to teaching and learning, which can bring with it an increase in self-esteem (Wollman-Bonilla, 1997) that can provide impetus for more formal professional development programmes.

The professional development opportunities enabled by mentoring work at a number of scales, from the level of individual teachers through to department, school or trust level. The wider geography department within which you work can gain from working with a beginning teacher. Geography is a vibrant and wide-ranging discipline (Parkinson, 2020) and teachers need to keep up with the latest developments. Whilst this provides an excitement for geography teachers, the reality of being able to stay engaged with developments in the discipline of geography or education more broadly can be a challenge and so an influx of recently graduated beginning teachers into a department can be of real benefit. As Butt and Collins (2018) explain, beginning teachers are able 'to translate or transform their recently gained geographical knowledge, understanding and skills to the classroom... in some sense each ITE student acts as a conduit, bringing aspects of recently acquired geography content from their university courses into schools' (pp. 297-298). As Tapsfield (2019) argues, beginning teachers can 'invigorate departmental practice by providing a stimulus for discussion, (and) development of new pedagogy and curriculum innovation' (p. 5). An example is geographical information systems (GIS), which is a growth area in geography education (as discussed in Fargher, 2017) which some teachers and schools have found a challenge to keep up with (Walshe, 2017). GIS is part of the Geography National Curriculum (DfE, 2013) and, as such, is part of contemporary Geography ITE courses. Many teachers currently teaching geography in schools may not have had the experience of using GIS when they began teaching, so a beginning teacher with this knowledge can bring measurable benefits that will enhance the professional development of the whole department (Fargher and Healy, 2021), although Walshe (2017) identifies variations in the experiences and enthusiasm of beginning teachers towards GIS.

At the whole-school level, mentoring can bring tangible benefits too. As Tapsfield (2019) identifies, mentoring 'can lead to recruitment of a good trainee as an NQT' (p. 5) or early career teacher. Having beginning teachers training in your school can ease recruitment, as often they will be in a strong position to apply for any vacancy and there is the added benefit that beginning teachers will understand the school and departmental ethos before applying. Recruiting a trainee to a full-time position can help to bring the latest pedagogical ideas into the school. It is through the critical reflection of these ideas that you can develop yourself and your department and potentially see benefits across the whole school. There is often a financial incentive to take on beginning teachers, which can be a real benefit to many schools by enhancing the budgets for professional development, although, as Taspfield (2019) recognises, the ways schools choose to allocate this funding may or may not benefit the department or individual teachers.

The success of working as a mentor, and realising the potential of that role as a form of professional development, relies on the relationship between you as a mentor and the beginning teacher. A key challenge within this relationship is the role that geographical knowledge plays. In Hudson's (2010) model of mentoring five key attributes for successful teaching were identified:

- *personal attributes* of the mentor including their ability to be supportive and comforting;
- *system requirements* include an understanding of national curricula and school policies;
- *pedagogical knowledge* includes generic classroom skills such as behaviour management and questioning;
- *modelling* identifies the key role that the mentor plays in displaying effective teaching; and
- *feedback* includes the advice and follow-up that a beginning teacher is given.

Yet none of these attributes signifies the importance of a beginning teacher's or mentor's subject specialism. *Content knowledge* is mentioned briefly as part of Hudson's (2010) pedagogical knowledge but only insofar as mentors are asked to 'check on the mentee's content knowledge to ensure it is in keeping with system requirements' (p. 32). This suggests that the content of school geography lessons plays a small role in the mentoring and beginning teacher relationship, and is something external that is determined by the needs of a *system* such as a national curriculum or examination criteria. Much work in the field of geography education has identified a more ambitious role for subject knowledge in the classroom (Young and Lambert, 2014). Roberts (2010, p. 112) famously asked 'where's the geography?' in her work as an external examiner[1] on PGCE (Postgraduate Certificate of Education) courses, and the same could potentially be asked of mentors and beginning teachers. She worked with beginning teachers who on paper were highly successful, 'where classroom management and relationships were outstanding but in which the geography was weak, unchallenging or even inaccurate' (p. 112). If mentoring is to be effective as a form of geography education professional development, rather than generic professional development, the status of geographical knowledge, pedagogy and values needs to be part of the discussion between you and the beginning teacher. The next section discusses this further.

Realising the potential of geography education mentoring as a professional activity

The place of subject knowledge, pedagogy and values in mentoring beginning teachers, and by extension affording opportunities for professional development, is an area of research in geography education. Lambert (2018) identifies a tendency in schools towards the promotion of generic rather than subject specific aspects of teaching:

> teachers' attention is drawn to general practices and principles of 'effective teaching' (such as lesson structure, use of data, techniques purporting to promote assessment for learning) and away from questions relating to the quality of what is taught and learned in this or that subject.
>
> (p. 363)

As Palombo et al. (2020) identify in their survey of 87 mentors, 'mentor training in teacher education is often focused on technical and managerial elements, with limited opportunities to consider the role and value of the subject' (p. 10), a sentiment also acknowledged by Rawlings Smith (2020) in her work on supporting beginning geographer teachers. In his seminal paper *On Taking the Geography Out of Geographical Education*, Marsden (1997) identified a struggle at the heart of geography education which has a relevance to the success of you as mentors working with beginning teachers today and the extent to which such activities can provide professional development opportunities. For Marsden (1997), three components of a successful geography curriculum exist which must be kept in balance: the *subject* component, including subject knowledge from the academic discipline of geography; the *educational* component with a focus on pedagogical practices and the role of the child; and the *social education* component with its focus on contemporary issues and *good causes*. For him, 'unhealthy stresses arise when the three basic components of curriculum planning are not kept in reasonable balance' (p. 241). Marsden drew on Wooldridge (1949), who, nearly 50 years previously, identified pressures on geographical knowledge in schools, arguing that the *Ge-* was being taken out of geography in favour of cross-curricular endeavours such as social studies.

A quarter of a century after Marsden's work, striking the right balance between ensuring good-quality geographical knowledge, enabling pupils to flourish, and teaching with and through geographical issues continues to be a useful framework to consider successful geography teaching, and therefore successful mentoring. Each beginning teacher will arrive with their own set of criteria about which of these are important and you can help them think through and make sense of these ideas and the relationships or *balance* between them. When guiding beginning geography teachers, balancing these ideas becomes important not only to help the beginning teacher develop, but also for you to enable good-quality geography teaching to be at the heart of your professional discussions. It is by reflecting on these ideas that you can clarify your own position and it is through this self-reflection that mentoring can become a powerful tool for professional development in geography education.

Subject expertise plays only a small role in Huling's (2001) ideas about successful mentoring, appearing as part of the professional 'competencies' (p. 2) of mentors. Brooks (2016) researched the role that subject expertise, including knowledge, subject pedagogies and values, plays in forming the identity of geography teachers, how teachers see and relate to their profession, and how this changes throughout their careers. In her work she interviewed a series of geography teachers over a number of years and discovered that they 'connected with the subject at different points of time' (p. 130). It is by reflecting on these ideas, and identifying the extent to which you are deeply connected to your subject, that enables you to identify the extent to which you model geographical, subject-specific behaviours, alongside more generic professionalism to beginning teachers.

Task 6.3 Mentor reflection: subject-specific feedback

Think about the last feedback you gave to a beginning teacher after observing them teach. Reflect on how much of it was focussed on the generic aspects of teaching (pacing, pitch, timing, behaviour management) and how much of it was focussed specifically on the geography being taught and learnt. Reflect on how the balance between these two aspects of feedback changes as a beginning teacher improves.

A framework to enable this reflection about the place of geographical knowledge in the school curriculum can come from the work of Young and Muller (2010) on curriculum futures. The thinking this can afford for you as mentors can help clarify a range of roles for geographical knowledge, and thus an opportunity for professional development. An over-emphasis on the learning of geographical facts for the sake of it, or simply for the passing of exams, turns geography into a tick-list of content, what Young and Muller (2010) call their 'Future 1' curriculum. This would be an over-emphasis of Marsden's (1997) subject component. This position echoes the stance Hudson (2010) takes on knowledge when he writes about content knowledge being checked against external 'system requirements' (p. 32). Yet equally as uninspiring for pupils is the removal of knowledge from the curriculum, and a focus on generic skills and competencies, what Young and Muller (2010) call a Future 2 curriculum. It is this that would over-emphasise the 'educational' component from Marsden's (1997) work. Here it is the maturation of the child that forms the central objective of teaching. Another key tension that Marsden (1997) identifies is the role played by the social education component in the geography curriculum. Too much curriculum dominated by what he calls 'good causes' (p. 242) can ignore the geography and just focus on pupil behaviour and response; classroom activities would focus on action plans to save the planet and to alter behaviours at the expense of developing real understanding of the issues. Yet too little focus on good causes and the subject can seem out of touch with the lives of young people, especially given the immediacy of climate change and ideas of 'The Anthropocene' (Castree, 2015).

Much has been written about the balance of values in the geography classroom. Standish (2007) argued that 'students are not only being taught about how the world is, but how it ought to be' (p. 29). By actively promoting certain values in the geography classroom 'geography is seen as some sort of action that has social or environmental consequences rather than an academic discipline that requires abstract thought and understanding' (Standish, 2009, p. 120). As a mentor, by clarifying your own position on the role of contemporary issues you can also help beginning teachers to explore the various benefits and challenges of teaching geography with and through such issues. One framework for your own self reflection, which might aid your own professional development and which can also be used with beginning teachers, is that on curriculum ideologies, from Rawling (2000). The ideological perspective through which a teacher thinks impacts not only on the way they see their subject, but also on the outcomes they want to achieve with their pupils. Bustin (2018) showed that a lesson on the impacts of climate change can look very different for students if planned through different ideological perspectives. Finding opportunities to develop your own understanding of these different perspectives can be of value when mentoring, as it can help to frame discussions about why beginning teachers choose to make certain curricular and pedagogical decisions. The deeper insight and challenge that come from discussing this with a beginning teacher have the potential to be a key form of your own professional development.

It is in the professional development space created by quality reflection and discussion about knowledge, skills and values that the idea of Future 3 curriculum thinking (Young and Muller, 2010) may be of use, as an alternative the Future 1 and 2 perspectives described earlier. At the heart of Future 3 thinking is powerful knowledge (Young, 2008). This is not a tick-list of content to be learnt (which would be akin to Future 1) but a way of attending to how knowledge is socially constructed by expert geographers and so this framing acknowledges that geographical knowledge can evolve as more research takes place, and greater diversity of expert voices is brought to the fore. The ways in which the powerful knowledge of school geography can be practically applied to the school curriculum, such as through sequencing and revisiting ideas throughout a student's school career, has been considered by Enser (2020), and these ideas could be a useful starting point for discussion between you and your beginning geography teachers. Reading and engaging with these ideas, as well as their critique (e.g. Catling and Martin, 2011; White, 2019) can facilitate your own professional development.

The power of geographical knowledge means geographically educated young people can be equipped to understand and respond to the challenges the planet faces. Children and young people have capabilities to think about the world in new ways and to work out their place in an ever-changing world. These GeoCapabilities can be used as a means to express the potential of geography as a school subject (Bustin, 2019). A focus on capabilities enables teachers to link geographical knowledge, through expert pedagogy, to the lives of young people. The thinking afforded through GeoCapabilities encourages teachers to take responsibility for curriculum thinking, and as such teachers become curriculum leaders (see Lambert et al., 2015; Bustin et al., 2017). Exploring these ideas will aid your own professional understanding; modules of teacher development on the GeoCapabilities (n.d.) website created as part of the GeoCapabilities 2^2 project are specifically designed as a form of structured professional development. Thinking in this way takes us beyond the simple idea that mentors checking beginning teachers' knowledge is meeting system requirements (as Hudson, 2010, describes), towards the idea that they are active curriculum makers (e.g. Lambert and Morgan, 2010). It is the collaborative discussions exploring the potential of school geography in this way that can provide an example of professional development.

Conclusion

In this chapter, I have outlined the many ways that working as a mentor in geography education to support beginning teachers also offers professional rewards. These can be in the form of tangible opportunities to take on further academic study at a university and to be formally recognised with qualifications, but also in the many intangible benefits that arise from thinking deeply about geography teaching and learning. By actively engaging with ideas in geography education you can clarify your own understanding, but also challenge and engage beginning teachers, enabling you to realise the opportunities for the *educative mentoring* experiences described in this chapter. There is a balance to be sought between the need to create generically trained teachers, and nurturing the sorts of teachers for whom the subject of geography is an integral part of their role. This is where the notion of professional identity (e.g. Brooks, 2016) can be of use. Reflecting on the role of geography as part of your professional identity can be an ongoing aspect of your mentor professional development. Smith (2001) describes mentors as *gatekeepers* to the teaching profession and as such you have a significant role in modelling and providing curriculum leadership. Opportunities to develop your own thinking, through formal and informal professional development opportunities, are key to ensuring a high level of professional and subject-based competency, which will benefit you, your beginning teachers and your students.

For discussion

- What role does geography play in your professional identity as a mentor of beginning geography teachers, and how does this manifest itself in the behaviours you are modelling?

- What are the main differences between mentoring with a focus on the more generic aspects of teaching and mentoring geography teachers and how can we provide opportunities for beginning geography teachers to identify themselves as geographers?
- What role might the ideas around powerful knowledge, curriculum futures and GeoCapabilities play in your own professional development as a geography teacher mentor and how might this shape your own thinking and that of the beginning teachers you work with?

Notes

1. External examining is the process by which a professional from one institution is invited to observe students in another to ensure a parity of standards is maintained. In this specific case, as part of this role, Roberts (2010) visited trainees on other university ITE courses.
2. The GeoCapabilities 2 project was an EU (Comenius) funded project led by UCL Institute of Education between 2013 and 2017 with partners in Europe and the USA.

Further reading and resources

1. Hudson, P., 2010. Mentors report on their own mentoring practices. *Australian Journal of Teacher Education*, 35(7), 30–42.

This is an original research paper which specifically asks experienced mentors to reflect on the role of mentoring as a professional development activity. The empirical basis of the report results in the five-stage model discussed in this chapter. The paper is based around Science and Mathematics teaching, and is embedded in the Australian School context. You can read it critically to contrast the experiences reported with those within your own context, as well as to reflect on the ideas from a geographical subject specialism.

2. Cajkler, W., Wood, P., Norton, J., and Pedder, D., 2013. Lesson study: Towards a collaborative approach to learning in initial teacher education? *Cambridge Journal of Education*, 43(4), 537–554.

This paper outlines the notion of Lesson Study, as discussed in this chapter, as an effective form of professional development. Lesson Study involves a mentor and beginning teacher working together to identify a curricular or pedagogical problem, co-constructing a lesson plan to address that problem, critically reflecting together on the success of the lesson then using this to inform further lessons. The processes and nature of the iterations, as well as the development of the idea, are explored in this paper and as such can be modelled.

3. Bustin. R., 2019. *Geography Education's Potential and the Capabilities Approach: GeoCapabilities and Schools*. Cham: Palgrave Macmillan.

Engaging with the ideas in this book will help you and beginning teachers to consider the bigger questions underpinning practice, and as such is a form of professional development. The book engages with questions about what we choose to teach in school geography and why. It provides a framework of thought around why geography teaching matters and can be used to conceptualise the role of geographical knowledge in geography education. It explores powerful knowledge as explained in this chapter, as well as notions of GeoCapabilties.

References

Brooks, C., 2016. *Teacher Subject Identity in Professional Practice: Teaching with a Professional Compass*. Abingdon: Routledge.

Bustin, R., 2018. What's your view? Curriculum ideologies and their impact in the geography classroom. *Teaching Geography*, 43(2), 61-63.

Bustin, R., 2019. *Geography Education's Potential and the Capabilities Approach: GeoCapabilities and Schools*. Cham: Palgrave Macmillan.

Bustin, R., Butler, K., and Hawley, D., 2017. GeoCapabilities: Teachers as curriculum leaders. *Teaching Geography*, 42(1), 17-19.

Butt, G., and Collins, G. 2018. Can geography cross 'the divide'? In D. Lambert and M. Jones (eds), *Debates in Geography Education*. Abingdon: Routledge, 291-301.

Cajkler, W., Wood, P., Norton, J., and Pedder, D., 2013. Lesson study: Towards a collaborative approach to learning in initial teacher education? *Cambridge Journal of Education*, 43(4), 537-554.

Castree, N., 2015. The Anthropocene - a primer for geographers. *Geography*, 100(2), 66-75.

Catling, S., and Martin, F., 2011. Contesting powerful knowledge: The primary geography curriculum as an articulation between academic and children's (ethno) geographies. *The Curriculum Journal*, 22(3), 317-335.

Clinard, L. M., and Ariav, T., 1998. What mentoring does for mentors: A cross-cultural perspective. *European Journal of Teacher Education*, 21(1), 91-108.

Department for Education, 2011. *Teachers' Standards: Guidance for school leaders, school staff and governing bodies*. London: DfE. Available at: https://assets.publishing.service.gov.uk/government/uploads/system/uploads/attachment_data/file/665520/Teachers__Standards.pdf [accessed 19 February 2021].

Department for Education, 2013. *Geography National Curriculum*. London: DfE. Available at: www.gov.uk/government/publications/national-curriculum-in-england-geography-programmes-of-study [accessed 30 March 2021].

Dewey, J., 1938. *Experience and Education*. New York: Collier Books.

Enser, M., 2020. *Powerful Geography: A Curriculum with Purpose in Practice*. Carmarthen: Crown House.

Fargher, M., 2017. GIS and the power of geographical thinking. In C. Brooks, G. Butt and M. Fargher (eds), *The Power of Geographical Thinking*. Cham: Springer, 151-164.

Fargher, M., and Healy, G., 2021. Empowering geography teachers and students with geographical knowledge: Epistemic access through GIS. In N. Walshe and G. Healy (eds), *Geography Education in the Digital World: Linking Theory and Practice*. London: Routledge, 102-116.

Feiman-Nemser, S., 2001. Helping novices learn to teach: Lessons from an exemplary support teacher. *Journal of Teacher Education*, 52(1), 17-30.

Ganser, T., 1997. Promises and pitfalls for mentors of beginning teachers. Paper presented at the Conference on Diversity in Mentoring, Tempe, AZ. Available at: https://files.eric.ed.gov/fulltext/ED407379.pdf [accessed 19 February 2021].

GeoCapabilities, n.d. GeoCapabilities. Available at: www.geocapabilities.org [accessed 31 March 2021].

Geographical Association, 2018. Geography initial teacher education (ITE) and teacher supply in England: 2018 update. Available from: www.geography.org.uk/write/MediaUploads/Advocacy%20Files/GA_Geography_ITE_training_and_supply_2018.pdf [accessed 1 December 2020].

Gholam, A., 2018. A mentoring experience: From the perspective of a novice teacher. *International Journal of Progressive Education*, 14(2), 1-12.

Healy, G., and Walshe, N., 2022. Navigating the policy landscape: Conceptualising subject-specialist mentoring within and beyond policy. In G. Healy, L. Hammond, S. Puttick and N. Walshe (eds), *Mentoring Geography Teachers in the Secondary School*. Abingdon: Routledge, 13-30.

Holloway, J., 2001. The benefits of mentoring. *Educational Leadership*, 58(8), 85-86.

Hudson, P., 2010. Mentors report on their own mentoring practices. *Australian Journal of Teacher Education*, 35(7), 30-42.

Hudson, P., 2013. Mentoring as professional development: 'Growth for both' mentor and mentee. *Professional Development in Education*, 39(5), 771-783.

Huling, L., 2001. Teacher mentoring as professional development. ERIC Digest. Available from: https://files.eric.ed.gov/fulltext/ED460125.pdf (accessed 19 February 2021).

Kinder, A., 2022. Mentoring within the geography subject community. In G. Healy, L. Hammond, S. Puttick and N. Walshe (eds), *Mentoring Geography Teachers in the Secondary School*. Abingdon: Routledge, 102-118.

Lambert, D., 2018. Editorial: Teaching as a research-engaged profession: Uncovering a blind spot and revealing new possibilities. *London Review of Education*, 16(3), 357-370.

Lambert, D., and Morgan, D., 2010. *Teaching Geography 11-18: A Conceptual Approach*. Maidenhead: OUP.

Lambert, D., Solem, M., and Tani, S., 2015. Achieving human potential through Geography education: A capabilities approach to curriculum making in schools. *Annals of the Association of American Geographers*, 105(4), 723-735.

Lopez-Real, F., and Kwan, T., 2005. Mentors perception of their own professional development during mentoring. *Journal of Education for Teaching* 31(1), 28-31.

Marsden, B., 1997. On taking the geography out of geographical education. *Geography*, 82(3), 241-252.

Mena J., Hennissen, P., and Loughran, J., 2017. Developing pre-service teachers' professional knowledge of teaching: The influence of mentoring. *Teaching and Teacher Education*, 66, 47-59.

Office for Standards in Education (Ofsted), 2020. Initial teacher education (ITE) Inspection framework and handbook. Available at: www.gov.uk/government/publications/initial-teacher-education-ite-inspection-framework-and-handbook [accessed 30 March 2021].

Palombo, M., Hammond, L., and Mitchell, D., 2020. The findings of the survey of mentoring in geography education. *Teaching Geography*, 45(1), 9-11.

Palombo, M., and Daly, C., 2022. Educative mentoring: A key to professional learning for geography teachers and mentors. In G. Healy, L. Hammond, S. Puttick and N. Walshe (eds), *Mentoring Geography Teachers in the Secondary School*. Abingdon: Routledge, 208-223.

Parkinson, A., 2020. *Why Study Geography?* London: The London Publishing partnership.

Rawling, E., 2000. Ideology, politics and curriculum change: Reflections on school geography 2000. *Geography*, 85(3), 209-220.

Rawlings Smith, E., 2020. Techniques for mentors to support early career teachers reflective practice. *Teaching Geography*, 45(2), 53-55.

Roberts, M., 2010. Where's the geography? Reflections on being an external examiner. *Teaching Geography*, 35(3), 112-113.

Smith, P., 2001. Mentors as gate-keepers: An exploration of professional formation. *Educational Review*, 53(3), 313-324.

Standish, A., 2007. Geography used to be about maps. In R. Whelan (ed), *The Corruption of the Curriculum*. London: Civitas.

Standish, A., 2009. *Global Perspectives in the Geography Curriculum: Reviewing the Moral Case for Geography*. London: Routledge.

Tapsfield, A., 2019. *Effective Geography ITE Training and Mentoring*. Sheffield: The Geographical Association.

Tonna, M. A., Bjerkholt, E., and Holland, E., 2017. Teacher mentoring and the reflective practitioner approach. *International Journal of Mentoring and Coaching in Education*, 6(3), 210-227.

UCL Institute of Education (IOE), n.d. Masters modules. Available at: www.ucl.ac.uk/module-catalogue/modules/developing-mentoring-practices-CPAS0114 [accessed 19 February 2021].

Walshe, N., 2017. Developing trainee teacher practice with geographical information systems (GIS). *Journal of Geography in Higher Education*, 41(4), 608-628.

White, J., 2019. The end of powerful knowledge? *London Review of Education*, 17(3), 429-438.

Wollman-Bonilla, J., 1997. Mentoring as a two-way street. *Journal of Staff Development*, 18(3), 50-52.

Wooldridge S. W., 1949. On taking the 'Ge-' out of Geography. *Geography*, 34(1), 9-18.

Wood, P., and Rawlings Smith, E., 2017. Lesson Study: A collaborative approach to teacher growth. *Geography*, 102(2), 91-94.

Young, M., 2008. *Bringing Knowledge Back In: From Social Constructivism to Social Realism in the Sociology of Education*. Abingdon: Routledge.

Young, M., and Muller, J., 2010. Three educational scenarios for the future: Lessons from the sociology of knowledge. *European Journal of Education*, 45(1), 11-27.

Young, M., and Lambert, D., 2014. *Knowledge and the Future School: Curriculum and Social Justice*. London: Bloomsbury.

7 Mentoring that makes a difference
Perspectives from beginning geography teachers

Gemma Collins

Introduction

In launching a survey of geography mentors, Hammond et al. (2019, p. 6) asked whether geography mentors have been 'given a voice to share their ideas and experiences'. The findings of the survey (Palombo et al., 2020) furthered our understanding of who geography mentors are, how they mentor and why, and it can be argued that there is much to be gained by beginning teachers also being given a voice in these contemporary discussions of learning to teach geography with the support of *expert colleagues* (DfE [Department for Education], 2019). Shoyer and Leshem (2016) asked student-teacher candidates to voice their *hopes and fears* for their future practice, resulting in insights into self-efficacy, aspirations, identity and apprehensions; the strength of student voice in their research is distinctive and powerful. This chapter features the voices of seven beginning teachers interviewed in 2021, following the completion of their ITE (Initial Teacher Education) in 2019/20. The rationale for hearing beginning teachers' voices in this chapter is to help you challenge the assumptions that can be made by mentors about what beginning teachers find useful, valuable and supportive. By giving beginning teachers some agency in their development and actively involving them in dialogue about their progress we can hear, in their own words, what they need from their mentors. The series of vignettes that follow illuminate key aspects of the mentoring process that made a significant difference to these beginning teachers and are examined through the lens of threshold concepts (Meyer and Land, 2003; Cousin, 2006; Meyer et al., 2006).

Threshold concepts and liminal space

The narratives presented in this chapter include moments the beginning teachers experienced as troublesome and challenging yet also integrative – allowing beginning teachers to make connections between varying aspects of practice – and transformative, leading to more consistent and coherent ways of thinking and practising as teachers. Literature surrounding threshold concepts is complex and extensive, but consistently highlights similar characteristics; threshold concepts are bounded, integrative, transformative, troublesome and irreversible (Meyer and Land, 2003). Cousin (2006) offers a succinct and useful overview, describing the main features of threshold concepts, as well as a helpful articulation of the idea of 'liminal space', describing it as:

an unstable space in which the learner may oscillate between old and emergent understandings.

(p. 4)

This state of liminality was explored by Wood (2012), who used blogs as a *liminal space* in which beginning teachers could begin to capture shifts in identity and practice as they negotiated their ITE. Wood (2012, p. 86) describes liminality as a state of being 'betwixt and between' and highlights the role of 'elders' – in the context of initial teacher education, perhaps mentors as 'expert colleagues' (DfE, 2019) – in guiding learners through a period of transition. Ellsworth's (1997, p. 71) notion of learners experiencing 'stuck places' and Meyer and Land's (2003) framework of threshold concepts and liminality are helpful reminders of the importance of empathy and compassion in mentoring. The following are accounts, in the words of the beginning teachers, of mentoring that made a difference.

Introducing the research

The interviews took place in January 2021 via Zoom. All participants were beginning teachers who completed ITE in 2019/20. The process began with a written task, typically taking the participant approximately 10 minutes to complete. The written task asked the participant to simply to reflect on their ITE, and to create a visual, graphical representation of their perceived trajectory over time. Capturing conceptual change is complex; commonly used methods have included qualitative interviews (Wood, 2000), blogs (Wood, 2012), and concept mapping (Buitink, 2009; Hay et al., 2008; Kinchin et al., 2019), where the concept map itself is often the object of interest. This research followed the approach of Heron et al. (2018) by using a written task – in this case, not a concept map, but a similarly visual representation of change over time – as a stimulus for discussion in the interview, with the qualitative data generated as the main object of interest. The interview itself therefore began with the participant talking through the outcomes of their written task and elaborating on any critical incidents or events. The process took no more than an hour, and was audio-recorded to aid data analysis.

I transcribed all of the interviews in full, beginning with the text that was automatically generated through Zoom, which I checked and edited for accuracy while re-listening to the interviews. Then I used the theoretical framework of threshold concepts to code the transcripts, and I found them featuring moments that could be considered threshold-crossing, from troublesome moments to transformative experiences to irreversibly grasping new ways of practising. However, within this broad framework for analysing the data, more individual stories, rooted in practice, began to emerge. It is through these practical examples that the participants' voices are heard most strongly, and through which you might determine, as a mentor, how you can facilitate similar moments of conceptual change in your beginning teacher. Therefore, the initial coding was revised; analysis no longer sought to establish common themes across the interviews – for example, to identify examples from each participant of concepts that were bounded, transformative, integrative and so on – but rather to identify, in the distinctive and individual accounts of the participants, examples of threshold-crossing of any nature

Ethical considerations

Guided by BERA (2018), ethical approval was obtained from the individual participants, who gave informed consent and were given the right to withdraw their data. Participants were offered access to the interview recording and transcripts, as well as the opportunity to review my interpretation of the data in the form of their individual vignette. Though entitled to waive their own right to anonymity, participants recognised that they were reflecting on the actions of mentors who had not given consent, and that by identifying themselves, they would also be revealing the identities of others. Pseudonyms have therefore been used to maintain anonymity. As suggested by Hammond (2021), the use of pseudonyms in research involving personal narratives can help to maintain identity and agency for the participants, and, in light of this, my participants were given the opportunity to choose their own pseudonyms in order to allow them control over their representation.

The process of data collection built on an extensive, pre-existing relationship with the participants, and so started from a place of understanding and trust. All beginning teachers from my 2019/20 ITE cohort were invited to take part in the research, with no obligation to engage and, with my formal involvement in their qualification now concluded, with no fear of detriment to their ongoing development should they decline to take part. It is assumed therefore that the participants volunteered willingly and that their consent indicates a relationship of trust and respect between us, which in turn created an environment in which participants felt able to be open and honest.

Kerry

Before the start of her first school placement, Kerry felt many of the apprehensions reported by beginning teachers before they join a new school. For Kerry, the experiences of that first day – being welcomed at the school reception, meeting members of staff, touring the school, and observing some teaching – were an essential part of the confidence-building that beginning teachers need to flourish. Kerry's account implies that how you describe your motivations for mentoring and how you set expectations for your availability are likely to make a difference for a beginning teacher, who will need your guiding hand as the expert, as she describes here:

> It's so new to you, and you're learning.... You know, no one tells a mentor how to mentor... you have you just naturally have to want to help somebody become better at something....

For Kerry, this inclusive and welcoming approach extended beyond the initial weeks of a new attachment. She recounts, from a different context, a less purposeful experience of being involved in supporting the history department with an educational visit. Whilst it was in some respects a positive and enjoyable experience, Kerry was left feeling that this experience had not extended as far as any meaningful learning for her personally as a beginning teacher:

> It was a history trip... I had my own little group and they seemed like they were loving it so that was really nice, but... I also didn't feel like that trip was to better me and to help

me become a better teacher. It was just like 'oh you'll be an easy person to put on the trip, and we won't miss you too much in school'. Although obviously I did myself reflect on it and get a lot out of it, I don't think that's what the intentions of the trip were.

In contrast, another earlier opportunity to engage with an educational visit was structured in such a way that it acted as a valuable learning episode for Kerry. Kerry recounts several steps in the process, from goal-setting, to speaking to other staff with expertise in the area, to a thorough debrief following the experience. Task 7.1 has been designed to help you as a mentor in constructing a similar learning episode based around geographical fieldwork, although similar principles can be applied to an educational visit or other kinds of outdoor learning. Hammond (2018) sets out the importance of geographical fieldwork in geography education, and therefore your contribution as a geography mentor to help to 'inform, and thus empower' (p. 175) your beginning teacher to integrate fieldwork into their practice cannot be overestimated.

Task 7.1 Involving your beginning teacher in planning geographical fieldwork

Consider these prompts for creating more active involvement from your beginning teacher when there are opportunities to engage with fieldwork:

- What personal goals does your beginning teacher have for the experience? These are likely to be different to the learning outcomes you plan for students.
- What actions can your beginning teacher take, perhaps with your support, to achieve these personal goals?
- Which aspects of the process can your beginning teacher be involved in, with your support and expert oversight? Consider, for example: obtaining quotes for travel; the drafting of information and consent letters to parents and carers; supporting in the completion of a risk assessment; the design of learning materials; or the negotiation of a programme of activities with an external organisation such as the Field Studies Council.
- Who else in your school might facilitate some learning in this area for your beginning teacher? Could you arrange a meeting with the Educational Visits Coordinator, the teacher in charge of the Duke of Edinburgh scheme, teaching assistants who have experience of supporting students in out-of-classroom settings?
- How can you help your beginning teacher take ownership of some aspects of the experience? Could they join you in taking registers and carrying out head counts? Are they first-aid trained?
- What form might a review of the beginning teacher's personal goals take? When and how can the experience be de-briefed and their own learning outcomes be reviewed?

Kerry recognised the contribution that she had made to the department in supporting the educational visit, but also that the experience had been mutually beneficial:

> it does benefit them as well, but because they want to help you – because that's what a mentor does, they want to help you because you're new to it – they tried to make... not everything about you, but that everything has a purpose for you as a [beginning] teacher.

The role of the mentor was clear in Kerry's narrative, in helping to make visible the otherwise hidden aspects of running an educational visit. This relates to the 'transformative' nature of threshold concepts (Meyer and Land, 2003) in this context revealing to beginning teachers the understanding of the role of a geography teacher in facilitating fieldwork that was previously invisible to them. A useful analogy to use with your beginning teacher might be that of an iceberg; it is likely that your beginning teacher can easily observe your surface-level actions, qualities and characteristics and can, to a greater or lesser extent, mimic these themselves (Cousin, 2006). Seeing students enjoying the educational visit was rewarding, but not as transformative to Kerry's practice as the earlier opportunity she had been given to co-construct and participate in an educational visit from conception to evaluation.

Sam

Analysis of the language in Sam's account revealed the importance of being made to feel like an active and valued part of the geography department in his placement school. In particular, Sam identified the weekly mentor meeting as an opportunity to engage in professional and scholarly dialogue about geography teaching and learning (Rawlings Smith, 2022). Sam recalls some of his earliest mentor meetings with remarkable clarity, despite his interview taking place over 12 months since many of those meetings occurred. This reveals the often deeply affective nature of the mentor meetings you will have with your beginning teachers; indeed, I still recall vividly one particularly harrowing lesson debrief from my own initial teacher education almost 20 years ago! Sam's accounts were of a two-way exchange and development of ideas, for example a reflection on his mentor's approach to a lesson debrief; Sam described his mentor asking him to reflect first on his own progress before they added their own views, then moving into a dialogue around a key theme arising from the observation. In the case of individual lesson debriefs, your beginning teacher may be keen to know what you thought of their lesson, but asking your beginning teacher to reflect on the lesson before the debrief takes place – what Biddulph et al. (2015, pp. 79–80) describe as having 'a conversation with yourself' about the learning that has taken place – can offer the time and space required for critical evaluation, not only for your beginning teacher, but for you as the mentor. Sam recognised and valued the place of the mentor as expert colleague, and needed their help to develop the skills of reflection and evaluation. Without early modelling of what you expect to see and early directed feedback on their practice, your beginning teacher could be left 'guessing' what a good geography lesson might look like, as Sam describes in these terms:

at that point, I didn't really know too much of what teaching was. [So]what's the point of you watching me if you're not going to give me your view as a teacher and a mentor of how to improve? Which kind of sounds a bit harsh... but as a [beginning teacher] you are very new to what to look for and [a mentor] telling you what they saw kind of opens your eyes.

Your greatest value as a subject mentor to a beginning teacher of geography is that you can facilitate a rich discussion focused strongly on the 'geography' - the geographical concepts, contexts and data - of the lesson (Roberts, 2010). The danger of a lesson debrief that is too reliant on the beginning teacher's evaluation - often, an evaluation that we ask to be made immediately following the lesson, with little or no time for real reflection, or an examination of the learning outcomes through the review of students' work, for example - is that discussion can focus only on the surface observations which tend towards the generic, such as classroom management, and that the 'geography' and focus on geographical learning is lost (Roberts, 2010). Kagan (1992, p. 161) concluded from a review of 40 'learning to teach' studies that novice teachers experience a 'shift in concerns from self to pupils' and that, 'novices... also need to be acquiring knowledge of pupils' (Kagan, 1992, p. 163), and the mentoring described by Sam appeared to have supported him in shifting his gaze from self to pupils. In describing his own experiences of this valuable subject-specific dialogue with his mentor, Sam focused less on individual lesson debriefs, and more on the weekly mentor meetings as an opportunity for a holistic view of his progress. For Sam, an effective mentor meeting was about introducing a cycle of target-setting and review:

> We would have a weekly focus, where I would observe a teacher - doing good differentiation, for example - and I would try to put that into practice in my lesson.... And that would be our cycle of observation, to see what I can improve on, meet about it, and discuss how.... Observe someone doing it very well, then put it into practice.

As a mentor, you have an essential role in helping your beginning teacher to learn what good practice looks like in the context of your school and your geography department. This idea of 'mentor as expert colleague' (DfE, 2019) reinforces the importance of creating for your beginning teacher a balanced timetable of learning opportunities, including classes which may be initially challenging, to expose them to a range of experiences from which they can learn. This provides opportunities for your beginning teacher to develop the willingness to seek advice and support from colleagues, and to negotiate some of the 'stuck places' (Ellsworth, 1997, p. 71) and most *troublesome* moments of learning to teach (Meyer and Land, 2003; Cousin, 2006). Wood (2012, p. 87) suggests that beginning teachers occupy a state of 'extended and ambiguous' liminality throughout their ITE, experiencing the uncomfortable existence in the space between 'knowing that...' but not yet 'knowing how to...'. That liminal space is conceptually and emotionally challenging, but a necessary space through which your beginning teacher must travel, in order for their understanding to be transformed.

Ahmed

For Ahmed, his early school experience was a time to find his feet and to build confidence. For beginning teachers enrolled on ITE programmes that feature school experience in at least two schools (typically a requirement for university-led ITE programmes, but that at the time of writing had been temporarily removed by the DfE (2021) in light of the impact of coronavirus (COVID-19) pandemic on schools), the transition to a contrasting school setting can be difficult, and as a mentor it is worth reflecting on the ways in which you might adapt your practice not only to the needs of an individual beginning teacher, but also to the stage of development at which they find themselves. For Ahmed, this transition from working with one mentor to another was a formative experience, as described here:

> I do feel like they're two amazing mentors, but they were so different as well. My second mentor was, you know, more by the book… he was down to earth… where he felt there was an area of improvement, he would tell me straight up and I really, really appreciated that because it did help me improve.

Ahmed demonstrates a key quality you will require of your beginning teacher, which is a willingness to ask for and act on your advice as a mentor. Importantly, Ahmed also demonstrates self-reflection and good humour throughout his interview, and, as evidenced in the quote above, a genuine desire for honesty from his mentor.

Ahmed's story suggests that building a strong foundation of trust between you and your beginning teacher can create the right environment for your beginning teacher to develop their reflective practice, which in turn can sustain them through the most challenging stages of their teaching careers. The reflective practice that both Ahmed's mentors developed in him allowed him to negotiate his first term as a newly qualified teacher (NQT):

> I don't know what happened… I was unsure of myself… I felt like a [beginning teacher] all over again, I didn't feel like I was in my NQT year. It was like that, for one or two weeks [but] I bounced back, you know things started to improve again. I did some reflection myself… I realised more time needs to go into my planning… I feel like that's something that my mentor helped me with, just to be really reflective of our practice. I always do that now. I told this to a few of the [beginning teachers at school] as well; as long as you can reflect, you're going to do really well in your career.

The impact of good mentoring extends far beyond the individual, as exemplified by Ahmed sharing the same advice with a new group of beginning teachers based in the school where he now works as an early career teacher.

Jean

In this reflection, Jean describes the impact of a guided 'learning walk' with her mentor, during which they observed together short periods of teachers' practice, with a particular focus. For Jean, the role of the experienced teacher was essential in making these learning walks an effective learning opportunity. There were aspects of classroom practice that would have remained 'hidden' for Jean, had the mentor not drawn attention to subtle behaviours such as tone of voice or positioning in the classroom, or even the choice of activities. Here, Jean describes observing a more experienced colleague teaching a class with which Jean struggled:

> They were like a different class... great... they're doing everything she's asking them to... they know what she expects. It kind of becomes more frustrating, because you think 'what actually are you doing to have this effect?'

In a second observation of the same teacher, this time carried out on the learning walk with the mentor, Jean was given greater insight into what was helping the teacher to manage the class so positively:

> when you go round with your mentor they can tell you those things that the teachers are doing that you just don't even realise, because they're more experienced.

It can be helpful to a beginning teacher for you as the mentor to give some insight into the origin of those classroom practices; are they dictated by school-wide policy, and therefore something that the beginning teacher would see happening in almost every classroom, or are these practices particular to you? If they are particular to you, how did you develop those practices and what do you believe makes them effective? To what extent are you happy for the beginning teacher to adapt or change those practices, or to try new approaches of their own?

As a more experienced teacher, and often even as an experienced mentor, you might take for granted much of the embedded good practice your beginning teacher will observe, as Jean describes here:

> I think sometimes maybe it's hard for people who are experienced to realise that they need to be really specific.

Meyer and Land (2003), when describing threshold concepts, suggest that grasping such concepts is 'irreversible'; that once something has been learned it cannot be unlearned or forgotten. Much of your role as an effective mentor may be to make explicit the previously tacit practices that your beginning teacher has observed from you and other expert teachers.

Charlie

It was immediately apparent from Charlie's account how formative her 'firsts' as a beginning teacher were:

> I don't think you can replace or forget, you know, your first lesson....

Successful first interactions, with you as their mentor and with the young people they teach, can be crucial moments for your beginning teacher. The experience of their first taught lesson, whenever that occurs, will be – as Charlie noted – a memorable event for your beginning teacher. What worked well for Charlie was an approach that could be described as 'jumping in at the deep end':

> I couldn't have learned more than by just teaching. So for me, that wasn't a negative experience, that was a really positive experience. I would say, based on my personality I'm just that sort of person that would 100% be positive, would 100% throw themselves into it…

but this approach might not work as well for a different beginning teacher. This reinforces the value of an approach to mentoring that is personalised, flexible, and takes into account the personality, characteristics, confidence and prior experiences of your beginning teacher. It is through open dialogue and negotiation between you and your beginning teacher that you can, as a mentor, determine the best approach to these early, formative experiences.

Knowing when to introduce new challenges to your beginning teacher is again, to some extent, a judgement that you might make as a mentor. Charlie made excellent progress early in her first school experience, and therefore her mentor began to adapt their mentoring practice accordingly:

> They were like… 'Oh, we can actually push you to do these things that we would expect [later in ITE]'… I really liked the challenge because, again that personality type, I always love a challenge. I think though maybe it made me less sure of my progress, because I was being given targets that were becoming less attainable, less easy than maybe the first targets were.

As your beginning teacher's practice develops, the nature of your feedback and targets will change, often becoming increasingly sophisticated and more conceptually challenging for the beginning teacher:

> I guess in your life you're never constantly criticised are you… You know, things are highlighted to you that you aren't doing right and no human being likes to hear that! That made my progress felt a little bit knocked, because… I thought I'd made good progress and… it's like they moved the goalposts.

Your beginning teacher will look to you as their mentor for reassurance that this change in feedback is a typical part of the process of learning to teach geography; Cousin (2006, p. 5) describes the need for 'recursiveness and excursiveness' in the learning journey, suggesting that

> in the insistence that there needs to be a number of 'takes' and looping back on the conceptual material to be grasped, the threshold concept perspective refreshes the critique of a simplistic, linear, learning outcomes approach.

You will, as a mentor, choose (in Charlie's words) to 'move the goalposts', in order to facilitate further development in your beginning teacher's practice, but this can be achieved with some transparency, negotiation and reassurance. It is likely – and desirable – that your feedback will move between the generic (how to manage a classroom environment, for example) and more subject-specific (what good geographical learning looks and sounds like and how to assess that progress, or focussing on the nuances of subject knowledge, for example), leading to some rich disciplinary discussion between you and your beginning teacher. Task 7.2 draws from a variety of feedback mechanisms that Charlie described as being effective in developing trust between her and her mentors; the task presents you with an opportunity to reflect on the ways in which you might use observation and feedback with your beginning teacher.

Task 7.2 Developing communication in the observation and feedback process

Reflect on these approaches to the observation and feedback process between you and your beginning teacher. Consider the strengths and limitations of each approach, in the context of your own practice, as well as practical ways of communicating and enacting these approaches.

- Formal observations of the beginning teacher are made by a variety of teachers in your department, and not always by you as the mentor.
- Not all feedback is written.
- Not all written feedback is structured in the same way.
- Not every lesson will be observed; usual class teachers may take on more of a coaching role, or a teaching assistant role, within some lessons.
- Feedback is distinctly *and* distinctively geography specific.

Emma

Like many beginning teachers of geography, Emma started ITE having graduated with a good geography degree; 82% of postgraduates training to teach geography in 2020/21 held a first or upper second-class degree (DfE, 2020). For beginning teachers like Emma there is a need to recontextualise geography subject knowledge (Puttick, 2014; 2015), and to consider the level at which subject knowledge should be taught across the phase(s) and age range in which the beginning teacher is working. In her interview, Emma described the challenge of having to pitch content at different levels than she had previously been used to, from her own educational background and other school experiences. Related to this was the transformative moment for Emma of realising – with commendable honesty – that not every young person is the successful learner she had herself been at school:

> I find it very difficult to relate to a low attainer because it's not something that I have experienced or even saw – because I was in the top set when I was in school. I struggle to engage them when they don't understand the content to access the… what I would describe as the high-level, more interesting aspects of geography. If they don't understand the basics they struggle to access the bits that I find interesting or that I think they might find interesting.

To support them in recognising and addressing subject misconceptions, your beginning teacher may find it useful to read around the idea of threshold concepts in the discipline of geography (Fouberg, 2013) as well as to consider what it means to make progress (Taylor, 2018) and the nature of conceptual development in geography (Brooks, 2018).

Jo

Jo's experience reveals another often pivotal moment for a beginning teacher: obtaining their first teaching post. At whatever stage this occurs, you should not underestimate the impact that this may have on your beginning teacher, from the time and energy required for job applications and interviews to the negative impact on self-confidence arising from not being successful. Mentors generally anticipate the need to raise morale and to build back confidence for a beginning teacher following an unsuccessful application or interview. Jo's experience, however, reveals that the mentor's role is just as important following success in obtaining a first teaching post.

Jo made excellent progress early in her ITE and was interviewed for and secured a full-time teaching post in January 2020. Reflecting back on this milestone, it would seem that Jo was surprised by the impact that it had on her subsequent progress:

> I was learning quite a lot and I felt more confident. Bizarrely, I think part of it was that I had a job… I think that made a massive difference. I [still] wanted to do really well and pass, but it just took that pressure off a bit… I was much more relaxed.

Of particular note is the feeling of relaxation – not complacency – that Jo reports. She goes on to describe an increased willingness to take risks in her practice, to make mistakes, and to learn from those mistakes. As a mentor, knowing when to encourage that informed risk-taking can be a difficult judgement, and it may be useful to consider the role played by success for your beginning teacher in the job market, as a catalyst for further development.

Conclusion

Seven beginning teachers have shared their personal experiences of being mentored through the process of learning to teach geography, and analysis has revealed some of their most transformative moments. Kerry and Sam both highlighted the impact of being an active participant in their learning and development and the importance of feeling like a valued part of the geography department. The mentor-mentee relationship was a key focus for Ahmed, who described the value gained from working with two contrasting mentors during his ITE year, and the ways in which both mentors, in different ways, developed him as a reflective practitioner. Jean and Charlie shared key aspects of the mentoring process which enabled them to refine their practice: in Jean's case, the value of observing expert colleagues with the support of a mentor as 'guide', and for Charlie, the personalised and negotiated approach to feedback as a mechanism to develop her practice. Emma started her ITE as an academically successful geographer, and she provided us with an honest account of how, with the support of her mentor, she recognised and addressed the struggles that many young people experience in their geography education. Finally, Jo reminded us of the affective nature of ITE, and how pivotal moments such as gaining a first teaching post can add to the contextual complexity of mentoring beginning teachers.

Common threads run through each narrative – a sense of belonging, of being welcomed and guided, of being valued, and of making a contribution to the geography departments in which these beginning teachers were placed – yet each individual account tells us something different about the mentoring practices that make a difference to beginning teachers.

Learning to teach geography is a deeply personal, emotional and affective experience, at times troublesome and difficult, but also transformative. In describing conceptual change, Cousin (2006, p. 5) states:

> in short, there is no simple passage in learning from 'easy' to 'difficult'; mastery of a threshold concept often involves messy journeys back, forth and across conceptual terrain.

As a mentor, you are central to the development of your beginning teacher and will be valued as the 'expert guides' on this necessary journey. This chapter ends as it should, with sincere thanks not only to the beginning teachers who took part in interviews, but also to their mentors who enabled them to flourish and to continue to thrive.

For discussion

- This chapter shared the voices of beginning teachers. To what extent and in what ways do these narratives suggest that compassion and empathy are important elements of mentoring?
- Every narrative in this chapter included some reflection on feeling welcomed into a new community. How can you welcome and induct your beginning teacher into their subject community at different scales: your geography department? Your wider subject network within and between local schools, and at a much larger scale, subject associations and learned societies?

Further reading and resources

1. Brooks, C., 2017. Pedagogy and identity in initial teacher education: developing a 'professional compass'. *Geography*, 102(1), 44–50.

Many of these beginning teachers' narratives are underpinned by the complexities of a shifting identity; from geographer, to beginning teacher of geography, but also a student of geography education. You may find it useful to further consider the notion of teacher identity in relation to you as a mentor, and this article is an excellent starting point.

2. Cousin, G., 2006. An introduction to threshold concepts, *Planet*, 17(1), 4–5.

Gaining some understanding of the nature of threshold concepts might enable you to note and act on pivotal moments in your beginning teacher's progress, and to develop an awareness of liminality as well as an empathy for those occupying the liminal space of ITE. This short summary is an excellent and accessible introduction to threshold concepts.

References

British Educational Research Association (BERA), 2018. *Ethical Guidelines for Educational Research*. 4th edn. Available at: www.bera.ac.uk/publication/ethical-guidelines-for-educational-research-2018-online [accessed 18 May 2021].
Biddulph, M., Lambert, D., and Balderstone, D., 2015. *Learning to Teach Geography in the Secondary School: A companion to school experience*. 3rd edn. Abingdon: Routledge.
Brooks, C., 2018. Understanding conceptual development in school geography. In M. Jones and D. Lambert (eds), *Debates in Geography Education*. 2nd edn. Abingdon: Routledge, 103–114.

Buitink, J., 2009. What and how do student teachers learn during school-based teacher education. *Teaching and Teacher Education*, 25(1), 118-127.

Cousin, G., 2006. An introduction to threshold concepts. *Planet*, 17(1), 4-5.

Department for Education [DfE], 2019. Early career framework: January 2019. Available at: https://assets.publishing.service.gov.uk/government/uploads/system/uploads/attachment_data/file/913646/Early-Career_Framework.pdf [accessed 31 March 2021].

Department for Education [DfE], 2020. Initial teacher training: trainee number census 2020 to 2021. Available at: https://explore-education-statistics.service.gov.uk/find-statistics/initial-teacher-training-census/2020-21 [accessed 31 March 2021].

Department for Education [DfE], 2021. Initial teacher training (ITT): criteria and supporting advice. Available at: www.gov.uk/government/publications/initial-teacher-training-criteria/initial-teacher-training-itt-criteria-and-supporting-advice#contents [accessed 31 March 2021].

Ellsworth, E., 1997. *Teaching Positions: Difference Pedagogy and the Power of Address*. New York: Teachers College Press, 297-324.

Fouberg, E. H., 2013. "The world is no longer flat to me": student perceptions of threshold concepts in world regional geography. *Journal of Geography in Higher Education*, 37(1), 65-75.

Hammond, L., 2018. The place of fieldwork in geography. In M. Jones and D. Lambert (eds), *Debates in Geography Education*. 2nd edn. Abingdon: Routledge, 171-183.

Hammond, L., 2021. London, race and territories: Young people's stories of a divided city. *London Review of Education*, 19(1), 1-14.

Hammond, L., Mitchell, D., and Palombo, M., 2019. Mentors in geography education: An underused resource and under-represented community? *Teaching Geography*, 44(1), 6.

Hay, D. B., Kinchin, I. M., and Lygo-Baker, S., 2008. Making learning visible: The role of concept mapping in higher education. *Studies in Higher Education*, 33(3), 295-311.

Heron, M., Kinchin, I. M., and Medland, E., 2018. Interview talk and the co-construction of concept maps. *Educational Research*, 60(4), 373-389.

Kagan, D. M., 1992. Professional growth among preservice and beginning teachers. *Review of Educational Research*, 62(2), 129-169.

Kinchin, I. M., Möllits, A., and Reiska, P., 2019. Uncovering types of knowledge in concept maps. *Education Sciences*, 9 (2), 131.

Meyer, J. H. F., and Land, R., 2003. Threshold concepts and troublesome knowledge: Linkages to ways of thinking and practising. In C. Rust (ed), *Improving Student Learning – Theory and Practice Ten Years On*. Oxford: Oxford Centre for Staff and Learning Development (OCSLD), 412-424.

Meyer, J. H. F., Land, R., and Davies, P., 2006. Conclusion: implications of threshold concepts for course design and evaluation. In J. H. F Meyer and R. Land (eds), *Overcoming Barriers to Student Understanding: Threshold concepts and troublesome knowledge*. London: Routledge, 195-206.

Palombo, M., Hammond, L., and Mitchell, D., 2020. The findings of the survey of mentoring in geography education. *Teaching Geography*, 45(1), 9-11.

Puttick, S., 2014. Space-times of teachers' journeys for knowledge. *Teaching Geography*, 39(3), 114-115.

Puttick, S., 2015. Recontextualising knowledge for lessons. *Teaching Geography*, 40(1), 29-31.

Rawlings Smith, E., 2022. Mentoring meetings and conversations supporting beginning teachers in their development as geography teachers. In G. Healy, L. Hammond, S. Puttick and N. Walshe (eds), *Mentoring Geography Teachers in the Secondary School*. Abingdon: Routledge, 137-155.

Roberts, M., 2010. Where's the geography? Reflections on being an external examiner. *Teaching Geography*, 35(3), 112-113.

Shoyer, S.. and Leshem, S., 2016. Students' voice: The hopes and fears of student-teacher candidates. *Cogent Education*, 3(1), 1.

Taylor, L., 2018. Making progress in learning geography. In M. Jones and D. Lambert (eds) *Debates in Geography Education*. 2nd edn. Abingdon: Routledge, 89-102.

Wood, K., 2000. The experience of learning to teach: Changing student teachers' ways of understanding teaching. *Journal of Curriculum Studies*, 32(1), 75-93.

Wood, P., 2012. Blogs as liminal space: student teachers at the threshold. *Technology, Pedagogy and Education*, 21(1), 85-99.

8 Mentoring within the geography subject community

Alan Kinder

Introduction

Despite the fact that teachers of geography share a physical space with young people, a school building with colleagues, and now have a dizzying range of online connections available to them on a '24/7' basis, teaching can still be a rather isolated professional experience. Most approaches to teacher preparation and induction recognise this and devote significant time and resources to ensuring that beginning teachers are not left to their own devices at this critical stage in their careers. Providers of Initial Teacher Education (ITE) and many induction programmes encourage and to some extent require beginning teachers to collaborate with both experienced and novice colleagues and to engage with the wider profession. However, not every route and setting, currently or historically, addresses the need for wider *subject-specialist* interactions, and in England the fragmentation of routes into teaching in recent years has produced instances where, even within the secondary phase, very limited specialist subject support has been available (Geographical Association [GA], 2015; 2018; Ofsted, 2020).

More positively, mentoring a beginning teacher represents an opportunity to widen or strengthen your connections with the geography subject community, an approach which can benefit you and your mentees, and which ultimately helps to sustain the community itself. The term *geography subject community* is used in the context of this chapter to refer principally to geography teachers and educators, to academic geographers in higher-education institutions (HEIs) and to the institutions supporting these professionals, although it can also be considered to include graduates using geographical knowledge and skills in other fields and professions. The significance of subject community connections receives relatively little consideration in policy-making or research relating to mentoring, where the focus tends to be - understandably enough - on the relationship that lies at its heart. The purpose of this chapter is not to downplay the importance of the mentor/mentee pairing, but to place it in its wider context and to examine how it relates to the reservoir of expertise represented and offered by the geography subject community.

The mentor's subject specialism and community

In this section, we consider the significance of subject knowledge and expertise for geography mentors and the ways in which the subject community can be used to develop these. These questions relate in part to the way in which a teacher's knowledge is conceptualised, which is explored more fully elsewhere in this book (Brooks, 2022; Healy and Walshe, 2022; Wood and

DOI: 10.4324/9781003157120-10

Mentoring within the subject community 103

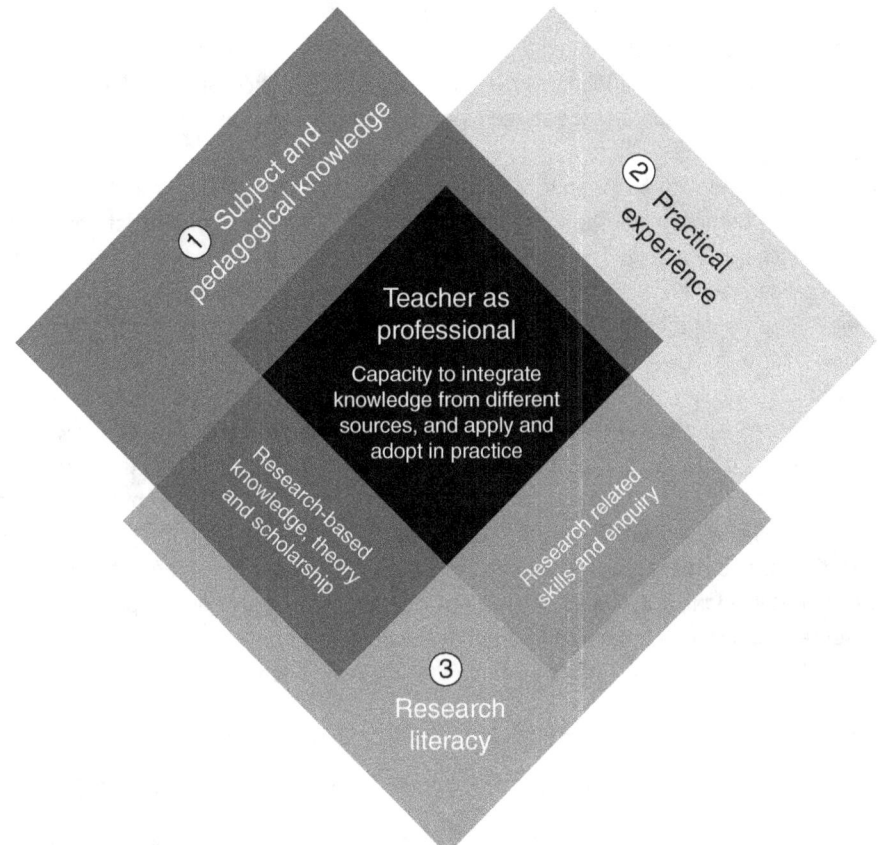

Figure 8.1 Dimensions of a teacher's professional knowledge.
Source: BERA, 2014, p. 10.

Quickfall, 2022). Suffice to say here that the notion of teachers' knowledge as a kind of practical craft or wisdom over-emphasises their first-hand experience without recognising that this can be made explicit and shared more widely (Winch et al., 2013). On the other hand, the view of teachers as technicians who need only follow *best practice* protocols established elsewhere overlooks their professional responsibility to interpret evidence from multiple sources and decide whether and how to apply it to their own, unique educational setting (Winch et al., 2013). The model of expertise shown in Figure 8.1 better reflects the dialogic relationship between the individual teacher's experience and knowledge generated elsewhere. Here, the teacher combines subject and pedagogical knowledge with practical experience and research literacy, integrating knowledge, ideas and information from these sources in order to apply and adopt them in practice (British Educational Research Association [BERA], 2014).

The significance of subject knowledge

I would argue that particular attention should be paid to the role of *the subject* in the dialogue between the individual their wider context, and concur with the view that good teachers 'have a clearly-developed view of the purposes and nature of their subject and an appreciation of their subject discipline as a resource, which sustains them throughout their career by providing a moral and intellectual basis for their practice' and which enables them to plan for progress, evaluate students' thinking and identify and respond to misconceptions (GA, 2015, p. 5).

Brooks' (2016) narrative research, which examined teachers' identities and relationships with geography, demonstrated how significant this ongoing process of subject construction can be to teachers' practice. The subject identity of each teacher in Brooks' study helped them to 'navigate through complex and sometimes contradictory contexts' in unique ways and appeared to guide these teachers' practice to the extent that she likened it to 'acting as a professional compass' (Brooks, 2017, pp. 45-46). It could be said that the *internal workings* of Brooks' (2016) professional compass are not yet fully understood, since the precise relationship between teachers' knowledge of the discipline of geography (by which I mean knowledge of content, concepts or methods with its origins in the academic discipline) and their conception of the subject in schools is under-researched. However, several recent accounts of geography teachers engaging with disciplinary knowledge describe a process of knowledge transformation. The majority of these accounts apply Bernstein's (2000) ideas of *recontextualisation* and *reproduction* (Lilliedahl, 2015) in attempts to explain how teachers of geography make use of the systematic knowledge produced through academic research to help inform their teaching and curriculum development (see for example Puttick, 2015; Firth, 2018).

Task 8.1 Mentor reflection: conceptualising the subject discipline

Write down a short summary of your own view of the purposes and key concepts of geography in education. From where do you think your thoughts and ideas originate? Have they been influenced by particular individuals, by things you have read or by networks or organisations with which you have had contact?

Although the language used is sometimes a little ambiguous, in recent years a number of policy documents in England have begun to recognise the process of subject construction and to acknowledge Young's assertion that the knowledge acquired by students at school does not rely solely on the authority of the individual teacher, but on the teacher as a member of a specialist subject community (Young, 2013). The non-statutory *National Standards for school-based initial teacher training (ITT) mentors* (Department for Education/National College for Teaching and Leadership [DfE/NCTL], 2016), referred to hereafter as the *National Standards*, states that mentors should 'have excellent subject knowledge' and 'keep their subject knowledge up-to-date' (DfE/NCTL, 2016, p. 7-8). The same *National Standards* urge mentors to 'continue to develop their own mentoring practice and subject and pedagogical expertise' (DfE/NCTL, 2016, p. 10) and identify two means by which this might be achieved: 'appropriate professional development' and 'robust research' (DfE/NCTL, 2016, p. 12). They also specify areas where mentor support for mentees is expected, such as to 'access, utilise and interpret robust educational research to inform teaching' (DfE/

NCTL, 2016, p. 12). The *Early Career Framework* (DfE, 2019) distinguishes *subject* from *curriculum* knowledge and describes expectations for both in some detail. It requires early career teachers, with help from their mentors, to learn how to craft the 'essential concepts, knowledge, skills and principles of the subject' into a sequenced and coherent curriculum (DfE, 2019, p. 12).

In England, the 2019 *Education Inspection Framework* (Ofsted, 2019) and changes to the inspection framework for ITE in England from 2020 also place increased weight on teachers acquiring and applying robust disciplinary and specialist pedagogical knowledge to their practice (Kinder and Owens, 2019). School and college inspection reports from Ofsted (the school inspectorate for England) have also become increasingly forthright about the need for such knowledge in teaching, and about the effects on teaching and training quality when it is absent or insufficient. Ofsted has expressed concern that some school-led ITE providers do not develop the 'crucial training role' of the subject mentor and has criticised practice where trainees lack understanding of subject pedagogy because they are 'not encouraged to develop a deeper understanding through probing questions about why and how to teach aspects of the subject' (Ofsted, 2014, p. 16). Of course, none of these policy documents or inspection reports, whether they be statutory or otherwise, should be read uncritically. For example, whilst the *National Standards* define a mentor as a 'suitably experienced teacher' (DfE/NCTL, 2016, p. 7), survey evidence from schools suggests 'decisions about when a teacher is ready to mentor are likely to be subjective and context-specific' (Palombo et al., 2020). Likewise, the use of geographical and educational research to inform geography teaching is less straightforward than suggested and can be highly problematic (Butt, 2020). A more productive approach is to read sources of this kind in conjunction with some authoritative geography-specific advice for mentors (see for example Tapsfield, 2019), reflect on their relevance to your own position and use them to help you identify aspects where your own subject expertise would benefit from further development.

Task 8.2 Mentor reflection: existing contacts with the wider geography subject community

Make a list of the points of contact you already have with the wider geography subject community. How frequently are you able to make use of these, and for what purposes? Are any of the external relationships you have *sharing-exploring* and if so, what aspects of geography or geography education have you explored together?

Subject knowledge development through community connections

If the importance of an ongoing *discourse* with your discipline is accepted by this point, then as a geographer your natural next steps might be to think about the *scale* at which this can operate and the *interconnections* that can facilitate it. It has been argued that the complex choices faced by individual teachers of geography are only likely to be satisfactorily addressed when large numbers of teachers engage with their fellow geographers and geography educators, since these choices concern curriculum content, contexts for study and approaches to teaching which frequently involve contested ideas about the world, as well as challenging moral dimensions (Kinder, 2017). Rawlings Smith (2020) makes a similar point in relation to mentoring geography teachers, by suggesting that the 'state of mind' needed for reflecting on and sharing practice 'is best developed collaboratively: education is deeply social and cannot be isolated from the broader cultural influences of school and society' (p. 53). This reference to societal influence is highly relevant to the ways and means by which you might derive benefits from engaging with your subject community.

In today's networked society, the range of opportunities for you and your mentees to engage in collaborative discourse across the subject community is wider than ever before. Online interaction, especially via social media platforms, is an increasingly popular means of professional communication and learning. This approach has the appeal of being (potentially) global and almost instantaneous, as well as appearing freely available to users. Popular social media accounts and online professional diaries or logs (*blogs* and *vlogs*) offer opportunities for reading, listening or downloading opinions, resources and information offered by others. Internet use also facilitates 'sharing-exchanging relationships', i.e. ones that are made and unmade quickly (Huxham and Hibbert, 2008, p. 505). Whilst these connections may be short-lived, they can nevertheless help spread practical advice and create opportunities to compare ideas and experiences with others. Sharing-exchanging as a form of interaction also has its limitations. As with any use of unmediated online sources or social media, particular attention needs to be paid to questions of accuracy, bias and provenance. Less obvious risks are also present. The algorithms underpinning many online platforms are designed to show us more of what we have already demonstrated we like to read. The end result is a modern form of confirmation bias – with ideas, topics and information that run counter to our existing world view hidden from our searches and social media feeds. Another modern twist on a well-researched problem concerns the weight we give to individuals or organisations with a large social media following. Unconsciously, we can interpret online popularity as a form of social mandate for their views, forgetting that social media following often accrues to energetic, controversial or polemical voices, not necessarily those expressing authoritative or well-founded ideas. The ready availability of online resources and connections also raises questions as to whether teachers are encouraged to simply pass these on at the expense of deeper reflection, and whether they are being made to feel inadequate when they see what others claim to be doing in their classrooms (Parkinson, 2018).

More sustained interactions, especially those involving face-to-face components, are credited by researchers with the creation of so-called *sharing-exploring relationships* in which participants learn to work with one another, establish norms of professional behaviour and distribute various tasks, including those connected to leading the group or network in its learning (Huxham and Hibbert, 2008; Stott et al., 2006). The conjunction of personal and professional dimensions in non-hierarchical *shared spaces* can facilitate the exchange of tacit (difficult-to-codify) knowledge and therefore help create new professional knowledge by and for network members (Stott et al., 2006). Over time, the evolution of trust leads to the production of social capital, the 'connections among individuals [e.g. flows of knowledge

Mentoring within the subject community 107

and ideas] which form a catalytic network by which individual, group and community-wide efforts are made more effective' (Dudley, 2004). In the pre-internet era, *communities of practice* (see Lave and Wenger, 1991; Wenger-Traynor and Wenger-Traynor, 2015) of this kind included groups of geography mentors working with an ITE tutor in relatively stable and well-established HEI-school partnerships, which were collaborative in nature and held in high regard (GA, 2015). School geography departments or networks of geography educators across a local authority area might also have worked in this fashion. Today, the landscape is more complex. Intermediate scales of geography subject community have been constructed across some multi-academy trusts (see for example David Ross Education Trust, n.d.) and network affiliations appear to be becoming more fluid, with some geographers and geography educators connecting with a range of teaching and research communities in order to develop different aspects of their knowledge and practice. Face-to-face networking now tends to be supplemented by online exchange, with the result that many communities have evolved a *blended* existence combining online *and* offline activity, adding to the evidence that has existed for some time that something richer and deeper is evolving online, not limited to transmission and consumption but about interacting, repurposing and co-creating (Mason and Rennie, 2009).

The geography subject community in the UK also features long-established and organised structures, including a teachers' subject association, the GA, and a learned and academic society, the Royal Geographical Society with Institute of British Geographers (RGS-IBG). Equivalent bodies serve Scotland, in the shape of the Scottish Association of Geography Teachers (SAGT) and Royal Scottish Geographical Society (RSGS). These charitable organisations play a particularly important role in advocating the subject and in incorporating and disseminating new geographical and educational knowledge, as well as defining and developing ideas relating to the intellectual and moral scope and potential of geography in education. A simplistic but useful way to understand their work is to distinguish between the teaching associations that focus on geography in education (the GA and SAGT) and the learned societies, which also seek to support advances in the academic discipline (RGS-IBG and RSGS). For mentors, they offer potentially important reference points or sources of guidance against which practice may be better understood. For example, the GA drew on expertise from across the geography teacher education community to produce its quality standards for ITE in geography, which articulate expectations for mentoring and help to contextualise the government's generic standards (GA, 2016). These bodies also convene networks of teachers and academics and look to these communities of practice to develop new insights in geography and education (see for example West et al., 2020; Finn et al., 2021). In the case of the GA, its committees and local Branches offer opportunities for you and your mentees to work with other geography educators; through its events, journals and subject advocacy the Association invites contributions from beginning teachers and experienced mentors (see Table 8.1 and Table 8.2). Taken together, these activities help teachers of geography refine and share their ideas and experiences and find their 'professional voice' within the national community (GA, 2017, p. 2). The main perceived barriers to engaging with these organisations appear to be knowing how to contribute through their formal channels and the costs associated with joining as a member, purchasing a publication or attending a conference or event, where these are not available on a free-of-charge basis. The challenge for each of these subject organisations is therefore to create as vibrant, diverse and connected a community as possible (Kinder, 2020) and to make entry and participation as straightforward as possible, whilst also ensuring that what is written and said across the community represents a kind of shared intelligence or capacity to 'face up to problems that confront us collectively and to develop collective solutions' (Lacey, 1988, p. 94).

The theoretical and national policy points raised above have important implications for your practice as a geography mentor, as they not only help you think about the focus of the work you might undertake with mentees (which we address in the next section), but also help clarify the kinds of knowledge you might look to the geography subject community to help you build or extend. For example, in thinking about the most valuable and impactful subject

Table 8.1 A selection of opportunities for mentors and mentees to engage with the geography subject community

Opportunity	For mentors	For mentees	Note
Opportunities for professional development and subject knowledge opportunities			
The GA annual conference, which includes a 'beginning teacher pathway' www.geography.org.uk/GA-Ann'ual-Conference-and-Exhibition	✓	✓	A pathway of workshops, lectures and fieldwork for beginning teachers, as part of the GA Annual Conference.
The Geography Teacher Educator conference www.geography.org.uk/Geography-Teacher-Educators-Conference	✓		An annual conference which brings together those researching and working in geography teacher education from across the UK and further afield to discuss research and current issues within geography education.
The Geography Teacher Educator e-newsletter www.geography.org.uk/Initial-Teacher-Education/Support-for-ITE-trainers	✓		A free GA e-newsletter, with news and information relevant to those training and inducting geography teachers.
GeogPod - The GA's Podcast www.geography.org.uk/GeogPod-The-GAs-Podcast	✓	✓	A series of free podcasts introducing the work and interests of a diverse range of geography academics and educators.
RGS-IBG Ask the geographer podcasts www.rgs.org/schools/teaching-resources/ask-the-expert-podcasts/	✓	✓	A series of podcasts with geographers sharing their geographical research for geography teachers and A-level geography students.
RGS-IBG Monday night lectures www.rgs.org/events/	✓	✓	Featuring renowned speakers discussing the latest geographical research.
Opportunities to contribute to the geography education community			
Submit an article for publication, for example in a journal published by the GA www.geography.org.uk/write-for-GA	✓	✓	An open invitation to any geography teacher to write for one of the GA's two professional journals, its magazine or its peer-reviewed academic journal.

Table 8.1 Cont.

Opportunity	For mentors	For mentees	Note
Present a session at a conference (for example, at the GA, SAGT, RGS-IBG annual conference) www.geography.org.uk/GA-Annual-Conference-and-Exhibition https://sagteach.org/cpd/ www.rgs.org/research/annual-international-conference/	✓	✓	Depending on the conference and session type, you might share research or ideas about teaching geography.
Become a peer reviewer for Routes journal https://routesjournal.org	✓	✓	Geography teachers can review submissions and support opportunities for A-level and undergraduate geographers to develop their scholarship.
Join your local GA Branch www.geography.org.uk/Get-Involved/GA-Branches	✓	✓	GA local branches host lectures by academics and run CPD in their locality.
Join a GA phase committee or special interest group www.geography.org.uk/Volunteer-Groups	✓	✓	Groups of teachers across the range of experience which meet to discuss different phases of education and areas of expertise and which provide advice to teachers and the GA. Open to GA members.
Join an RGS-IBG research group and/or their mailing list www.rgs.org/research/research-groups/	✓	✓	The RGS-IBG currently has 32 research groups, including one focussed on 'Geography and Education'.
Opportunities for recognition of professional development or achievement			
GA professional passport www.geography.org.uk/GA-Professional-Passport-and-Award	✓	✓	An online tool and award to support and recognise geography teachers who reflect deeply and critically on the professional development that they undertake.
GA Rex Walford Geography Student Teacher Award www.geography.org.uk/GA-Rex-Walford-Geography-Student-Teacher-Award		✓	This award is open to trainees and ECTs and recognises inspirational and innovative practice in primary or secondary geography ITE.
RGS-IBG Chartered Geographer (Teacher) accreditation www.rgs.org/professionals/chartered-geographer/	✓		A professional accreditation for geography teachers who have been teaching for at least six years.
RGS-IBG Rex Walford Award www.rgs.org/schools/competitions/rex-walford-award/		✓	This award is open to trainees and ECTs and entrants are asked to produce a scheme of work that focusses on the theme of the RGS-IBG's Young Geographer of the Year competition.

Table 8.2 Readings and professional development opportunities in relation to mentors in geography education from the GA

Opportunity	Description
Geography mentoring www.geography.org.uk/Geography-mentoring	GA web section for mentors.
Effective Geography ITE Training and Mentoring www.geography.org.uk/eBooks-detail/ 21763557-75cf-42e7-9538-5f722ddc2024	GA e-book relevant to those training or mentoring early career teachers and other geography teachers.
Techniques for mentors to support early career teachers' reflective practice www.geography.org.uk/Journal-Issue/ 712aa985-6fd2-4835-b928-bfa20ee0c3c9	*Teaching Geography* article focussed on reflective practice with techniques for mentors to use.
Mentoring www.geography.org.uk/eBooks-detail/ f8523569-614e-40a8-8a71-4e65e27413f0	GA Handbook chapter exploring ways to mentor geography teachers throughout their professional careers.
Resourceful geography mentoring www.geography.org.uk/Journal-Issue/ e804099d-068c-46dd-bb08-7b858d50d749	*Teaching Geography* article identifying where to start if you are asked to be a mentor and the skills that you need.
High quality Initial Teacher Education in secondary geography www.geography.org.uk/ Providing-high-quality-geography-ITE	A set of criteria for high-quality ITE in geography, with references to mentoring.

reading you could access via the *geography subject community*, the following possibilities emerge:

- reading and engaging with research, or summaries of recent academic thinking and its relevance to teaching (e.g. Gurnell, 2018; Lane, 2019);
- critical reflections on subject-specialist teaching approaches (e.g. Roberts, 2013);
- different perspectives on contemporary and controversial issues (e.g. Willis, 2014);
- critical assessments of the applicability of geographical information and ideas in the public realm to the geography classroom (e.g. Trolley, 2020).

Finally, it is also important to acknowledge the constraints you might be facing when seeking to develop your subject-specific knowledge and skills using the avenues described thus far. Uppermost is the fact that your primary commitment must be, quite rightly, to the children and young people under your care and that managing the demands of mentoring is likely to depend to some extent on the time and support made available to you by your school or college. Research and inspection evidence suggest that, in this important respect, more support for geography mentors is needed and that geography mentor training within ITE often neglects disciplinary knowledge in favour of the technical and managerial concerns of course delivery (GA, 2015; Palombo et al., 2020). Another all-too-frequent constraint relates to the prior subject knowledge of some mentors and mentees: analysis shows geography, in comparison with other secondary-school subjects, as having the third-lowest proportion of teachers with a relevant post-A-level qualification (National Audit Office, 2017).

> **Task 8.3 Mentor reflection: developing subject expertise through the subject community**
>
> Write down the key aspects of subject expertise and knowledge you think could be further developed through engaging with others in the geography subject community. Now write down the main constraints on you developing subject-specific knowledge and skills. Can you identify any quick wins or ways in which the subject community could help you better manage these constraints?

Connecting mentees with their geography subject community

Before we turn to your role in respect of modelling and brokering connections across the geography subject community for your mentees, let us consider briefly the way in which the mentor/mentee pairing can operate as a subject *community of two*, albeit with a porous boundary that allows it to draw in expertise from elsewhere.

Within the geography education community, it has been acknowledged for some time that we create new knowledge and make sense of the world by discussing how we understand things with other people (Roberts, 2013), that 'internal reflection and "monologues"' follow on from social interactions (Chalmers and Keown, 2006, p. 109). More broadly, the contribution towards continuing professional development (CPD) in education made by collaborative activities such as 'planning, practising, experimenting, adapting, reviewing and debriefing' has also been recognised over time (Centre for the Use of Research and Evidence in Education [CUREE], 2012, p. 12). More recently, the features of effective teacher CPD have emerged with increasing clarity from a growing body of research evidence (see for example Cordingley et al., 2015; DfE, 2016; Scutt and Harrison, 2019; Perry et al., 2019; Fletcher-Wood and Zuccollo, 2020). In brief: *domain-specific* (including subject-specific) professional development is more effective where it is underpinned by robust evidence and expertise, sustained over time, focussed on improving and evaluating pupil outcomes and supported through external expert challenge. Research focussed on subject-specific CPD suggests it is effective when it is focussed directly on developing knowledge or practice unique to a subject area (e.g. a signature pedagogy such as geography fieldwork), or on developing an aspect of teaching in ways which are contextualised for that subject (Cordingley et al., 2018; Coe, 2020).

Not surprisingly, mentoring emerges from the research literature as a particularly impactful suite of practices, particularly when it involves sustained, collaborative activity between the mentor and mentee, incorporating critical reflection and expert challenge. Mentor/mentee dialogue as a source of professional development is examined in some detail within Rawlings Smith (2022) and so it is probably sufficient here to re-emphasise the value of mentors drawing on and applying the subject expertise discussed in the first section of this chapter in order to develop their reflective practice with mentees. Indeed, a strong case has been made that reflective practice in teaching and mentoring is only transformative if and when it is founded on subject expertise (Brooks, 2017; Rawlings Smith, 2020) and that teacher training or induction lacking high-quality subject dialogue 'is in danger of replicating mediocre geography teaching and not providing trainees with a vision of the highest quality geography teaching to which they should aspire' (Tapsfield, 2016, p. 108). Ideas for questions and approaches to help you focus dialogue on subject teaching quality are shared very regularly within the geography subject community (see for example Tapsfield, 2019; Rawlings Smith, 2020) but whatever approach is taken, a useful question to consider is, 'who constitutes the expert in the community of two?'. In many instances, recent graduates or individuals switching to teaching from another career can arrive with more recent academic knowledge, fresh ideas around content selection and curriculum design or with their own 'address book' of external sources and expertise. Their capacity for co-creating, leading initiatives and adding to their mentor's professional knowledge and skills should therefore not be underestimated (Rosenthal, 2014). Skilful mentors take account of this, adapting their stance from direct instruction and modelling practice through to collaboration, reflective dialogue and co-construction with the mentee-as-expert, as appropriate to the circumstance (Tapsfield, 2019).

This potential for reciprocity in the mentee/mentor relationship also extends to the idea of promoting or brokering relationships across the geography subject community. Although the *National Standards* ask you to 'support the trainee in accessing expert subject and pedagogical knowledge' (DfE, 2016, p. 12), we must also acknowledge that many ITE students and Early Career Teachers (ECTs) may already have ready access to communities of practice elsewhere, for example through shared, scholarly reading with fellow beginning teachers. Whilst it is true that high-quality ITE provision models good practice and develops subject knowledge by 'helping trainees to identify their knowledge gaps [and] by inculcating a scholarly approach to reading widely about the subject' (GA, 2015, p. 5), many beginning teachers have a great deal to offer to schools and mentors in return. Healy describes her excitement at joining a community of trainee geography teachers in *their* shared subject reading, something she chose to do as she

> felt that as a mentor I needed to read the same geography education scholarship as my trainees, and that in so doing, this scholarship could be deployed to shape trainees' targets and training activities, in both shared discussions and dialogue around lesson observations.
>
> (Healy, 2019, p. 52)

However, it appears that academic reading as a joint enterprise between mentors and mentees is still a neglected area of activity (Palombo et al., 2020). Where trainees do undertake extensive reading, ITE inspectors have nevertheless emphasised the need for follow up to help them apply the ideas to their teaching (Ofsted, 2014).

Despite the non-hierarchical account of mentoring described above, mentors do of course provide the opportunity for beginning teachers to work directly with a *suitably experienced* geography teacher, and can also open up access to subject community connections and expertise not otherwise easily available to new entrants. The *National Standards* task the mentor with signposting trainees to 'other expertise and knowledge, for example subject associations' (DfE, 2016, p. 8). I would advocate more than just signposting, but a range of actions that, taken together, help to model to beginning teachers how professionals gain their agency through engaging actively with the values, purposes and acquired wisdom of the wider profession. As we saw in the first section of this chapter, communities of practice play a crucial role in creating professional knowledge, by which I mean new insights in geography education or gains in knowledge and skills for individual community participants. They can also generate a shared identity and encourage greater risk-taking and innovation, through the creation of a 'safety in numbers' effect and by ensuring members keep to commitments they have made in the presence of others (Gollwitzer and Sheeran, 2006). These 'good habits', which lead to 'deep and consequential change in classroom practice' (Coburn, 2003, p. 4), seem to me to be of particular value to teachers in the early phase of their careers. Nor should we overlook the psychological value that can come from participation, particularly at the beginning of a teaching career. Feeling part of a larger movement for geography education and knowing that others face similar (or different) circumstances and challenges to ourselves provides encouragement as well as allowing a degree of benchmarking against which expectations can be adjusted. Critically, it is the breadth of the community with which we connect that helps to mitigate the risk of *groupthink*, which often constrains the practice and effectiveness of small networks (Dudley, 2004).

As we saw in the first section of this chapter, navigating the complexity of the wider subject community requires some knowledge of its components and the ways in which these interrelate. A comprehensive account of the many opportunities for mentors to broker subject community connections for mentees is beyond the scope of this chapter. However, the subject associations for teachers of geography (such as the GA or SAGT) and the learned societies for geography (including the RGS-IBG and RSGS) do provide sound and structured means of engaging with academic geographers, the discipline of geography, with geography educators and with subject specialist pedagogy. The GA's professional journal *Teaching Geography*, for example, provides a 'good place to start' for mentors searching for good, evaluative writing about geography teaching and learning (Rawding and Tapsfield, 2017, p. 331). It also publishes contributions from beginning teachers, and therefore provides an opportunity for you and your mentee to reflect on and share your ideas and practice with others. Table 8.1 sets out a range of other ways in which you could model engagement with the wider community to your mentees, through something as simple as subscribing to the GA's Geography Teacher Educator e-newsletter, opportunities to share your joint experiences and ideas with the community, or by joining a community of practice together.

Task 8.4 Mentor reflection: exploring opportunities to engage with the geography subject community

Read Table 8.1 and Table 8.2. Are any of these opportunities available and used by you already, through the GA or through alternative means? Which of the opportunities look distinctive and important to you, and how might you go about using these to support the development of beginning geography teachers? What obstacles might you need to overcome?

Conclusion

For new teachers of geography to acquire agency and learn to make sound judgements about practice for themselves (e.g. to interpret a curriculum framework rather than simply implement it), they need to consider very carefully the *why* as well as the *how* of what they do. This view of pedagogy, not as mere technical mastery but as 'the discourse which informs and justifies the act of teaching' (Alexander, 2004, p. 11), implies an ongoing need to reflect upon their own experience in the light of evidence and experience from elsewhere. It also implies a need to sustain a discourse with the discipline and, as geographers, to keep knowledge and ideas about the world up to date. Beginning teachers otherwise risk repeating or reproducing too narrow a range of approaches (whether appropriate to their own context or not), which weakens their capacity to equip school students with a framework for understanding themselves in the world. As Tapsfield rightly points out, mentees must not become a 'clone' of their mentor, however good a geography teacher you are, and looking beyond your own school or department to exploit opportunities for your mentee to work with geography colleagues elsewhere is the best way to ensure they are not (Tapsfield, 2015, p. 10).

The geography subject community represents a rich reservoir from which new ideas and insights may be derived and a sense of purpose recalibrated and renewed. It is most certainly not a single, monolithic body or an army of *clones*, but is better thought of as a range of nested and overlapping local, regional and national networks and communities – face-to-face and virtual, formal and informal – which have evolved over a long period of time. From the perspective of a mentor, this landscape may look more complex than the one in existence before the onset of the 'internet age', but it also offers choices for mentors and mentees which range from consumption and adoption of external ideas, through interpretation and discussion, to full participation – either individually or in tandem. Understanding how these networks and communities function and the types of benefit that can be derived from interacting with them is key to navigating the choices on offer successfully.

For discussion

- In what ways do you think you could benefit from developing your own engagement with the wider geography subject community?
- In the past, how have you introduced your mentees to the wider geography subject community? Is there anything you will do differently after reading this chapter?

Further reading and resources

1. Kinder, A., 2017. Belonging to a subject community. In M. Jones (ed), *Handbook of Secondary Geography*. Sheffield: Geographical Association, 330-343.

An examination of the reasons the geography subject community relies on 'the participation of the many, not the few', why teachers of geography should belong to and contribute towards a wider community of practitioners and others with subject expertise, and what individual and collective benefits result.

2. Tapsfield, A., 2019. *Effective Geography ITE Training and Mentoring*. Sheffield: Geographical Association.

Guidance and support for tutors training beginning secondary geography teachers but also relevant for those training or mentoring ECTs and other geography teachers, including returning teachers and non-specialists. Includes chapters on mentoring and school-based training strategies.

References

Alexander, R., 2004. Still no pedagogy? Principle, pragmatism and compliance in primary education. *Cambridge Journal of Education*, 34(1), 8-33.

Bernstein, B., 2000. *Pedagogy, Symbolic Control, and Identity: Theory, research, critique* (No. 4). Rowman & Littlefield: London.

British Educational Research Association, 2014. *Research and the Teaching Profession: Building the capacity for a self-improving education system*. London: BERA. Available at www.thersa.org/globalassets/pdfs/bera-rsa-research-teaching-profession-full-report-for-web-2.pdf [accessed 15 September 2020].

Brooks, C., 2016. *Teacher Subject Identity in Professional Practice: Teaching with a professional compass*. Abingdon: Routledge.

Brooks, C., 2017. Pedagogy and identity in initial teacher education: Developing a 'professional compass'. *Geography*, 102(1), 44-50.

Brooks, C., 2022. Mentoring as a spatial practice. In G. Healy, L. Hammond, S. Puttick and N. Walshe (eds), *Mentoring Geography Teachers in the Secondary School*. Abingdon: Routledge, 31-41.

Butt, G., 2020. *Geography Education Research in the UK: Retrospect and prospect*. Cham, Switzerland: Springer Nature Switzerland.

Chalmers, L., and Keown, P., 2006. Communities of practice and the professional development of geography teachers. *Geography*, 91(2), 109-116.

Coburn, C., 2003. Re-thinking scale: Moving beyond numbers to deep and lasting change. *Educational Researcher*, 32(6), 3-12.

Coe, R., 2020, January. *The Case for Subject-Specific CPD*. London: Institute of Physics (IoP).

Cordingley, P., Higgins, S., Greany, T., Buckler, N., Coles-Jordan, D., Crisp, B., Saunders, L., and Coe, R., 2015. *Developing Great Teaching: Lessons from the international reviews into effective professional development*. London: Teacher Development Trust. Available at: https://tdtrust.org/wp-content/uploads/2015/10/DGT-Summary.pdf [accessed 16 September 2020].

Cordingley, P., Greany, T., Crisp, B., Seleznyov, S., Bradbury, M., and Perry, T., 2018. *Developing Great Subject Teaching: Rapid Evidence Review of Subject Specific Continuing Professional Development in the UK*. London: Wellcome Trust. Available at: https://wellcome.org/sites/default/files/developing-great-subject-teaching.pdf [accessed 17 September 2020].

Centre for the Use of Research & Evidence in Education, 2012. *Understanding What Enables High Quality Professional Learning: A report on the research evidence*. Coventry: CUREE. Available at: www.curee.co.uk/files/publication/%5Bsite-timestamp%5D/CUREE-Report.pdf [accessed 17 September 2020].

David Ross Education Trust, n.d. The DRET way: secondary. Available at: https://drive.google.com/file/d/1XHp_XwL-kKFre7PjUN6JhLbdnkpm78Fi/view [accessed 21 September 2020].

Department for Education, 2016. Standard for teachers' professional development. Available at: www.gov.uk/government/publications/standard-for-teachers-professional-development [accessed 16 September 2020].

Department for Education/National Centre for Teaching and Leadership, 2016. National Standards for school-based initial teacher training (ITT) mentors. Available at: www.gov.uk/government/publications/initial-teacher-training-government-response-to-carter-review [accessed 15 September 2020].

Department for Education, 2019. *Early Career Framework*. London: HM Government. Available at: www.gov.uk/government/publications/early-career-framework [accessed 15 September 2020].

Dudley, R., 2004. The dynamic structure of social capital: how interpersonal connections create community wide benefits. *On-line Proceedings of the 22nd International Conference of the System Dynamics Society*, University of Oxford, Oxford. 25-29 July 2004.

Finn, M., Hammond, L., Healy, G., Todd, J., Marvell, A., McKendrick, J., and Yorke, L., 2021. Looking ahead to the future of GeogEd: Creating spaces of exchange between communities of practice. *Area*.

Firth, R., 2018. Recontextualising geography as a school subject. In M. Jones and D. Lambert (eds), *Debates in Geography Education*. 2nd edn. Abingdon: Routledge, 275-286.

Fletcher-Wood, H., and Zuccollo, J. 2020. The effects of high-quality professional development on teachers and students. A rapid review and meta-analysis. Education Policy Institute (EPI)/Wellcome Trust. Available at: https://epi.org.uk/publications-and-research/effects-high-quality-professional-development/ [accessed 16 September 2020].

Geographical Association, 2015. *Geography Initial Teacher Education and Teacher Supply in England: A national research report by the Geographical Association*. Sheffield: Geographical Association. Available at: www.geography.org.uk/write/MediaUploads/Advocacy%20Files/GA_ITE_REPORT-final_web.pdf [accessed 15 September 2020].

Geographical Association, 2016. High quality Initial Teacher Education in secondary geography. Available at: www.geography.org.uk/Providing-high-quality-geography-ITE [accessed 15 September 2020]

Geographical Association, 2017. The specialist role of the Geographical Association. Available at: www.geography.org.uk/write/MediaUploads/About%20us/GA_The_specialist_role_of_the_GA.pdf [Accessed 16 September 2020].

Geographical Association, 2018. *Geography Initial Teacher Education (ITE) and Teacher Supply in England: 2018 update*. Sheffield: Geographical Association. Available at: www.geography.org.uk/write/MediaUploads/Advocacy%20Files/GA_Geography_ITE_training_and_supply_2018.pdf [accessed 15 September 2020].

Gollwitzer, P., and Sheeran, P., 2006. Implementation intentions and goal achievement: A meta-analysis of effects and processes. *Advances in Experimental Social Psychology*, 38, 69-119.

Gurnell, A., 2018. Twenty-five years of progress in physical geography: A personal view of its antecedents and trajectory. *Geography*, 103(3), 122-136.

Healy, G., 2019. Subject scholarship as a mechanism for developing trainees' reflective practice and teachers' curricular thinking. *Impact: Journal of the Chartered College of Teaching*, 6, 52-54. Available at: https://impact.chartered.college/article/subject-scholarship-developing-trainees-reflective-teachers/ [accessed 16 September 2020].

Healy, G., and Walshe, N., 2022. Navigating the policy landscape: conceptualising subject-specialist mentoring within and beyond policy. In G. Healy, L. Hammond, S. Puttick and N. Walshe (eds), *Mentoring Geography Teachers in the Secondary School*. Abingdon: Routledge, 13-30.

Huxham, C., and Hibbert, P., 2008. Manifested attitudes: intricacies of inter-partner learning in collaboration. *Journal of Management Studies*, 45(3), 502-529.

Kinder, A., 2017. Belonging to a subject community. In M. Jones (ed.), *Handbook of Secondary Geography*. Sheffield: Geographical Association, 330-243.

Kinder, A., 2020. The GA's strategic plan 2020-25. *GA Magazine*, 46(3), 6-7.

Kinder, A., and Owens, P., 2019. The Education Inspection Framework – through a geographical lens. *Teaching Geography*, 44(3), 97-100.

Lacey, C., 1988. The idea of a socialist education. In H. Lauder and P. Brown (eds), *Education: In Search of a Future*. London: Falmer Press, 91-98.

Lane, S., 2019. Critical physical geography. *Geography*, 104(1), 49-53.
Lave, J., and Wenger, E. 1991. *Situated Learning: Legitimate peripheral participation*. Cambridge: Cambridge University Press.
Lilliedahl, J., 2015. The recontextualisation of knowledge: Towards a social realist approach to curriculum and didactics. *Nordic Journal of Studies in Educational Policy*, 2015(1), 40-47.
Mason, R., and Rennie, F., 2009. Social networking as an educational tool. In J. Arthur and I. Davies (eds), *The Routledge Education Studies Reader*. London: Routledge.
National Audit Office, 2017. *Retaining and Developing the Teaching Workforce*. London: NAO. Available at: www.nao.org.uk/wpcontent/uploads/2017/09/Retaining-and-developingthe-teaching-workforce.pdf [accessed 17 September 2020].
Ofsted, 2014. University of St Mark and St John Teacher Education Partnership Initial Teacher Education inspection report, Re-inspection: 23-26 June 2014. Available at: http://reports.ofsted.gov.uk/inspection-reports/find-inspection-report/provider/ELS/70131 [accessed 16 September 2020].
Ofsted, 2019. *The Education Inspection Framework*. London: Ofsted. Available at: https://assets.publishing.service.gov.uk/government/uploads/system/uploads/attachment_data/file/801429/Education_inspection_framework.pdf [accessed 22 December 2020].
Ofsted, 2020, January 20. Building great teachers? Initial teacher education curriculum research:phase2.Availableat:www.gov.uk/government/publications/initial-teacher-education-curriculum-research/building-great-teachers [accessed 15 September 2020],
Palombo, M., Hammond, L., and Mitchell, D., 2020. The findings of the survey of mentoring in geography education. *Teaching Geography*, 45(1), 9-11.
Parkinson, A., 2018. How has technology impacted on the teaching of geography and geography teachers? In D. Lambert and M. Jones (eds), *Debates in Geography Education*. 2nd edn. Abingdon: Routledge, 184-196.
Perry, E., Boylan, M., and Booth, J., 2019. *Quality Assurance of Teachers' Professional Development: Rapid evidence review*. London: Wellcome Trust. Available at: https://wellcome.org/sites/default/files/quality-assurance-of-teachers-continuing-professional-development.pdf [accessed 16 September 2020].
Puttick, S., 2015. Recontextualising knowledge for lessons. *Teaching Geography*, 40(1), 29-31.
Rawding, C., and Tapsfield, A., 2017. Mentoring. In M. Jones (ed), *Handbook of Secondary Geography*. Sheffield: Geographical Association, 306-317.
Rawlings Smith, E., 2020. Techniques for mentors to support early career teachers' reflective practice. *Teaching Geography*, 45(2), 53-55.
Rawlings Smith, E., 2022. Mentoring meetings and conversations supporting beginning teachers in their development as geography teachers. In G. Healy, L. Hammond, S. Puttick and N. Walshe (eds), *Mentoring Geography Teachers in the Secondary School*. Abingdon: Routledge, 137-155.
Roberts, M., 2013. *Geography Through Enquiry*. Sheffield: Geographical Association.
Rosenthal, R., 2014. How does student teacher research contribute to knowledge creation within the secondary school? PhD, University of Sussex.
Scutt, C., and Harrison, S., 2019. Teacher CPD, International *Trends, Opportunities and Challenges*. London: Chartered College of Teaching. Available at: https://my.chartered.college/wp-content/uploads/2019/11/Chartered-College-International-Teacher-CPD-report.pdf [accessed 16 September 2020].
Stott, A., Jopling, M., and Kilcher, A., 2006. *How Do School-to-School Networks Work?* Nottingham: National College for School Leadership. Available at: www.researchgate.net/publication/253469781_How_do_school-to-school_networks_work [accessed 15 September 2020].
Tapsfield, A., 2015. Resourceful geography mentoring. *Teaching Geography*, 40(1), 8-10.

Tapsfield, A., 2016. Teacher education and the supply of geography teachers in England. *Geography*, 102(2), 44-50.

Tapsfield, A., 2019. *Effective Geography ITE Training and Mentoring*. Sheffield: Geographical Association.

Trolley, S., 2020. Prisoners of Geography? How contextualising a book can develop students' understanding of geography. *Teaching Geography*, 45(2), 72-74.

Wenger-Trayner, E., and Wenger-Trayner, B., 2015. Introduction to communities of practice: A brief overview of the concept and its uses. Available at: https://wenger-trayner.com/introduction-to-communities-of-practice/ [accessed 15 April 2021].

West, H., Hill, J., Finn, M., Healey, R., Marvell, A., and Tebbett, N., 2020. GeogEd: A new research group founded on the reciprocal relationship between geography education and the geographies of education. *Area*. https://doi.org/10.1111/area.12661.

Willis, K., 2014. Development: Geographical perspectives on a contested concept. *Geography*, 99(2), 60-66.

Winch, C., Oancea, A., and Orchard, J., 2013. *The Contribution of Educational Research to Teachers' Professional Learning – Philosophical Understandings*. London: BERA. Available at: https://socialsciences.exeter.ac.uk/media/universityofexeter/collegeofsocialsciencesandinternationalstudies/education/research/groupsandnetworks/educaationtheoryreadingnetwork/BERA-Paper-3-Philosophical-reflections.pdf [accessed 15 April 2020].

Wood, P., and Quickfall, A., 2022. Working with the complexity of professional practice and development. In G. Healy, L. Hammond, S. Puttick and N. Walshe (eds), *Mentoring Geography Teachers in the Secondary School*. Abingdon: Routledge, 59-74.

Young, M., 2013. Overcoming the crisis in curriculum theory: A knowledge-based approach. *Journal of Curriculum Studies*, 45(2), 101-118.

9 Supporting the development of geography mentors – the potential of professional learning at Masters level

Ann Childs

Introduction

This chapter explores a two-year part-time programme of professional learning for teacher educators, the Masters in Teacher Education. The rationale for the development of the programme is captured well from an observation made by Zeichner (2005), who said:

> Many universities today treat teacher education as a self-evident activity for both school and university-based teacher educators who mentor prospective teachers in clinical experiences and for the instructors and faculty who teach the courses in a teacher education program. Anyone who has ever worked with prospective teachers knows that, although there are some similarities in teaching children and young adolescents, there are many important ways which the two kinds of teaching differ and where one's expertise as a teacher does not necessarily translate into expertise as a mentor.
>
> (Zeichner, 2005, p. 118)

Here Zeichner is fundamentally questioning the assumption that teachers necessarily make good teacher educators and, from this, we began to explore what the distinctive knowledge base of a teacher educator (TE) might be and, most importantly, what a Masters-level programme of professional learning for a TE might look like. This chapter begins by exploring some of the key issues and challenges reported in geography teacher education and in the education of geography mentors. It then goes on to explore the ways and extent to which the Masters in Teacher Education might address these issues by first exploring the history and development of the programme and then the detail of the programme itself. Here themes in the literature around what constitutes the knowledge base of a TE and how TEs learn will be woven into the account before considering the implications for the future professional learning of geography mentors in the current context.

Issues and challenges in geography teacher education

This section explores some of the key issues and challenges in geography teacher education. A key issue reported by the Geographical Association (2015) is how much subject specialist input in geography occurs in the education of trainee teachers:

> The development of subject knowledge and subject-specific pedagogy is an important element of effective ITE training; however, the evidence in geography ITE is that the amount of subject-specialist input is very variable.
>
> (p. 3)

The literature in England emphasises major concerns with the development of subject knowledge and subject-specific pedagogy in geography trainee teachers and this is echoed in the USA (see for example Witham Bednarz et al., 2005; Brooks, 2010). A key way suggested in this literature to address these concerns is through the education of school-based TEs – mentors who work with beginning teachers. For example, Witham Bednarz et al. (2005), in outlining the guiding principles for the development of their new approach to educating new geography teachers, lay emphasis on developing the competences of mentors 'to help beginning geography teachers acquire appropriate content and pedagogical content knowledge' (p. 108). This is also reported as a key aim in teacher education in England (Tapsfield, 2016). However, in England, the quality of geography-specific mentoring has been questioned by Tapsfield (2016), and one issue raised to explain the lack of quality is the fragmentation and proliferation of routes into teaching in England and the introduction, in particular, of school-based, school-led initial teacher education (ITE). In a research report by the Geographical Association (2015), it is suggested that the effects of moving to more school-based, school-led routes has resulted in more generic and less geography-based training of geography teachers:

> The emergence of several hundred new geography ITE providers has brought new schools into the system. This expansion has also reduced average geography cohort size, with the result that geographers in small cohorts are more likely to be trained generically. Extreme fragmentation – the single trainee model – limits opportunities for trainee geography teachers to work together and learn from one another. Small cohort allocations have also contributed to the closure of several long-standing university geography ITE courses.
>
> (p. 3)

This view is supported by Tapsfield (2016), who argued that the 'expansion of school-led routes' resulted in reduction in the quality of mentoring where mentors failed 'to set trainees subject-related areas for development' (p. 106). Tapsfield (2016) goes on to suggest that to improve mentoring in geography mentors need 'up-to-date subject and pedagogical knowledge' (p. 106) but she also reports that there were few opportunities for geography teachers to do so. A recent survey of geography teachers and mentors found that they perceived that there were significant challenges in the training they received for the role (Palombo et al., 2020). They reported that the emphasis of the training was more focussed 'on technical and managerial elements' whereas they placed much more value on 'further training and development focussed on geography, teaching geography and mentoring in geography' but that current training did not 'reflect these aspirations' (Palombo et al., 2020, p. 11).

In summary, the literature suggests the ongoing importance of developing new geography teachers' subject and subject-specific pedagogy but raises concerns about the expertise and training of the school-based geography mentors who are key to this development.

The Masters in Teacher Education – a programme of professional learning for teacher educators

History and development

The view, see Zeichner (2005) above, that a teacher's expertise does not necessarily translate into a TE's expertise is shared by others (see for example Cochran-Smith, 2003; Lunenberg et al., 2007; Goodwin and Kosnick, 2013) and was also supported by academics and TEs in the Department of Education at Oxford University. We perceived that those making the transition into teacher education would benefit from education themselves and this was one of the key reasons we developed the Masters in Teacher Education in 2015. A second reason was that, as science and mathematics TEs, we were frequently asked to run one-off training in many parts of the world to educate TEs. This conflicted with our own understanding that professional learning is better done on an ongoing basis bringing TEs together into a community rather than these short one-off courses. These two key drivers led to the development of the two-year, part-time online Masters in Teacher Education, initially in the subjects of mathematics and science, but, as demand rose, in all subjects from September 2019. The course currently attracts TEs from all over the world who work in schools, universities and as consultants, and these TEs also work at primary, secondary and tertiary level. What holds them all together is that they have responsibility for developing either beginning teachers' or in-service teachers' practice. Details of the course and its structure will be discussed later in the chapter.

As articulated above, the development of the Masters in Teacher Education was prompted by our concern to provide education for TEs. In designing the course, we had in mind what knowledge we wanted to develop in our TEs and how to facilitate their learning. The next two sections consider firstly what has been written about the knowledge base of TEs and, secondly, the models for teacher and TE learning which informed the approach we adopted to develop TEs' knowledge.

What is the knowledge base of a teacher educator?

There is an extensive literature which describes a teacher's knowledge base. The seminal work of Shulman (1986), for example, introduced pedagogical content knowledge (PCK), the knowledge a teacher needs to transform their subject context knowledge to make it accessible to pupils which includes:

> The most useful forms of representation of those ideas, the most powerful analogies, illustrations, examples, explanations and demonstrations – in a word, the ways of representing and formulating the subject that make it comprehensible to others.
>
> (p. 9)

But also:

> what makes the learning of specific topics easy or difficult; the conceptions and preconceptions that students of different ages and backgrounds bring with them to the learning of the most frequently taught topics and lessons.
>
> (Shulman, 1986, p. 9)

PCK seemed to particularly resonate in teacher education and over time, through the work of others, it has evolved, developed and been critiqued. For example, Cochran et al. (1993), in their critique of PCK, were concerned that it suggested that a teacher's knowledge was static and fixed; as such, they adopted a more flexible notion of knowledge to describe pedagogical content knowing. In terms of evolution of PCK Barnett and Hodson (2001) focussed more on PCK in context when they proposed pedagogical context knowledge. There is also literature in geography education where PCK has been used as a framework to analyse both beginning and experienced teachers' PCK and to identify key areas for development and implications for TE's practice (see, for example, Lane, 2009; 2015; Reitano and Harte, 2016).

However, a literature which describes a TE's knowledge base is more elusive, as Cochran-Smith (2003) comments:

> Enormous attention has been devoted over the last two decades to what K-12 teachers need to know and be able to do in order to be effective in their work with students. In fact, to a great extent, 'the knowledge question' has driven the field of teacher education... and dominated the literature. Much less attention at the policy level, however, has been devoted to what teachers of teachers need to know.
>
> (p. 6)

The literature does report on some efforts to describe a TE's knowledge base, for example Loughran (2008), who argues that a TE's knowledge base would include:

> a knowledge of teaching about teaching and a knowledge of learning about teaching and how the two influence one another in the pedagogic episodes that TEs create to offer students of teaching experiences that might inform their developing views of practice.
>
> (p. 1180)

Other writers, such as Murray and Male (2005), focus on new TEs moving into higher education and acknowledge that, in making this move, they bring knowledge from their school teaching background, what they term *first-order knowledge* including knowledge of the academic discipline, their knowledge of schooling, 'experiential knowledge and understanding of school teaching' (p. 2). However, they also argue that in order to be TEs, in higher education, they also need to develop *second-order knowledge*, which includes:

> Knowledge of the 'discipline' or 'subject' of education and the pedagogical knowledge of how to teach that 'subject' in HE.
>
> (p. 3)

Murray and Male's (2005) article focusses more on TEs in HE but they do consider school-based mentors being involved in this second-order work too when they say:

> Significantly, however, this experience of mentoring happens within a school setting and is often focused on the mentor supporting the student teacher in acquiring the context

specific knowledge of how to teach a particular class. Drawing on the conceptual framework for this research, we define such mentors as being involved in second-order work (in that they are inducting student teachers into the profession), but it is important to note that this work takes place within the first-order settings of their schools, drawing on their localised, practitioner knowledge of those settings in order to induct student teachers. (p. 5)

What is interesting about this quote is Murray and Male's (2005) characterisation of mentors' knowledge as TEs as localised, practitioner knowledge, which resonates with the knowledge base that the Oxford Internship Scheme values in a mentor where 'the mentor is primarily required to discuss suggestions for practice in the context of their school' (Hayward, 1997, p. 20). Others have questioned whether this knowledge base is sufficient for effective mentoring. For example, Jones and Straker (2006) argue that, if the focus of a mentor's knowledge is only on their own knowledge and repertoire, this may be 'at the expense of other equally important aspects of professional training and development, such as making sense of wider educational issues' (p. 182). They see the dangers of this, particularly where teacher education has become more school-based as a move towards 'an apprenticeship training' and a 'de-intellectualisation of teacher education' (pp. 181-182). In the Oxford Internship Scheme this is avoided because TEs from the university work alongside school-based mentors and the role of the university tutor is to bring in these wider theoretical perspectives which, with the contextualised knowledge from mentors, are brought together in a reflective process by trainee teachers (interns) called practical theorising. However, in the English system, as in the USA where Jones and Straker's (2006) concerns are expressed, there is a move to entirely school-led and school-based teacher education where there is a genuine danger of the narrowing of the knowledge base new teachers will have access to.

Beyond this knowledge base others have argued that TEs need to develop their affective and emotional knowledge in developing effective relationships with their beginning teachers in areas which require sensitivity, building trust, being honest and valuing the independence of their beginning teachers (see for example Vonk, 1993; Loughran, 2006). Vonk (1993) articulates this well when it is said that:

> a good mentor must have the following personal qualities: open-mindedness, reflectiveness, flexibility, listening skills, empathy, creativity and a helping attitude.
>
> (p. 8)

In summary, supporting Zeichner's (2005) contention that a teacher's expertise does not necessarily translate directly to a TE's expertise, this section has shown that there is much a TE needs to learn and that this 'knowledge is complex and multifaceted'. The next section discusses some of the influential ways reported in the literature that TEs have developed their knowledge and practice.

How do teacher educators learn?

Having considered what the knowledge base of a TE might be our next challenge was to reflect on how to facilitate the professional learning of TEs. We were aware that the literature consistently reports that the education of new TEs is often neglected (van Velzen et al., 2010; Zeichner, 2005; Cochran-Smith, 2003).

> The limited research indicates that the induction of beginning teacher educators is usually a neglected issue that results in the lack of formal induction, and the induction of teacher educators is often haphazard depending on the good will, time and effort of experienced colleagues. Most beginning teacher educators have to find their own way.
>
> (van Velzen et al., 2010, p. 62)

Initially we were informed in our decision about how to construct the course through our work on the Oxford Internship scheme (OIS) and the underpinning idea of professional learning of beginning teachers through a process of practical theorising. To expand briefly from above on the process of practical theorising in ITE, this was conceived of beginning teachers drawing on different kinds of knowledge – contextualised knowledge from school teachers (mentors) and more decontextualised from university-based TEs. A key principle of the OIS is that these are different kinds of knowledge but they are of equal importance (McIntyre, 1993). A second key principle of the OIS was that no knowledge, whatever the nature or source, should be assumed to be valid, but instead should be questioned (McIntyre, 1993, p. 2). Hayward (1997) then describes the process of practical theorising where:

- suggestions for practice derived from, say, product-process research or national/international examples of 'good practice', usually provided by the university tutor, can be tested against practice in the school using criteria like the ideas' feasibility, social acceptability and effectiveness;
- contextualised ideas for practice from school can be tested against more academic criteria of, for example, theoretical coherence, general ideas of good practice, the educational and social values implicit in different practices, their generalisability in terms of effectiveness, and their impact on the long-term learning of children, in the university. (p. 19)

It is the testing of evidence by student teachers from the school and the university that is at the heart of practical theorising and that is intended to facilitate the ongoing professional learning of the beginning teachers. How then might we adapt this as a model to develop the Masters in Teacher Education? We decided that the masters would offer the decontextualised knowledge in teacher education (see below for more details of what this constituted) and this would be set against contextualised knowledge of the teacher education context that the TEs would gather through inquiry tasks they carry out in the first year of the course. More details on how this was operationalised is discussed in the next section. Inquiry, as a means to facilitate TE learning, has been proposed by others; for example, it is certainly resonant with Cochran-Smith's (2003) inquiry as stance, where she argues that:

> The education of teacher educators with inquiry as stance occurs within the context of inquiry communities wherein everyone is a learner, a researcher, a seeker of new insights, and a poser of questions for which no one in the group already has the answers.
>
> (p. 23)

The suggestion of TEs working together in an inquiry community is one that we adopted in the Masters in Teacher Education, as will be seen below. Finally, we drew on the work from the self-study movement where self-study is seen a tool to promote the professional learning of TEs:

> By self-study, I mean intentional and systematic inquiry into one's own practice. Included in this definition is inquiry conducted by individual teacher educators as well as groups working collaboratively to understand problems of practice more deeply.
> (Dinkelman 2003, p. 8)

Loughran (2004) also argues that although reflection on practice is an important element of self-study for the individual teacher educator, self-study should also go beyond this and the reflections that teacher educators undergo in the process of self-study should be accessible to the wider audience of teacher educators to inform their thinking too.

Self-study is a movement that has had a powerful influence in developing TEs' practices and can be seen as a ground-up movement of inquiry, collaboration and investigation by TEs that goes beyond reflection and can use standard research methods to understand and develop teacher education practice.

The structure and rationale for the current course

The Masters in Teacher Education was developed in 2015 for TEs in mathematics and science; we began by setting out its aims (see Box 9.1), which, with the later development of the course for all TEs, we retained. As the course is for both pre-service and in-service TEs, we used the generic term learner teachers to designate the beginning and experienced teachers they were educating.

Box 9.1 The aims of the Masters in Teacher Education

1. To develop familiarity with research and professional debates associated with teacher education, in particular debates and issues about teaching, learning and assessment education.
2. To learn about pedagogy for teacher education in these subjects in a variety of settings.
3. To acquire a repertoire of methods for transforming the subject knowledge of teachers and educators for teaching purposes.
4. To introduce participants to the quality assurance and research standards and methods that characterise the research fields of subject education.
5. To equip participants to continue professional and academic dialogue with others in the field.

In describing and analysing the current course I will draw on these aims, the literature and our own professional knowledge to explore how the course was designed to educate new TEs and to provide continuing professional learning for those already in the profession. In the final section of this chapter, I will reflect on the ways and the extent to which the current course could be flexible enough to address the issues and challenges raised above for the development of geography mentors.

Year one: the taught units

Year one of the course begins with a face-to-face residential to induct TEs into the online units of the course, to meet their study group and to begin to develop their academic reading and writing. After the residential the students return to their educational contexts to study three taught online units:

- Unit 1: Understanding your learner teachers and their actions: implications for your practice as a teacher educator.
- Unit 2: What knowledge does a teacher need?
- Unit 3: Teacher and teacher educator learning: implications for the design of a teacher education session.

I will describe Unit 1 in some detail to show how the online taught element of the course works before outlining more briefly Units 2 and 3. The decision to focus the first unit on understanding learner teachers came from our knowledge of the literature and our own practice as TEs of the importance of exploring the beliefs learner teachers bring to the teacher education process. However, we also hoped that this would inevitably lead TEs to explore their own beliefs about teaching, learning and teacher education too, as we recognised both beginning and experienced TEs would also bring beliefs about effective teaching, learning and teacher education to their professional learning on the course. This is supported by Male and Murray (2005), who indicate that particularly beginning TEs will bring beliefs about teacher education from their own experiences:

> Teacher educators in England tend to have limited experience with their new role before entering HE. As schoolteachers, who have experienced ITE themselves at the beginning of their careers, they tend to have ingrained memories and attitudes to the professional induction experience. Later in their school teaching careers they may also have acquired experience of teacher education through being a mentor to ITE students on school experience (teaching practice).
>
> (p. 5)

The first inquiry task of Unit 1 asks the TEs to elicit their learner teachers' beliefs about teaching and learning and, where appropriate, the nature of the subject. They record the findings of their inquiry on a template called a Reflection and Activity portfolio (RAP). This activity has been adapted for use with your beginning teachers in Task 9.1.

Task 9.1 Mentoring reflection: what beliefs do beginning geography teachers have?

Stage 1: firstly, reflect on your own beliefs about teaching, learning and the nature of geography as a school subject. How have these beliefs changed and developed over the course of your career as a teacher and mentor?

Stage 2: explore with your beginning teacher their beliefs about teaching and learning and the nature of geography as a school subject. This could be done in a number of ways:

(i) Talking them through a lesson plan and, by doing so, attempt to understand why they have planned the lesson in the way they did and explore what it says about what they perceive their role as a teacher is, what the learners will be doing and what it says about how they perceive the subject geography should be taught. Ask them if they can think about where their ideas come from.
(ii) Asking beginning teachers to draw their ideal classroom and then use their drawing to talk about the elements they draw and why. Does their drawing say anything about how geography itself should be taught?
(iii) Asking beginning teachers to draw or talk about what they think the discipline of geography is and how this relates to school geography.

Stage 3: in eliciting beginning teachers' beliefs consider what implications this has for you as a mentor. For example, the literature shows that beginning teachers often base their initial planning and teaching on their own experiences as a learner. In what ways are their beliefs productive and helpful and in what ways might they need to be developed?

In the RAP on the Masters in Teacher Education the TEs also read some key literature on teachers' beliefs about teaching, learning and the nature of the subject to bring together decontextualised knowledge from the readings with contextualised knowledge from their own professional experience and the eliciting of their own beginning teachers' beliefs to look at implications for their developing professional thinking in the process of practical theorising (McIntyre, 1993; Hayward, 1997). This contributes to meeting aim 1: 'To develop familiarity with research and professional debates associated with teacher education in particular debates and issues about teaching, learning and assessment education'. The final section of the RAP then engages the student with methodological issues in relation to the inquiry task and again begins to work toward meeting the aim of introducing 'participants to the quality assurance and research standards and methods that characterise the research fields of subject education' through their own work (aim 4). The RAPs are posted on to a forum and TEs are asked to read and give feedback to their study group's work. Each study group then meets synchronously with their study group supervisor (a tutor on the course) to discuss the issues that have arisen from the inquiry task and hence help meet the aim 'To equip participants to continue professional and academic dialogue with others in the field' (aim 5). These study group meetings also resonate with the tenets of inquiry as stance in that they often involve discussions where each member of the study group 'is a learner, a researcher, a seeker of new insights, and a poser of questions for which no one in the group already has the answers' (Cochran-Smith, 2003, p. 23).

The second inquiry task then asks the TEs to extend the task on eliciting beliefs to observing their learner teachers' teaching. This again gives the TE further insights into their learner teachers' beliefs about teaching and learning and the extent to which these beliefs are enacted in practice. It also raises methodological issues about how to observe a teacher (and then interview them) to understand their practice rather than to judge them. The RAP is again posted, fed back on and discussed in the study group, encouraging practical theorising by exploring the contextualised findings from the inquiry undertaken with the learner teachers, alongside the relevant literature (decontextualised knowledge). The RAP also raises key methodological issues including ethical issues such as the difference between judgement and understanding of a learner teachers' practice and how to observe. It also begins to engage the TEs with discussing their positionality on the course as both a researcher and a learner TE, developing their practice through practitioner inquiry and research.

The third inquiry task in Unit 1 then asks the TEs to reflect on their own beliefs about teaching and learning, how these have changed over time and what influenced these changes; responses are posted and fed back on within study groups as described above. All three inquiry tasks are then brought together in the first examined assignment of 5000 words. TEs are encouraged, through this assignment, to look at a wider range of literature (decontextualised knowledge) and bring this together with the findings from their inquiry tasks (contextualised knowledge) to consider the implications for their professional thinking and practice as TEs in the process of practical theorising. This process of practical theorising is intended to engage them with how they would work with their learner teachers to develop their beliefs and practice and, therefore, ultimately with aim 2 'to learn about the pedagogy of teacher education'.

Unit 2 has a similar structure to Unit 1, but this time looks at teacher knowledge and draws on the work of Shulman and others. It also requires the TEs to complete RAPs and work in their study groups in the same way as in Unit 1. Units 1 and 2 are therefore designed to get the students to engage with what their learner teachers are bringing to the teacher education process in terms of their beliefs and knowledge. Unit 3 then focuses on teacher learning, a key knowledge base Loughran (2008) suggests a TE needs. The TE is required to analyse their practice in promoting teacher learning through analysing a session they have conducted with their beginning teachers, culminating in a 10,000-word assignment. The analysis for the assignment closely resonates with the processes of self-study specifically akin to requiring the TE 'to do an intentional and systematic inquiry into' their own practice (Dinkelman, 2003, p. 8). The assignment draws on evidence from the session and theoretical perspectives, which form the backbone of the taught part of the unit. These theoretical perspectives include the role of theory in teacher learning, stage theory, principles in informing the design of teacher education programmes and the role of collaboration in teacher learning. Sessions chosen by school-based mentors have generally focussed on observation and feedback sessions of their beginning teacher. A final plank of the assignment is for the TEs to reflect themselves on their learning and their own knowledge development.

Year two: the research and development project

Year two of the course begins with a week's residential in August to develop the TE's research skills to carry out a research and development project, the main focus for study in year two, which results in a 20,000-word dissertation. The project requires the TE to carry out an intervention to develop teacher education in their context and to research its effectiveness in collaboration with his/her own colleagues. The TE's choice of focus for the intervention very often comes from issues that are raised in year one. For example, a TE, drawing on work from Unit 3 on professional learning communities, sought to develop a professional learning community in their department focussing on developing teachers' subject knowledge and pedagogical content knowledge in areas where they were less familiar, drawing on work from Unit 2. This focus was chosen in discussion with the department.

Conducting the research and development project has significant resonances with the process of practical theorising as the contextualised evidence collected through the research is interrogated with the research literature to develop teacher education practice in the TE's context. The process of undertaking the research and development project also has significant resonances with inquiry as stance. For example, the case above of the development of an ongoing professional learning community resonates with Cochran-Smith's (2003) inquiry as stance of communities where everyone is a 'learner, a researcher, a seeker of new insights, and a poser of questions for which no one in the group already has the answers' (p. 23). In addition, the research and development project also resonates with the tenets of self-study in that it involves intentional and systematic inquiry into the TE's own practice 'conducted by individual TEs as well as groups working collaboratively to understand problems of practice more deeply' (Dinkelman, 2003, p. 8). Finally, some of the TEs, on completing their masters, have gone a step further, consistent with Loughran's (2004) view that self-study also involves an outward-facing function, to disseminate their work through conferences and in journal articles.

The potential for the Masters to develop mentors' practice in geography education

The final section considers the potential of study on the Masters in Teacher Education to address the issues raised in geography teacher education above. These issues coalesce around the need in geography education to strengthen new teachers' subject knowledge and pedagogical content knowledge and the concomitant need to strengthen geography mentors' practice to support learner teachers to develop these areas.

The move in the Masters to a more generic programme, from one in mathematics and science to all subjects, may seem to weaken the focus on the subject, precisely against what the literature above in geography education suggests is needed; however, the flexibility in the course still offers a strong focus on the subject dimension. For geography mentors on the course the focus on the learner teachers' beliefs about the nature of the geography would allow a rich exploration of key literature in geography education on the nature school and academic geography (see for example Harrison et al., 2004; Mitchell and Lambert, 2015; Puttick, 2015a; 2015b). We have found, in previous cohorts, that when TEs explore the beliefs of their learner teachers they also challenge and develop their own beliefs. For example, in Unit 1 a group of TEs in their RAPs indicated that their own understanding about the nature of their academic discipline and school subject had developed almost as much as their learner teachers. Eliciting beginning teachers' beliefs about geography requires a shift away from generic mentoring and towards a much stronger focus on subject-specific pedagogy of mentoring, as advocated by Brooks (2017).

Task 9.2 Mentor reflection: the balance between generic and subject-specific guidance for beginning geography teachers

This task asks you to think about your interactions as a mentor with beginning teachers and the balance between generic guidance, for example on behaviour and classroom management, and that focussed on subject knowledge and subject-specific pedagogy in geography.

Stage 1: Subject specificity in mentor sessions

Think about a recent session with your beginning teacher that could be, for example, a mentor meeting where you were supporting the planning of a lesson or where you observed the beginning teacher and gave feedback. What was the balance in the session between generic guidance and that focussed on subject knowledge and subject-specific pedagogy in geography? Why?

Stage 2: Balance over time

For experienced geography mentors think about a beginning teacher you worked with over time and consider and reflect on how the balance in the content of your interactions (generic vs geography-specific) changed over the course of working with the beginning teacher? Why?

For all mentors, after your interactions with a beginning teacher over a period of six (or more) weeks, reflect on the balance in the content of your interactions (generic vs geography-specific) and how it changed over the course of working with the beginning teacher? Why?

Stage 3: Implications

From your reflections in stages 1 and 2 are there any implications for your future practice as geography mentor? How will you develop your practice in the area(s) you have identified?

Similarly, in Unit 2 the focus on teacher knowledge allows for an exploration by the geography mentors of their learner teachers' subject matter knowledge (SMK) and PCK, thereby focusing on geography-specific literature (see for example Pattison, 1964; Harrison et al., 2004; Bonnett, 2008). Again, the strong focus on geography serves the dual purpose of the mentor understanding their own learner teachers' current knowledge, and their areas for development, whilst also allowing them to reflect on and develop their own SMK and PCK by drawing on a range of literature in geography education (see for example Lane, 2009; 2015; Jo and Witham Bednarz, 2014; Blankman et al., 2015; Reitano and Harte, 2016).

Unit 3 requires the mentor to analyse a session they have conducted with their beginning teacher; school-based mentors tend to focus on analysis of a session which involves joint planning, observation of the lesson and then feedback. This can easily focus on the subject and, in developing the analysis framework for the session, the TE could draw on geography education literature. Even if the focus of the session is on more generic issues, such as behaviour management, the role of the TE's supervisor would be to bring in the subject-specific focus. For example, as a supervisor with a science mentor the original focus was on the classroom management of science practical work. In discussing this focus with the TE, we realised that the issues the beginning teacher faced were as much about using appropriate practical work. This allowed a focus on science education literature addressing what constitutes effective practical work for learning in science.

Finally, the research and development project has potential for the mentor to focus on subject pedagogy development for their learner teacher. Many school-based mentors focus on developing subject knowledge and pedagogy and this often involves collaboration and inquiry with the whole department. For example, one project involved developing the effectiveness of practical work as a key science strategy in the mentors' science department. A second example involved a TE and head of science, working to develop their use of assessment for learning across the department. Although initially this did not have a strong subject focus, it became so because, as the department started to inquire into what constituted good assessment practice in learning science, they engaged with science education literature addressing what constitutes learning in science. These two projects exemplified collaboration between the mentor and learner teachers and interrogation of the key literature, both of which are consistent with the tenets of practical theorising, inquiry as stance and self-study as key ways to promote TEs' learning.

Task 9.3 Mentor reflection: your own self-study/investigation

Stage 1: What is your area of concern?

What in your experience is a key challenge for you as a geography mentor? For example, in your professional experience as a geography teacher and geography mentor what key areas of subject knowledge and subject-specific pedagogy in geography need enhancing? If you are currently mentoring a beginning teacher what challenges are they experiencing? Why? Reflecting on these questions may help you identify an area of your practice that, over time, you want to develop.

Stage 2: Addressing the concern

If you were to work with your beginning teacher on the area you have identified in stage 1 what evidence would you collect to:

(i) be able to reflect on how the beginning teacher's practice was developing (e.g. by lesson observations, their plans, pupil work and so on);
(ii) be able to reflect on the effectiveness of your guidance as a mentor (e.g. making notes or audio recording mentoring and feedback sessions and reflecting on these)?

In stage 2 more systematic reflection on this evidence over time could allow you to, for example, reflect on the balance between your support of more generic issues of practice like behaviour management and/or subject-specific pedagogy, and to specifically notice where that balance lies, and to reflect on how you want to work with your beginning teacher in the future.

Further thoughts

Exploring the potential for collaboration: how could you collaborate with mentor colleagues in other subject areas to work on issues related to subject knowledge and subject-specific pedagogy? What would be the benefits/challenges of cross-subject collaboration between mentors? Is this something you might consider?

Conclusion

The course originally developed for mathematics and science TEs now admits those from a much wider range of subjects and levels. However, as illustrated, subject and subject-specific teacher education is very much alive and well and at the heart of the Masters in Teacher Education. In addition, the TEs, in engaging with the inquiry tasks and the literature, as well as developing their learner teachers, also significantly develop their own beliefs and knowledge as teachers and TEs. For these reasons, I would argue that the Masters in Teacher Education has significant potential for geography mentors to develop their practice in geography mentoring as they work in their study groups and supervisors to address the challenges identified in geography teacher education identified in the discussion above.

For discussion

- What expertise/knowledge did you bring to the role of a geography mentor? How much training did you receive for the role?
- In the course of mentoring what aspects of your knowledge and skills as a mentor have developed? How have these developed? What key advice would you give to a new geography mentor?
- On reflection, what more education/training would be helpful to make you more effective in your role as a mentor?

Further reading and resources

1. Allsop, T., and Benson, A., 1996. *Mentoring for Science Teachers*. Buckingham: Open University Press.

Although this is about mentoring in science education, and written some time ago, there are some interesting case studies and insights into the real lives of mentors. Chapters include exploring principles for school-focussed ITE and how these can be put into action in designing a programme of ITE. There are two chapters on case studies of mentoring in action in *normal* times and *difficult* times dealing with a range of mentoring issues, with a follow-up chapter on solutions. Finally, there is a chapter where beginning teachers reflect on their own experiences of mentoring.

2. Palombo, M. Hammond, L., and Mitchell. D., 2020. The findings of the survey of mentoring in geography education. *Teaching Geography*, 45(1), 9-11.

This is a recent survey of mentoring in geography education and deals with some of the issues raised in this chapter about the balance between generic and subject-specific issues in geography mentoring for you to reflect on further. How does this research, for example, reflect your own experiences of mentoring in geography?

References

Barnett, J., and Hodson, D., 2001. Pedagogical context knowledge: Toward a fuller understanding of what good science teachers know. *Science Education*, 85, 426-453.

Blankman, M., van der Schee, J., Volman, M., and Boogaard, M., 2015. Primary teacher educators' perception of desired and achieved pedagogical content knowledge in geography education in primary teacher training. *International Research in Geographical and Environmental Education*, 24(1), 80-94.

Bonnett, A., 2008. *What is Geography?* London: SAGE.

Brooks, C., 2010 Why geography teachers' subject expertise matters. *Geography*, 95(3), 143-148.

Brooks, C., 2017. 'Pedagogy and Identity in initial teacher education: developing a professional compass,' *Geography*, 102(1), 44-50.

Cochran, K. F., King, R. A., and DeRuiter, J. A., 1993. Pedagogical content knowledge: An integrative model for teacher preparation. *Journal of Teacher Education*, 44(4), 263-272.

Cochran-Smith, M., 2003. Learning and unlearning: The education of teacher educators. *Teaching and Teacher Education*, 19, 5-28.

Dinkelman, T., 2003. Self-study in teacher education: A means and ends tool for promoting reflective teaching. *Journal of Teacher Education*, 54(1), 6-18.

Geographical Association, 2015. *Geography Initial Teacher Education and Teacher Supply in England: A National Research Report.* Sheffield: Geographical Association.

Goodwin, A. L., and Kosnick, C., 2013. Quality teacher educators = quality teachers? Conceptualising essential domains of knowledge for those who teach teachers. *Teacher Development*, 17(3), 334-346.

Harrison, S., Massey, D., Richards, K., Magilligan, F. J., Thrift, N., and Bender, B., 2004. Thinking across the divide: Perspectives on the conversations between physical and human geography. *Area*, 36, 435-442.

Hayward, G., 1997. Principles for school focused initial teacher education: Some lessons from the Oxford internship scheme. In T. Allsop and A. Benson (eds), *Mentoring for Science Teachers*. Buckingham: Oxford University Press, 11-26.

Jo, I., and Witham Bednarz, S., 2014. Developing pre-service teachers' pedagogical content knowledge for teaching spatial thinking through geography. *Journal of Geography in Higher Education*, 38(2), 301-313.

Jones, M., and Straker, K., 2006. What informs mentors' practice when working with trainees and newly qualified teachers? An investigation into mentors' professional knowledge base. *Journal of Education for Teaching*, 32(2), 165-184.

Lane, R., 2009. Articulating the pedagogical content knowledge of accomplished geography teachers. *Geographical Education*, 22, 40–49.

Lane, R., 2015. Experienced geography teachers' PCK of students' ideas and beliefs about learning and teaching. *International Research in Geographical and Environmental Education*, 24(1), 43–57.

Loughran, J. J., 2004. A history and context of self-study of teaching and teacher education practices. In J. J. Loughran, M. L. Hamilton, V. K. LaBoskey and T. Russell (eds), *International Handbook of Self-Study of Teaching and Teacher Education Practices*. Dordrecht: Kluwer Academic, 7–30.

Loughran, J., 2006. *Developing a Pedagogy of Teacher Education: Understanding teaching and learning about teaching*. Abingdon: Routledge.

Loughran, J., 2008. Toward a better understanding of teaching and learning about teaching. In M. Cochran-Smith, S. Feiman-Nemser and J. McIntryre (eds), *Handbook of Research on Teacher Education: Enduring Questions in Changing Contexts*. 3rd edn. New York: Routledge, 1177–1182.

Lunenberg, M., Korthagen, F., and Swennen, A., 2007. The teacher educator as a role model. *Teaching and Teacher Education*, 23, 586–601.

McIntyre, D., 1993. Theory, theorizing and reflection in initial teacher education. In J. Calderhead and E Gates (eds), *Conceptualizing Reflection in Teacher Development*. London: Falmer Press.

Mitchell, D., and Lambert, D., 2015. Subject knowledge and teacher preparation in English secondary schools: The case of geography. *Teacher Development*, 19(3), 365–80.

Murray, J., and Male, T., 2005. Becoming a teacher educator: Evidence from the field. *Teaching and Teacher Education*, 21, 125–142.

Palombo, M. Hammond, L., and Mitchell. D., 2020. The findings of the survey of mentoring in geography education. *Teaching Geography*, 45(1), 9–11.

Pattison, W. D., 1964. The four traditions of geography. *Journal of Geography*, 63, 211–216.

Puttick, S., 2015a. Geography teachers' subject knowledge: An ethnographic study of three secondary school geography departments (unpublished PhD thesis). University of Oxford.

Puttick, S., 2015b. Chief examiners as Prophet and Priest: Relations between examination boards and school subjects, and possible implications for knowledge. *The Curriculum Journal*, 26(3), 468–487.

Reitano, P., and Harte. W., 2016. Geography pre-service teachers' pedagogical content knowledge. *Pedagogies: An International Journal*, 11(4), 279–291.

Shulman, L. S., 1986. Those who understand: Knowledge growth in teaching. *Educational Researcher*, 15(2), 4–14.

Tapsfield, A., 2016.Teacher education and the supply of geography teachers in England. *Geography*, 101(2), 105–109.

van Velzen, C., van der Klink, M., Swennen, A., and Yaffe, E., 2010. The induction and needs of beginning teacher educators. *Professional Development in Education*, 36(1–2), 61–75.

Vonk, J. H. C., 1993. Mentoring Beginning Teachers: Development of a Knowledge Base for Mentors. Paper presented at the Annual Meeting of the American Educational Research Association, Atlanta, GA, April 12–16.

Witham Bednarz, S., Bockenhauer, M. H., and Walk, F. H., 2005. Mentoring: A new approach to geography teacher preparation. *Journal of Geography*, 104(3), 105–112.

Zeichner, K., 2005. Becoming a teacher educator: A personal perspective. *Teaching and Teacher Education*, 21, 117–124.

SECTION 3
Being a geography mentor

10 Mentoring meetings and conversations supporting beginning teachers in their development as geography teachers

Emma Rawlings Smith

Introduction

Beginning geography teachers have much to gain from experienced school mentors; because of the ways they model high-quality teaching and professionalism, provide opportunities for observations, collaboration and guidance, and enable innovation and creativity. Stanulis and Bell (2017) stress the importance of quality mentoring:

> The kind of mentoring beginning teachers experience during their first few years of teaching can make or break their desire to remain in teaching and their potential to impact student learning. Because mentors are seen as the most influential participants in helping novices learn to teach, the way they perform the mentoring role is of critical importance. (p. 59)

Stanulis and Bell's (2017) suggestion that a mentor can *make or break* a beginning teacher's desire to stay in the profession is not a single story: it is echoed in empirical research, professional literature and the Carter Review of Initial Teacher Training (ITT; Hobson and Malderez, 2013; Coe et al., 2014; DfE, 2015; Ofsted, 2020). Mentors observe, feed back, question, listen and initiate dialogue in order to set appropriate developmental targets, and broaden the focus of reflective practice beyond singular lessons in order to develop subject knowledge, pedagogical reasoning and identity (Loughran, 2019). They also provide opportunities and information to orient new members of the geography department into the school's culture in terms of shared professional behaviours (Weber, 1930). This can be transformative in terms of increasing the motivation, confidence and self-efficacy of beginning teachers (Caspersen and Raaen, 2014; Hill et al., 2020), who may otherwise leave the profession due to concerns such as high workload, school accountability, disillusionment and not feeling a sense of belonging (Noble-Rogers, 2021). As Bustin (2022) suggests, people who take on the role of mentor have the opportunity to shape the thinking of beginning teachers. Mentoring meetings are key to this process, as they provide the space for conversations focussed on geography education, which can be intensely satisfying.

This chapter will first consider the qualities effective mentors bring to formal mentoring meetings and why these are key to successful teacher growth and development. The second part of the chapter will then set out a number of strategies such as reflective practice, teacher noticing, listening, dialogue and learning conversations through geographical enquiry which can be used during mentoring meetings to support beginning geography teachers in their professional development. Central to any mentoring strategy is the subject and for this reason the chapter also provides practical examples from the geography classroom which focus on the question Roberts (2010, p. 112) would put at the heart of everything – 'Where's the geography?'

The qualities of effective mentors

Creating the conditions for a positive mentor-mentee relationship requires a particular skill set. According to the National Standards for school-based ITT mentors, personal qualities such as being approachable, making time for the beginning teacher and offering support with integrity, honesty and respect (DfE, 2016) are the minimum expectation. Kaplan (2019, p. 121) suggests that 'a good mentor should do everything to allow the student to succeed'. They use the term *frientoring* to suggest that successful mentors befriend mentees by getting to know them beyond their work, rather than keeping them at an emotional distance while managing the dual role of supervision and evaluation of progress against the Teachers' Standards (DfE, 2011). With a love of your subject, you can motivate and inspire beginning teachers to develop their own ways of knowing and beliefs about the nature of knowledge, otherwise known as their epistemic identity.

A positive working relationship also requires the mentee to have the necessary affective dispositions to expand their capacity to learn and, ultimately, to reach their potential. Claxton (2006, p. 6) suggests that a capable learner is one who is resilient, resourceful, reflective and reciprocal: see Figure 10.1. Beginning teachers with these dispositions are better equipped to learn and cope with the reality shock of their new role, and therefore persist when teaching gets challenging (Caspersen and Raaen, 2014).

In a small-scale case study with 70 PGCE Geography students exploring who and where they turn to for guidance and knowledge about teaching (Rawlings Smith, 2021), findings

Resilient	Resourceful
proactive, adventurous, determined, flexible, observant, focused	questioning, open-minded, playful, imaginative, integrating, intuitive
Reflective	**Reciprocal**
clear-thinking, thoughtful, self-aware, methodical, opportunistic, evaluative	collaborative, independent, open to feedback, attentive, empathic, imitative

Figure 10.1 Positive learning dispositions.
Adapted from Claxton, 2006, p. 6.

indicate that the attributes mentees value most in their mentors include the following key themes:

- personal or **affective qualities**, for example giving time and support freely and their empathy, approachability and active listening skills.
- professional **competences** or cognitive qualities, for example their teaching expertise, being knowledgeable, awareness of the subject and school context to prompt learning and change and having a critical stance willing to challenge the status quo.
- professional **collaboration** or sociality; explicit opportunities for co-planning, team teaching and shared reflective practice embedded in the everyday work of teaching to allow beginning teachers to partner with more established teachers and be part of the curriculum conversation during pre-lesson preparation, the lesson itself and post-lesson evaluation.
- **mutual dialogue**, for example the mentor involves beginning teachers in all aspects of school life from whole-school staff meetings, break duty and extra-curricular activities and champions their mentees for their efforts with school colleagues and senior leaders.

By emphasising the importance of the cognitive and affective qualities of mentors, this study complements Mcnally and Martin's (1998) research with mentors which finds that beginning teachers require a balance between support and challenge to achieve continuous growth as 'a good mentor furnishes direction: the map, the timetable, the means of locomotion, and somebody to help them when lost' (Kaplan, 2019, p. 116). Mcnally and Martin (1998, p. 42) suggest that you can provide support by identifying strengths, offering counsel and help, being sensitive to feelings, collaboratively planning and teaching, providing opportunities to observe others, making time for them and being approachable. They also describe the ways in which mentors find challenge harder to identify because it should be appropriate to a teacher's stage of development; examples include increasing criticality and moving the focus of reflection from teaching to learning. Figure 10.2 demonstrates how mentors

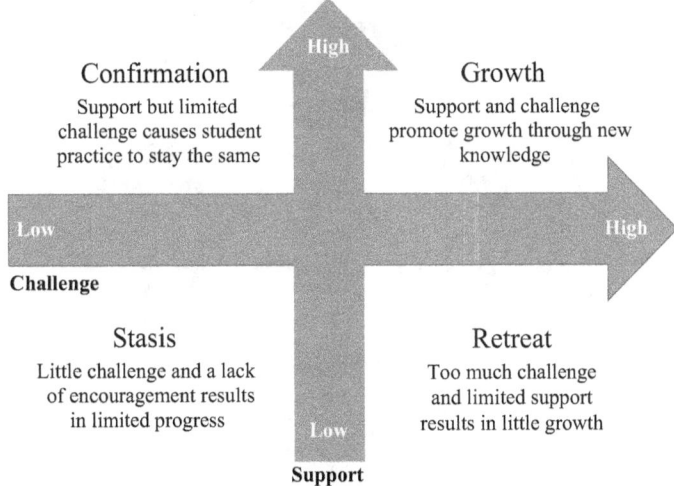

Figure 10.2 Balancing support and challenge for beginning teachers.
Adapted from Martin, 1996.

support, challenge and provide vision, with the ideal conditions to promote growth through new knowledge using both support and challenge.

> **Task 10.1 Mentor reflection: support and challenge**
>
> Have you ever considered the support you provide a mentee? Write two lists: one describing how you support mentees and the second how you challenge them. Now read on to understand why balancing support and challenge is important.

With many competing workplace demands, it is vital that you make the most of timetabled mentoring meetings. This chapter responds to this need by conceptualising four key elements of mentoring meetings which support the professional learning of beginning teachers.

Four aspects of mentor meetings: reflecting, noticing, listening and dialogue

Having set out the importance of quality mentoring and the attributes mentees value most in their mentors, this chapter now shifts to explore four aspects of mentoring – reflecting, noticing, listening and conversing – which you can use to help beginning teachers better understand and develop their teaching practice. These aspects of praxis incorporate ideas from research and theory in the field of geography education and, more broadly, the discipline of education, and can be used to give balance and structure to mentoring meetings. Each aspect is represented in Figure 10.3 and will be addressed as this chapter progresses.

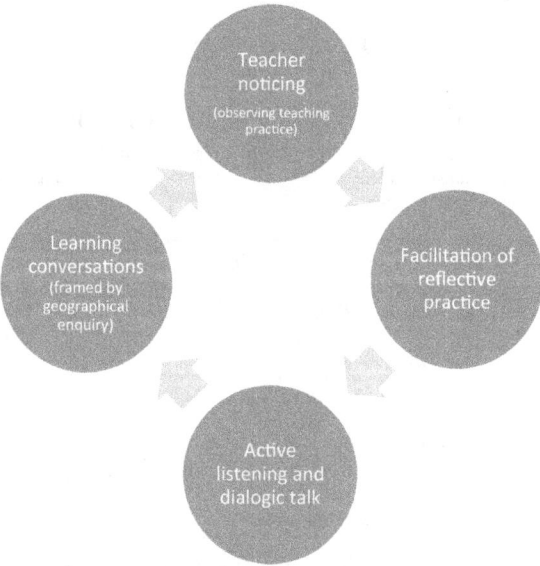

Figure 10.3 Mentors involvement in the learning cycle.

Attention to reflective practice

Teaching is a complex activity, and the classroom is a complex social space. Beginning teachers need much more than classroom experience to make sense of their teaching role and responsibilities. According to Dewey (1933, p. 9), the act of reflection is emancipatory as it is key to learning, and is the 'active, persistent, and careful consideration of any belief or supposed form of knowledge in the light of the grounds that support it and the further conclusions to which it tends'. For teaching to be better considered, Dewey (1933) suggests that the essential skill of thinking reflectively should be taught and embedded in professional practice as a systematic process. In order to effectively consider reflection in the context of teacher education, we need clarity around its meaning. Rodgers (2002) worries that reflection as defined by Dewey has 'suffered from a loss of meaning... and [has] lost its ability to be seen' (p. 843). In an attempt to make Dewey's thinking more accessible, Rodgers (2002, p. 845) outlines the following four criteria which characterise reflection and its purpose:

1. Reflection is a meaning-making process that moves a learner from one experience into the next with a deeper understanding of its relationship with and connections to other experiences and ideas.
2. Reflection is a systematic, rigorous, disciplined way of thinking, with its roots in scientific enquiry.
3. Reflection needs to happen in community, in interaction with others.
4. Reflection requires attitudes that value the personal and intellectual growth of oneself and others.

Drawing on Rodgers' (2002) ideas, you can foster this deliberative and systematic reflective practice with your mentees to support deep introspective analysis and encourage thinking about learning or metacognition. Opfer and Pedder (2011) remind us that the process by which teachers learn from professional development is still rather obscure. This is possibly due to it not always being subject-specific or directly transferable to classroom practice. It is therefore important to keep subject knowledge central to reflective discussions. For example, when making sense of a recently taught year 9 geography lesson on the Global Atmospheric Circulation Model, you might ask a beginning teacher to talk through the lesson planning process and the decisions they made around lesson sequencing, pitch and pace, subject knowledge, source materials, learning approach, activities, assessment, and so on. As a consequence of reflecting on the lesson, you might encourage them to consider what they would revise if they had the opportunity to repeat the lesson. As a mentor, you could then review these new lesson plans to check for appropriate objectives, substantive knowledge (such as latitude, solar insolation, differential heating, air pressure and the Hadley, Ferrell and Polar cells), and teaching and learning activities which are designed to be increasingly challenging.

Looking back in order to move practice on

Later theorists influenced by Dewey, as well as Lewin, Piaget and James, all encourage practitioners to look back on experience before moving practice on (Hargreaves and Page, 2013). This process of reflection has been imagined as cyclical, as illustrated by Kolb's (1984) experiential learning cycle and Gibbs' (1988) reflective cycle. Kolb's (1984) work refers to experiential learning to highlight the importance of experience in the learning process. He also utilises Piaget's idea that knowledge is constructed through interaction with more experienced others in a particular context, an idea Lave and Wenger (1991) define as situated learning. Gibbs' (1988) reflective cycle (Figure 10.4) adds in an affective dimension. Drawing on Gibbs' work, Table 10.1 sets out debriefing questions which you can use to initiate reflective practice. Due to the complexity of the classroom, what works well in one context may not work well elsewhere; therefore, a continual process of teach-reflect-evaluate-revise helps move beginning teachers towards transformative and emancipatory learning (Mezirow et al., 1990; Biesta, 2007).

Brookfield's (1998, p. 2) four lenses of critical reflection are a useful tool to scrutinise our 'taken-for-granted beliefs' or assumptions about society, education and those we educate by viewing what we do in the classroom through the eyes of our students, colleagues, personal experiences, and theory and research. This systematic process can uncover distorted or incorrect assumptions (Brookfield, 2017) and help develop practical wisdom or *know-how*

Figure 10.4 Gibbs' (1988, pp. 53-54) cyclical model of reflection.

Table 10.1 Developing reflective practice

Description	Feelings	Evaluation and analysis
• What did you do? • What did others do? • What instructions were given? • Was geography central to this lesson? • What was the sequence of events? • Who was involved? Did this change? • What learning occurred? • What was the outcome?	• What were you thinking during the lesson? • Did your feelings change before and after the lesson? • What do you think other people were feeling? • What do you think about it now? • What do you think other people feel about it now?	• What was your intention? • What were the strengths and weaknesses? Why? • Did you forget anything? • What did you contribute? • To what extent did the pupils follow your instructions? • Did you teach everything as per the lesson plan? What changed? Why? • Did the resources, i.e. maps, illustrations and texts, effectively support learning? • What additional skills or knowledge were needed?

by framing analytical and evaluative thinking about teaching and learning (Biesta, 2012). To ensure reflection is critical, Brookfield (2017, p. 9) argues that reflection should focus on 'teachers understanding power and hegemony'. In order to provoke critical thinking, you should shift between discussing technical matters of teaching to questioning the framing of educational processes and interactions by broader structures of power and dominant ideology at work in schools (Brookfield, 2017). A critically engaged mentor is well-placed to explore contemporary issues with beginning teachers, such as:

- the structure and content of the geography national curriculum;
- diversity, equity and inclusion;
- the attainment gap; and
- decolonising geography.

Attention to teacher noticing

In every lesson, a hundred or more decisions about what and how to move learning on are made. Because of this, responsive teaching is challenging as teachers instruct pupils for particular educational purposes while dealing with the unpredictability and synchronicity of the classroom environment (Doyle, 1986). A teacher's ability to rapidly read and respond to classroom situations requires a certain level of teacher competence and automaticity which develops with practice, reflection and learning. As part of Eraut's (2004) critique of reflective practice, he problematises how reflection is often enacted as recollection, arguing that any focus on a discrete experience will be bounded as a single episode or incident, whereas when we talk about what we have learned from experience we are more likely to be 'referring to our accumulated learning from a series of episodes' (Eraut, 2004, p. 251). This matters in the context of teacher development because it is often the intersection of a number of elements which results in the ideal conditions for learning. For example, learning is more likely with a knowledgeable teacher, an ordered classroom environment, a well-planned and well-resourced lesson, and motivated pupils (Illeris, 2008).

An increasing amount of literature is being published on understanding teacher noticing and it is a key area of mathematics education research (Amador et al., 2021). Yet, teacher noticing is largely unexplored in geography education, with some exceptions including retrospective video analysis in pre-service teacher education (Walshe and Driver, 2019). The term teacher noticing is used to refer to the skills of perception, interpretation and informed decision-making (Scholten et al., 2020) which teachers use during instruction to interpret teaching situations and respond appropriately. Sherin et al. (2011, p. 5) describe noticing as the process during instruction 'through which teachers manage the "blooming, buzzing confusion of sensory data" with which they are faced'. During the first few weeks of a school placement, this sensory data might involve beginning teachers noticing the rules and routines of the classroom, behaviour management, school sanction (and praise) systems, and the institutional culture and social norms of the school, whereas, during the consolidation and extension phases, beginning teachers may turn their attention from technical know-how to the blend of subject content and pedagogy knowledge that Shulman (1987) describes as pedagogical content knowledge, such as geographical misconceptions, conceptual progression and the significance of everyday and disciplinary knowledge to pupils (Lane, 2009; Firth, 2011; Rata, 2016).

In the context of geography education, Walshe et al. (2021) argue that the government's systematic move to school-centred Initial Teacher Education (ITE) in England has resulted in beginning teachers spending less time engaging with educational theory and more time observing classroom practice. What they learn from these experiences is uncertain because 'the relative inexperience of a trainee often means they lack an epistemological framework which would enable understanding and identification of significant classroom events' (Scherr and Hammer, cited in Walshe et al., 2021, p. 27). Orchard and Winch (2015) are also concerned with the shift from teacher education to teacher training, asserting that teachers as professionals 'must understand what they are doing and why they are doing it, and must be able to think intelligently about how to do it better' (p. 3). In order to master situated understanding, it is essential for beginning teachers to develop epistemic and pedagogical reasoning and the ability to notice factors affecting pupil behaviour and learning (Sherin, 2017; Loughran, 2019), without which they can struggle to make ethically sound judgements (Orchard and Winch, 2015).

What does an attention to noticing look like in a mentoring meeting?

Noticing or being aware of what you actually do, rather than what you think you are doing, can be overwhelming, challenging and draining for a novice because it is a cognitive, affective and emotional process. In research using video vignettes of geography instruction, Scholten et al. (2020) suggest that the skill of managing the complexity of classroom interactions by *noticing* and maintaining a focus on learning can be learned. Observing a video of a colleague teaching and having them unpack what is happening and the multiple stimuli they respond to can make this aspect of teacher cognition more explicit. Beginning teachers can learn a great deal if you make visible your thinking around the three message systems of curriculum, pedagogy and assessment, which Bernstein (2000) argues are of most importance in schools.

> **Task 10.2 Mentor reflection: what would you do in this scenario?**
>
> Consider the following situation. A mentor is observing a mentee's year 8 lesson and mid-way through, when most pupils are writing an answer to the question 'How did the Turkish earthquake impact the people of Izmir?', the mentor notices a pupil quietly doodling in the back of their book. In the debrief, the mentor must decide what approach to take. You could be prescriptive, but this provides little space for the mentee to be reflective. It would be better to guide the mentee and allow them to reflect and learn from their experience (Table 10.2). Sometimes you might choose not to provide any feedback. For example, when a lesson does not go to plan, a beginning teacher may benefit from emotional support and the space to reflect on their own in preparation to try again. What would you do in this situation?

The degree of direction you provide in lesson feedback depends on the stage of development of the mentee (see Table 10.2). Prescriptive advice might focus on the pitch and pace of the lesson or question whether sufficient and increasingly challenging tasks were provided. As mentees increasingly understand the complexities of teaching, then you can facilitate deeper reflective practice by asking probing questions and stimulating discussion. In this case a non-directive, coaching approach might simply be to ask *Why was the student off-task?*

Moving from noticing to improved practice via instructional coaching

Through the Core Content Framework and Early Career Framework (DfE, 2019a; 2019b), there is support available for beginning teachers in England for mentoring and professional

Table 10.2 From directive to non-directive approaches to lesson feedback

Intervention	Purpose	Detail
Directive (prescriptive)	Inform the beginning teacher about what they noticed and what they would do in the same situation	The mentor might say this: 'there was a pupil who finished their work before the others in the group, make sure you have a range of activities prepared should you notice quick finishers. You are lucky they did not start to talk or disrupt the others working!'
Non-directive (guiding)	Describe what they saw and ask the beginning teacher whether they noticed this issue and what (on reflection) they might do if it happened again.	A more guided discussion might start by the mentor saying: 'During the lesson Pupil A finished the task ahead of the others. What could you have done if you had noticed this? How would you change your lesson plan if you were to reteach this exact lesson?'
Supportive	Boost confidence, especially for areas of teaching the beginning teacher is struggling with.	The mentor might say: 'The pace of your lesson was faster than last week and you were much swifter with the transitions between activities. Tell me what else went well today.'

development with the aim of encouraging teacher retention. Instructional coaching (Bambrick-Santoyo, 2018) is increasingly used as a form of sustained, structured, subject-specific and incremental professional development which might be arranged along the following lines:

1. See it: identify an area of teaching needing development;
2. Name it: suggest manageable steps for improvement;
3. Do it: practise each step, gain feedback, then trial it in the classroom. Over time, the complexity of practice is increased until the teacher masters it.

Explicit instruction therefore improves practice in manageable steps. It might be that you identify teaching needs common across all beginning teachers such as building on prior knowledge, developing spatial skills and revising subject content to create instructional coaching tools ready to support teaching practice. Instructional coaching also offers the opportunity to consider your own teaching. If you were going to explain to a colleague how you teach a particularly difficult geographical concept, you could consider how you would break the task down into manageable steps.

> **Task 10.3 Mentor reflection: instructional coaching**
>
> Imagine you need to teach tropical storm formation or the causes of desertification with a higher level of challenge: follow the steps above to plan how you would do this with your mentee.

Attention to listening

At the end of a meeting I recently attended, the host thanked those who spoke and also those who listened. In that moment the value of being silent and listening was elevated to that of being vocal. This balance is essential for successful mentoring. Brookfield (2017, p. 97) notes that 'of all the pedagogic tasks teachers face, getting inside student's heads is one of the trickiest. It's also one of the most crucial'. The next best thing to getting into a mentee's head is for you to be an active listener and provide a safe learning space for a teacher to express their raw reflections, ideas, problems and difficulties without fear of you cutting in, commenting or judging. Active listening also provides the space for thinking about education, professional identity and a whole host of other issues. Kline (1999) identifies ten behaviours which improve the way people think in a system called a Thinking Environment (see Table 10.3). Listening underpins every behaviour. Conceptualising teachers involved in mentoring as thinking partners attends to the power dynamics at play when a more experienced teacher mentors a subordinate.

By applying these behaviours in meetings, you can model active listening, which Kline (1999, p. 102) suggests 'frees people to think faster and say less'. Furthermore, by utilising

Table 10.3 Thinking environment components

Behaviour	Meaning
Attention	The quality of attention determines the quality of other peoples' thinking.
Equality	Everyone is valued equally as a thinker.
Ease	An internal state free from rush or urgency creates the best conditions for thinking.
Appreciation	Focus on things that work well, as the human mind works best in the presence of appreciation.
Encouragement	Competition can be dangerous, so replace it with a search for good ideas.
Feelings	Thinking stops when we are upset. If we express feelings just enough, thinking resumes.
Information	Full and accurate information results in intellectual integrity.
Difference	A diverse group which welcomes different points of view is more likely to achieve accurate, cutting-edge thinking.
Incisive questions	A wellspring of good ideas lies just beneath an untrue limiting assumption. Incisive questions will remove it, freeing the mind to think afresh.
Place	When the physical environment affirms our importance, we think more clearly and boldly, and when our bodies are cared for and respected, our thinking improves.

Adapted from Kline, 1999, p. 35.

Kline's incisive questions you can help mentees to consider limiting assumptions, which Brookfield (2017) distinguishes as:

- causal assumptions are the assumptions about how things work and the conditions under which these can be changed. For example, a beginning teacher might believe that experienced teachers know everything about a subject. It is important for them to understand that new knowledge needs to be learned and this is why continued professional development is important for all teachers;
- prescriptive assumptions – the assumptions we hold about what we think ought to happen in a particular situation. These might include assumptions about how pupils should behave. For example, you might spend time in class revising a specific volcanic eruption. However, when marking the end-of-unit assessment, a pupil might score poorly if they wrote about an alternative eruption which made the news headlines. This reminds us that what we teach is not always what is learned or assessed; and
- paradigmatic assumptions – the structuring assumptions we use to order our world. These assumptions about the nature of reality frame how we see and understand the world. For example, some teachers believe that education systems are democratic, while others believe that there is always a political dimension to education.

According to Brookfield (2017), it is much easier to unpack causal assumptions with beginning teachers, as prescriptive or paradigmatic assumptions are more deeply embedded and may not even be recognised as assumptions, even when pointed out.

Task 10.4 Mentor reflection: active listening

A school day can be very busy, but it is important to give time to beginning teachers. A good listener is someone who is fully present, focussed, interested, and listens to learn without interrupting. Do you consider yourself to be an active listener or is this a skill that you might want to further develop?

Attention to dialogue

Dialogue or the 'oral exchange and deliberative handling of information, ideas and opinions' (Alexander, 2020, p. 128) can support powerful learning by encouraging beginning teachers to unpick their teaching practice, share their thinking about the cognitive and social aspects of teaching and learning, and better understand the purpose and philosophy of education. Teachers and students have much to benefit from working in a dialogic classroom where thinking about thinking, learning, knowledge and understanding enables teaching to become more visible to students and learning to become more evident for teachers. Alexander (2020) has spent the last two decades, initially in the primary classroom and latterly in secondary schools, developing dialogic teaching and improving the quality of classroom talk. Dialogic teaching is 'a pedagogy of the spoken word that harnesses the power of dialogue to stimulate and extend students' thinking, learning, knowing and understanding, and to enable them to discuss, reason and argue' (Alexander, 2020, p. 128). Drawing on research from 500 classes in five countries, Alexander (2008) outlines the theory, principles and indicators of dialogic teaching, then suggests that the dialogic classroom involves talk that is collective, reciprocal, supportive, cumulative and purposeful:

1. Collective - Participants address learning tasks together;
2. Reciprocal - Participants listen to each other, share ideas and consider alternative viewpoints;
3. Supportive - Pupils express their ideas freely, without fear of embarrassment over 'wrong' answers, and they help each other to reach common understandings;
4. Cumulative - Participants build on answers and other oral contributions and chain them into coherent lines of thinking and understanding;
5. Purposeful - Classroom talk, though open and dialogic, is also planned and structured with specific learning goals in view.

Dialogic mentoring can be supported by engaging with Alexander's (2020, p. 127) eight dialogic teaching repertoires. Focusing on dialogic repertoires rather than Teachers' Standards can shift attention from performance judgements to a productive pedagogy of talk. The eight dialogic repertoires include:

- Interactive Culture (1)
- Interactive Settings (2)
- Learning Talk (3)
- Teaching Talk (4)
- Questioning (5)
- Extending (6)
- Discussing, Deliberating and Arguing (7 and 8)

As an example, the dialogic repertoire Interactive Culture echoes components of Kline's (1999) Thinking Environments and can support teachers to set the routines, rules and rituals of interactive classroom culture and the dialogic repertoire. In a second example, Extending can help us prompt reasoning to open up and sustain dialogue in the classroom (see Table 10.4).

Table 10.4 Dialogic repertoire for beginning teachers

Repertoire 1: Interactive Culture	**Repertoire 6: Extending**
Productive dialogue requires a shared understanding of the way talk should be managed (Alexander, 2020, pp. 138-139).	Extending beyond the typical three-part model of questioning (Initiate-Response-Evaluate) can open up student thinking (Alexander, 2020, pp. 150-151).
• Communicative norms - concern the transactional character of discourse; i.e., we listen, we don't interrupt or talk over people. • Deliberative norms - govern the handling of discussion and argumentation; i.e., we give evidence for claims, we state our position, we are prepared to move and to challenge. • Epistemic norms - these are the norms for managing domain-specific discussion, a process of paradigmatic socialisation; i.e., how we represent others or approach controversial issues such as inequality and Britain's colonial past.	Share, expand and clarify thinking • Time to think • Say more • Are you saying? Listen carefully to one another • Rephrase • Repeat Deepen reasoning • Evidence of reasoning • Challenge • Counter example Think with others • Agree/disagree • Add on • What others mean

Enacting dialogue which focusses on collective and reciprocal tasks such as co-planning and co-teaching can support mentoring as a dyadic relationship between two individuals. Working together helps a mentee to learn more about pedagogical reasoning and share their specialist disciplinary knowledge with you (Loughran, 2019). It can also set the scene for purposeful dialogic feedback, which combines dialogue and feedback to build coherent lines of thinking around subject content, pedagogy and assessment before new targets are set with the purpose of improving specific elements of practice. Woodhouse and Wood (2020), in research with doctoral students focussed on creating dialogic spaces, found that it is important to acknowledge the affective dimension of receiving feedback. We know that learning to teach is demanding, so when you provide structured, supportive and formative feedback in a sensitive manner, it can significantly boost a beginning teacher's confidence.

Learning conversations framed by geographical enquiry

It is widely accepted that teacher professional development is more effective when it is sustained, collaborative, subject-specific, draws on expertise and is practice-based (Timperley et al., 2007; Timperley, 2015). To allay Deng's (2018, p. 371) concern that 'content as a topic of conversation has disappeared from current global policy discourse', learning conversations in school geography should focus on the question Roberts (2010, p. 112) puts at the heart of everything - 'Where's the geography?' Roberts' (2003) framework for *Learning Through Enquiry* includes four stages (Figure 10.5), the last of which involves reflecting on learning. Focussing on reflection has led me to think about how learners can be critical in relation to data, knowledge, pedagogy and the enquiry process itself (Rawlings Smith, 2020). Expanding this idea here, you can use the questions set out in Box 10.1 to initiate learning conversations with a subject-specific focus. For example, when reflecting on whose voices are not heard in the classroom, issues of invisibility and stereotyping of marginalised groups could be discussed.

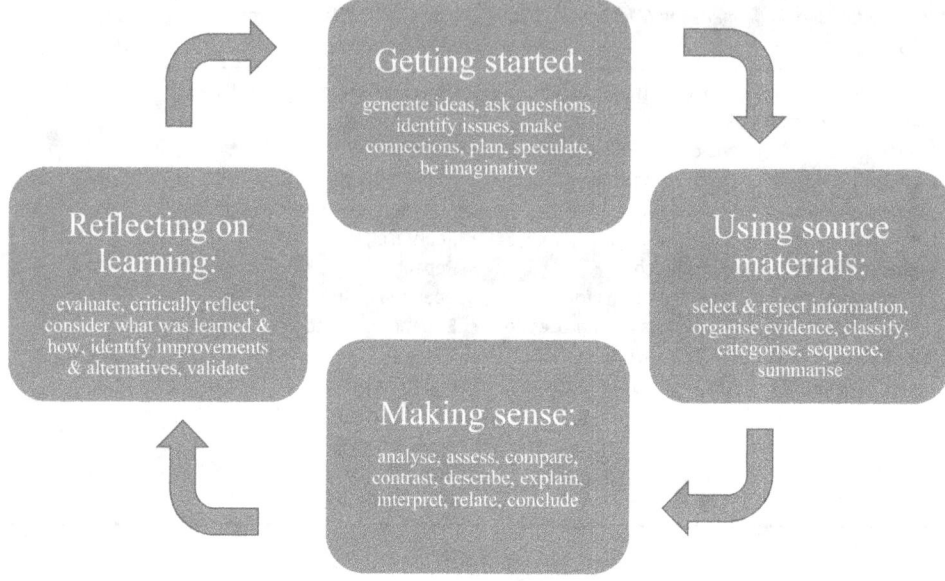

Figure 10.5 Framework for learning and reflecting through enquiry.
After Roberts, 2003, p. 44.

Box 10.1 Reflecting on learning through enquiry (after Roberts, 2003, and Rawlings Smith, 2020)

Reflecting on data

- Were you able to locate, collect and select appropriate evidence?
- Were the data used in the lesson contemporary, relevant and accessible?
- Were students able to sort, classify or sequence the data you provided?
- Does your evidence and data represent or distort the world?
- How could teaching materials be improved?

Reflecting on knowledge and skills

- Does geographical knowledge build on the last lesson or unit?
- What has been learned? How has it been learned?
- How is pupils' conceptual understanding being developed?
- How is learning progressing your students' geographical thinking?
- What is the value of what has been learned?
- What skills and techniques have been used?

- How could the lesson be improved or further developed?
- What alternative approach could be taken if the lesson was repeated?

Reflecting on pupils

- How did you consider pupils' individual needs?
- Whose opinions were voiced in the lesson?
- Whose voices are not heard in your classroom?
- Do pupils understand the enquiry process?
- Do pupils think about the learning process?

Maintaining high-quality learning conversations with structuring mentoring meetings

There are many approaches you can take to structuring mentoring meetings. Typically meetings focus on monitoring progress and target setting and might run as follows:

In the week prior to the mentoring meeting:

- Ensure all members of the department are aware of the beginning teacher's targets, especially if they are observing lessons.
- Record evidence of key strengths from lesson observations and the wider staff body.
- Review previous targets and consider potential targets arising from classroom practice.
- Share the agenda, so there is an awareness of what will be discussed. This could include progress towards goals, personal achievements, current challenges, potential new targets and actions from the week before.

During the meeting:

- Start with a catch up, review of wellbeing, evidence of strengths and positive praise.
- Reflect on the *big picture* of progress to date to put into context any recent challenges.
- Negotiate key discussion points and what your mentee wants to focus on. For example, lesson debriefing might address how assessment is being used across all year groups or how spatial thinking is being developed with some of the younger pupils rather that a brief review of every lesson. Note key points discussed.
- Ask open questions such as 'Tell me what you learned from teaching year 8 about the impact of climate change yesterday'.
- Discuss relevant aspects of any practitioner research taking place.
- Explore any struggles or new challenges the mentee is facing and discuss possible interventions to trial. You might ask how they would teach it differently or suggest some alternative approaches.
- Review previous actions and targets ready to revise these for the following week. Target-setting should focus on subject and curriculum knowledge, pedagogy, pupil progress and outcomes, use of assessment, scaffolding and differentiation, managing behaviour, safeguarding and professional responsibilities.

- Discuss challenge and support. If a mentee is not feeling challenged, you could ask them to take on more responsibility, create a lesson from scratch, teach a revision lesson or run a geography club session. If a mentee needs more support, you might co-plan or co-teach some lessons, or arrange them to observe another teacher who models a particular teaching skill well.
- At this point bring in feedback from other teachers to broaden the discussion to whole-school roles and responsibilities which the mentee may wish to take advantage of.

After the meeting:

- The mentee should record a summary of the discussion, targets and confirm the date and time for the next meeting.
- You should provide details for any resource discussed or make necessary connections with colleagues so lesson observations or other teaching opportunities can be arranged.

Conclusion

As a mentor, you work with beginning teachers on a daily basis, to observe, notice, encourage, champion, induct and challenge – all with the purpose of improving classroom practice. You hold responsibility for supporting your beginning teacher in making progress towards QTS (Qualified Teacher Status) or completion of their early career induction. As this role often involves reviewing targets, assessing progress and communicating with colleagues (for example, the school's lead ITE tutor or a university-based tutor) to celebrate successes and identify challenges and areas in which the beginning teacher requires additional support, this dual role can cause tension, anxiety and stress. For example, if the beginning teacher perceives that assessment is prioritised over support, or that their guidance is not approached in a sensitive, compassionate and professional manner the mentor-mentee relationship can experience challenges, or, in a worst-case scenario, it may even break down. Reflective practice, teacher noticing and active listening can all help you to structure thinking and learning conversations focussed on teaching and learning in the geography classroom to successfully induct beginning geography teachers into the profession.

For discussion

- Why is it important to be a critically reflective teacher and how can this be embodied in your mentoring conversations?
- Why might beginning teachers benefit from drawing on theory and research while developing their classroom practice? In what ways might this be developed/supported during mentoring conversations?
- To what extent do you agree that subject specificity should be the most important focus within learning conversations for beginning geography teachers?
- How can you encourage wider departmental staff to engage in professional conversations with beginning geography teachers?

Further reading and resources

1. Alexander, R., 2019. Dialogic teaching. Available at: https://robinalexander.org.uk/dialogic-teaching/.

Robin Alexander has a website which supports his recent book on dialogic teaching and sets out how we can harness the power of talk in education.

2. Brookfield, S., 2017. *Becoming a Critically Reflective Teacher*. San Francisco: Jossey-Bass.

Stephen Brookfield helps the reader to understand why it is important to see classroom practice through the eyes of others to uncover assumptions and become a more informed practitioner.

3. Rawlings Smith, E., 2020. Techniques for mentors to support early career teachers' reflective practice. *Teaching Geography*, 45(2), 53-55.

In this *Teaching Geography* article, the author provides additional techniques which mentors can use to encourage reflective practice.

References

Alexander, R., 2008. *Towards Dialogic Teaching: Rethinking Classroom Talk*. 4th edn. York: Dialogos (5th edition available 2017).

Alexander, R., 2020. *A Dialogic Teaching Companion*. London: Routledge.

Amador, J., Bragelman, J., and Castro Superfine, A., 2021. Prospective teachers' noticing: A literature review of methodological approaches to support and analyze noticing. *Teaching and Teacher Education*, 99. https://doi.org/10.1016/j.tate.2020.103256.

Bambrick-Santoyo, P., 2018. *A Principal Manager's Guide to Leverage Leadership 2.0: How to Build Exceptional Schools Across Your District*. San Francisco: Jossey-Bass.

Bernstein, B., 2000. *Pedagogy, Symbolic Control and Identity*. New York: Rowman and Littlefield.

Biesta, G. J. J., 2007. Why 'What Works' won't work: Evidence-based practice and the democratic deficit in educational research. *Educational Theory*, 57(1), 1-22.

Biesta, G. J. J., 2012. Giving teaching back to education: Responding to the disappearance of the teacher. *Phenomenology and Practice*, 6(2), 35-49.

Brookfield, S., 1998. Critically reflective practice. *The Journal of Continuing Education in the Health Professions*, 18, 197-205.

Brookfield, S., 2017. *Becoming a Critically Reflective Teacher*. San Francisco: Jossey-Bass.

Bustin, R., 2022. Mentoring as a professional development opportunity. In G. Healy, L. Hammond, S. Puttick and N. Walshe (eds), *Mentoring Geography Teachers in the Secondary School*. Abingdon: Routledge, 75-87.

Caspersen, J., and Raaen, F. D., 2014. Novice teachers and how they cope. *Teachers and Teaching*, 20(2), 189-211.

Claxton, G., 2006. Expanding the capacity to learn: A new end for education? Opening Keynote Address, British Educational Research Association Annual Conference, Warwick University, 6 September. Available at: http://44btwo16ocnidz2x81qvjzsf.wpengine.netdna-cdn.com/wp-content/uploads/2014/11/BERA-Keynote-Update-Feb10.pdf [accessed 21 April 2021].

Coe, R., Aloisi, C., Higgins, S., and Major, L. E., 2014. What makes great teaching? review of the underpinning research. Project Report. Sutton Trust, London. Available at: http://dro.dur.ac.uk/13747/1/13747.pdf [accessed 21 April 2021].

Department for Education (DfE), 2011. *Teachers' Standards: Guidance for school leaders, school staff and governing bodies.* London: HMSO. Available at: www.gov.uk/government/publications/teachers-standards [accessed 21 April 2021].

Department for Education (DfE), 2015. *Carter Review of Initial Teacher Training (ITT).* London: HMSO. Available at: https://assets.publishing.service.gov.uk/government/uploads/system/uploads/attachment_data/file/399957/Carter_Review.pdf [accessed 21 April 2021].

Department for Education (DfE), 2016. *National Standards for School-Based Initial Teacher Training (ITT) Mentors.* London: HMSO. Available at: https://assets.publishing.service.gov.uk/government/uploads/system/uploads/attachment_data/file/536891/Mentor_standards_report_Final.pdf [accessed 21 April 2021].

Department for Education (DfE), 2019a. *Initial Teacher Training (ITT) Core Content Framework.* London: HMSO. Available at: www.gov.uk/government/publications/initial-teacher-training-itt-core-content-framework [accessed 20 December 2020].

Department for Education (DfE), 2019b. *Early Career Framework.* London: HMSO. Available at: https://assets.publishing.service.gov.uk/government/uploads/system/uploads/attachment_data/file/913646/Early-Career_Framework.pdf [accessed 21 April 2021].

Dewey, J., 1933. *How We Think: A Restatement of the Relation of Reflective Thinking to the Educative Process.* New York: D.C. Heath and Company.

Deng, Z., 2018. Rethinking teaching and teachers: Bringing content back into conversation. *London Review of Education*, 16(3), 371-383.

Doyle, W., 1986. Classroom organization and management. In M. C. Witttrock (ed), *Handbook of Research on Teaching.* 3rd edn. New York: Macmillan, 392-431.

Eraut, M., 2004. The practice of reflection. *Learning in Health and Social Care*, 3(2), 47-52.

Firth, R. 2011. Making geography visible as an object of study in the secondary school curriculum. *The Curriculum Journal*, 22(3), 289-316.

Gibbs, G., 1988. *Learning by Doing: A Guide to Teaching and Learning Methods.* London: Further Education Unit at Oxford Polytechnic.

Hargreaves, J., and Page, L., 2013. *Reflective Practice.* Cambridge: Polity Press.

Hill, J., Bass, E. L., and Stewart, T. T., 2020. Promoting preservice teacher efficacy through dialogic problem-posing seminars. *English in Education*, 54(4), 358-370. DOI: 10.1080/04250494.2019.1626195.

Hobson, A. J., and Malderez, A., 2013. Judgementoring and other threats to realizing the potential of school-based mentoring in teacher education. *International Journal of Mentoring and Coaching in Education*, 2(2), 89-108.

Illeris, K., 2008. *How We Learn: Learning and Non-Learning in School and Beyond.* London: Routledge.

Kaplan, D., 2019. What mentoring means to me. *Journal of Geography in Higher Education*, 43(1), 116-124.

Kline, N., 1999. *Time To Think.* London: Cassell Illustrated.

Kolb, D. A., 1984. *Experiential Learning.* Englewood Cliffs, NJ: Prentice.

Lane, R., 2009. Articulating the pedagogical content knowledge of accomplished geography teachers. *Geographical Education*, 22, 40-50.

Lave, J., and Wenger, E., 1991. *Situated Learning: Legitimate peripheral participation.* Cambridge: Cambridge University Press.

Loughran, L., 2019. Pedagogical reasoning: The foundation of the professional knowledge of teaching. *Teachers and Teaching*, 25(5), 523-535.

Martin, S., 1996. Support and challenge: Conflicting or complementary aspects of mentoring novice teachers? *Teachers and Teaching: Theory and Practice*, 2, 41-56.

Mcnally, P., and Martin, S., 1998. Support and challenge in learning to teach: The role of the mentor. *Asia-Pacific Journal of Teacher Education*, 26(1), 39-50.

Mezirow, J., and Associates, 1990. *Fostering Critical Reflection in Adulthood: A Guide to Transformative and Emancipatory Learning.* San Francisco: Jossey Bass.

Noble-Rogers, J., 2021. The recruitment and retention of teachers in England. In T. Ovenden-Hope and R. Passy (eds), *Exploring Teacher Recruitment and Retention: Contextual Challenges from International Perspectives*. Abingdon: Routledge, 34–45.

Opfer, D., and Pedder, D., 2011. Conceptualizing teacher professional learning. *Review of Educational Research*, 81, 376–407.

Orchard, J., and Winch, C., 2015. What training do teachers need? Why theory is necessary to good teaching. *Impact: Philosophical Perspectives on Education Policy*, 22, 1–43.

Ofsted, 2020. *Building Great Teachers? Initial teacher education curriculum research: phase 2*. Manchester: HMSO. Available at: www.gov.uk/government/publications/initial-teacher-education-curriculum-research/building-great-teachers [accessed 21 April 2021].

Rata, E., 2016. A pedagogy of conceptual progression and the case for academic knowledge. *British Educational Research Journal*, 42(1), 168–184.

Rawlings Smith, E., 2020. Techniques for mentors to support early career teachers' reflective practice. *Teaching Geography*, 45(2), 53–55.

Rawlings Smith, E., 2021. Who or where do beginning geography teachers turn, when sourcing information and developing knowledge of how to teach? University of Leicester, School of Education Research Seminar, 18 February.

Roberts, M., 2003. *Learning Through Enquiry*. Sheffield: Geographical Association.

Roberts, M., 2010. Where's the geography? Reflections on being an external examiner. *Teaching Geography*, 35(1), 112–113.

Rodgers, C., 2002. Defining reflection: Another look at John Dewey and reflective thinking. *Teachers College Record*, 104(4), 842–866.

Scholten, N., Höttecke, D., and Sprenger, S., 2020. How do geography teachers notice critical incidents during instruction? *International Research in Geographical and Environmental Education*, 29(2), 163–177.

Sherin, M. G., Jacobs, V. R., and Philipp, R. A., 2011. Situating the study of teacher noticing. In M. G. Sherin, V. R. Jacobs and R. A. Philipp (eds), *Mathematics Teacher Noticing: Seeing through Teachers' Eyes*. New York: Routledge, 3–13.

Sherin, M. G., 2017. Exploring the boundaries of teacher noticing: Commentary. In E. O. Schack, M. H. Fisher and J. A. Wilhelm (eds), *Teacher Noticing: Bridging and Broadening Perspectives, Contexts, and Frameworks*. New York: Springer, 401–408.

Shulman, L., 1987. Knowledge and teaching: Foundations of the new reform. *Harvard Educational Review*, 57(1), 1–23.

Stanulis, R. N., and Bell, J., 2017. Beginning teachers improve with attentive and targeted mentoring. *Kappa Delta Pi Record*, 53(2), 59–65.

Timperley, H., 2015. Leading teaching and learning through professional learning. *Australian Educational Leader Journal*, 37(2), 6–9.

Timperley, H., Wilson, A., Barrar, H., and Fung, I., 2007. *Teacher Professional Learning and Development: Best Evidence Synthesis Iteration*. Wellington: Ministry of Education.

Walshe, N., and Driver, P., 2019. Developing reflective trainee teacher practice with 360-degree video. *Teaching and Teacher Education*, 78(1), 97–105.

Walshe, N., Driver, P., and Keenoy, M.-J., 2021. Navigating the theory-practice divide: Developing trainee teacher pedagogical content knowledge through 360-degree immersive experiences. In N. Walshe and G. Healy (eds), *Geography Education in the Digital World: Linking Theory and Practice*. Abingdon: Routledge, 26–37.

Weber, M., 1930. *The Protestant Ethic and the Spirit of Capitalism* (T. Parsons, Trans.). London: Routledge.

Woodhouse, J., and Wood, P., 2020. Creating dialogic spaces: Developing doctoral students' critical writing skills through peer assessment and review. *Studies in Higher Education*. Advance online publication. DOI: 10.1080/03075079.2020.1779686.

11 Planning in geography education

A conversation between university-based tutors and school-based mentors in Initial Teacher Education

Faizaan Ahmed, Lauren Hammond, Sara-Anne Nichols, Steve Puttick and Amy Searle

Introduction

Education is a 'political activity' (Catling, 2014, p. 350): decisions about what to teach in this day and age (Lambert and Solem, 2017), how to teach it and why, are all unavoidably political. Those involved in curriculum design at all levels make some things visible – judging them to be worth knowing – and others invisible – judging them as being less worthy of knowing. These questions are particularly challenging for geography because of its scope and scale as a discipline that seeks to better understand the world in all of its complexity and wonder (Matthews and Herbert, 2008): how can it be 'anything but political in its narratives about the world' (Yusoff, 2018, p. 103)? Geography's concern with urgent and important societal, environmental and political issues offers significant potential to inform and empower children in their everyday lives and futures, and so there is great responsibility surrounding decisions about what and how to teach.

Geography education, including how policy-makers, teachers and academics represent and teach children to investigate the world and the people who call it home, matters. For example, as Dorling and Tomlinson (2019) demonstrate through their examination of the relationships between race and education from Empire to Brexit, the representation of people and places has, at times, fostered imperialist attitudes and had a profound impact on peoples' geographical imaginations and socio-political values (Dorling and Tomlinson, 2019; Morgan and Lambert, 2001; 2020; Puttick and Murrey, 2020; Hammond, 2021a). So, how can beginning teachers be supported to address these significant challenges? How do beginning teachers develop the knowledge and skills to plan geography lessons and curricula that enable children to better understand and act in the world?

In this chapter, we come together as three school-based mentors who also work as full-time geography teachers, and two university-based tutors who work in ITE (Initial Teacher Education), to critically reflect upon our experiences of, and perspectives on, planning in school geography. In addition to the weighty political dimension about choices around what knowledge is worth teaching, planning offers practical assistance for classroom pedagogy, enabling the teacher to be 'freer' and better able to respond to children and their needs within lessons (Biddulph et al., 2015). Focussing on planning gives us an opportunity to examine how planning is understood and valued by beginning teachers, mentors and tutors, and how geography is conceptualised and represented in plans. Although we focus mainly on planning at the level of individual lessons, the arguments put forward also relate to medium- and longer-term planning, highlighted at points throughout.

We begin with a literature review focussed on planning in geography education and education more broadly. Following hooks (1994), and specifically her dialogue with Ron Scapp, we then engage in a dialogic conversation to explore some of the ways in which beginning teachers are taught to plan in schools and universities during ITE. We conclude the chapter by arguing for the importance of ongoing and open dialogue between tutors, mentors and beginning teachers to support and inform geography teacher education for high-quality planning in school geography.

Lesson planning

Planning is the process through which teachers make decisions about what and how to teach, from choices about individual activities and lessons through to whole schemes of work and across years of education. Planning is widely regarded as a vital skill for teaching – in Chizhik and Chizhik's (2018, p. 67) terms, 'every teacher-credential program would argue that lesson planning is an essential part of its curriculum'. However, there has been limited research attention given to how planning is taught, conceptualised and practised during ITE (König et al., 2020). Insights into the amount of time teachers spend on planning – for example, over an hour per day for Chinese teachers, and less than half an hour for American teachers (Shen et al., 2007) – show a considerable range, and in all contexts the length of time is presumably increased for beginning teachers. Research, particularly in mathematics education (Li et al., 2009; González et al., 2020), demonstrates the value of close empirical work on teachers' planning, providing insight into their thinking and professional development in the context of specific topics (such as teaching fraction division). In geography education there has been limited empirical research attention to planning: previous chapters are mainly based on *in principle* arguments combined with individuals' own experiences, such as Biddulph's (2017) descriptions of planning as:

> A technical, intellectual and moral process. Pragmatically you organise material (content, teaching approaches, resources) into a form that you feel will make sense to your students. You decide an appropriate teaching sequence that is progressive in terms of students' learning. You create year-by-year plans, termly plans and shorter, more manageable units.
>
> (p. 35)

This immediately raises challenges for beginning teachers who might be tasked with planning an activity or a lesson, because these individual events are not isolated: they come within the context of a significant body of work (technical, intellectual, moral) that others have already worked through. A single lesson also plays a role within the medium- and longer-term planning that was previously undertaken: ultimately, contributing to the body of geographical knowledge, ideas and skills that the teacher and department believe it is most important to introduce children and young people to.

The dominant model of lesson planning in ITE is argued by John (2006) to focus on rationalistic and technical aspects which he argues 'leads to a limited view of teaching and learning as well as a restricted approach to learning to teach' (p. 483). He characterises this dominant model as 'linear', beginning with the creation of lesson objectives and finishing with an evaluation. Such an approach may well be very familiar to you, and might be illustrated by a series of steps which are often presented in text boxes on lesson plan pro formas:

- objective;
- vocabulary;
- resources;
- starter;
- main activity; and
- plenary.

This list varies between programmes and at different times has included assessment, differentiation, students' needs, links to previous lessons, homework, and so on. John's (2006) critique of this linear model opens up a key challenge around planning – and particularly within the context of teaching beginning teachers how to plan – that is, the tension between written plans (teaching as *intended*) and lived classroom experience (teaching as *reality*):

> The model does not take into account the contingencies of teaching. Plans constructed according to the rational model may look fine on paper, but classrooms tend to be more uncertain places: time-pressures, organizational issues, attitudes, moods, emotions, and serendipity all impinge on the closed structures of the model... it tells us very little about the substance of the particular activity we apply [the model] to. In sum, it does not say enough about the uniqueness of teaching and learning.
>
> (p. 487)

These tensions around planning were illustrated by the comments that Puttick and Warren-Lee (2020) and Puttick and Wynn (2021) found in their analysis of the written lesson observation feedback given to beginning teachers (explored further in Puttick, 2022). They found that planning was mentioned frequently in feedback throughout the ITE year and across both strengths and areas of development. The tensions between structure, strongly echoing the technical linear model, and a desire for flexibility are illustrated in the following feedback:

> Peter has made great progress towards a more ordered, structured and controlled learning environment. Having achieved this successfully, he now needs to work on ways to maintain it with less rigid planning and with more potential within that planning for pupil-centred learning.
>
> (Written lesson observation example, in Puttick and Wynn, 2021, p. 158)

There are tensions between the aspects that are praised (order, structure and control) and the 'flexibility' that is presented as an area for development: subtle nuances between these potentially contradictory principles that are presented to beginning teachers. Within the sample of beginning geography teachers (n = 31), planning was in the top four most frequently mentioned topics in feedback, and most of the comments related to planning were brief evaluative statements. For example: 'Very well-planned lesson, which built on students' prior learning well...' (Puttick and Warren-Lee 2021, p. 102). Beyond the general statement that the lesson builds on students' prior learning, it would be hard for the beginning teacher to understand why the planning was seen as being good: what aspects contributed to it being *well-planned*? How can we best support all beginning teachers to consistently plan well? Through a dialogic conversation between mentors and tutors, we now critically examine these tensions further.

A conversation between tutors and mentors working in ITE

In her book *Teaching to Transgress: Education as the Practice of Freedom*, hooks (1994) engages in a rich dialogue with Ron Scapp (her colleague and friend) to discuss their roles as professors and critical thinkers in the academy. The dialogue between hooks and Scapp enables them to explore how philosophy, knowledge and dialogue can bring people together to develop shared values in education, to challenge one another's thinking, and to stimulate discussion as to how systems and praxis might be improved.

We highlight this here because the importance of partnerships between schools and universities described in policy (including in England: DfE, 2016; 2019; Healy and Walshe, 2022) can be experienced through a tension as beginning teachers sometimes struggle to reconcile the school and university elements of their teacher education programme. This may be due to the existence of different *communities of practice* (Lave and Wegner, 1991; Finn et al., 2021) that school teachers and academics sometimes occupy, for example, drawing on different theories, and literatures serving different purposes. Beginning (and experienced) teachers also sometimes face challenges in connecting theory and practice, and considering the complex relationships between what Bernstein (2000) conceptualises as *reservoirs* of knowledge and *repertoires* of practice.

In the dialogue that follows, we draw on our individual experiences and perspectives to examine the mentoring of planning in school geography. Faziaan Ahmed (FA) is Head of Research at Oaks Park High School in London, Lauren Hammond (LH) is Lecturer in Geography Education at UCL Institute of Education, Sara-Anne Nichols (SN) is Second in Charge of Geography at Didcot Girls' School, Steve Puttick (SP) is Associate Professor of Teacher Education at the University of Oxford and Amy Searle (AS) is Curriculum Coordinator: Research and Development Lead at Burford School in Oxfordshire. This dialogue is a record of a 'slow conversation', conducted through asynchronous writing online following (synchronous) online meetings during which we critically discussed the purposes, processes and challenges of planning with beginning teachers. During the slow conversation several key themes emerged: beginning teachers' and mentors' perspectives on, and use of, planning in their practice; the use (and mis-use) of lesson plans in ITE; the relationships between theory and practice in geography education; the relationships between geography education and inclusion in schools and everyday life; and consideration of progress in geography and how planning can support students to make progress within lessons, across sequences of lessons and throughout their education. To represent our slow conversation we share the text as it was written, meaning themes are explored concurrently, allowing the relationships between them to be examined. We also integrate three tasks into the narratives, which you can use to support and inform your mentoring on planning. AS begins the conversation by sharing a short reflection on an experience of planning with a beginning teacher.

Questioning the purposes and (mis)uses of planning in initial teacher education

AS: For some beginning teachers, writing a lesson plan is a means to an end, with the end being a 'thanks' from the class teacher when they receive the plan for the upcoming lesson, or being another page to add to the ever-growing evidence file. Used well, a lesson plan is essential to support classroom learning and teacher development. John (2006) argues that lesson planning must be seen as a practice in itself, instead of to prepare for the teaching practice.

Occasionally, beginning teachers may write their lesson plans after teaching their lessons, potentially because they see lesson plans as a course requirement, rather than to support lesson preparation. This approach means beginning teachers can be underprepared to teach and unable to accurately answer student questions. It must be recognised, however, that lesson planning is a skill that is both difficult to learn and difficult to teach. I often structure conversations on planning around:

- the geography you wish to deliver;
- the reasons for teaching this geography; and
- how the geography will best be taught.

I think lesson plans should be written ahead of the lesson to consider the geographical journey of the lesson and the activities best suited for this. Beginning teachers should be encouraged to be reflective of their practice, and specifically the geography in their lessons, using questions such as 'where is the geography?' (Roberts, 2003). As mentors we should model this reflective practice, such as by adapting lessons or updating case studies as we engage with recent research and respond to current events (Rawlings Smith, 2020).

As the beginning teacher's confidence and competence grows, they can adapt the depth and format of the plan to best suit their needs and also embrace mid- and long-term planning too: similar to Myatt's (2018) comments on the ways that individual lesson plans can interrupt the flow of the planning of fuller sequences of learning. Giving beginning teachers autonomy over the format of their lesson planning is imperative to ensure that their plan is the best possible working document for themselves, rather than anyone else.

SN: Can we discuss the purpose of documentary evidence in respect to lesson planning? The lesson plan is a valuable diagnostic tool for the beginning teacher and their mentor. From my perspective, a lesson plan is ever-changing and fluid, a 'living' working document, rather than just evidence for QTS (Qualified Teacher Status). However, I think

Planning in geography education 161

we should also appreciate that some forms of evidence (including lesson plans) are more accessible and available than others. I have found that the quality of lesson plans created by beginning teachers can be incredibly varied, in respect to quality and quantity. How could we address this?

FA: I think the three-step approach is excellent. Framing planning around several key questions, such as the ones outlined, is a practical and manageable way of developing the skill of lesson planning. Beginning teachers range in terms of their initial knowledge of planning and interests in both geography and education: some have excellent ideas on activities; others have outstanding subject knowledge. However, it is only by marrying content, purpose and approach that beginning teachers can begin to master the lesson planning process.

AS: Beginning teachers often either write overly detailed plans which, whilst useful, are incredibly time-consuming (Tapsfield, 2019), or they write brief, superficial plans whose usefulness is minimal. Consequently, the triangulation of communication between the beginning teacher, mentor and tutor is imperative. By taking guidance from the tutor, mentors are best placed to support beginning teachers with appropriate lesson planning.

Task 11.1 Exploring lesson plan pro formas

Share a variety of lesson plan pro formas with the beginning teacher such as your departmental/school lesson plan and their university lesson plan. Critically examine how the pro formas represent and structure geographical knowledge and teaching. Together, consider the strengths and limitations of each pro forma, and if, how and why each pro forma is of value to planning geography lessons. You might conclude by asking the beginning teacher which pro forma they would most like to use in their planning and why.

Planning for 'delivery' and connecting with children's geographies

LH: I agree that considering the purposes of planning, and having ongoing dialogic conversations between mentors, tutors and beginning teachers is of critical importance to avoid planning becoming a 'tick box' activity.

Amy, I am interested in your choice of term 'delivery' for geography. Do you perceive there are any challenges with this term and/or any differences between teaching and delivery, and how you might explore these ideas with beginning teachers through your mentoring? I am also interested that you don't identify the children and young people we teach as an area of consideration in planning. I find a model developed by the GeoCapabilities project (GeoCapabilities, n.d.; Lambert et al., 2015) and originally shared via a newsletter in 2016 helpful here in considering what might be conceptualised as *critical questions* underpinning both planning and what Lambert and Morgan (2010) term *curriculum making*. The model represents the critical questions in concentric circles that have equal value, but which should be read and considered from the outside in:

- Who are the children we teach?
- Why teach geography, in this day and age?
- What shall we teach, how shall we teach it, and why?

In the version of the model shown in Figure 11.1, I have adapted the original model and situated the critical questions in place and time-space, to represent that everyday life, education and schooling are shaped by place and time-space, just as people and education shape place and time-space. In my research – through listening to children and drawing on research in children's geographies – I have argued that exploring the question of 'who are the children we teach?' requires active consideration not only of learning needs and prior attainment, but also of children's everyday knowledge and identities, along with consideration of the communities that we serve as teachers and academics (Hammond, in review). I am interested to hear whether these areas are considered in your discussions about planning with beginning teachers.

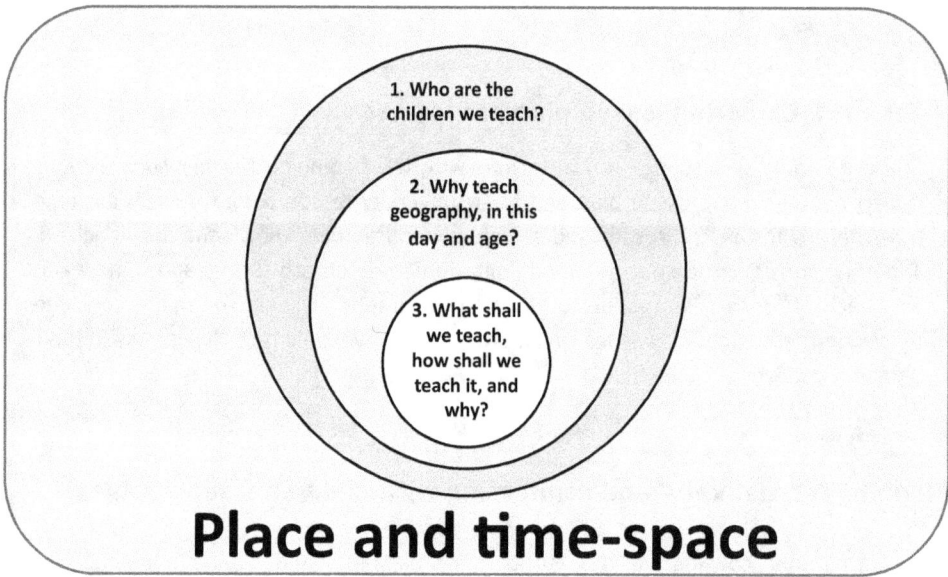

Figure 11.1 Critical questions underpinning curriculum-making in geography (informed by the GeoCapabilities approach).
Source: Hammond, 2021b.

AS: I think the term 'delivery' is helpful to encourage beginning teachers to consider what geographical knowledge they need to teach their students, but this does perhaps oversimplify things as the geography is not a parcel being handed from teacher to students. However, it encourages the beginning teacher to think of the end goal of their students' geographical journey through a topic or course, helping them to see the bigger picture – what is the geography? The other two key areas of consideration (listed above) encourage the beginning teacher to consider how this delivery should occur and why their chosen methods are most appropriate. Mentors must help beginning teachers to navigate this initially, with the beginning teacher later taking the lead.

SP: That's really interesting, because the metaphor of 'delivery' is often critiqued for representing a reduced, simplistic notion of teaching – but the way you are using it in relation to thinking about slightly longer-term plans beyond the individual lesson makes sense. For me this raises questions about power: who gets to make these decisions about what and how it's taught, and the extent to which teachers' and students' involvement is encouraged or constrained?

AS: The integration of students' geographies into our curriculum is important. Learning needs and prior attainment must be considered in lesson planning to ensure good progress and outcomes are promoted, but teachers must also feel empowered to go beyond the specification and teach a curriculum tailored to their students. An inclusive curriculum and inclusive lesson planning should create equitable opportunities for all students that reflect the whole school community. All teachers must ensure that students feel acknowledged and reflected in their geography curriculum. It is, therefore, appropriate to add a fourth key consideration – the geographies of the students to be taught.

FA: Asking 'who are we teaching?' is an important part of the lesson planning process as this directly feeds into the other questions and informs the kind of geographies we teach. Developing an inclusive curriculum is a welcome goal. However, it also raises challenges. Society has arguably moved from being diverse to super-diverse where we now not only have a diversity of minority groups, but also greater awareness of diversity within minority groups (Vertovec, 2007). Planning lessons that anticipate and engage with such a range of personal geographies requires skill and judgement, both of which take time to develop and put into practice. Beginning teachers need support with this to help avoid the risks of homogenising or caricaturing groups, and different school and teacher demographics will face different kinds of challenges anticipating and implementing this. It is also worth considering some systematic barriers in creating an inclusive curriculum. Fieldwork and specifically residential fieldwork are an integral part of geography. However, some might argue the value placed on residential fieldwork is an ethnocentric view. For parents of students from more conservative communities, the importance of residential fieldwork may conflict with their norms and practices which perhaps may be more protective. As a result, care must be taken to ensure curricula, including fieldwork, are planned not to exclude these students from vital geographical experiences.

SP: That is a really interesting point, because while some attention has been given to the ways in which planning for fieldwork might better anticipate issues of accessibility (Stokes et al., 2019), it feels like we are at a fairly early stage in addressing some of the more fundamental norms in school geography education that have been taken as the neutral or natural position, but which actually represent a fairly narrow (White) position (Hamilton, 2020). Students' geographies come, in part, from the geographies of their communities. There is a real challenge in making the connections with these communities and geographies more explicit.

SN: One way we could do this is through planning that pays close attention to the ways in which people (such as stakeholders in a decision-making exercise) are named: where are these names from, and how do they connect with the names and communities of our students? Another example is to break misconceptions by starting from popular culture, such as within the lyrics from the song by Band Aid, *Do They Know It's Christmas?* There are so many opportunities to unpick really unhelpful stereotypes about Africa, aid, dependency and white-saviour narratives. Explicitly planning to address misconceptions seems to be really important across a range of geographical topics (Dove, 2016).

SP: I agree, and this also helps to develop planning in quite theoretically informed but also very practically relevant ways. Enabling students to deconstruct this kind of popular culture – through geography to 'see' it better – seems a more important gauge of the success of their geography education than the use of locational knowledge tests which have been quoted as a proxy for the success (or otherwise) of geography education in the media (Morgan, 2017). There are probably connections between the work on misconceptions more broadly and children's geographies that we would want to draw out.

AS: The curriculum must reflect the school community, whilst also awakening students to a world beyond their school gates. I have used Adichie's (2009) TED Talk, *The Danger of a Single Story*, to discuss the concept of stereotypes. Students asked questions, shared ideas and challenged their own stereotypes and misconceptions.

Planning, observation and structure

SN: I have found that beginning teachers often expect to use pre-existing resources, rather than planning a lesson for themselves. To address this, I have set beginning teachers a challenge of planning a lesson without using any pre-existing resources. An example of this was a lesson on the Global Atmospheric Circulation Model, where they used balloons to represent the Earth and felt-tip pens to label and draw the Hadley, Ferrel and Polar cells. As the mentor, observing the lesson, I felt that the students were able to describe and explain the atmospheric model more accurately than they would have done if they had used the pre-existing lesson. I felt that the beginning teacher took *ownership* of the lesson, rather than just presenting (or *delivering*) the lesson from available resources. In this case, they also became more adventurous with their own planning and more proficient at adapting resources with purpose.

Another avenue which I have explored with beginning teachers is planning a lesson or series of technology-free lessons, which demonstrates that technology-based lessons are not the only way of planning and subsequently delivering a geography lesson.

LH: It's interesting that you raise this Sara-Anne, as sometimes as a tutor I navigate different schools having different amounts of prepared materials, and mentors having different philosophies as to the extent to which beginning teachers can change and/or should adapt these materials in their planning and teaching. I have experience of beginning teachers being unable to apply different ideas in their planning, due to being required to teach very specific geographical knowledge using a predefined lesson structure and pedagogies by their placement schools. Anecdotally, I have found that sometimes beginning teachers like the structure to start with, but then they often begin to find this approach quite restrictive and/or that it does not match with their own philosophies or enable them to explore the complex relationships between theory and practice.

Planning in geography education 165

As Burn and Mutton explain (2018, n.p.), 'teachers need to be effectively equipped so that they can interrogate their own practice to identify why it is not working, learn from new ideas and adapt them to particular situations'. Through rationalising in their planning how they are applying theory to practice, and why, and then critically evaluating the successes and challenges of the approach (in that particular context, with those particular children), beginning teachers develop their knowledge and skills to plan to teach different geographies, in different ways, in different contexts and with different children.

Task 11.2 Co-planning with your beginning teacher

In collaboration with your beginning teacher, agree an area of geography and class that you will co-plan a lesson for. Use the critical questions in Figure 11.1, to frame a discussion with your beginning teacher on planning for that particular class, on that particular area of geography. With your beginning teacher, you might use these questions to underpin your planning of the geography lesson that you will teach, also taking into account national and longer-term curricula in the school. After the lesson has been taught, you might critically evaluate both the use of the questions as underpinning foci of planning, along with the differences and relationships between teaching as *intended* and teaching as *reality*.

SN: I have found it useful for beginning teachers to start observing lessons and teaching, with a discussion of basics of how to observe a lesson and how to plan a lesson. As mentors, we must appreciate the level of school-based experience the beginning teachers have. I do agree that it is fundamental to give beginning teachers a clear structure in order to actively observe a lesson or indeed plan a lesson, especially during the beginning stages of their teaching experience.

FA: I also think this is an issue of scaffolding. Each beginning teacher brings their own strengths and areas for development and so the amount of structure and freedom they need will vary: getting the right balance is key. However, for many beginning teachers, the access to prepared lessons can stymie creativity. By seeing a prepared lesson, beginning teachers unfairly compare their initial ideas to fully prepared lessons and this comparison can lead them to dismiss their ideas before they are fully developed. So, sometimes, there is value in only providing aims and objectives, allowing beginning teachers greater freedom in their planning.

SN: I would like to suggest that we – as mentors – use our professional judgement when we provide beginning teachers with aims and objectives. These are essential, but if a beginning teacher has had little to no prior experience, they may require more structure and support, in order to develop an effective lesson plan. Conversely, a beginning teacher may use the aims and objectives, but plan a lesson which is wholly off-focus or indeed even inappropriate.

AS: Initially, beginning teachers may benefit from using pre-prepared lessons that they tailor for their classes, providing examples of good practice that help them focus on building routines and relationships. Over time, the need for planning from scratch increases. A dialogue between the mentor and the department ensures that the benefits of planning from scratch for the beginning teacher, department and students are clearly illustrated. This should reduce the reluctance of teachers to 'let go'. Beginning teachers deserve freedom to explore approaches to teaching and learning without unnecessary constraints.

Sara-Anne, how do you give beginning teachers freedom to develop their own teaching style when you share your teaching and learning non-negotiables?

SN: Examples of our non-negotiables include hands-down questioning, independent working-time and one voice (Fletcher-Wood, 2018). These are also geographical in focus: using compass directions, scale and skills within lessons. Within the geography department I feel like we embrace these principles and incorporate them across the planning and delivery of our curriculum, not only supporting the development of beginning teachers, but developing everyone's skill, reflection and responsiveness. I would discuss the purpose of one voice, for example, which is beneficial for explicit instruction and explain why hands-down can be a powerful Assessment for Learning (AfL) tool. I would then take a gradual release approach, where the beginning teacher has a copy of the non-negotiables on the desk as a visual reminder, to then removing this support over time.

SP: This idea of gradually removing support over time also came up in research on the feedback beginning teachers are given (Puttick and Wynn, 2021); there is an individual, personalised balance that needs to be struck between support and freedom in planning. The way in which departments and schools operate on a continuum between freedom and autonomy obviously varies, but I can see there being useful ways of incorporating both at different times, including thinking about the ways in which examples above of technology, resources and pre-made plans might be intentionally used at different times for different purposes.

FA: We separate aspects of teaching that require skill development, such as differentiation and AfL, and those which are habits, such as meeting students at the door or handing our resources out at the beginning of lessons. This approach was influenced by cognitive load theory but does potentially suffer from being mentor-led and removing the opportunity for beginning teacher-led in some cases. Nonetheless, the goal was to make non-skilled aspects unconscious and committed to long-term memory to ease the burden on working memory. To ensure buy-in, I often use the analogy of learning to drive. When first learning, everything is novel and overwhelming, but over time less so until it becomes second nature. Furthermore, presenting beginning teachers with a list of expectations provides clarity. These are then shared in the department and feedback is requested on these, as well lesson feedback. Finally, modelling expectations raises beginning teachers' level of commitment to them.

AS: I love your analogy, Faz. I think many beginning teachers become frustrated when they observe excellent teaching and learning but are unable to immediately replicate this. Your list of expectations sounds helpful, particularly before many aspects of teaching become automated.

Planning and curriculum thinking

FA: Thank you Amy. I would like to introduce our final challenge: beginning teachers often struggle to find the right balance between breadth and depth and this manifests itself in lessons which are over-resourced. One reason is beginning teachers are concerned with maintaining student interest. This can have ramifications, such as oversimplification, and lead to an unsustainable workload; to address this, in the past I have asked beginning teachers to plan a lesson using one curriculum artefact. One beginning teacher chose to use a newspaper article which contained information, a map and an image. They identified a series of key ideas they wanted students to leave the lesson with. These ideas ranged from specific geographical elements to broader skills. They then developed a series of objectives to enable progression. Finally, they included three hinge questions to assess learning. One of the challenges was the time it took the beginning teacher to find the resource. We discussed the use of different resources (including limitations of using just one), and through this discussion tried to build the beginning teachers' ability to better make decisions about resources for geography teaching.

Task 11.3 Developing critical awareness of curriculum artefacts

Select with your beginning teacher a lesson plan and its associated curriculum artefact(s) and resources. Engage in a critical discussion about how geography and (different) people and places are represented in the lesson, considering the impacts that the lesson may have on children's and young people's geographical knowledge and imaginations. You might also critically consider how geography teachers can support children to better understand how inequalities and injustices have been (re)produced in and constructed in society, and openly and actively consider how they might be attended to.

AS: Exactly, the students may be busy, but with limited geography learned. Finding high-quality resources to use in the classroom can be challenging when lesson planning. For example, care must be taken to ensure the geographical accuracy of the resource and that the resource reading age is appropriate for the students you are intending to use it with; one particular challenge is that many academic articles are hidden behind a paywall, with few secondary schools having access as a result. *Routes: The Journal for Student Geographers* (2021) is an excellent source of open-access articles that can develop beginning teachers' geographical knowledge or be used as a stimulus for discussions in lessons.

SN: Have we considered professional geographical bodies, to support lesson planning and us as mentors? For example, the Royal Geographical Society with Institute of British Geographers and the Geographical Association are incredible repositories of information, resources and materials. One resource I have used with beginning teachers is the Subject Audit tool (Geographical Association, 2020). I was able to use this to plan the teaching experience timetable and consequently support the beginning teachers' planning in differing areas of their subject development.

LH: Thank you all for these really helpful personal reflections and exemplars from your wealth of experience as mentors. Most of the discussion so far has focussed on lesson planning. I wondered if it might be helpful to share some examples of how you support beginning teachers in planning sequences of lessons and/or how you begin to explore wider ideas or theories about curriculum planning with beginning teachers. For example, through one Masters assignment we ask student teachers to plan, teach and evaluate a series of lessons to support them in connecting, and exploring the complex relationships between, theory and practice, and to further consider what it means to make progress in geography.

FA: We begin by discussing the organisation and rationale that underlie the curriculum. We aim to raise beginning teachers' awareness of a curriculum as intentional and interconnected as opposed to discrete topics. In addition, we hope to expose beginning teachers to a range of curriculum models including linear, topic, themed and the spiral curriculum. The lesson planning assignment our ITEs undertake as part of their training is helpful in exploring curriculum planning at a scheme of work level. Beginning teachers are asked to consider the aims of schemes of work and the best approach to teaching these. Further conversations take place during the planning process focussed on other lesson planning considerations.

AS: We explore curriculum thinking using our Key Stage 3 Geography curriculum map. We discuss topic choices, sequencing and the synoptic concepts that underpin our curriculum. As part of this, we discuss the importance of using fertile questions to structure each lesson, make connections between topics and add intrigue to learning (Harpaz, 2005; Enser, 2020). In addition, these fertile questions ensure students know the what and the why in their geographical curriculum (Enser, 2020). Harpaz (2005) suggests six key characteristics of fertile questions, including being open, connected and practical. Myatt (2018) complements this thinking, suggesting that best practice uses overarching questions that form the road map and framework of learning.

When teaching, as a department we collate a list of adaptations to be made before we reteach the unit and I encourage the beginning teacher to get involved in this. This illustrates the importance of long-term planning and curriculum thinking rather than seeing lessons as discrete learning episodes. In addition, trainees complete a curriculum assignment where they choose a controversial topic, identify preconceptions, plan a small sequence of lessons to address misconceptions and then evaluate this. The beginning teacher decides on the issue to teach and has autonomy to decide the best evidence-informed approach to combat said misconceptions.

SN: PGCE assignments can often be used to showcase the beginning teacher how to sequence lesson plans. Long-term planning is essential, and I have included several opportunities in mentor meetings to discuss this explicitly. To support the beginning teacher with lesson planning at Key Stage Three, I shared the curriculum map. I would demonstrate how a single lesson is planned, how a unit is planned and how a unit fits into the curriculum map. The essential step is that we discuss the lesson and how their planning directly relates to the curriculum map.

Conclusion

Through critical engagement with literature about geography education and planning, and an open conversation between mentors and tutors, in this chapter we have examined the complexities of supporting beginning teachers in planning lessons and curricula in school geography. The chapter has brought to the forefront the tensions that beginning geography teachers and their mentors and tutors face in planning (and learning to plan) a geography curriculum that is rich, inclusive and enabling to, and for, society's children. As we have demonstrated in this chapter, these tensions include, but are not limited to: tensions about the purposes of planning and the *place* of planning in (initial) teacher education; tensions about the purposes of teaching geography; tensions about the relationships between school and university systems and policies in both ITE, and planning and teaching; tensions about personal values in, and experiences of, geography education; and tensions about the relationships between research, policy and praxis. Our slow conversation about planning in school geography has shown how these tensions interweave and come alive in mentor meetings, lesson feedback, university lectures and seminars, and ultimately in the experiences of beginning teachers as they sit down to plan a lesson or wider curricula.

Recognising and exploring these tensions matters to mentoring in geography education. A richer understanding of the experiences of beginning teachers, mentors and tutors, and how these experiences relate to research, policy and praxis, can inform mentoring practices. For example, being informed about research into lesson planning and curriculum design can inform mentor discussions with beginning teachers about the relationships between teaching as *intended* and teaching as *reality*, and support critical examination of lesson plans and wider curricula. This knowledge can also enable mentors to contribute to debates about geography teacher education – specifically with regard to considering how we can best support beginning teachers in their planning. The contribution of mentors – as colleagues who work with beginning teachers every day during their school placements – is critically important to the development of true partnership, and a mutually beneficial relationship, between universities and schools. In the case of planning, we argue that this would include active consideration of the relationships between *reservoirs* of knowledge (about planning and geography education) and *repertoires* of practice (Bernstein, 2000) in school geography, and the role of mentors and tutors (and the relationships between them) in supporting the development of beginning teachers. For example, in mentors supporting beginning teachers to use the ideas of methods of geography and geography education to inform their planning, and evaluate the successes and challenges of their planning and teaching.

For discussion

- Reflect on the theories and values that underpin the planning documents and policies that you use in your practice: consider how and why you examine the relationships between theory and practice in planning with beginning teachers.

- Reflect on how ideas about progress in geography are set out and examined in lesson plans and longer-term curricula. In doing so, consider what strategies and ideas you can use (and how) to support beginning teachers to critically consider what it means to make progress, and how they can plan for students to make progress, in geography.

Further reading and resources

1. hooks, b., 1994. *Teaching to Transgress: Education as the Practice of Freedom*. Abingdon: Routledge.

In this book, hooks draws on her experiences as a student and academic, along with theories about teaching and education, to challenge the biases that have shaped teaching practices in society and to examine the power and possibility of both pedagogy and education.

2. John. P. D., 2006. Lesson planning and the student teacher: Re-thinking the dominant model. *Journal of Curriculum Studies*, 38(4), 483-498.

This conceptual paper has played an important role in research attention on lesson planning and is widely cited in the literature. The way in which 'rationalistic, technical curriculum planning' (John, 2006, p. 483) is defined offers useful insights into what is argued to be the dominant model. By making the norms associated with this model explicit it helps to stimulate more critical attention on some of the assumptions about how we might approach planning.

References

Adichie, C. N., 2009. The danger of a single story. Available at: www.ted.com/talks/chimamanda_ngozi_adichie_the_danger_of_a_single_story?language=en [accessed 26 February 2021].

Bernstein, B., 2000. *Pedagogy, Symbolic Control and Identity: Theory, Research, Critique* (revised edn). Oxford: Rowman & Littlefield.

Biddulph, M., 2017. What do we mean by curriculum? In M. Jones (ed) *The Handbook of Secondary Geography*. Sheffield: The Geographical Association.

Biddulph, M., Lambert, D., and Balderstone, D., 2015. *Learning to Teach Geography in the Secondary School: A Companion to School Experience*. Abingdon: Routledge.

Burn, K., and Mutton, T., 2018. Constructing the curriculum of (initial) teacher education: When should new teachers be encouraged to ask critical questions?' *Impact*, 4. Available at: https://impact.chartered.college/article/constructing-curriculum-initial-teacher-education-when-new-teachers-encouraged-ask-critical-questions/ [accessed 15 February 2021].

Catling, S., 2014. Giving younger children a voice in primary geography: empowering pedagogy – a personal perspective. *International Research in Geographical and Environmental Education*, 23(4), 350–372.

Chizhik, E. W., and Chizhik, A. W., 2018. Using activity theory to examine how teachers' lesson plans meet students' learning needs. *The Teacher Educator*, 53(1), 67–85.

Department for Education [DfE], 2016. *National Standards for School-Based Initial Teacher Training (ITT) Mentors*. London: Department for Education.

Department for Education [DfE], 2019. *Early Career Framework*. London: Department for Education.

Dorling, D., and Tomlinson, S., 2019. *Education and Race: From Empire to Brexit*. Bristol: Polity Press.

Dove, J., 2016. Reasons for misconceptions in physical geography. *Geography*, 101(1), 47–53.

Fletcher-Wood, H., 2018. *Responsive Teaching: Cognitive Science and Formative Assessment in Practice*. London: Routledge.

Enser, M., 2020. Are you asking fertile questions? If not, you should be. Available at: www.tes.com/news/are-you-asking-fertile-questions-if-not-you-should-be [accessed 26 February 2021].

Finn, M., Hammond, L., Healy, G., Todd, J., Marvell, A., McKendrick, J. H., and Yorke, L., 2021. Looking ahead to the future of GeogEd: Creating spaces of exchange between communities of practice. *Area*/ DOI: 10.1111/area.12701.

GeoCapabilities, n.d. GeoCapabilities. Available at: www.geocapabilities.org/ [accessed 24 February 2021].

Geographical Association, 2020. Subject knowledge audit. Available at: www.geography.org.uk/write/MediaUploads/Teacher%20education/GA_ITE_TE_Audit_subject_knowledge.pdf [accessed 16 December 2020].

González, M. J., Gómez, P., and Pinzón, A., 2020. Characterising lesson planning: A case study with mathematics teachers. *Teaching Education*, 31(3), 260-278.

Hamilton, A. R., 2020. The white unseen: On white supremacy and dangerous entanglements in geography, *Dialogues in Human Geography*, 10(3), 299-303.

Hammond, L., 2021a. London, race and territories: Young people's stories of a divided city. *London Review of Education*, 19(1), 1-14. https://doi.org/10.14324/LRE.19.1.14.

Hammond, L., 2021b. Connecting with Children's Geographies in Geography Education lecture at Utrecht University.

Hammond, L., in review. Who are the children we teach? considering identities, place and time-space in education.

Harpaz, Y., 2005. Teaching and learning in a community of thinking. *Journal of Curriculum and Supervision*, 20(2), 136-157.

Healy, G., and Walshe, N., 2022. Navigating the policy landscape: Conceptualising subject-specialist mentoring within and beyond policy. In G. Healy, L. Hammond, S. Puttick and N. Walshe (eds), *Mentoring Geography Teachers in the Secondary School*, Abingdon: Routledge, 13-30.

hooks, b., 1994. *Teaching to Transgress: Education as the Practice of Freedom*. Abingdon: Routledge.

John, P. D., 2006. Lesson planning and the student teacher: Re-thinking the dominant model. *Journal of Curriculum Studies*, 38(4), 483-498.

König, J., Bremerich-Vos, A., Buchholtz, C., Fladung, I., and Glutsch, N., 2020. Pre-service teachers' generic and subject-specific lesson-planning skills: On learning adaptive teaching during initial teacher education. *European Journal of Teacher Education*, 43(2), 131-150.

Lambert, D., and Morgan, J., 2010. *Teaching Geography 11-18: A Conceptual Approach*. Maidenhead: Open University Press.

Lambert, D., Solem, M., and Tani, S., 2015. Achieving human potential through geography education: A capabilities approach to curriculum making in schools. *Annals of the Association of American Geographers*, 105(4), 723-735.

Lave, J., and Wenger, E., 1991. *Situated Learning: Legitimate Peripheral Participation*. Cambridge: Cambridge University Press.

Lambert, D., and Solem, M., 2017. Rediscovering the teaching of geography with the focus on quality. *Geographical Education*, 30, 8-15.

Li, T., Chen, X., and Kulm, G., 2009. Mathematics teachers' practices and thinking in lesson plan development: A case of teaching fraction division. *ZDM Mathematics Education*, 41, 717-731.

Matthews, J. A., and Herbert, D. T., 2008. *Geography: A Very Short Introduction* Oxford: Oxford University Press.

Morgan, J., 2017. The making of geographical ignorance? *Geography*, 102(1), 18-25.

Morgan, J., and Lambert, D., 2001. Geography, 'race' and education. *Geography*, 86(3), 235-246.

Morgan, J., and Lambert, D., 2020. Black Lives Matter and geography teaching. Available at: https://impolitegeography.wordpress.com/2020/07/20/black-lives-matter-and-geography-teaching/[accessed 7 September 2020].

Myatt, M., 2018. *The Curriculum: Gallimaufry to Coherence*. Woodbridge: John Catt Educational.

Puttick, S., 2022. Lesson observations at the interface between research and practice. In G. Healy, L. Hammond, S. Puttick and N. Walshe (eds), *Mentoring Geography Teachers in the Secondary School*. Abingdon: Routledge, 173-186.

Puttick, S., and Murrey, A., 2020. Confronting the deafening silence on race in geography education in England: Learning from anti-racist, decolonial and Black geographies. *Geography*, 105(3), 126-134.

Puttick, S., and Warren-Lee, N., 2021. Geography mentors' written lesson observation feedback during initial teacher education. *International Research in Geographical and Environmental Education*, 30(2), 95-111. DOI:10.1080/10382046.2020.1757830.

Puttick, S., and Wynn, J., 2021. Constructing 'good teaching' through written lesson observation feedback. *Oxford Review of Education*, 47(2), 152-169.

Rawlings Smith, E., 2020. Techniques for mentors to support early career teachers' reflective practice. *Teaching Geography*, 45(2), 53-55.

Roberts, M., 2003. *Learning Through Enquiry*. Sheffield: Geographical Association

Routes, 2021. *Routes: The Journal for Student Geographers*. Available at: https://routesjournal.org/ [accessed 26 February 2021].

Shen, B., Poppink, S., Cui, Y., and Fan, G., 2007. Lesson planning: A practice of professional responsibility and development. *Education Horizon*, 85(4), 248-258.

Stokes, A., Feig, A. D., Atchison, C. L., and Gilley, B., 2019. Making geoscience fieldwork inclusive and accessible for students with disabilities. *Geosphere*, 15(6), 1809-1825.

Tapsfield, A., 2019. *Effective Geography ITE Training and Mentoring*. Sheffield: Geographical Association.

Vertovec, S., 2007. Super-diversity and its implications. *Ethnic and Racial Studies*. 30(6), 1024-1054.

Yusoff, K., 2018. *A Billion Black Anthropocenes or None*. Minneapolis: University of Minnesota Press.

12 Geography lesson observations at the interface between research and practice

Steve Puttick

Introduction

I wonder if you can remember your first observed lesson. Who was observing you? Why were they observing you? What do you remember about the feedback they gave you? What did they say? What did they write? What happened as a result of this feedback?

Lesson observations have a mixed past. I hope your experiences have been positive and useful, but some people reading this book will have quite unpleasant memories of being judged and categorised through lesson observations (with the main memory being the judgement that you're *inadequate*; you *require improvement*; you're merely *satisfactory*). Lesson observations have been used as a powerful tool to make consequential judgements about individual and school performance. At their best, they offer a fascinating opportunity to reflect on practice and engage with a rich process of questioning how and what we should teach, and also about how we know these things: based on what evidence, and for what kinds of reasons? In this chapter I introduce some of the findings from recent research on written lesson observation feedback during Initial Teacher Education (ITE) in order to stimulate questions for reflection, particularly about certainty and blind spots. My aim is to argue for using lesson observations in a way that draws on a wide range of knowledges and experiences, actively seeks different perspectives, and is comfortable holding them in creative tension, allowing space for genuinely professional dialogue between observers and beginning teachers. Conceptualising lesson observations and feedback in this way – as complex, epistemologically contested interactions in applied professional contexts – means that lesson observations are not easy, and, as the saying goes, if it feels easy then you are not doing it right!

Power, knowledge and lesson observations

There are many different reasons for observing a lesson, and much has been written on the way in which the 'performative nature of observed lessons constructs highly charged events' (Puttick, 2017a, p. 49).

Power / Knowledge			
Asymmetries between observed and observer	On the relative importance of different aspects of the lesson	About what 'good teaching' looks like	About what sources of information are most relevant to this situation
Power over / for / with…	How you can and should 'see' and through what 'lens'	About what counts as valid knowledge in this situation	Held with what degree of certainty / uncertainty

Figure 12.1 Possible power/knowledge relations around lesson observations (presented as illustrative possibilities, not organised around rows/columns).

Task 12.1 Mentor reflection: experiences of observed lessons

Take a moment to think back to the lesson observation you experienced as the teacher being observed. For example, you might consider the following questions: how did you feel before? What planning did you do? How did this compare to your normal lesson planning? How did you feel after the lesson? Can you remember any other lesson observations that your colleagues have experienced? In what ways do your experiences, reactions and feelings compare with theirs?

Then, list six factors that might contribute to lesson observations being 'highly charged events'.

What factors did you come up with? In what ways are your factors related to *power* and *knowledge*? Figure 12.1 shows some of the ways in which power and knowledge might be interrelated, experienced and performed in the context of lesson observations.

Research on the written feedback given to beginning teachers following lesson observations suggests that most feedback is given with a high degree of certainty. In our analysis of the written feedback given to beginning teachers across a one-year ITE programme, we (Puttick and Wynn, 2021) found this certainty illustrated by the explicit ways in which observers claimed that things were *clear* or *clearly evident*, illustrated in this example of written feedback:

> Relationships with pupils – High levels of mutual respect clearly evident. Appropriate use of humour, regular use of praise and responding positively to pupils' questions and comments all helped with this.
>
> (p. 11)

Throughout, we found little evidence of observers' claims being qualified or hedged, such as through terms like *it seems*, or *which might…*, and there seemed to be two aspects related to this certainty:

1. The general level of descriptions (in the example above: 'mutual respect').
2. The generic (rather than subject-specific) nature of descriptions (such as 'responding positively').

In both of these aspects, the general and generic level of comments seem to be linked with the certainty because of their 'non-objectionable' nature. *Of course* responding positively is a good thing, and *of course* it will be associated with mutual respect. Possibly, the regular use of highly certain accounts is related to the broader cultural context in which 'performative schooling systems demand objectivity and reliability of judgements, whether of learners or teachers...' (Puttick, 2017a, p. 62). There are tensions between the kinds of certainty of judgement required of professional standards and institutional accreditation, and a more tentative epistemological perspective that is not quite so certain that we actually do know what we think we can see. In the example above, we might ask how an observer can know about mutual respect. What kinds of proxies for this were used? And how confident are we that these (presumably behavioural) performances and interactions relate to authentic notions of respect? Why do we think that we should be reinforcing these apparently easily observable insights for beginning teachers? How might we make our reasoning – the evidence base on which we are drawing these conclusions – more explicit and accessible for beginning teachers?

Some of these questions are opened up through a blog post that Aldridge (2016) wrote about *The girl who fell off her chair*. Recalling a memory from his own ITE experience, he describes an observed lesson that he taught. At one point during this lesson he asked a question to the class, and, when one girl raised her hand to answer the question, she fell onto the floor. Going over to investigate, Aldridge saw that the girl did not have a chair. Rather than telling him that she did not have a chair, she had decided to adopt a crouching position supported with a hand on the table! Aldridge believes this lasted for at least 10 minutes until the falling incident, and then:

> After the lesson came the inevitable 'debrief'. The girl was apparently unhurt, but the incident had caused not inconsiderable amusement to her peers and clearly loomed large in our shared consciousness for the remainder of the lesson. My school-based observer could hardly have missed it... I think I opened the dialogue with some remark to the effect that I had been thrown somewhat by the chair incident (as indeed I had)... my observer eventually cleared her throat and said, 'And now, over to the learning' – and that was all we ever said about the matter. The next item on the agenda was very likely that – as usual, but perhaps with more reason on this occasion – my 'timings were off', and that I 'hadn't got as far as I planned'.
>
> (Aldridge, 2016)

He reflects on how we might distinguish between what counts as educationally significant events and an 'unremarkable diversion'. You will only have limited amounts of time available for lesson observation feedback, and there are hard decisions to be made about what counts as significant: what should you spend your time observing and feeding back? Or, to put it another way: what should you be trying to *see*? Geographical analyses of 'gaze' and 'positionality' have a lot to say about the ways in which people (particularly geographers and researchers) often assume they are able to look from a *neutral* and *objective* perspective: the disinterested observer making a purely rational judgement (Lossau, 2005). These critiques highlight the very particular ways in which we all see through the lens of our own histories, perspectives, beliefs and experiences. One psychological take on this is to ask whether you see a duck or a rabbit when looking at that famous silhouette. The main argument that I hope to make through the following sections might be summarised in this way: human observation – even by experts – is limited and partial, and so we should be cautious about making strong claims about lesson observations, and instead approach them with humility and inquisitiveness.

Do observers agree?

Research on lesson observations suggests that we are likely to disagree about how 'good' lessons are, which has some important implications for the areas of the lesson that we highlight to the beginning teacher either as a strength or as an area of development. Gargani and Strong's (2014) work is a good example of the significant time and resources, and also the narrowness of observation tool, that is necessary to achieve both high inter-observability agreement and high levels of accuracy. Whether this kind of consistency would necessarily be a good thing during ITE is an open question, and they note some examples, in the context of the United States of America, of the highly contested nature of lesson observations when used as part of teacher-evaluation systems (for example, see Gargani and Strong, 2014, p. 399). Similarly, the question over the extent to which very narrow or restricted observation tools might have a role to play during ITE (or more broadly) is also worth exploring further. Towards the end of this chapter, I discuss the kinds of pro formas that might support observation and feedback; thinking about the structure of these forms offers an opportunity to revisit these questions.

In a study designed to answer the question 'Do we know a successful teacher when we see one?', Strong et al. (2011) ran three experiments to: firstly, test under increasingly more favourable conditions whether judges can correctly rate teachers of *known ability* to raise student achievement; secondly, inquire about what criteria judges use when making their evaluation; and thirdly, determine which criteria are most predictive of a teacher's effectiveness. They conclude that, 'in every case, judges achieved relatively high levels of agreement but were absolutely inaccurate, leading us to question whether educators can identify effective teachers when they see them' (p. 378). Because of the relatively high levels of agreement, they argue these were not likely to have been arrived at by chance, but instead were because of systematic influences, and

> At the same time, the judgements made by both expert and nonexpert judges were inaccurate in ways that also reflected systematic influences – certain teachers were inaccurately rated by a significant majority of judges while others were not, and the accuracy of judges overall was significantly lower than would have been produced by chance.
>
> (p. 374)

Their study involved participants deciding, based on observing teachers' lessons, whether the teacher was either high or low performing. Testing these judgements against the actual value-added scores of each teacher is what led Strong et al. to question 'whether educators can identify effective teachers when they see them' (p. 378). Commonly held assumptions about what counts as *good teaching* seemed to play a powerful role, and in ways that were not well-aligned with the *actual* effectiveness of the teaching being observed. You might be able to think of a number of commonly held beliefs about teaching that have been promoted in the past, but which are now widely questioned (and replaced by other shared ideas). Three-part lessons, maximum amounts of teacher talk (regardless of content or purpose), particular arrangements of students and tables, explicit attention to learning styles and so on have all featured widely in CPD (continuing professional development), Ofsted reports, National Strategies, and so on. The argument made elsewhere is that, because of the complexity of education, and the connectedness of the field, homogenising forces or *isomorphism* (Puttick, 2017b) result in these kinds of similarities. Strong and colleagues' work found agreement at the general level of what looks like effective teaching, but alarming discrepancies between these judgements and the effectiveness (at least as judged by students' grades).

Exploring a similar question about consistency between observers, Hudson's (2016) study provides an interesting example of the ways in which mentors' feedback and judgements might compare in the context of more specific issues. Hudson asked 20 mentors to watch a video of the same lesson: nine of the mentors praised the teacher's instructions for their clarity, while 12 criticised the very same instructions for being too complex.

The assumption underpinning much work that has been carried out on lesson observations is that standardisation and agreement between observers is (obviously) the ideal that is being pursued. You do not want observers to say different things that might contradict and confuse the person being observed. Or, do you? Should observers always agree? For an example of disagreement over an observed lesson in the particular context of a research project, and the possible ethical implications arising from this situation, see Puttick (2017a). That account describes a situation in which two observers came to quite different conclusions about a lesson: a non-specialist senior leader judged it as requires improvement – with significant implications for the Newly Qualified Teacher being observed – whereas I believed that it was a good lesson. The high-stakes and evaluative nature of the judgement is brought into sharp focus through the account, arguing these aspects marginalise the opportunities for rich and useful subject-specific professional dialogue.

Research on the impact of dealing with multiple sources of information has indicated that students who believe that knowledge is complex, uncertain and actively constructed report higher levels of enjoyment and curiosity, and lower levels of confusion, anxiety and boredom. For example (in the context of climate change):

> Students who believed that the justification of knowledge about climate change requires critical evaluation of multiple sources experienced higher levels of enjoyment and curiosity, and lower levels of boredom when confronted with conflicting information. A belief in the complexity of this knowledge was related to lower levels of confusion, anxiety, and boredom. A belief in the uncertainty of this knowledge predicted lower levels of anxiety

and frustration, and a belief in the active construction of knowledge predicted lower levels of confusion.

(Muis et al., 2015, p. 168)

There seem to be good reasons to introduce beginning teachers to some sense of knowledge about teaching as complex, partial and plural. Or, to use the language of performativity, we might think through ways in which to 'disturb the assumed epistemological objectivity with which observers make judgements... blunt[ing] some of the tools of performativity and hopefully open[ing] a little more space for professional dialogue' (Puttick, 2017a, p. 62).

Are you sure you saw what you think you saw?

Research on lesson observations has highlighted some of the concrete ways in which different observers might *see* quite different things within the same lesson. In the examples discussed above this includes very different interpretations of the efficacy of the same teacher instructions. One aspect of our tendency to see different things is related to the limits of our attention and the finite capacity that we have for looking at things. In the language of cognitive load theory this might be described as the limits of working memory. A classic psychology experiment illustrating the ways in which our attention is highly selective involves showing participants a video of a group of six people passing a basketball. (Spoiler alert! If you would like to try this exercise out for yourself, stop reading and head to this video: https://youtu.be/vJG698U2Mvo.)

Three of the players are wearing black t-shirts, and the others are wearing white t-shirts. Watching the video, you are asked to count the number of passes made by the players in white t-shirts. At the end of the video, the number of passes is revealed. Then comes the punchline: but did you notice the gorilla?! The video is replayed to show that, while the passes were being made (and you were concentrating hard on the white t-shirts' passes), a person in a big gorilla suit casually wandered through the middle of the video, pausing in the middle to beat their chest! In their experiment, Chabris and Simons (2011) found that half of the people watching the video did not notice the gorilla. So, while everyone *saw* the same video, they did not *see* the same things. Their study involved naïve observers, that is, it was an activity they had never done before: they were not expert basketball-pass-counters! Maybe they would be more aware of other things if they were engaged in activity that they were familiar with, and experts in? To find out whether this finding also holds for experts, Drew et al. (2013) asked 'what about expert searchers who have spent years honing their ability to detect small abnormalities in specific types of images?' They invited 24 radiologists to do an activity that they were expert in (a lung-nodule detection task). Similar to Chabris and Simons' gorilla video, they added a big gorilla to the image, then asked the participants a technical observation question (similar to counting the basketball passes). Afterwards, the participants were asked if they saw the gorilla. They found that an even higher number (83%) of these experts did not see the gorilla. The eye-tracking Drew et al. (2013) used also showed that these participants actually looked at the gorilla, but their concentration on the activity they thought they were doing meant that they did not *see* it. Therefore, Drew et al. (2013) conclude that 'even expert searchers, operating in their domain of expertise, are vulnerable to inattentional blindness' (p. 1848). The shared difficulties faced by expert and novice observers is also replicated in Strong et al.'s (2011) work introduced above. What might we, in geography education, be blind to? In some ways this is a very hard question: how can you know what you do not know? Longstanding critiques have suggested that geographical knowledge has rarely featured in post-lesson observation feedback, and some recent work has highlighted the ways in which we have often been blind to colonialism and race, and so I briefly discuss these examples in relation to lesson observations.

Geographical knowledge

School geography lessons have been critiqued for the limited attention that has been given (including by observers) to the content of lessons. For example, Roberts' (2010) reflections on her experiences as an external examiner:[1] 'What particularly struck me from written feedback on lessons was the large amount of attention given to generic matters and the very limited feedback on the actual geography' (p. 112). Instead of focussing on 'the actual geography', the focus has – according to these critiques – been on generic ideas like *engagement* and *progress*. In Morgan and Lambert's (2011, p. 281) terms, 'thinking skills, learning to learn and the emotional dimensions of learning assumed more immediate or urgent attention than a critical gaze on the material content of lessons'. Elsewhere, they describe this as a *pedagogic adventure* which is argued to have dominated discussion about school geography. Similarly, Firth (2011) describes how

> in post-observation discussion... my experience has been that geographical knowledge has rarely, if ever, figured in such discussion. It has been marginalised by the exigencies of everyday practice and the imperatives of policy.
>
> (p. 312)

In this quote from Firth, we might ask some critical questions about the university-based ITE tutor's role in these discussions: if they were a part of these three-way discussions, is this also a self-reflective critique? Whose responsibility is it to construct these discussions in particular ways? If everyone involved is a part of the conversation, then no one party can have the sole responsibility to bring in particular themes. As those involved with mentoring beginning geography teachers, and across ITE partnerships, this presents us with a challenge: how might we facilitate better subject-specific conversations about *the geography*?

Our research on written lesson observation feedback (Puttick and Warren-Lee, 2020; Puttick and Wynn, 2021) broadly supports these claims about subject-specific issues having received relatively limited attention. However, our data also 'qualify and soften these previous concerns by suggesting that it seems to be an overstatement to claim that there is a complete "absence" of attention to the geography' (Puttick and Warren-Lee, 2020, p. 14): in the geography-specific lessons (n = 31), one-third of the comments in the written feedback did make explicit reference to geography. We located these subject-specific comments along a continuum from simpler references that only identified or named something geographical, then including an evaluative description, specific improvements, and through to more complex framings aimed at prompting reflection (p. 7).

Our implication in this presentation of a continuum of subject-specific references is that moving to more complex engagement is a good thing. Over the course of an ITE programme, we want beginning teachers to be challenged by increasingly complex discussion around their teaching: asking hard questions and having challenging conversations about knowledge and curriculum, and not just technical questions or tips about particular techniques. Developing work on this is also an ongoing challenge for geography education research more broadly: in Healy et al.'s (2020, p. 22) terms, 'there needs to be more attention to how teacher educators and mentors can develop mentoring practices that place the subject curriculum at the heart of their work with trainee teachers'.

Colonialism and race

One area of geographical knowledge that has recently been argued to need far greater attention involves colonialism and race (Esson, 2020; Puttick and Murrey, 2020). Part of the argument about the importance of addressing these issues is based on geography's past as a subject of empire whose origin has messy entanglements with deeply racist projects of empire that have actively marginalised certain peoples and knowledges (Hamilton, 2020). In addressing this past we must, in Daley et al.'s (2017) terms,

> include voices, ideas, scholarship, and places in the world that have been under-represented in geography's publication venues over the years. After all, politics and struggles over the future of the economy, society, and the environment are localized and also profoundly globalized.
>
> (p. 3)

During teaching with doctoral and PGCE geographers I have informally asked the question 'what did you learn about colonialism or race from your geography education?' to start the conversation. Overwhelmingly, the answer is either *nothing*, or romanticised ideas about the ways in which European nations brought benefits to colonised nations: do not worry about the famines and looting, now you have railways! Naïve understandings of empire are deeply engrained in geography education, which means that critical questions unravelling geography's past are rarely considered. For example, Roberts' (2013) discussion of 'controversial issues' includes the impact of the British Empire as a 'controversial issue' because of the different interpretations that exist:

> Some issues are controversial because of differences of interpretation, for example, there are different interpretations of the impact of the British Empire on Britain's former colonies; some accounts emphasise the positive impacts while others the negative.
>
> (p. 114)

The weakness of defining issues *as controversial* because of differences of interpretations has been well explored by Hand (2008): just because some people think that racism is a good thing does not mean that it should be taught *as* a controversial issue. In the example of the British Empire, the very framing of these countries – Britain's former colonies – reveals highly problematic relations (including their continuing positioning *as Britain's*) and has been strongly critiqued by academic geographers among others. But how might this be enacted in the classroom? What kinds of inattentional blindness might there be that we can usefully apply lesson observations to? Following the theme of how places are represented, we might ask 'In what ways did you represent different places?' There have been several recent parodies of the colonial gaze which might be painfully close to some representations in school geography resources. For example, see the *discovery* of the River Gulu.[2] Lesson observations offer a brilliant opportunity to explore these questions: to what extent does representation of places and peoples in geography teaching resources reproduce the kinds of problematic portrayals that are so well parodied in these accounts?

Task 12.2 Focussing on 'the geography' in lesson observation feedback

- How can you raise good questions about 'the geography'? (including for some beginning teachers who might have very little choice about what they teach).
- In what ways can you help to stimulate careful reflection on geographical knowledge?
- How might you prompt more critical and reflective consideration of the ways in which echoes of empire and race continue to be reproduced in school geography?
- What are the possible implications of the ways in which peoples and places are portrayed in the lesson?

Use these prompts to create six questions that you might use to stimulate critical discussion about geographical knowledge through lesson observation feedback.

Observation pro formas

Research discussed above (Gargani and Strong, 2014; Hudson, 2016) on observers' consistency and the accuracy of their judgements strongly suggests that we should be cautious about the certainty with which our observational judgements are framed. This work also argues that having a clear focus for observations affects the feedback. In Hudson's (2016) study, mentors watched a video-recorded lesson twice. During the first viewing they were given an open-form observation pro forma, whereas for the second viewing they were directed to feedback on one aspect of the teachers' practice (questioning). In the open-observation mode only one mentor gave constructive criticism about questioning, whereas, when asked to focus on questioning, all mentors offered one or more positive responses, and 'all but three mentors wrote at least one constructive criticism with this specific focus' (Hudson, 2016, p. 232). While we might expect an increase in comments during the second viewing, the extent of this increase is striking. The general claim that a clear focus increases feedback on specific areas is also well supported by Soares and Lock's (2007) intervention on subject-specific mentoring. Their intervention was motivated by the apparent lack of science-specific feedback for beginning teachers, which is echoed in the critiques of the (apparently) limited attention given to geographical knowledge. To increase the subject-specificity of mentors' feedback, they provided enhanced professional development for a small group of specialist mentors who were also banned from giving any lesson observation feedback on generic issues, such as *presence* or *classroom management*, except where these dimensions were explicitly related to the subject. They ran their evaluation with a group of PGCE Science beginning teachers (n = 29), generating data through the beginning teachers' perceptions of the written feedback they received following observed lessons. Comparing the feedback that the beginning teachers received from their science mentor and the specialist mentor, they report a massive shift in the beginning teachers' perceptions of the attention given by mentors to topic-specific pedagogy. Only three per cent of science mentors (according to the beginning teachers' perceptions) addressed topic-specific pedagogy, whereas nearly all (95%) of the specialist mentors were perceived to address topic-specific pedagogy (by the same measure). In part, this emphasises the importance of questions that clarify the vision, aim or purpose of observation and feedback: how should we structure observation templates? There are also important issues to explore around the relationships between these kinds of pro formas and the approach and structure of mentoring conversations, for

Table 12.1 Aspects of lesson observation pro formas

Aspect	Description	Discussion
Structure	Continuum from open/free to highly structured. At the open/free end, an observation form might be a blank sheet of paper. The highly structured end might be set of tick-box questions or include Likert-scale responses.	Greater freedom has the potential for mentors to work without the constraint of pre-determined framing and scales. Greater structure makes aspects that might otherwise be hidden become explicit, and possibly aids consistency and the potential to see changes over time.
Focus	Similar continuum from no-focus to a tightly defined focus.	Clear focus seems to ensure that this area (such as questioning) is given attention, whereas it might otherwise not be. Tightly defined focus, if adhered to, will limit feedback on other (potentially significant) areas.
Subject/generic	Decisions over the extent to which lesson observation pro formas explicitly address subject-specific questions, or more generic issues.	Much of the research suggests that observers give limited attention to subject-specific issues, which supports an argument for adopting geography-specific observation pro formas.
Sources of information	On what evidence are the decisions/judgements/comments from the observer made?	Observers often seem to make evaluative statements that might be enhanced by giving the beginning teacher access to the sources of information on which the comments are based.
Areas of development	Most observation pro formas give space for areas to develop / action plans: to what extent do they make the sources of information explicit?	What sources of knowledge are included? There are great opportunities for thoughtfully engaging with a wide range of knowledges, including research evidence such as through having a prompt question: what articles/papers might be useful to consider in relation to this?

example, thinking through the ways in which Rawlings Smith's (2022) useful distinction between reflecting, noticing, listening and dialogue might be complemented by the pro formas. Table 12.1 presents some aspects of pro formas that you might consider.

Task 12.3 Constructing lesson observation pro formas

Look back over the different arguments that I have tried to make in this chapter about:

- observation
- agreement
- certainty
- knowledge and
- sources of information.

If you already have a lesson observation pro forma, take a moment to reflect on it against these criteria, and against the aspects outlined in Table 12.1. Where does it sit against these aspects of lesson observations? What might the implications be? How might you refine it further? If you do not have a lesson observation pro forma that you already use, try to use the aspects in Table 12.1, plus your responses to the previous tasks, to design one. What questions/areas will you prioritise? What kind of approach (structure/focus/subject/generic, and so on) will you include?

Much of the preceding discussion has implied that lesson observation feedback is based on a model involving a lone beginning teacher and a mentor-observer. However, it is worth noting that other configurations often exist, particularly involving other members of a department who might also be observing the beginning teacher with their classes. To what extent might you be able to support their observations of and feedback for the beginning teacher? How might you model and share different ways of giving feedback that draw on the different areas for reflection highlighted in this chapter? In terms of the hierarchical configuration of beginning teacher / observer, what scope might there be to create different opportunities to co-construct ideas about good geography teaching? Co-teaching, switching roles between observer and teacher, varying who writes feedback so that the beginning teacher takes ownership of this at points, and shaping reflective questions together might all offer some potential to vary the dominant observed/observer structure. Lesson Study (Wood and Rawlings Smith, 2017) also offers a well-developed approach to structure co-enquiry and collaboratively support beginning teachers' ownership over their own growth.

Conclusion

In this chapter I hope to have explored a number of different questions around lesson observation feedback, and to have done so in a way that also leaves these questions open. An important aspect running throughout these arguments involves the tentative nature of knowledge that is possible through lesson observations. Teaching is incredibly complex, particularly in the context of beginning teachers' development, and there are few obvious answers about what *good teaching* looks like (even if there are widely held assumptions about what this looks like). So, I have tried to argue that lesson observations should try to make explicit the basis on which you are making any judgements, comments and suggestions about teaching. This approach is less about telling the beginning teacher how they should teach, and more about introducing them to a wider and richer conversation that draws on multiple sources of knowledge: modelling expansive, inquisitive critical professional reflection. In Boyd et al.'s (2015) terms, teaching is:

> too complex, too situated in particular settings, too dependent on the identity and personality of the teachers and learners for us to be able to simply tell you how to do it… as a professional you must learn to question, evaluate and test policy, theory, professional guidance and research evidence, while keeping your eye firmly on the needs of your learners.
>
> (pp. 2-3)

And, in the same spirit of critical inquiry that I have tried to use throughout, we might also probe Boyd and colleagues a little further: why finish with (only) the needs of the learners? And who decides what these needs are? To what extent should we also be keeping our eye firmly on *the geography*?

For discussion

- What kinds of evidence do you cite, and what arguments do you make in your feedback? Drawing on an example from your own feedback, you might consider: what are you showing beginning teachers about the ways in which knowledge is produced and navigated in geography teaching?
- Do you use one lesson observation pro forma, or do you take a different approach at different times? For example, in what ways might different points in the beginning teacher's development be better suited to different approaches?

Notes

1. Higher-education institutions use external examiners as one way of ensuring consistency of standards across institutions and to contribute to course development. In the context of ITE programmes the role often involves observing lessons, holding discussions with mentors and beginning teachers, scrutinising a range of written assignments and evidence submitted towards QTS recommendations, and attending examination boards. For example, see: www.heacademy.ac.uk/system/files/downloads/Fundamentals%20of%20External%20Examining%20AHE%20-%20%20Feb%202019%20v2.pdf.
2. https://thewire.in/the-sciences/gulu-river-london-thames-colonialism, and @gathara's Twitter feed (see: https://twitter.com/gathara/status/1352151084006072320?s=20).

Further reading and resources

1. Puttick, S., and Wynn, J., 2021. Constructing 'good teaching' through written lesson observation feedback. *Oxford Review of Education*, 47(2), 152-169.

Introduced in this chapter, Puttick and Wynn (2021) describe in further detail the methodological design of our study that analysed over 500 written lesson observation forms, exploring a number of themes that may be useful to reflect further on, including a framework of different conceptions of 'good teaching', and the ways in which strengths, areas for development and action plans, and planning are presented in written lesson observation feedback.

2. Puttick, S., and Warren-Lee, N., 2021. Geography mentors' written lesson observation feedback during initial teacher education. *International Research in Geographical and Environmental Education* 30(2), 95-111. doi:10.1080/10382046.2020.1757830.

Focussing on the geography-specific data from our larger study, Puttick and Warren-Lee (2020) explore the ways in which subject-specific concerns in geography might be made more explicit in written lesson observation feedback by analysing data from 31 geography lesson observations. We conclude by suggesting a number of areas for further research to explore: it would be great to see some of these explored further (including through Masters research, and reported in the pages of *Teaching Geography*).

3. Healy, G., Walshe, N., and Dunphy, A., 2020. How is geography rendered visible as an object of concern in written lesson observation feedback? *The Curriculum Journal*, 31(1), 7-26.

Asking 'how is geography rendered visible as an object of concern in written lesson observation feedback?', Healy, Walshe and Dunphy (2020) argue for the importance of lesson observations as a key mechanism for beginning teachers' development. Their analysis of findings from their research with mentors and teacher educators raises important questions about the role of the subject and curriculum in lesson observations.

References

Aldridge, D., 2016. The girl who fell off her chair. Available at: https://zudensachen.wordpress.com/2016/11/26/the-girl-who-fell-off-her-chair/ [accessed 15 December 2020].
Boyd, P., Hymer, B., and Lockney, K., 2015. *Learning Teaching: Becoming an Inspirational Teacher*. St Albans: Critical Publishing.
Chabris, C., and Simons, D., 2011. *The Invisible Gorilla*. London: Harper Collins.
Daley, P., McCann, E., Mountz, A., and Painter, J., 2017. Re-imagining politics & space: Why here, why now? *Environment and Planning C: Politics and Space*, 35(1), 3-5.
Drew, T., Vo, M. L., and Wolfe, J. M., 2013. The invisible gorilla strikes again: Sustained inattentional blindness in expert observers. *Psychological Science*, 24(9), 1848-1853.
Esson, J., 2020. "The why and the white": Racism and curriculum reform in British geography. *Area*, 52, 708-715.
Firth, R., 2011. Making geography visible as an object of study in the secondary school curriculum. *The Curriculum Journal*, 22(3), 289-316.
Gargani, J., and Strong, M., 2014. Can we identify a successful teacher better, faster, and cheaper? Evidence for innovating teacher observation systems. *Journal of Teacher Education*, 65(5), 389-401.
Hamilton, A. R., 2020. The white unseen: On white supremacy and dangerous entanglements in geography. *Dialogues in Human Geography*, 10(3), 299-303.
Hand, M., 2008. What should we teach as controversial? A defense of the epistemic criterion. *Educational Theory*, 58(2), 213-228.
Healy, G., Walshe, N., and Dunphy, A., 2020. How is geography rendered visible as an object of concern in written lesson observation feedback? *The Curriculum Journal*, 31(1), 7-26.
Hudson, P., 2016. Identifying mentors' observations for providing feedback. *Teachers and Teaching: Theory and Practice*, 22(2), 219-234.

Lossau, J., 2005. The body, the gaze and the theorist: Remarks on a strategic distinction. *Cultural Geographies*, 12, 59-76.

Morgan, J., and Lambert, D., 2011. Editors' introduction. *The Curriculum Journal*, 22(3), 279-287

Muis, K. R., Pekrun, R., Sinatra, G. M., Azevedo, R., Trevors, G., Meier, E., and Heddy, B. C., 2015. The curious case of climate change: Testing a theoretical model of epistemic beliefs, epistemic emotions, and complex learning. *Learning and Instruction*, 39, 168-183.

Puttick, S., 2017a. Performativity, guilty knowledge, and ethnographic intervention intervention. *Ethnography and Education*, 12(1), 49-63.

Puttick, S., 2017b. You'll see that everywhere: Institutional isomorphism in secondary school subject departments. *School Leadership & Management*, 37(1-2), 61-79.

Puttick, S., and Murrey, A., 2020. Confronting the deafening silence on race in geography education in England: Learning from anti-racist, decolonial and Black geographies. *Geography*, 105(3), 126-134.

Puttick, S., and Warren-Lee, N., 2021. Geography mentors' written lesson observation feedback during initial teacher education. *International Research in Geographical and Environmental Education*, 30(2), 95-111. doi:10.1080/10382046.2020.1757830.

Puttick, S., and Wynn, J., 2021. Constructing 'good teaching' through written lesson observation feedback. *Oxford Review of Education*, 47(2), 152-169.

Rawlings Smith, E., 2022. Mentoring meetings and conversations supporting beginning teachers in their development as geography teachers. In G. Healy, L. Hammond, S. Puttick and N. Walshe (eds), *Mentoring Geography Teachers in the Secondary School*. Abingdon: Routledge, 137-155.

Roberts, M., 2010. Where's the geography? Reflections on being an external examiner. *Teaching Geography*, 35(3), 112-113.

Roberts, M., 2013. *Geography Through Enquiry: Approaches to Teaching and Learning in the Secondary School*. 2nd edn. Sheffield: Geographical Association.

Soares, A., and Lock, R., 2007. Pre-service science teachers' perceptions of written lesson appraisals: The impact of styles of mentoring. *European Journal of Teacher Education*, 30(1), 75-90.

Strong, M., Gargani, J., and Hacifazliog, Ö., 2011. Do we know a successful teacher when we see one? Experiments in the identification of effective teachers. *Journal of Teacher Education*, 62(4), 367-382.

Wood, P., and Rawlings Smith, E., 2017. Lesson study: A collaborative approach to teacher growth. *Geography*, 102(2), 91-94.

13 Geography and geography education scholarship as a mechanism for developing and sustaining mentors' and beginning teachers' subject knowledge and curriculum thinking

Grace Healy

Introduction

This chapter focusses upon exploring how and why geography and geography education scholarship can be powerful for mentors and beginning geography teachers. As mentors and geography teachers, you might consider the sources you can draw upon to develop and sustain your subject knowledge and curriculum thinking, and whilst there are benefits of engaging with generic curriculum theory or other forms of education research, there can also be challenges if this is prioritised. If we take teaching a subject as a specialised activity (Lambert, 2018), then it is important to draw upon geography and geography education scholarship, because research focussed on generic principles will never address the core subject-specific concerns of teachers as they wrestle with 'curricular choices about structure and sequence in light of their students' understandings' (Burn, 2016, p. 240). The term scholarship is used here to more broadly encompass theoretical and empirical research undertaken by geographers and geography educators, practitioner research pursued by geography teachers, and outputs from geography teachers' scholarly teaching. As Brooks (2010) states, scholarly teaching[1] 'goes beyond the interactions that take place in the classroom and into an understanding of teaching that is grounded in intellectual endeavour and considered decision-making' (p. 69). This broad conception of scholarship embraces the complexity of the relationship that exists between research and practice for subject-specialist teaching and acknowledges that 'judgment in education is not simply about what is possible (a factual judgment) but about what is educationally desirable (a value judgment)' (Biesta, 2007, p. 11) at a subject level.

In this chapter, I will initially set out how this chapter conceptualises subject knowledge and curriculum thinking, and the ways in which subject knowledge and teachers' subject expertise have been characterised within the field of geography education. I will then go on to explore in greater detail the various means and reasons for engaging with geography and geography education scholarship within the context of mentoring geography teachers.

Subject knowledge and curriculum thinking

Teacher subject knowledge and curriculum thinking have been characterised in various ways within policy, as well as in professional and academic literature. For example, the Teachers' Standards in England outline the expectation that teachers 'have a secure knowledge of the relevant subject(s) and curriculum areas, foster and maintain students' interest in the subject, and address misunderstandings' and 'demonstrate a critical understanding of developments in the subject and curriculum areas, and promote the value of scholarship' (DfE, 2011, p. 5). Shulman (1986) identified a domain of 'content knowledge in teaching' which includes 'subject matter content knowledge', 'pedagogical content knowledge' (PCK) and 'curricular knowledge' (pp. 9-10); these categories, outlined in more detail in Table 13.1, have become widespread ways of discussing teachers' knowledge for teaching. However, there are extensive critiques about these categorisations; for example, McEwan and Bull (1991) question whether it is possible to distinguish between PCK and subject matter content knowledge,[2] and Fordham (2016) has argued that there has been insufficient attention to subject-specificity of teachers' curricular knowledge. So, whilst acknowledging that these categorisations are not unproblematic, they are used here to allow for appreciation of the different aspects of content knowledge that you, as a mentor, can support the development of. Alongside conceptions of subject knowledge and subject expertise, this chapter also attends to teachers' curriculum-making and curriculum thinking. Lambert and Morgan (2010) outline the three sources of energy that can influence geography teachers' curriculum-making: student experiences, school geography and student experiences; the curriculum-making model presented by Lambert and Biddulph (2015) builds on Lambert and Morgan's (2010) original model by showing the three sources of energy framed 'in the context of the discipline of geography' (Lambert and Biddulph, 2015, p. 215). Geography curriculum-making brings together concern for the local ownership that geography teachers have for curriculum and pedagogy for their geography students (Brooks, 2006). In this chapter, questions of curriculum are foregrounded because this allows for the curricular purpose to drive the method and avoids 'an intransitive pedagogy, a pedagogy without an object' (Counsell, 2016, p. 245). This echoes the sequencing of Lambert's (2018, p. 367) central questions for curriculum leadership:

- Who are the students?

    (What is their prior experience and knowledge? What are their aspirations?)

- Why teach this subject?

    (How does it justify curriculum space? What is its educational value?)

- What should be taught?

    (On what basis do we select what to teach? How is this sequenced?)

- How do we best teach this subject?

    (What pedagogic approaches are suited to serving the purposes identified above?)

Table 13.1 Shulman's (1986) categorisation of 'content knowledge in teaching' (p. 9)

Shulman's categorisation	Description
Subject matter content knowledge	'This refers to the amount and organization of knowledge per se in the mind of the teacher' (Shulman, 1986, p. 9).
Pedagogical content knowledge	This 'goes beyond knowledge of subject matter per se to the dimension of subject matter knowledge *for teaching*' (Shulman, 1986, p. 9).
Curricular knowledge	This includes knowledge of how 'the curriculum is represented by the full range of programs designed for the teaching of particular subjects and topics at a given level, the variety of instructional materials available in relation to those programs, and the set of characteristics that serve as both the indications and contraindications for the use of particular curriculum or program materials in particular circumstances' (Shulman, 1986, p. 10).

Task 13.1 Mentor reflection: reflecting on content knowledge for geography teaching

Before moving on, it would be helpful to consider how you have thought about *content knowledge in teaching* for your own teaching and within your mentoring by reflecting on the following questions:

1. In what ways have you thought about *content knowledge in geography teaching*?
2. To what extent do you find Shulman's (1986) categories of knowledge a helpful way to frame discussion and development of the *subject expertise* that geography teachers require?
3. Do you find the *curriculum-making model* includes the sources that shape your own geography curriculum-making and thinking?
4. When mentoring geography teachers, in what ways do you make explicit to beginning geography teachers what is influencing your *decision-making*?

Geography teachers' subject expertise and curriculum making

Brooks' (2007; 2016) narrative research provides an articulation of the subject-specificity of teachers' professional knowledge; this includes making explicit the role of subject expertise in geography teachers' planning and teaching (Brooks, 2010), and the importance of the subject expertise of mentors (Brooks, 2017). Within education more broadly there has been attention to the curriculum principle of powerful knowledge, whereby curriculum based on an entitlement and access to subject knowledge has been argued for (Young, 2009). Within this framing, powerful knowledge is perceived to be distinct from common-sense knowledge, as it is systematic (related to each part of a discipline), specialised (developed by specialists within defined fields of expertise) (Young, 2011) and fits within a Future 3 scenario (as shown in Table 13.2). Young (2020) argues that this not just about teachers having subject knowledge, but requires teachers to hold 'an understanding of their role as members of a virtual community of specialists' (p. 25); this has implications for how as mentors we induct

Table 13.2 Three futures for subject knowledge adapted from Young and Muller, 2010

Future scenario	View of knowledge	Implication for school subject
F1	Under-socialised Knowledge for the powerful	Elitist - subject boundaries are fixed and maintained. Knowledge is fixed, backward-looking.
F2	Over-socialised Knowledge lacks power	Subject boundaries are removed. Generic learning outcomes, such as skills, become the aim - a turn away from knowledge.
F3	Social realist Powerful knowledge	Subject knowledge boundaries are maintained but also crossed for the creation and acquisition of new knowledge. Subject knowledge is dynamic and forward-looking.

Source: Mitchell, 2017, p. 68.

beginning geography teachers into the geography subject community in ways that support the development of their subject expertise.

Within the geography education community, this characterisation of subject knowledge has been debated and critiqued (e.g. Catling and Martin, 2011; Firth, 2011; Roberts, 2014; Maude, 2016; Healy, 2021a) and also furthered through the work of GeoCapabilities (Lambert, 2016). The GeoCapabilities approach draws upon the curriculum-making model and the principles of Young's (2009) powerful knowledge and Future 3 curriculum, as outlined by Young and Muller's (2010) curriculum futures' framework (Lambert, 2016).[3] Lambert (2016) acknowledges that 'everyone has a geographical existence and everyday experiences from which to draw that have geographical dimensions' (p. 393) and concurs that in the curriculum-making process, there needs to be due consideration given to young people's everyday knowledge as set out by Roberts (2014). Firth (2011) also illuminates that academic geographers producing research in the areas of children's and young people's geographies are often doing this through the co-construction of knowledge, and so a concern for knowledge is more than just a concern for geographical content, but ones that takes account of the epistemic nature of geographical knowledge (Firth, 2015). This more clearly highlights that as teachers we can benefit from being attentive to the everyday knowledge that students might hold (that is not drawn upon geographically) and the everyday knowledge that is marshalled through a geographical lens within the classroom (Firth, 2011). This means there is capacity to appreciate the relationship between the geography that is taught in school and the everyday geographies that make up students' own geographical knowledge and perspectives (Catling and Martin, 2011; Firth, 2011) as an important aspect of the subject expertise of geography teachers. The implications of this are twofold; firstly, that beginning teachers themselves will have different everyday geographical knowledge they bring alongside their academic geographical knowledge, and secondly, that beginning teachers need to appreciate the multiple experiences of their students.

In order to achieve a Future 3 curriculum, Morgan, Hordern and Hoadley (2019) argue that the relationship of subjects to their disciplines should be held alongside sociality, whereby knowledge 'acquires its special character as a consequence of systematic (and yet ideally inclusive, participatory and democratic) social processes' (p. 121). In particular, they suggest a need for addressing efforts to 'ensure those whose are alienated find greater access to disciplines and engagements with curriculum, and that broader and more diverse social groupings contribute to the reshaping of knowledge over time' (p. 121). Within our own discipline and subject, we need to be aware that there are significant concerns that might hinder sociality, such as the diversity of who studies geography at A-level and undergraduate level (RGS, 2020), and the diversity of academics who are that are in a position to contribute to the discipline (Rose, 2020). This requires a continued conversation about diversity and inclusivity that takes account of the intersectionality of geographers' identities, including, but not limited to, matters of class, disability, gender and gender diversity, sexuality and race (Finn et al., 2021). In order to sustain subject expertise and engage in curriculum-making, and support beginning geography teachers in this endeavour too, it is necessary to be alert to who is (re)shaping geographical knowledge both in the academy and for school geography.

Engaging with geography and geography education scholarship as a mechanism to sustain geography teachers' subject expertise

As beginning and experienced geography teachers have varied conceptions of geography (Walford, 1996; Brooks, 2006; Walshe, 2007; Mitchell and Lambert, 2015; Puttick, 2015), it can be fruitful to reflect on your own subject expertise and that of your mentees. We can be mindful of the concern that the 'increasingly fragmented, research-focused university discipline… produces geography graduates with varied and unpredictable conceptions of what constitutes geographical knowledge' (Mitchell and Lambert, 2015, p. 273), but at the same time recognise the subject expertise of beginning teachers that we work with. In particular, you might reflect on whether individuals' subject expertise can provide opportunities for geography teachers within your department to model their readiness to engage with developing their subject expertise. For example, a beginning geography teacher might be supported to set up a reading group for the department based on their expertise in geography, work collaboratively with several members of the department on curriculum development based on their geographical expertise, or lead a seminar for sixth-formers and department colleagues based on geographical research they have undertaken.

Many Initial Teacher Education (ITE) programmes have ways of auditing and tracking beginning geography teacher's subject knowledge, and these can be very helpful ways of ensuring that beginning teachers have the opportunity to develop subject knowledge across the breadth and depth of geography throughout their training year. However, it is important to reflect upon how this is framed, as Puttick (2018) has argued that beginning geography teachers can be positioned as either knowing or not knowing subject knowledge. He goes on to describe a tension between 'having – and being judged to have – strong and secure subject knowledge, whilst also being self-critical' (p. 39). In the context of history, Burn (2007) has also argued for the importance of mentors and beginning teachers being able to acknowledge existing expertise and the limitations of what they know:

> an appreciation of the range of types of knowledge on which they are constantly drawing may make mentors more willing to go on working in genuinely collaborative ways with

student teachers, even as they unpick and re-evaluate their own subject knowledge, examine more closely pupils' preconceptions or reject the use of particular analogies.

(pp. 462–463)

This emphasises that you might want to consider carefully how you frame subject knowledge development with beginning teachers. For example, do you highlight that this is part of career-long commitment? How do you model your own and colleagues' continued subject knowledge development to beginning teachers? As you look at Table 13.3, you will see that by introducing beginning geography teachers to a range of ways that they can develop their subject expertise, this will in turn empower them to navigate sustaining their subject expertise as they move through their career. In some cases, this might be about:

- accessing geography research directly (e.g. the Royal Geographical Society's (RGS) 'Ask the Geographer' podcast);
- using geography education scholarship to help develop a critical approach to teaching geography (e.g. engaging with Taylor (2017) and Winter (2018) to consider how you might examine textbooks before use with school students);
- discussing geography and geography education scholarship within the professional conversations that fellow geography teachers have with beginning geography teachers as you co-plan and discuss geography teaching.

There are various points during mentoring in which signposting or engaging with geography and geography education research can be used to develop subject expertise and geography teaching. As you enter into shared dialogue around lesson planning, observations and evaluations, geography and geography education scholarship can be a means by which you can 'make explicit the basis on which you are making any judgements, comments and suggestions about teaching' and provide a way of introducing beginning geography teachers 'to a wider and richer conversation that draws on multiple sources of knowledge: modelling expansive, inquisitive critical professional reflection' (Puttick, 2022, p. 184). For example, you might:

- signpost a piece of geography scholarship and ask a beginning teacher to consider whether after reading it they might explain a particular concept to students differently;
- ask a beginning geography teacher to read some geography education scholarship and then ask them to reflect on a task they used or a particular question they posed to students;
- both read a recent piece of geography scholarship and set aside time to discuss this as you co-plan a lesson sequence;
- ask a beginning teacher to reflect upon geography scholarship focussed on children's and young people's geographies as a way of considering the possibilities for students' perspectives and geographical imaginations around a particular aspect of geography;
- ask a beginning geography teacher to engage with a piece of geography education scholarship on misconceptions and alternative conceptions in respect to a particular aspect of geography and use this to inform the formative assessment used within the lesson;

- after teaching a lesson, spend time making explicit some of the decisions that you made in the planning and/or teaching of the lesson that were informed by geography scholarship and geography education scholarship;
- before asking students to teach a departmental scheme of work, share with them a reading list of geography and geography education scholarship that informed its development.

Table 13.3 Subject knowledge development for beginning geography teachers

Shulman's (1986) categorisation of 'content knowledge in teaching' (p. 9)	Examples
Subject matter content knowledge	**Royal Geographical Society's (RGS) 'Ask the Geographer' podcast** - Podcasts that provide geography teachers with access to contemporary geographical research. www.rgs.org/schools/teaching-resources/ask-the-expert-podcasts/ **RGS's Monday night lecture series** - Lectures that provides geography teachers with access to contemporary geographical research. www.rgs.org/geography/online-lectures/ **Geographical Association (GA)'s GEO platform** - The GEO platform is for students studying for GCSE geography and A-level geography, but the academic lectures can be useful for geography teachers. https://geographyeducationonline.org/live-events/lectures **Local GA branches** - Some local GA branches offer a lecture series. See information about local GA branch activity within GA news and on the GA website. www.geography.org.uk/Journals/GA-Magazine www.geography.org.uk/Get-Involved/GA-branches ***Geography* journal** - The GA's *Geography* journal provides access to contemporary geography scholarship and includes contributions from geographers and geography educators. www.tandfonline.com/action/journalInformation?show=aimsScope&journalCode=rgpy20 ***Routes* journal** - Routes is a peer-reviewed journal for sixth-form and undergraduate geographers looking to read and publish geographical knowledge, and so can provide access to contemporary geographical scholarship. https://routesjournal.org **Academic journals** - There are a range of journals that geographers publish in; these can cover the whole discipline (e.g. *Area, Geo:Geography and Environment*), or focus on specific areas (e.g. *Children's Geographies, Economic Geography, Quaternary Science, Progress in Human Geography, Progress in Physical Geography*).[1] **GeoCapabilities phase 3 vignettes** - As part of the GeoCapabilities phase 3 project, geography teachers have developed vignettes based on geographical scholarship in migration. www.geocapabilities.org/vignettes/ **Royal Meteorological Society (RMetS) and University of Reading MOOC** - MOOCs can provide opportunities to develop subject knowledge; this particular one allows participants to explore the physical processes behind the weather. www.futurelearn.com/courses/come-rain-or-shine

(continued)

Table 13.3 Cont.

Shulman's (1986) categorisation of 'content knowledge in teaching' (p. 9)	Examples
	Connections with your local university department – The RGS holds a directory of universities currently offering geography courses; you might want to explore what outreach and connections your local geography department has with schools. www.rgs.org/geography/choose-geography/geography-at-university/directory-of-geography-courses/
Pedagogical content knowledge	Co-planning (including collectively development of questions, explanations, resources) in relation to a particular aspect of geography.
	Observing and post-lesson debrief with an experienced teacher around a particular aspect of geography with a focus on unpacking teachers' decision-making in relation to what and how they are teaching.
	Engaging with textbooks and lesson resources with a focus on thinking how about geographical knowledge (including knowledge of people and places) has been represented and made accessible for students.
	Engaging with a *Teaching Geography* article that has foregrounded how geography teachers have taught a particular topic to inform future planning and teaching. For example, Corbridge and Hawley's (2020) development of a case study of the coastal management of the Fylde coast.
	Looking at extended written responses from students and exploring what this shows about what students appear to be finding easier or more difficult, identifying misconceptions that appear to be arising, and what the implications there might be for future lessons and evaluating lessons previously taught.
Curricular knowledge	Engaging with schemes of work/programmes of study around a topic (across Key Stage 3 – Key Stage 5) within your department and from other schools or organisations (e.g. www.geography.org.uk/teaching-resources/Secondary-and-post-16-resources www.rgs.org/schools/teaching-resources/)
	Critically engaging with textbooks and resources around a particular topic. For example, you might examine how places are represented and issues positioned; this might be informed by Taylor's (2017) and Winter's (2018) approaches to analysis of geography textbooks.
	Engaging with resources that render teachers' curriculum thinking and decision-making visible. For example:
	GeoCapabilities 2 materials (The Capability approach and powerful disciplinary knowledge, Curriculum making by teachers, Video case studies) www.geocapabilities.org/geocapabilities-2/
	GeoCapabilities 3 Vignettes constructed by geography teachers on migration www.geocapabilities.org/vignettes/
	Routes lesson resources https://routesjournal.org/peer-review/lessonresources/

1 There are acknowledged barriers to accessing geography research via academic journals (e.g. paywalls).

In these examples, the role of geography and geography education scholarship has been foregrounded, but in practice it is often more powerfully considered in conjunction with the other sources and aspects of professional knowledge. For example, when exploring your decision-making after a lesson, you might explain why you chose to phrase a set of questions as you did by making explicit your knowledge of the class and their prior learning, and your experience of teaching this lesson sequence before, alongside drawing upon geography or geography education scholarship.

There is also value in considering how beginning teachers 'learn from (and contribute to) the distributed forms of knowledge held and developed by' (Burn et al., 2007, p. 442) your subject department. Burn et al. (2007) found that the subject departments in their research provided a rich learning environment for beginning teachers, which was achieved through collaboration and a supportive culture around teacher learning. As illustrated in Healy (2019), there are examples of beginning teachers in other subjects reading subject and subject education scholarship, alongside experienced colleagues, to address a practical teaching issue and thus disrupting and developing all teachers' curriculum thinking over time (e.g. Murrey et al., 2013). This opportunity for collective professional development can be underpinned by an educative mentoring approach, which is further explored by Palombo and Daly (2022), whereby teachers are positioned as learners (Langdon and Ward, 2015) and where mentors can benefit through professional learning alongside beginning teachers.

Task 13.2 Mentor reflection: reflecting on how geography teachers can remain engaged as geographers

Biddulph, Lambert and Balderstone (2021) illuminate *why* they see value in engaging with a geography seminar within a local university department:

> This is not because we feel that ideas from a seminar event can be translated directly into a lesson the following morning, but more because it is an opportunity for you to connect with new ideas emerging at the research frontier and also still feel engaged as a geographer. (p. 284)

1. In what ways do you engage with geography that make you feel *engaged as a geographer*?
2. As a department, are there routinely things you do that enable you and your colleagues to connect with new ideas emerging at *the research frontier*?
3. Drawing on Table 13.3 and your own practice, how might you support beginning teachers to feel *engaged as geographers*?

As a mentor, you play an important role in helping beginning teachers appreciate geography as an ever-evolving disciplinary resource (Lambert and Walshe, 2018) and in navigating the demand to keep up to date with contemporary developments given that geography is a dynamic subject (Roberts, 2021). Navigating what has been termed an 'untidy and unruly'

(Lambert, 2019, p. 260) or 'sprawling, ragged, gorgeous' (Geoghegen et al., 2020, p. 462) discipline can be a complex endeavour for geography teachers. I have suggested that Hordern's (2019) notion of delocating concepts from one discipline or subject to another is important for geography and geography teachers, as geography draws on ideas from beyond the discipline of geography, and so as geography teachers we can use our subject expertise to transform and mediate such content (Healy, 2021a). This is something that does not neatly fit within a subject knowledge audit but is something that can be made explicit through mentoring.

Engaging with geography education scholarship as a means of critical engagement within the curriculum policy context

Geography education scholarship can enable beginning geography teachers to understand how the past curriculum policy context has influenced their own experiences of geography education and the relationship that exists between current curriculum policy and practice of the geography teachers they are working with. To illustrate this, we can look at how Rawling's (2001; 2003; 2015; 2016; 2020) extensive geography education scholarship illuminates the complexities in the social construction of the geography curriculum, through analysis of curriculum policy and curriculum change. Rawling (2018a), drawing on the approaches to studying place proposed by Creswell (2015), provides a helpful exploration as to how place is understood and represented in the 2013 Geography National Curriculum (GNC) (DfE, 2013) and in GCSE and A-level specifications in England. This more focussed exposition exemplifies how, within the 2013 GNC, there is strong representation of 'understanding places (*descriptive*)' approaches, whereas other approaches to studying place such as 'investigating processes (*social constructivist*)' approaches and exploring being in the world (*phenomenological*)' approaches are given less attention (Rawling, 2018a, p. 57). Rawling's (2018b) in-depth narrative of how the discipline has kept the concept of place in motion, alongside a critical discussion of how approaches to place have been represented in the curriculum over time, provides a persuasive argument for the need for dialogue that crosses the borders between school and academic geography.

> **Task 13.3 Supporting the development of beginning teachers: how is place characterised and represented in school geography?**
>
> As a mentor, you might want to engage a beginning geography teacher with Rawling's (2018a) *Teaching Geography* article and (2018b) *Debates in Geography Education* chapter as a springboard to consider:
>
> 1. In what ways was place characterised within your mentee's geographical education to date?
> 2. In what ways is place characterised within the curriculum documents and in the teaching that your mentee has observed within the geography department?
> 3. In what ways do we want place to be understood and represented within school geography for children and young people?

To provide another example of how geography education scholarship can support critical engagement with curriculum policy, we can explore how Puttick and Murrey (2020) have turned the spotlight on the absence of race within formal curriculum documents in England (e.g. GNC (DfE, 2013), General Certificate of Secondary Education [GCSE] Subject Content (DfE, 2014a) and A-level subject content (DfE, 2014b)). Puttick and Murrey (2020) have emphasised how this 'stands in contrast to important strands of thought in the discipline at-large, and there is potential for important lessons from anti-racist conversations and internal debates within geography' (p. 127). Such geography education scholarship provides a catalyst for you to explore with beginning geography teachers how different aspects of school geography are characterised within national curriculum frameworks, and to document where there might be absent knowledge(s) within geography curricula. Attention to who studies and contributes to the discipline of geography (RGS, 2020; Rose, 2020) and knowledge-exchange across the *borderland* between school and academic geography matters here too (Castree et al., 2007).

Whilst acknowledging the role of teachers in curriculum-making, Rawling (2020) argues that this can never 'compensate for poor curriculum development decisions at national or sub-national level' (p. 72). Instead, 'for intellectual re-engagement to take place, there needs to be a regular process of debate and discussion, at national level, about subject knowledge and its interpretation in the school curriculum' (p. 75). As geography teachers, we can be aware that as Winter (2012) has clearly explicated there are various 'knowledge teams' that hold 'responsibility for shaping the discourses (en)framing the geography curriculum, for influencing what school geography is' (p. 278):

> The first is interested in the school geography curriculum and influenced (inevitably) by the state (Department for Education [DfE], Geographical Association [GA], Royal Geographical Society [RGS]/Institute of British Geographers [IBG] and Ofqual). The second is dominated by academia (journal editors, research council referees, university appointment and promotion committees, journal reviewers and conference proposal reviewers). The third team consists of publishers, the media and Awarding Bodies comprising the commercial sector. Finally, there is the team that has increased in scope and size in recent years, of educational consultants, non-government organisations, think tanks, interest groups, educational charities and philanthropists.
>
> (Winter, 2012, p. 278)

Geography education scholarship can bring to the fore and help geography teachers think critically about the relationship between policy and practice in particular place and time-space contexts. Mitchell (2020) has emphasised how teachers' curriculum-making is now framed by a societal context of late capitalism, whereby individualism, accountability and new technologies can hinder geography curriculum thinking, and yet if 'teachers are able to recognise the hyper-socialised situation of their work, they are better placed to make sound curriculum making decisions based on independent professional judgements as subject specialists' (p. 175). As a mentor, you can enable beginning geography teachers to actively take account of how the national context of curriculum policy might enable and constrain their curriculum-making as geography teachers.

Engaging with geography education scholarship as a means of situating beginning geography teachers' practice and illuminating other teachers' curricular theorising and problem-solving

This section focusses on how as a mentor you can routinely draw on geography education scholarship to enable beginning teachers to situate their teaching practice within the *reservoir* (Bernstein, 1999) of the teaching practice of others found within the wider geography education community. As illustrated in Table 13.4, there are different forms of insights that can be gained from engaging with geography education scholarship that is written by geography teachers or illuminates geography teachers' curricular theorising and problem-solving. In some cases, this geography education scholarship can help beginning teachers navigate scholarship from the wider discipline of education and from other subject-specialist communities, as the authors engage with this scholarship as geographers and geography educators (e.g. Vernon, 2016; Healy, 2018).

In the cases set out in Table 13.4, you will see that scholarship can become a way of revealing how geography educators respond to the challenges of teaching geography with concern for *what* and *how* geography is being taught. Ellis (2007) has acknowledged the complexity of developing beginning subject teachers through drawing upon Lave and Wenger's (1991) notion of 'the community-displacement contradiction' (p. 115) whereby:

> Newcomers are caught in a dilemma. On the one hand, they need to engage in existing practice, which has developed over time: to understand it, to participate in it, and to become full members of the community in which it exists. On the other hand, they have a stake in its development as they begin to establish their own identity in its future.
>
> (p. 115)

In response to this *dilemma*, as mentors and geography teachers we can reflect on the ways in which we might help beginning geography teachers understand and participate in existing practice, and at what points we can make explicit what is up for debate and ripe for beginning teachers to contribute to within the geography subject community. Geography education scholarship can provide insights into and stimulus for reflecting on these aspects of your mentoring. Within the journal *Teaching Geography*, we can see the benefits of *beginning geography teachers* being empowered to have a *stake in the development of geographical education*, by looking at the contributions Matthews (2020), Milner (2020) and Trolley (2020) have made to subject community discourse.

Engaging with geography and geography education scholarship to render visible the disciplinary dimension of school geography

Geography and geography education scholarship can also help us as mentors address the disciplinary dimension in geography with beginning geography teachers. I have proposed that:

> Disciplinary knowledge allows teachers and students to grasp that the practices of geographers have evolved over time, such that both the methods and foci of geographical study have changed (Lewin and Gregory, 2018), and therefore produce

Table 13.4 What types of insights can geography education scholarship provide?

What types of insights?	Examples of geography teachers' curricular theorising and problem-solving
Insights gained into the curricular language used within geography education through engaging beyond geography/geography education discourse	Vernon, E., 2016. The structure of knowledge: does theory matter? *Geography*, 101(2), 100-104. Vernon's (2016) spotlight article on the structure of knowledge explores questions that arise from Bernstein's (1999) theory around the structure of knowledge for geography teachers. This illustrates the importance of geography teachers and researchers in geography education working as a subject community to draw on literature beyond geography education but viewed through a subject-specific lens.
Insights into the value of children's and young people's geographies for geographical education	Hammond, L., 2019. Utilising the 'production of space' to enhance young people's understanding of place. *Geography*, 104(1), 28-37. Hammond's (2019) article provides insight into the value of geography teachers considering young people's understandings of the concept of space through 'applying a "geographical lens"... [that] could have significant impacts on exploring national identity with students' (p. 36).
Insights into the challenges of perceptions and representations of distant places	Kennedy, C., 2011. Imagining distant places: changing representations of Egypt. *Teaching Geography*, 36(2), 52-54. Taylor, L., 2014. Diversity between and within: approaches to teaching about distant place in the secondary school curriculum. *Journal of Curriculum Studies*, 46(2), 276-299. Kennedy (2011) and Taylor (2014) both illustrate the need to be aware of *othering* and *stereotyping* when teaching about distant places through their research on students' changing understandings of Egypt and Japan respectively.
Insights into geography teachers drawing on geographical scholarship to inform their curriculum planning and teaching	Healy, G., 2018. Using local organisations and geographical scholarship to support A-level place studies. *Teaching Geography*, 43(1), 13-15. Healy (2018) demonstrates how historical and geographical scholarship could be used directly with students to provide a way of contextualising place studies.
Insights into geography teachers using geographical scholarship with students	Trolley, S., 2020. *Prisoners of Geography?* How contextualising a book can develop students' understandings of geography. *Teaching Geography*, 42(2), 72-74. Trolley (2020) demonstrates how she drew upon geographical scholarship to help her A-level geography students contextualise Tim Marshall's book *Prisoners of Geography*.
Insights into what is up for debate and ripe for scholarship within the geography education community	Rawding, C., 2019. Putting Burgess in the bin. *Teaching Geography*, 44(3), 94-96. Puttick, S., 2020. Taking Burgess out of the bin. *Teaching Geography*, 45(1), 6-8. Puttick (2020) illustrates that whilst he agrees the criticisms of the use of the Burgess model within the geography classroom, there still can be debate around how and why geography teachers might still use it in their teaching when engaging with Rawding's (2019) article. Milner, C., 2020. Classroom strategies for tackling the whiteness of geography. *Teaching Geography*, 45(3), 105-107. Milner (2020) shares some small-scale research which was conducted with Black, Asian and minority ethnic geography teachers, and clearly recommends there is much more that needs to be done in terms of practice and research in this area.

> interpretations that "differ from different vantage points in time and space" (Daniels, Sidaway, Bradshore and Shaw, 2012, p. 2).
>
> (Healy, 2021a, p. 77)

Attending to the disciplinary dimension of geography can be part of teachers' subject expertise (Healy, 2021a). However, as the role of disciplinary knowledge has been under-examined in school geography (Firth, 2015) and school geography has been 'characterised by a certain epistemological certainty' (Puttick and Murrey, 2020, p. 131), it seems helpful to address why geography and geography education scholarship could be particularly valuable here for mentors and beginning teachers.

It has been long acknowledged that geography's big ideas are perceived as 'sites of contestation, and because of this are likely to possess multiple meanings that cannot be reduced to a single straightforward definition' (Lambert and Morgan, 2010, p. xi). Whilst Brooks (2018) has highlighted that concepts such as place and space provide a link between the school subject and academic discipline, I would emphasise that the way in which concepts remain in motion in the academic discipline of geography tells us something about how geographers are drawing upon these concepts in contemporary research. For example, Rawling (2018b) sets out the ways in which recent directions in place study have been drawing upon Deleuze and Guatarri's (1987) theories of assemblage (e.g. Anderson and MacFarlane, 2011). It is through geography scholarship where it is possible to see this new direction in motion; for example, Hope (2021) uses assemblage theory to research the Sustainable Development Goals (SDGs) in Bolivia, as this 'foregrounds the specific partnerships behind the SDGs (both institutional and between the human and non-human) to reveal the intricacies of consensus-building' (p. 218). In the context of Hope's (2019, n.p.) research, this allows greater attention to how the 'SDGs are primarily being operationalized by the state, by international NGOs and by their national partners' and 'brought into existing initiatives, rather than causing a wholesale reappraisal of development work'. At this specific level, engaging with this geographical research can help geography teachers more critically teach about SDGs and how the SDGs come into conflict with alternatives to development and alternative forms of development in specific places.

There have been significant provocations and questions in respect of the substance of school and academic geography. Puttick and Murrey (2020) have argued for:

> a more holistic and sustained anti-racist geography curriculum – including attention to Black, Indigenous and decolonial thought within the discipline from early childhood education to HE.
>
> (p. 132)

Whilst Finn et al. (2021) ask:

> to what extent do all of our students (present and potential) see themselves reflected in existing geography curricula and represented in nuanced ways? Whose places, bodies, voices and experiences are obscured or privileged? And how might we respond to the dis/advantaging nature of our curricula and pedagogies, and to some educators and students' relative privileges?
>
> (p. 4)

Both Puttick and Murrey's (2020) call and Finn et al.'s (2021) questions emphasise that as geography teachers we can have awareness of the *knowledge teams* that enframe the subject of geography (Winter, 2012), and be empowered to interrogate the positioning and nature of the geography we teach. The Decolonising Geography Educators group[4] has been making significant contributions within this area: for example, through engaging with awarding bodies in England and Wales in relation to racial bias within questions and through undertaking 'a voices project looking at the diversity and marginalisation of voices which should be included when teaching about different peoples and places around the world' (Ali, 2020, p. 14; Decolonise Geography, n.d.). The RGS's Race, Culture and Equality (RACE) working group has a key objective to 'encourage and support staff in developing pedagogical approaches and curricula to better understand geographies of race and eradicate racism' in higher education (Esson and Last, 2020, p. 668), which might provide scope for knowledge-exchange in relation to the teaching and learning about race and racism in geography (see Esson and Last, 2019). In introducing an *Area* special section on decolonising geographical knowledge, Noxolo (2017) concludes that:

> The invocation of both place and flow should alert us as geographers to the ways in which the discipline is not only able to effectively critique the ways in which the discipline is now inserted into ongoing dynamics of coloniality, but is also well- placed to respond to the call to decolonise knowledge.
>
> (p. 319)

This emphasises that for geography educators there is a necessity to develop a better understanding of knowledge production within geography, especially given that knowledge is 'deeply imbricated in power, and in the contingencies of its time, location and relations of production' (Noxolo, 2017, p. 319).

Rose (2021) argues 'as geographers, we understand the world much better if we are attentive to, and write about, a world that is diverse all the way down'. For mentors and beginning teachers, this is not only about being conscious of who 'writes the discipline' (Rose, 2021), now and in the past, but how we represent this for our students. It is important to recognise that there are blind spots due to absent knowledge(s) within the discipline; for example, Tooth and Viles (2021) illuminate that within geomorphology certain topics and knowledge have been privileged, as they question whether, for example, geomorphologists should be 'paying more attention to the "crappy landscapes" (Urban, 2018), where landscapes meet people and the full complexities of human-environment interactions are played out' (p. 8). Tooth and Viles (2021, p. 8) consider emerging actions, such as 'being honest about potentially problematic aspects of early disciplinary practices' and, whilst these suggestions are contextualised within undergraduate and postgraduate studies, how we frame geographical knowledge and attend to how geographical studies have been undertaken is just as pertinent within a school classroom. There is value in considering how beginning geography teachers can be enabled to:

- critically engage with how geographical knowledge is framed and represented within teaching resources and to students;

- develop their subject expertise with attention to disciplinary knowledge, such as how geographical knowledge is produced and constructed within the discipline of geography.

This is clearly illustrated in practice by a beginning geography teacher, Milner (2020), who explores strategies that could enable geography teachers to tackle the 'whiteness of the discipline' (p. 107). Milner's (2020) *Teaching Geography* article concludes with the following extremely pertinent questions for discussion: 'How do we approach geographical knowledge? How do we use case studies and represent the world? How do we approach colonial histories?' (p. 107). These are significant questions that geography teachers can reflect upon in their curriculum-making, and might be addressed in particular through engagement with the disciplinary dimension of geography.

Conclusion

Engaging with geography and geography education scholarship can contribute to the collective agency of geography teachers, through which beginning geography teachers can be empowered to draw upon the *reservoir* of practice found within the wider geography subject community. This chapter also recognises the importance of mentors and beginning teachers being able to engage with the broader domain of education, in terms of theory, research and practice, and the value of this engagement being shaped by a teacher's subject expertise. Priestley, Robinson and Biesta (2015), in their conceptualisation of teacher agency, propose that individuals' past experience enables them to achieve professional agency, and I have argued that individual teachers can benefit from the past experience found within their wider subject community (Healy, 2021b). Therefore, I propose that thinking explicitly about the role of geography and geography education scholarship can support beginning geography teachers' decision-making and empower future generations of geography teachers as professionals.

For discussion

- Reflect on any particular pieces of geography or geography education scholarship which may have empowered you in your own teaching and mentoring. How have you drawn on this to influence your practice?
- How do you model your own and colleagues' continued subject knowledge development to beginning teachers?
- In what ways could you engage beginning geography teachers with geography and geography education scholarship?

Notes

1. See Brooks (2010) for further discussion of the development of the Scholarship of Teaching and Learning from Higher Education and its applicability for geography teaching.
2. See both Brooks (2016) and Deng (2020) for a more detailed account of the issues that have then been raised around PCK.
3. For an in-depth exploration of GeoCapabilities see Bustin (2019).
4. See https://decolonisegeography.com for the Decolonising Geography Educators group's website.

Further reading and resources

1. Brooks, C., 2010. Developing and reflecting on subject expertise. In C. Brooks (ed), *Studying PGCE Geography at M Level: Reflection, research and writing for professional development*. Abingdon: Routledge, 66-76.

Clare Brooks' (2010) chapter examines the role of subject expertise more broadly for geography teachers and within the context of the planning and teaching of geography lessons. The chapter is written for beginning geography teachers, and so this is a chapter that might be useful to read with your mentee.

2. Catling, S., and Willy, T., 2018. *Understanding and Teaching Primary Geography*. 2nd edn. London: Sage.

This chapter has focussed on developing subject expertise and curriculum thinking within the secondary context; however, it can be beneficial for secondary geography teachers to engage with geography education scholarship that has focussed on primary geography. Catling and Willy's (2018) book provides a good starting point for anyone interested in such an endeavour.

3. Esson, J., and Last, A., 2019. Learning and teaching about race and racism in geography. In H Walkington, J. Hill and S. Dyer (eds), *Handbook for Teaching and Learning in Geography*. Cheltenham: Edward Elgar, 227-240.

This chapter establishes how learning and teaching about race and racism in academic geography can support understanding about racial inequality, and better equip geographers to understand how knowledge production perpetuates inequalities; you might want to consider the implications of this for your geography curriculum thinking and teaching.

References

Ali, R., 2020. Decolonising the geography curriculum WhatsApp group: Supporting geography teachers. *GA News*, 46(3), 14.
Anderson, B., and MacFarlane, C., 2011. Assemblage and geography. *Area*, 43, 124-127.
Biddulph, M., Lambert, D., and Balderstone, D., 2021. *Learning to Teach Geography in the Secondary School: A companion to school experience*. 4th edn. London: Routledge.
Bernstein, B., 1999. Horizontal and vertical discourse: An essay. *British Journal of Sociology of Education*, 20(2), 157-172.
Biesta, G. J. J., 2007. Why 'what works' still won't work: Evidence-based practice and the democratic deficit in educational research. *Educational Theory*, 57(1), 1-22.
Brooks, C., 2006. Geography teachers and making the school geography curriculum, *Geography*, 91(1), 75-83.
Brooks, C. 2007. Towards understanding the influence of subject knowledge in the practice of 'expert' geography teachers (PhD thesis). Institute of Education, University of London.
Brooks, C., 2010. Developing and reflecting on subject expertise. In C. Brooks (ed), *Studying PGCE Geography at M Level: Reflection, research and writing for professional development*. Abingdon: Routledge, 66-76.
Brooks, C., 2016. *Teacher Subject Identity in Professional Practice: Teaching with a professional compass*. Abingdon: Routledge.
Brooks, C., 2017. Pedagogy and identity in initial teacher education: Developing a professional compass. *Geography*, 102(1), 44-50.
Brooks, C., 2018. Understanding conceptual development in school geography. In M. Jones and D. Lambert (eds), *Debates in Geography Education*. 2nd edn. Abingdon: Routledge, 103-114.

Burn, K., 2007. Professional knowledge and identity in a contested discipline: Challenges for student teachers and teacher educators. *Oxford Review of Education*, 33(4), 445-467.

Burn, K., 2016. Sustaining the unresolving tensions within history education and teacher education. In C. Counsell, K. Burn and A. Chapman (eds), *MasterClass in History Education*. London: Bloomsbury, 233-242.

Burn, K., Childs, A., and McNicholl, J., 2007. The potential and challenges for student teachers' learning of subject-specific pedagogical knowledge within secondary school subject departments. *The Curriculum Journal*, 18(4), 429-445.

Bustin, R., 2011. The living city: Thirdspace and the contemporary geography curriculum. *Geography*, 96(2), 60-68.

Bustin, R., 2019. *Geography Education's Potential and the Capabilities Approach: GeoCapabilities and Schools*. Switzerland: Palgrave Macmillan.

Castree, N., and Lambert, D., 2007. Geography without borders. *Transactions of the Institute of British Geographers*, 32(2), 129-132.

Catling, S., and Martin, F., 2011. Contesting powerful knowledge: The primary geography curriculum as an articulation between academic and children's (ethno-) geographies. *The Curriculum Journal*, 22(3), 317-335.

Corbridge, A., and Hawley, D., 2020. 'Holding the line': A case study of the physical geography and coastal management of the Fylde coast. *Teaching Geography*, 45(2), 56-58.

Counsell, C., 2016. History teacher publication and the curricular 'What?': Mobilizing subject-specific professional knowledge in a culture of genericism. In C. Counsell, K. Burn and A. Chapman (eds), *MasterClass in History Education*. London: Bloomsbury, 243-252.

Cresswell, T., 2015. *Place: An Introduction*. 2nd edn. London: Wiley Blackwell.

Decolonise Geography, n.d. About. Decolonising Geography. Available at: https://decolonisegeography.com/about [accessed 10 April 2021].

Deleuze, G., and Guattari, F., 1987. *A Thousand Plateaus; Capitalism and Schizophrenia*. Minneapolis: University of Minnesota Press.

Deng, Z., 2020. *Knowledge, Content, Curriculum and Didaktik: Beyond Social Realism*. Abingdon: Routledge.

Department for Education [DfE], 2011. *Teachers' Standards: Effective from 1 September 2012*. London: DfE.

DfE, 2013. *Geography Programmes of Study Key Stage 3*. London: DfE.

DfE, 2014a. *Geography GCSE Subject Content*. London: DfE.

DfE, 2014b. *Geography GCE AS and A Level Subject Content*. London: DfE.

Ellis, V., 2007. *Subject Knowledge and teacher Education: The development of beginning teachers' thinking*. London: Continuum.

Esson, J., and Last, A., 2019. Learning and teaching about race and racism in geography. In H Walkington, J. Hill and S. Dyer (eds), *Handbook for Teaching and Learning in Geography*. Cheltenham, Edward Elgar, 227-240.

Esson, J., and Last, A., 2020. Anti-racist learning and teaching in British geography. *Area*, 52(4), 668-677.

Finn, M., Hammond, L., Healy, G., Todd, J., Marvell, A., McKendrick, J., and Yorke, L., 2021. Looking ahead to the future: key issues across the geography and education nexus. *Area*.

Firth, R., 2011. Debates about knowledge and the curriculum: Some implications for geography education. In G. Butt (ed), *Geography, Education and the Future*. London: Continuum, 141-164.

Firth, R., 2015. Constructing geographical knowledge. In G. Butt and S. Brindley (eds), *MasterClass in Geography Education: Transforming Teaching and Learning*. London: Bloomsbury, 53-66.

Fordham, M., 2016. Teachers and the academic disciplines. *Journal of Philosophy of Education*, 50(3), 419-431.

Geoghegen, H., Hall, S. M., Latham, A., and Leyland, J., 2020. Continuing conversations: Reflections on the role and future of Area from the new editorial team. *Area*, 52(3), 462–463.

Hammond, L., 2019. Utilising the 'production of space' to enhance young people's understanding of place. *Geography*, 104(1), 28–37.

Healy, G., 2018. Using local organisations and geographical scholarship to support A- level place studies. *Teaching Geography*, 43(1), 13–15.

Healy, G., 2019. Subject scholarship as a mechanism for developing trainees' reflective practice and teachers' curricular thinking. *Impact: Journal of the Chartered College of Teaching*, 6, 52–54.

Healy, G., 2021a. A call to view disciplinary knowledge through the lens of geography teachers' professional practice. In M. Fargher, D. Mitchell and E. Till (eds), *Recontextualising Geography in Education*. Cham, Switzerland: Springer, 71–88.

Healy, G., 2021b. Insights from professional discourse on GIS: a case for recognising geography teachers' repertoire of experience. In N. Walshe and G. Healy (eds), *Geography Education in the Digital World: Linking Theory and Practice*. London: Routledge, 89–101.

Hope, J., 2019. Why no change? Sustainable development, extractivism and the environment in Bolivia. Open University. Available at: www.open.ac.uk/ikd/blog/why-no-change-sustainable-development-extractivism-and-environment-bolivia [accessed 20 January 2021].

Hope, J., 2021. The anti-politics of sustainable development: Environmental critique from assemblage thinking in Bolivia. *Transactions of the Institute of British Geographers*, 46(1), 208–222.

Hordern, J., 2019. Exercise and intervention: On the sociology of powerful knowledge. *London Review of Education*, 17(1), 26–37.

Kinder, A., 2022. Mentoring within the geography subject community. In G. Healy, L. Hammond, S. Puttick and N. Walshe (eds), *Mentoring Geography Teachers in the Secondary School*. Abingdon: Routledge, 102–118.

Kennedy, C., 2011. Imagining distant places: Changing representations of Egypt. *Teaching Geography*, 36(2), 52–54.

Lambert, D., 2016. Geography. In D. Wyse, L. Hayward and J. Pandya (eds), *The Sage Handbook of Curriculum, Pedagogy and Assessment*. London: Sage, 391–407.

Lambert, D., 2018. Teaching as a research-engaged profession: Uncovering a blind spot and revealing new possibilities. *London Review of Education*, 16(3), 357–370.

Lambert, D., 2019. On the knotty question of 'Recontextualising' geography. *International Research in Geographical and Environmental Education*, 28(4), 257–261.

Lambert, D., and Biddulph, M., 2015. The dialogic space offered by curriculum-making in the process of learning to teach, and the creation of a progressive knowledge-led curriculum. *Asia-Pacific Journal of Teacher Education*, 43(3), 210–224.

Lambert, D., and Morgan, J., 2010. *Teaching Geography 11–18: A Conceptual Approach: A Conceptual Approach*. London: McGraw-Hill Education.

Lambert, D., and Walshe, N., 2018. How geography curricula tackle global issues. In A. Demirci, R. de Miguel González and S. W. Bednarz (eds), *Geography Education for Global Understanding*. Switzerland: Springer, 83–96.

Langdon, F., and Ward, L., 2015. Educative mentoring: A way forward. *International Journal of Mentoring and Coaching in Education*, 4(4), 240–254.

Lave, J., and Wenger, E., 1991. *Situated Learning: Legitimate Peripheral Participation*. New York: Cambridge University Press.

Matthews, A., 2020. It's virtually a glacier. *Teaching Geography*, 45(1), 34–36.

Maude, A., 2016. What might powerful geographical knowledge look like? *Geography*, 101(2), 70–76.

McEwan, H., and Bull, B., 1991. The pedagogical nature of subject matter knowledge. *American Educational Research Journal*, 28(2), 316-334

Milner, C., 2020. Classroom strategies for tackling the whiteness of geography. *Teaching Geography*, 45(3), 105-107.

Mitchell, D., 2017. Geography curriculum making in changing times (PhD thesis). University College London.

Mitchell, D., 2020. *Hyper-socialised: How Teachers Enact the Geography Curriculum in Late Capitalism*. Abingdon: Routledge.

Mitchell, D., and Lambert, D., 2015. Subject knowledge and teacher preparation in English secondary schools: the case of geography. *Teacher Development*, 19(3), 365-380.

Morgan, J., Hordern, J., and Hoadley, U., 2019. On the politics and ambition of the 'turn': Unpacking the relations between Future 1 and Future 3. *The Curriculum Journal*, 30(2), 105-124.

Murray, H., Burney, R., and Stacey-Chapman, A., 2013. Where's the other 'c'? Year 9 examine continuity in the treatment of mental health through time. *Teaching History*, 151, 45-54.

Noxolo, P., 2017. Introduction: Decolonising geographical knowledge in a colonised and re-colonising postcolonial world. *Area*, 49(3), 317-319.

Palombo, M., and Daly, C., 2022. Educative mentoring: A key to professional learning for geography teachers and mentors. In G. Healy, L. Hammond, S. Puttick and N. Walshe (eds), *Mentoring Geography Teachers in the Secondary School*. Abingdon: Routledge, 208-223.

Priestley, M., Biesta, G., and Robinson, S., 2015. *Teacher Agency: An Ecological Approach*. London: Bloomsbury.

Puttick, S., 2015. Geography teachers' subject knowledge: An ethnographic study of three secondary school geography departments (unpublished PhD thesis). University of Oxford.

Puttick, S., 2018. Student teachers' positionalities as knowers in school subject departments. *British Educational Research Journal*, 44(1), 25-42.

Puttick, S., 2020. Taking Burgess out of the bin. *Teaching Geography*, 45(1), 6-8.

Puttick, S., 2022. Lesson observations at the interface between research and practice. In G. Healy, L. Hammond, S. Puttick and N. Walshe (eds), *Mentoring Geography Teachers in the Secondary School:*. Abingdon: Routledge, 173-186.

Puttick, S., and Murrey, A., 2020. Confronting the deafening silence on race in geography education in England: Learning from anti-racist, decolonial and Black geographies. *Geography*, 105(3), 126-134.

Rawding, C., 2019. Putting Burgess in the bin. *Teaching Geography*, 44(3), 94-96.

Rawling, E., 2001. *Changing the Subject: The Impact of National Policy on School Geography 1980-2000*. Sheffield: Geographical Association.

Rawling, E., 2003. *Connecting Policy and Practice; Research in Geographical Education*, The BERA Professional User Review Series. British Educational Research Association.

Rawling, E., 2015. Spotlight on: Curriculum Change and examination reform for geography 14-19. *Geography*, 100(3), 164-167.

Rawling, E., 2016. The geography curriculum 5-19: What does it all mean? *Teaching Geography*, 41(1), 6-9.

Rawling, E., 2018a. Reflections on 'place'. *Teaching Geography*, 43(2), 55-58.

Rawling, E., 2018b. Place in geography: Change and challenge. In M. Jones and D. Lambert (eds), *Debates in Geography Education*. 2nd edn. Abingdon: Routledge, 49-61.

Rawling, E., 2020. How and why national curriculum frameworks are failing geography. *Geography*, 105(2), 69-77.

Roberts, M., 2014. Powerful knowledge and geographical education. *Curriculum Journal*, 25(2), 187-209.

Roberts, M., 2021. Geographical sources in the digital world. In N. Walshe and G. Healy (eds), *Geography Education in the Digital World: Linking Theory and Practice*. London: Routledge, 53-64.

Rose, G., 2020. Editorial introduction by Professor Gillian Rose: Diversity and Inclusion. *Routes*, 1(2), 138-141.

Royal Geographical Society [RGS], 2020. *The Geography of Geography Report*. London: RGS. Available at: www.rgs.org/geography/key-information-about-geography/geographyofgeography/report/geography-of-geography-report-web.pdf/ [accessed 20 January 2021].

Shulman, L. S., 1986. Those who understand: Knowledge growth in teaching. *Educational Researcher*, 15(2), 4-14.

Taylor, L., 2014. Diversity between and within: Approaches to teaching about distant place in the secondary school curriculum. *Journal of Curriculum Studies*, 46(2), 276-299.

Taylor, L., 2017. Handling heterogeneity in English geography textbooks 1850-2000. *Journal of Curriculum Studies*, 49(5), 683-702.

Trolley, S., 2020. Prisoners of geography? How contextualising a book can develop students' understandings of geography. *Teaching Geography*, 42(2), 72-74.

Tooth, S., and Viles, H. A., 2021. Equality, diversity, inclusion: Ensuring a resilient future for geomorphology. *Earth Surface Processes and Landforms*, 46(1), 5-11

Vernon, E., 2016. The structure of knowledge: Does theory matter? *Geography*, 101(2), 100-104.

Walford, R., 1996. 'What is geography?' An analysis of definitions provided by prospective teachers of the subject. *International Research in Geographical and Environmental Education*, 5(1), 69-76.

Walshe, N., 2007. Understanding teachers' conceptualisations of geography. *International Research in Geographical & Environmental Education*, 16(2), 97-119.

Winter, C., 2012. Enframing geography: Subject, curriculum, knowledge, responsibility. *Ethics and Education*, 7(3), 277-290.

Winter, C., 2018. Disrupting colonial discourses in the geography curriculum during the introduction of British Values policy in schools. *Journal of Curriculum Studies*, 50(4), 456-475.

Young, M., 2009. What are schools for? In H. Daniels, H. Lauder and J. Porter (eds), *Knowledge, Values and Educational Policy: A Critical Perspective*. London: Routledge, 10-18.

Young, M., 2011. Discussion to Part 3. In G. Butt (ed), *Geography, Education and the Future*. London: Continuum, 181-183.

Young, M., 2020. From powerful knowledge to the powers of knowledge. In C. Sealy (ed), *The ResearchED Guide to The Curriculum*. Woodbridge: John Catt, 13-17.

Young, M., and Muller, J., 2010. Three educational scenarios for the future: Lessons from the sociology of knowledge. *European Journal of Education*, 45(1), 11-26.

14 Educative mentoring
A key to professional learning for geography teachers and mentors

Maria Palombo and Caroline Daly

Introduction

Educative mentoring is argued in this chapter to be a core professional practice, one that enables the beginning teacher and the mentor to benefit from sustained collaboration in which both parties learn. Mentoring that is *educative* is a professional practice for both participants, set within an overall vision of effective teaching and learning. It therefore rejects *quick-fix* or solution-focussed strategies that are frequently based on the mentor passing on knowledge about 'how things are done' (Daly and Milton, 2017, p. 182) in particular geography classrooms. It is linked to a 'vision of good teaching and a developmental view of learning to teach' (Norman and Feiman-Nemser, 2005, p. 680). This makes it distinctive from mentoring approaches linked to psychological support and technical advice, as described by Wang and Odell (2002). The practice-focussed needs of beginning teachers are met by establishing a set of professional habits that emphasise they are *professional learners* alongside their mentor – and develop through shared enquiry approaches to developing as a teacher. Educative mentoring is based on the belief that both mentees *and* mentors deepen their professional knowledge and practice through shared, critical thinking about how to respond to learners' needs and the demands of learning in the subject. In analysing the benefits of educative mentoring, Langdon (2017, p. 531) argues that

> a collaborative self-development approach is likely to produce and reproduce teachers who understand that they, alongside their colleagues, are able to draw on their own and others' expertise to improve their practice throughout their careers.

In the discussion below, we begin by outlining the principles that underpin educative mentoring practices. Three common tasks completed by a geography mentor and beginning teacher are then explored through an educative mentoring lens. These practical examples suggest ways in which geography mentors can practise educative mentoring to develop collaborative planning, observation and post-lesson dialogue, and collaborative marking. We suggest how such an approach can support the career-long development of geography teachers.

What are the underpinning principles and characteristics of educative mentoring?

Ultimately, educative mentoring (like any mentoring process) aims to continuously improve learning for all pupils in the classroom. Figure 14.1 presents a model of the underpinning principles and characteristics of educative mentoring, demonstrating its inter-related components that sit within a vision of good teaching and learning that is jointly developed between mentor and mentee.

The model positions all teachers as learners within the classroom, including both you and the beginning teacher. Rather than an expert-novice relationship, there is a focus on a collaborative learning process.

Teachers as learners

At the heart of the process of educative mentoring is shared exploration of questions that develop practice, whereby both practitioners view the classroom as a site of enquiry (Norman and Feiman-Nemser, 2005). In viewing the classroom in this way and seeing the mentor-beginning teacher relationship as dynamic, both parties become involved in actively problematising everyday events and actions involved in teaching. They aim to build 'knowledge-of-practice' (Cochran-Smith and Lytle, 1999):

> implicit in the idea of knowledge-of-practice is the assumption that, through inquiry, teachers across the professional life span – from very new to very experienced – make problematic their own knowledge and practice as well as the knowledge and practice of others and thus stand in a different relationship to knowledge.
>
> (p. 273)

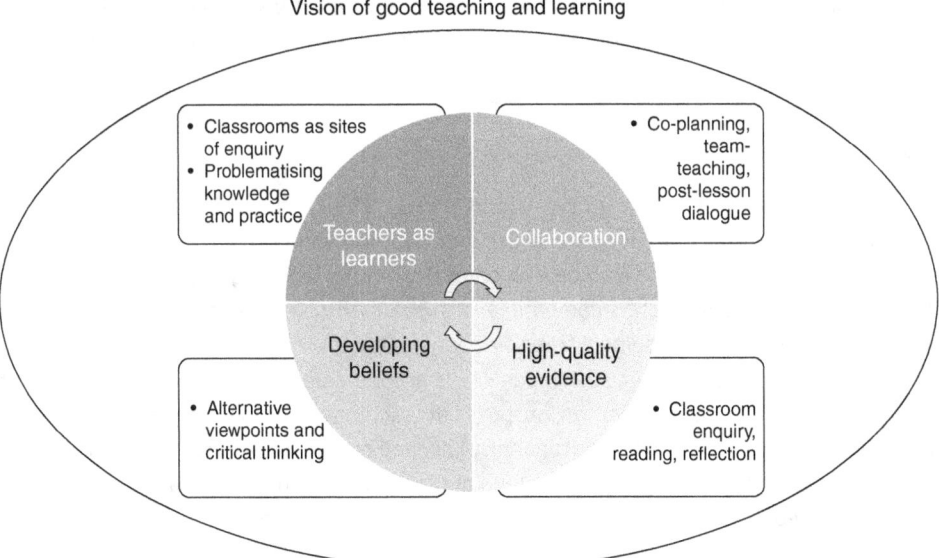

Figure 14.1 Underpinning principles and characteristics of educative mentoring

This represents teacher knowledge and practice as ongoing and continuously developing. It is different from 'knowledge-*for*-practice', where knowledge that has been generated elsewhere (such as through external research) is studied and applied. It is also different from knowledge-*in*-practice, where teachers build their knowledge from experience, observations and trial and error.

Collaboration

Knowledge-*of*-practice situates teachers as continuous learners, collaborating with others as co-learners and co-thinkers, working towards a vision of good teaching and learning (Cochran-Smith and Lytle, 1999; Langdon and Ward, 2015). Through the adoption of *inquiry-as-stance* (Cochran-Smith and Lytle, 2009) both the beginning teacher and the mentor are able to challenge assumptions about the norms of teaching and learning within their context, and in wider education (Daly and Milton, 2017). Collaboration is at the heart of unravelling problems of practice that face the beginning teacher and are relevant to all teachers. The quality and focus of mentoring dialogue are of critical importance here, focussed around specific collaborative practices that can involve co-planning, team teaching and post-lesson dialogue for example.

Generating high-quality evidence

The classroom as a site of enquiry can provide rich and meaningful evidence of pupil learning, as a core way of understanding the effects of pedagogical approaches and learning activities that are being tried out by mentees. Examples of this include: building case studies of how individuals or groups of pupils respond to particular teaching approaches in the beginning teacher classroom; observation of pupil learning by the mentor/mentee during team teaching episodes; gathering pupil views on aspects of the geography curriculum to inform planning to teach; and capturing beginning teacher reflection within post-lesson mentor dialogue.

Developing beliefs

Educative mentoring contrasts with an *expert-novice* relationship which may influence the beginning teacher to simply reproduce existing practice embodied by the mentor, rather than developing a thoughtful, nuanced vision of geography teaching that is developmental. This developmental approach is compatible with the mentor modelling effective practices for beginning teachers and demonstrating a range of established approaches to geography teaching and learning. However, such modelling is accompanied by critical reasoning by both parties, based on discussion about the purposes of teaching geography and the needs of specific pupils in particular classrooms, frequently linked to reading research. Beginning teachers need to locate the mentor's style of teaching and common features of established practices within wider debates about effective geography teaching (Tapsfield, 2019). Therefore, post-lesson dialogue and the ability of the mentor to articulate the thinking and reasoning behind pedagogical and curriculum decisions are important. It opens discussion about the principles and beliefs underpinning the choices made. This works both ways. Through mentor dialogue, the beginning teacher learns to articulate their reasoning for curriculum and pedagogical decisions and the changing understanding on which they are based.

Mentoring within an expansive learning environment

The educative mentoring relationship described here would be supported by cultural norms being present in a school, such as habits of open questioning, building curiosity about how pupils learn, and encouraging risk-taking as a joint endeavour among staff. Hodkinson's (2009) research in secondary schools identified features of *expansive* and *restrictive* environments for teachers' development, adapted from Fuller and Unwin's (2003) study of workplace learning (see Table 14.1).

Expansive environments are those which support the learning of all practitioners, recognising that collaboration is key. For mentors to be able to initiate and maintain educative mentoring relationships, the features of an expansive school workplace environment are essential. These affect the mentor's self-perception of what it means to be a learner as an experienced teacher. Expansive environments support teachers' development of enquiry approaches that enable them to question existing beliefs about how geography is taught and how pupils are experiencing it. In other words, educative mentoring can be unsettling. Indeed, it should be, because it supports the possibility of transformational professional learning, by which individual beliefs can shift and inform continually evolving practice. *Adaptive expertise* is identified as an advanced professional attribute among educative mentors (Langdon, 2017). It is the capacity to continually scrutinise

Table 14.1 Expansive-restrictive learning environments for teachers

Expansive	Restrictive
Close collaborative working	Isolated, individualist working
Colleagues mutually supportive of learning	Colleagues obstruct or do not support each other's learning
An explicit focus on learning as a dimension of normal working practices	No explicit focus on teacher learning, except to meet crises or imposed initiatives
Supported opportunities for personal development that goes beyond school or government priorities	Teacher learning mainly strategic compliance with government or school agendas
Out of school educational opportunities including time to stand back, reflect and think differently	Few out of school educational opportunities, only narrow, short training programmes
Opportunities to integrate off-site learning into everyday practice	No opportunity to integrate off-the-job learning
Opportunity to extend professional identity through boundary crossing into other departments, school activities, schools and beyond	Work restricted to home departmental team within one school. Opportunities for boundary crossing only come with a job changes
Support for local variation in ways of working and learning for teachers and work groups	Standardized approaches to teacher learning are prescribed and imposed
Teachers use a wide range of learning opportunities	Teachers use a narrow range of learning approaches

Source: Hodkinson, 2009, p. 165. Reproduced by permission of Taylor & Francis Group from: *Changing Teacher Professionalism*, by H. Hodkinson, Edited by S. Gewirtz, P. Mahony, I. Hextall and A. Cribb. Copyright (2009) by Routledge.

routines and behaviours in one's own teaching and to seek information on which to base new alternatives (Timperley, 2011). Adaptive experts are able to respond to situations where practice can be enhanced and are open to change. Such expertise is supported by a school environment in which it is safe to question existing routines and to seek new ways of working, based on rich evidence generated with the beginning teacher in the classroom, as well as found in external sources. It is clear that school leadership plays a vital role in creating the conditions that support educative mentoring. Educative mentoring can thrive in schools that function as effective learning communities, in which enquiry into practice is the norm and adaptive expertise is recognised as a key to effective teaching.

Educative mentoring in geography

This section aims to illustrate how educative mentoring might be approached in geography mentoring of beginning teachers. It draws on typical tasks that the beginning teacher and mentor are likely to carry out: collaborative planning, observations linked to post-lesson dialogue, and collaborative marking.

Collaborative planning

Planning is a central task for the beginning teacher and is essential to supporting pupils' geographical understanding and progress. The beginning teacher should consider individual lesson planning, but it is also important that they consider progress of pupils across sequences of lessons, and how these sequences build geographical knowledge and understanding across the geography curriculum. The topic *development*, a geographical concept that is often taught in the UK as it is featured in the Key Stage 3 National Curriculum (DFE, 2013), as well as in GCSE and A-level specifications (DFE, 2014a; 2014b), is used here to demonstrate how planning might be approached. The focus is on collaboration, situating the mentor and beginning teacher as co-thinkers, rather than the mentor checking and approving a lesson plan or scheme of work.

Development is a contested concept in geography, in the sense that it has been politicised in the past and continues to be a concept which is discussed in the academy and school geography (Lambert and Morgan, 2010). Much of the discussion is around the representations of different places, the ways in which development is taught in school geography, sometimes using a moralistic perspective, and how different geographical perspectives can support pupil understanding, enabling them to take a more critical view of the world (Standish, 2018; 2020; Willis, 2014). Lambert and Morgan (2010) put forward the argument that, drawing on the concept of interdependence, the nature of connections and relationships between people and places can broaden 'traditional and sometimes tired notions of "development" in the geography curriculum' (p. 108). Standish (2020) argues that teaching needs to move beyond, and away from, binary and reductionist notions of development. The Black Lives Matter movement and calls to decolonise the curriculum have increased awareness of the responsibilities of geography teachers to draw from a diverse range of perspectives, such as indigenous geographies, and question the structure of geographical knowledge which can be viewed as colonial control within the discipline (Clement, 2019; Barker and Pickerill, 2020).

These discussions indicate the dilemmas and professional learning opportunities for you and the beginning teacher in planning to teach this topic in the beginning teacher's classroom.

It is likely that your geography department in school will have a set of resources and a scheme of work or curriculum plan, outlining the content and skills to be taught in a unit about or incorporating development, with potential activities for teaching. A useful starting point would be for you and the beginning teacher to spend some time reviewing and discussing the materials, potentially problematising the plans and the resources, based on questions that explore the purpose of the curriculum and the ways in which pupils are able to make sense of the geography.

As co-thinkers and collaborators, both you and the beginning teacher can share your current understandings in order to construct the curriculum and then enact it. A useful way to frame the co-planning discussion would be to draw on the well-established curriculum-making model (Lambert and Biddulph, 2015) that enables us to consider the geography, the pedagogy and the student experience, represented as three sources of energy. By balancing these three sources of energy, curriculum-making supports pupils to think geographically, taking them beyond what they already know, and ensuring that learning is underpinned by key geographical concepts. It ensures that pupil knowledge and prior experience are considered carefully, whilst ensuring that geographical knowledge and understanding are central – pupils are not considered to be passive recipients. Such a model can ensure that co-planning is focussed on developing a shared vision of high-quality teaching and learning.

Using the curriculum-making model as a framework, the following questions can be considered as a basis for collaborative planning. These questions are illustrative and there is likely to be a wide range that you might discuss.

- What is development?

This is an essential starting point, linking to the academic discipline and the school geography elements of the curriculum-making model. By discussing understandings of a contested concept in geography education, both you and the beginning teacher are able to consider your own perspectives and agree on the ideas that can form a shared, inclusive vision of the curriculum. This is important to the development of beginning teachers of geography and a vital part of formulating a professional view of the purpose of geography education. In a beginning teacher's early stage of learning, demonstrating high expectations that teaching geography is an ongoing exploration of the subject helps to create an expansive environment (Table 14.1), normalising discussions focussed on the geography being taught and the pedagogical approaches to best support pupil learning. It also reiterates the importance of subject specialist knowledge and understanding in planning a unit, considering deeply the purpose of the subject matter and problematising that knowledge. In this instance, there might be discussions about the different perspectives on development such as postcolonial perspectives of development and criticisms of this (Nash, 2002), indigenous knowledge and the positionality of geographers in relation to this (Radcliffe, 2017; Briggs, 2013) and critical viewpoints of post-millennium development goals (Enns et al., 2014; Radcliffe, 2020). A beginning teacher will very likely have more recent engagement with the subject matter in academia, through either university studies or teacher education programmes, enabling deep discussions about the geography in the curriculum, considering how development is constructed for the teachers as well as pupils. Their knowledge of geography positions them as a valued participant in such a conversation, with the capacity to bring new or challenging insights to what has been formalised within particular geography departments. This educative focus for mentor dialogue can enable alternative perspectives (Figure 14.1) on what constitutes an aspect of the geography curriculum – it is essential that these are discussed as a basis for planning what pupils are to learn.

- What are the possible geographical imaginations that pupils bring to the classroom about development?

The term 'geographical imaginations' is used here to consider the knowledge and understandings that pupils bring to the classroom derived from media and popular culture. Very often these imaginations can be thought of as common sense, although might hide a multitude of assumptions (Gregory, 1994; Massey, 2005). These might also be based on their own direct experiences, such as family links with other countries or holidays. Utilising the curriculum-making model to structure the discussion, it is important to consider what pupils might already know, and the impact of this knowledge or geographical imagination on how pupils make sense of the geography within the lesson and wider unit. Here you are able to draw on your own experience of teaching pupils, to highlight misconceptions such as homogeneous and binary understandings of a place being poor or rich, developed or underdeveloped. The beginning teacher will be able to bring their own encounters with such misconceptions to the conversation. Further discussion might consider the representations across wider curricula which reinforce or challenge such misconceptions, examining the complex web of ideas that pupils bring to the geography classroom and which teachers need to explore with them. You and the beginning teacher can thus draw on the observations and reflections, as well as wider experiences, to co-construct your knowledge and understanding to build knowledge-*of*-practice.

- What pedagogical approaches can be tried?

Decisions of pedagogy must be in relation to the above questions about what is being taught, the prior knowledge of pupils and the overall purpose of the unit. If you and the beginning teacher are aiming to introduce alternative perspectives on development, enquiry-based learning approaches might be appropriate, enabling pupils to utilise a range of geographical data to reach an informed conclusion (Roberts, 2013). However, further discussion might be had about presenting development as a solution-focussed issue, situating places through a Western perspective of development mainly focussed on economic progress and drives to modernity. For example, decision-making activities, such as those featured in GCSE (General Certificate of Secondary Education) exams where pupils need to justify a particular decision in relation to a given issue, can allow pupils to demonstrate deep geographical thinking.[1] This can also, however, present development as a problem to be solved, consisting of people that need help. Even where small-scale, locally driven development projects are studied, there is a Western perspective that might need to be deconstructed, alongside the prominence of indigenous geographies (Briggs, 2013). Such reflections would directly impact on the types of activities planned, linking the geographical knowledge and the pedagogical decisions. There are no easy answers – that is at the heart of educative mentoring – but such discussions bring benefits for the mentor, beginning teacher and pupil learning.

The next step might be the construction of a sequence of lessons, either in the form of an overall plan or as a set of lesson plans. An educative mentor does not take 'the more traditional mentoring strategy of correcting and approving lesson plans' (Barnett and Friedrichsen, 2015, p. 655). Instead, there should be encouragement to discuss the rationale behind pedagogical decisions, talking through the plans and engaging in further co-construction.

As a result of this enquiry, a focus can be arrived at for the beginning teacher to observe your teaching, arising from questions of how a critical view of the world can be developed through a particular activity. A next step might be asking the beginning teacher to conduct a focussed observation of your lesson, based on identifying the choices made by the teacher and the pupils' responses. This is a good opportunity for the beginning teacher to begin to link their subject knowledge of development to the pedagogical knowledge employed in the classroom. It situates the classroom as a site of enquiry from the outset, problematising practice with a focus on how mentees perceive the pupils are learning about development. This provides a platform for the beginning teacher to contribute to a conversation about teaching the topic, drawing on observations of pupil learning. It provides a perspective that is informed by careful noting of which issues arise in the mentor's teaching. Such a conversation will allow both you and the beginning teacher to discuss and formulate your vision of what good teaching and learning within such a unit can look like. You are able to reflect on your experiences of teaching this topic, allowing you to deconstruct practice and highlight potential misconceptions that have previously come to light, as well as the particularly effective elements of the unit. In doing so, you are modelling reflective practice, but you also need to invite ideas and considerations from the beginning teacher, which, in turn, develops their own practice.

Such steps in educative mentoring are not exclusive to the example of development. Following from co-planning, ideally there would be the opportunity to team teach. This allows both you and the beginning teacher to experience the planning and teaching processes together, and share reflections on practice and pupil learning, thereby co-constructing 'knowledge-*of*-practice'.

Task 14.1 Enquiring into teaching about 'development': an educative mentoring approach

Look at the curriculum content and teaching materials provided by your geography department to teach *development* at Key Stage (KS) 3 or KS4. Design a series of questions that you can use to guide a mentoring conversation with your mentee. Ask your mentee to read the same materials beforehand and think of their own questions about teaching this topic.

Your questions might include:

- What view(s) of development do you think is represented in the materials we use in the department? Which materials suggest that and why?
- How do these ideas compare with how you learned about development at school?
- Is there anything here that is included or left out that surprises you?
- Why do you think development is considered to be such an important focus in the geography curriculum? What is your view on that?
- Which pupil learning activities do you find interesting or challenging? What could you find out about that, through observation?

Following your mentor dialogue about the materials, reflect together on similarities and contrasts in mentor/mentee questions about teaching development and use this to inform shared goals for the beginning teacher as they teach this unit.

These kinds of questions can be applied to any geography topic that your mentee will be expected to teach.

Observations and post-lesson dialogue

Lesson observation is recognised as a common strategy to enable the mentor to understand the educational practices of the beginning teacher (Wang et al., 2008; Healy et al., 2020; Puttick and Warren-Lee, 2020). A key feature of lesson observation is the feedback provided to the beginning teacher after an observation has taken place. However, this can be problematic, as noted by Hobson and Malderez (2013), who coined the phrase *judgementoring* in order to demonstrate how this practice can inhibit learning opportunities for beginning teachers – and for mentors.

> Judgementoring is perhaps most visible in the frequent use by mentors of a restrictive "feedback" strategy in post-lesson discussions, typically involving a mentor-led evaluation of the "positive" then "negative" features of a lesson, followed by suggestions for improvement.
>
> (Hobson and Malderez, 2013, p. 95)

Within educative mentoring, this feedback might be renamed a *learning conversation* or *post-lesson dialogue*, in order to shift the emphasis from the expert-novice dynamic to a learning opportunity for both parties. This is exemplified in Hodkinson's (2009) *expansive* school environment, allowing ideas to be discussed and encouraging mutual teacher learning.

Observation of a beginning teacher should be discussed beforehand to identify a clear focus for what is to be observed. This is another opportunity, before the observation takes place, for the beginning teacher to reflect on their practice and current understanding of how pupils learn geography. This should not be based around competencies or the performance of the beginning teacher as such. Norman and Feiman-Nemser (2005) argued that the focus of observations should be on pupil learning and understanding, summarising an argument from Dewey (1904/1965):

When observing an experienced teacher, for example, novices should not focus on the teacher's behaviour in order to 'accumulate a store of methods'. Rather they should pay close attention to the way students make sense of what they are studying.

(p. 680)

Focussed observations of the beginning teacher can draw on evidence of how pupils are making sense of the geography in the lesson, using either examples of work or observations of pupils during the lesson and their responses to the teaching. This can build up rich evidence of learning that can be analysed in the post-lesson dialogue. Stanulis et al. (2019) describe this as 'getting rid of the kitchen sink to focus on one aspect of effective teaching' (p. 574).

Post-lesson dialogue is far more effective if it is focussed on a worthwhile longer-term goal which can provide an educative foundation for specific adjustments to practice. An educative goal might be for the beginning teacher to deepen their understanding of the role of prior knowledge in pupils' learning in geography, learning how to explore this and current (mis)conceptions. It may be helpful to identify such a goal as an enquiry question that is explored through the beginning teacher's lesson. An enquiry question is one that requires deep consideration, is explored by using a range of evidence within the lesson, and is not focussed on simple solutions or finding easy answers. It helps to unravel the complexities of practice, always feeding into ongoing development. Most enquiry questions are never answered fully – they go on informing practice over time. They are questions that you might ask of your own practice, as well as the beginning teacher's practice.

During the lesson you should observe the pupils – their spoken and non-spoken reactions, responses to questions, levels of engagement and evidence of learning, in line with the focus/ enquiry question agreed beforehand. In the geography classroom, evidence of learning can be elicited in a variety of ways; pupils' writing, responses to teacher questioning, discussion with peers, labelled or annotated diagrams, maps, sorting activities and a range of other means. As the observer, you need to consider the extent to which pupils are making sense of the geography. This does not take the form of the mentor sitting at the back of the classroom taking notes. Instead, you get involved with the pupils, ask them questions about what they think they are doing, and look carefully at the activities they are working on and how well they are making sense of the geography. This can produce a range of reflections from you, which supports post-lesson dialogue based on insights into the pupils' learning. The collection of this rich evidence might be in the form of notes about pupils, observations about their responses, questions they ask and specific pieces of work.

The evidence supports the beginning teacher to reflect on the lesson in a critical way, possibly compiling further notes, using the focus of the observation as a central theme. Post-lesson dialogue becomes an opportunity for you and the beginning teacher to co-construct knowledge of how pupils learn in the geography classroom. You both bring a perspective to the dialogue, rooted within knowledge-*of*-practice. Within this dialogue, you should avoid offering simple advice such as 'I would have done it this way…'. Instead, the dialogue can focus on the evidence gathered, and how it demonstrates the relationship between the teaching behaviours of the beginning teacher and the pupils' learning. This allows you and the beginning teacher to maintain the relationship of collaborators and co-thinkers, building knowledge and understanding for both.

Task 14.2 Observing a lesson: using the classroom as a site of enquiry

The questions below are examples that could be used an as enquiry question in a focussed observation of a geography lesson.

- How is prior knowledge of pupils built upon in the lesson? Are pupils enabled to voice their perspectives in a constructive environment that allows them to be challenged and built upon?
- How does questioning support pupils in understanding the geography?
- How engaged are pupils? What helps engagement for all?
- How are learners' needs met? Are pupils able to engage with the geography in a way that is meaningful for them?
- How do we really know if pupils have achieved the lesson objectives? How reliable is the evidence of learning?
- How is formative assessment used to help the teacher (and pupils) to gain an understanding of pupils' learning?
- How are pupils given the opportunity to make sense of the geography?

This list is not exhaustive and the focus of the observation may require different questions. The key element of the observation should be a focus on pupil learning, leading to a discussion in the post-lesson dialogue which unpicks the rich evidence generated through the observation.

During the lesson observation, move around the room and look carefully at how pupils are responding to the teaching. Talk to the pupils about their learning, ask them to share what they are learning with you. Look at the evidence of learning, whether written or verbal. After the lesson observation, take some time to reflect on the learning that you observed and write some reflection notes, linking to the focus enquiry question that was agreed with the beginning teacher. The beginning teacher should also complete a reflection on pupil learning in the same way.

The post-lesson dialogue provides an opportunity for the mentor and beginning teacher to share their perspectives on the learning that has taken place in the lesson, and generate future questions. A possible structure for this might be:

1. Sharing reflections on pupil learning linked to the agreed enquiry question.
2. Examine the evidence of learning – through discussion of pupil responses and written work. What did the pupils learn? How reliable is the evidence of learning?
3. What is the relationship between the beginning teacher's decisions and the pupil learning?
4. What are the potential answers to the enquiry question?
5. What other questions about practice have been generated through the post-lesson dialogue? Which of these should be focussed on in order to best support pupils' geographical learning?

Collaborative marking

Marking pupil work in a collaborative way allows the beginning teacher to consider the impact of their teaching on pupil understanding. Equally important, they learn how to respond effectively to pupils' work in a variety of ways, in order to support further learning. It is also an opportunity for the mentor to consider the quality of the work being assessed, refine their own assessment skills, and consider the assessment practice that best supports learning. We use an example of a year 8 piece of assessed work, worth six marks in a test, in order to demonstrate how collaborative marking can be an educative mentoring strategy (see Figure 14.2).

Mentoring around this piece of work might inevitably feature many aspects of an expert-novice relationship, with the mentor holding the 'answers' to how to apply a particular mark scheme fairly and consistently. Collaborative marking, however, can have multiple foci. It can be a learning opportunity for both, analysing whether desired outcomes from the unit are evidenced, where any misconceptions may still exist, and considering the impacts of curriculum and pedagogical choices made by the teacher on pupils' learning. This is about how the mentor and mentee establish an *educative* agenda for their meeting to discuss *marking*. Crucially, collaborative marking should *feed forward* into future practice.

The example in Figure 14.2 is from a pupil described as *high prior attaining*. The evidence of geographical understanding that it provides at the end of a unit on rivers can stimulate a number of discussions between the mentor and beginning teacher. However, shorter non-assessed pieces of work might also be used in the same way, and these might come at any point in a sequence of lessons. This process can also be used in line with the post-lesson dialogue after an observation, when focussing on rich evidence of pupil learning.

With reference to a place you have studied, explain how human activity can increase the risk of flooding.

Due to developments in infrastructure, cities and town, humans may cover over large amounts of ground with concrete, a process known as concreting. Concreting increases surface run off, whilst decreasing infiltration in a particular area. Precipitation will then begin to fill drains and build up in puddles on top of the concrete, which may lead to flooding.

Furthermore, another common human activity is cutting down trees, a process called deforestation, which effectively catch water on their leaves and branches. Transpiration, water catching on plants and evaporating, then occurs. However, when trees and other plants are removed for structural development, the precipitation can infiltrate the surface of the ground and this can lead to more surface run off, which may lead to flooding.

Figure 14.2 An example of a year 8 response to an exam-style question, at the end of a unit on rivers

Stanulis et al. (2019) reported that mentors adopting educative mentoring strategies found that analysis of pupil work led to beginning teachers reflecting more deeply on their teaching, as opposed to blaming pupils for poor behaviour or lack of effort. The pupils' writing in Figure 14.2 demonstrates some understanding of human activity that can increase the risk of flooding, but this is presented in an abstract way, without the contextual example of a place that has been studied. This might be attributed to pupils forgetting to support their answers, or possibly not paying attention to instructions, despite it being explicit in the question. However, comparison with other pupil responses might identify whether this as a wider issue, thereby focussing the beginning teacher on how they can develop their teaching in order to support pupil learning rather than adopting a deficit view of the pupils. The inclusion of real places in geography lessons supports pupils' contextual knowledge, whilst also enabling them to deepen their understanding of geographical concepts. Analytical discussion of pupil work allows the beginning teacher to reflect on where they have introduced contextual examples, and how activities in the classroom may have supported pupils in using examples in their geographical writing. This is also a learning opportunity for the mentor to reconsider routinised assessment practice, evaluating how this is supporting pupil learning and how far assessment formats are constructed in a way which allows pupils to demonstrate their geographical understanding.

Figure 14.2 also highlights the pupil's use of some key terms related to a drainage basin system, such as *infiltration* and *surface run off*. However, the pupil has not clearly made the link between the increased surface run off and the impact on river levels. Discussion between you and the beginning teacher can open up potential reasons for the gaps in knowledge and understanding presented here. These might be related to the way in which the curriculum is sequenced or the focus of the learning activities. For example, the inclusion of the geographical terms in the pupil work demonstrates that geographical vocabulary has been picked up and is mostly being applied correctly. However, the lack of connection between the processes and the impacts on a river might be due to a lack of linking the processes to a real flood event, restricting opportunities for pupils to apply their understanding to the real world. Is it possible that the case study of flooding used in the unit did not emphasise the link to the processes that had been studied previously?

A mentor conversation based on collaborative marking goes beyond applying a mark scheme and generates further enquiry questions to be used by you and the beginning teacher. Mentor dialogue can probe into the content of the unit and how key concepts such as flooding are presented and taught, possibly seeking further guidance in research and literature. Such discussions between you and the beginning teacher are not only useful in demonstrating how to effectively use evidence of pupil learning to consider next steps in teaching, but are also powerful for the department in thinking about potential curriculum changes and how these might be put in place over the longer term. This allows for both you and the beginning teacher to continue to construct knowledge-*of*-practice, drawing on viewpoints from the geography discipline, as well as providing the opportunity to consider pedagogy. This is not a conversation that waits until beginning teachers are *competent*. It is the means by which they develop collaborative, enquiring habits that are essential to learning how to become a principled and knowledgeable professional.

Conclusion

The principles and characteristics of educative mentoring discussed in this chapter underpin the continual development of adaptive expertise, for both the mentor and beginning teacher. The practical examples demonstrate how educative mentoring can be used within activities that are part of many teacher education programmes, as well as whole school systems; for example, see Gu et al.'s (2018) analysis of collaborative planning as professional development within schools. In this way, educative mentoring is not seen as an approach to mentoring only beginning teachers. It can foster a professional learning community within and across departments and across schools, enabling mentors to build skills that can continue to improve the effectiveness of curriculum and pedagogy, with pupil learning at its heart. The model of educative mentoring presented in Figure 14.1 might also be used in co-constructing knowledge-*of*-practice when used as a reference point for beginning teachers' journal entries, discussing specific developmental areas, such as inclusion, or within regular mentor meetings. Educative mentoring is necessarily unsettling of taken-for-granted ways of doing things. By disrupting traditional expert-novice mentoring relationships, it has the potential to offer transformative learning experiences for both you and the beginning teacher.

For discussion

- What have you learned about teaching and learning through your mentoring role? How did this come about?
- Is your school environment and geography department mostly expansive or restrictive? How do you know this and what changes might be put in place to allow educative mentoring to take place?
- Other than the suggestions in this chapter, how else might you use the classroom as a site of enquiry?

Note

1. For an example of this, see AQA GCSE Geography Paper 3 – Sample Set 1, available at https://filestore.aqa.org.uk/resources/geography/AQA-80353-SQP.PDF.

Further reading and resources

1. Langdon, F., and Ward, L., 2015. Educative mentoring: A way forward. *International Journal of Mentoring and Coaching in Education*, 4(4), 240–254.

For an overview of educative mentoring, and the theory that underpins it, this article provides an outline of the knowledge, attitudes and skills required of an educative mentor. This is useful to consider your mentoring approach currently and the key changes needed to make it more educative.

2. Stanulis, R. N., Wexler, L. J., Pylman, S., Guenther, A., Farver, S., Ward, A., Croel-Perrien, A., and White, K., 2019. Mentoring as more than "cheerleading": Looking at educative mentoring practices through mentors' eyes. *Journal of Teacher Education*, 70(5), 567–580.

To consider how educative mentoring changes practice from the perspective of mentors, this article provides case studies with specific changes to mentor practice, outlining the benefits to beginning teachers, mentors and pupils. This is a useful article to consider specific practice-based changes in mentoring.

References

Barker, A., and Pickerill, J., 2020. Doings with the land and sea: Decolonising geographies, Indigeneity, and enacting place-agency. *Progress in Human Geography*, 44(4), 640-662.

Barnett, E., and Friedrichsen, P., 2015. Educative mentoring: How a mentor supported a preservice biology teacher's pedagogical content knowledge development. *Journal of Science Teacher Education*, 26(3), 647-668.

Briggs, J., 2013. Indigenous knowledge: A false dawn for development theory and practice? *Progress in Development Studies*, 13(3), 231-243.

Clement, V., 2019. Beyond the sham of the emancipatory Enlightenment: Rethinking the relationship of Indigenous epistemologies, knowledges, and geography through decolonizing paths. *Progress in Human Geography*, 43(2), 276-294.

Cochran-Smith, M., and Lytle, S., 1999. Relationships of knowledge and practice: Teacher learning in communities. *Review of Educational Research in Education*, 24(7), 249-305.

Cochran-Smith, M., and Lytle, S., 2009. *Inquiry as Stance: Practitioner Research in the Next Generation*. New York: Teachers College Press.

Daly, C., and Milton, E., 2017. External mentoring for new teachers: Mentor learning for a change agenda. *International Journal of Mentoring and Coaching*, 6(3), 178-195.

DfE, 2013, Geography programmes of study key stage 3. Available at: https://assets.publishing.service.gov.uk/government/uploads/system/uploads/attachment_data/file/239087/SECONDARY_national_curriculum_-_Geography.pdf [accessed 20 January 2021].

DfE, 2014a. Geography GCSE subject content. Available at: https://assets.publishing.service.gov.uk/government/uploads/system/uploads/attachment_data/file/301253/GCSE_geography.pdf [accessed 20 January 2021].

DfE, 2014b. Geography GCE AS and A Level subject content. Available at: https://assets.publishing.service.gov.uk/government/uploads/system/uploads/attachment_data/file/388857/GCE_AS_and_A_level_subject_content_for_geography.pdf [accessed 20 January 2020].

Dewey, J., 1904/1965. The relation of theory to practice in education. In R. D. Archambault (ed), *John Dewey on Education*. Chicago: University of Chicago Press.

Enns, C., Bersaglio, B., and Kepe, T., 2014. Indigenous voices and the making of the post-2015 development agenda: The recurring tyranny of participation. *Third World Quarterly*, 35(3), 358-375.

Fuller, A., and Unwin, L., 2003. Learning as apprentices in the contemporary UK workplace: Creating and managing expansive and restrictive participation. *Journal of Education and Work*, 16(4), 407-426.

Gregory, D., 1994. *Geographical Imaginations*. Oxford: Blackwell.

Gu, Q., Heesom, S., Williamson, R., and Crowther, K., 2018. Reducing teachers' unnecessary workload: the promise of collaborative planning. Transform Teaching School Alliance. Available at: https://dera.ioe.ac.uk/31215/1/Teaching_School_Alliance_-_Reducing_teacher_workload.pdf [accessed 20 January 2021].

Healy, G., Walshe, N., and Dunphy, A., 2020. How is geography rendered visible as an object of concern in written lesson observation feedback? *Curriculum Journal*, 31(1), 7-26.

Hobson, A. J., and Malderez, A., 2013. Judgementoring and other threats to realizing the potential of school-based mentoring in teacher education. *International Journal of Mentoring and Coaching in Education*, 2(2), 89-108.

Hodkinson, H., 2009. Improving schoolteachers' workplace learning. In S. Gewirtz, P. Mahony, I. Hextall and A. Cribb (eds), *Changing Teacher Professionalism: International Trends, Challenges and Ways Forward*. Abingdon: Routledge, 157-169.

Lambert, D., and Biddulph, M., 2015. The dialogic space offered by curriculum-making in the process of learning to teach, and the creation of a progressive knowledge-led curriculum. *Asia-Pacific Journal of Teacher Education*, 43(3), 210-224.

Lambert, D., and Morgan, J., 2010. *Teaching Geography 11-18: A Conceptual Approach*. Maidenhead: Open University Press.

Langdon, F., 2017. Learning to mentor: Unravelling routine practice to develop adaptive mentoring expertise. *Teacher Development*, 21(4), 528-546.

Langdon, F., and Ward, L., 2015. Educative mentoring: A way forward. *International Journal of Mentoring and Coaching in Education*, 4(4), 240-254.

Massey, D., 2005. *For Space*. London: Sage.

Nash, C., 2002. Cultural geography: Postcolonial cultural geographies. *Progress in Human Geography*, 26(2), 219-230.

Norman, P. J., and Feiman-Nemser, S., 2005. Mind activity in teaching and mentoring. *Teaching and Teacher Education*, 21(6), 679-697.

Puttick, S., and Warren-Lee, N., 2020. Geography mentors' written lesson observation feedback during initial teacher education. *International Research in Geographical and Environmental Education*. doi:10.1080/10382046.2020.1757830.

Radcliffe, S. A., 2017. Geography and indigeneity I. *Progress in Human Geography*, 41(2), 220-229.

Radcliffe, S. A., 2020. Geography and indigeneity III: Co-articulation of colonialism and capitalism in indigeneity's economies. *Progress in Human Geography*, 44(2), 374-388.

Roberts, M., 2013. *Geography Through Enquiry: Approaches to Teaching and Learning in the Secondary School*. Sheffield: Geographical Association.

Standish, A., 2018. Teaching about development in a post-development society: The case of geography. *International Research in Geographical and Environmental Education*, 27(3), 199-215.

Standish, A., 2020. Time for geography to catch up with the world. *Geography*, 105(3), 135-141.

Stanulis, R. N., Wexler, L. J., Pylman, S., Guenther, A., Farver, S., Ward, A., Croel-Perrien, A., and White, K., 2019. Mentoring as more than "cheerleading": Looking at educative mentoring practices through mentors' eyes. *Journal of Teacher Education*, 70(5), 567-580.

Tapsfield, A., 2019. *Effective Geography ITE Training and Mentoring*. Sheffield: Geographical Association.

Timperley, H., 2011. *Realizing the Power of Professional Learning*. New York: Open University Press.

Wang, J., and Odell, S.J., 2002. Mentored learning to teach according to standards-based reform: A critical review. *Review of Educational Research*, 72(3), 481-546.

Wang, J., Odell, S. J., and Schwille, S. A., 2008. Effects of teacher induction on beginning teachers' teaching: A critical review of the literature. *Journal of Teacher Education*, 59(2), 132-152.

Willis, K., 2014. Development: Geographical perspectives on a contested concept. *Geography*, 99(2), 60-66.

15 Well-being

Theory and practice for beginning geography teachers

Emma Clarke, Aimee Quickfall and Shaun Thompson

Introduction

Initial Teacher Education (ITE) programmes (including the one-year PGCE (Post Graduate Certificate in Education), which all of the authors teach on) have often been described by trainees as a *rollercoaster*. Emotional peaks and troughs are experienced by almost all trainees to a range of degrees and many express their time in ITE and the early years of their careers as the *toughest of their life*. Well-being and stress-management issues for those in training and early in their careers are often significant, with non-linear and high-stakes struggles – emotionally, financially and academically – common for many (Birchinall et al., 2019).

This chapter will consider well-being for beginning geography teachers, exploring potential sources of challenge and providing practical guidance for mentors supporting well-being which is underpinned by our own empirical research, alongside the wider literature on supporting mentors and other staff in school who are engaged in mentoring practices. In particular, this chapter aims to introduce recent research in well-being for trainee and early-career teachers, with a particular focus on geography teaching, share the well-being *see-saw* and how it can be used to support mentees, consider how reflecting on challenges and resources for beginning geography teachers can be supportive and develop strategies for positive well-being, and discuss key steps that can be taken to develop and maintain positive well-being for mentees.

What is well-being?

The term well-being now has a common currency in many professions, as well as in the popular psyche. In education, developing well-being for children and teachers has been a major policy drive, specifically in schools in England (Bonell et al., 2014; DfE, 2014; 2016; Ofsted, 2019). For example, the Department for Education in England (DfE, 2018) have highlighted their focus on ensuring schools promote pupils' mental health and well-being, and from 2020 teaching pupils to look after their well-being will be mandatory.

Hand-in-hand with the explicit focus on well-being for pupils has been a consideration of teachers' well-being, both nationally and internationally (DfE, 2014; 2016; Froese-Germain,

2014; Gallant and Riley, 2017; Public Health England, 2015; Roffey, 2012; Spilt et al., 2011). Teaching has been suggested to be one of the most stressful professions in the world, with high emotional labour and low job satisfaction (Johnson et al., 2005). Research suggests teacher well-being affects teaching, student motivation and retention, with well-being and workload the most commonly cited factors for leaving the profession (Collie et al., 2015; Ofsted, 2019). These factors are regularly reflected in rising international teacher attrition rates (Danilewitz and Rodger, 2017; DfE, 2018; 2019). A recent report by the English school inspections body noted low well-being in most of those surveyed, with well-being actually reducing over a teachers' career (Ofsted, 2019). In a study commissioned by the Department for Education, over half of teachers surveyed said they had considered leaving in the past two years due to pressures on health, and 45% felt they did not achieve the right balance between home and work lives (DfE, 2017). Reports by the Independent Teacher Review Groups (DfE, 2016) stated that all parts of the education system have a role to play in reducing unnecessary tasks for teachers, including ITE providers. The current Teachers' Standards (DfE, 2012) do not mention the well-being of pupils or teachers, but tie trainee and qualified teachers' personal and professional conduct to their regard for the ethos, policies and practice of the school where they work. However, more recent English documents (such as the ITT Core Content Framework [DfE, 2019] and the Early Career Framework [DfE, 2020]) do have a discrete focus on well-being. This was replicated in the policy documents in Finland (FNBE, 2016) and Denmark (Danish Institute for Human Rights, 2012) where we collected data for our research. This has significant implications, as it shifts the emphasis for developing trainee well-being onto mentors due to the dichotomy between the documentation for assessment (DfE, 2012) and the documents for content (DfE, 2019; 2020; Healy and Walshe, 2022).

A discourse of teachers taking ownership of their well-being to thrive, rather than survive, persists (Margolis et al., 2014); however, there seems little appetite at present, or in recent decades, to tackle systemic and cultural issues affecting well-being in the sector (Perryman and Calvert, 2020). This has resulted in a limited field of knowledge on what sustains and develops well-being for trainee and early-career teachers. Research on what may promote teacher well-being is scarce (Roffey, 2012), and what research exists has tended to focus on individuals and their survival characteristics (Margolis et al., 2014) as opposed to broader school-wide factors. Research into student well-being, including in higher education (Bates et al., 2017; Houghton and Anderson, 2017; Seldon and Martin, 2017; Universities UK, 2015), is also beginning to grow from a similarly small field, indicating that students at higher-education institutions (HEIs) are negatively affected by stress and as a result have lower well-being due to managing a range of responsibilities (Dwyer and Cummings, 2001). In the gap between student and teacher well-being there is a significant lack of research and guidance for those currently enrolled on ITE programmes (Thompson et al., 2020; Birchinall et al., 2019). If it is assumed that those on ITE programmes sit between these two bodies of research, it could be argued they are vulnerable to the stresses of both simultaneously. Even if trainees only experience the reported issues with well-being for one of these groups, they are still in a challenging position. As Roffey (2012, p. 9) suggests:

Training teachers who then leave because their lives are unfulfilled at best and miserable at worst is not only devastating to those individuals and damaging to students but also expensive on the public purse.

This leads to questions about what the mentor's role is in supporting the development of well-being for beginning and early-career geography teachers and reducing early-career teacher attrition.

Task 15.1 Mentor reflection activity: promoting individual resilience

Mentors have been suggested to be important in 'promoting individual resilience' (Margolis et al., 2014, p. 223) in an education system where reduced well-being and poor mental health are relatively common (Rumschlag, 2017; Skaalvik and Skaalvik, 2010), and burnout in specific cases of qualified teachers has been linked to the development of burnout symptoms as a trainee (Vaisanen et al., 2018).

- What do you think about this?
- Is this how you see your role?
- What might the advantages and limitations of this perception of mentoring be?
- How would this affect your work with a mentee?
- What conflicts are there between this view of 'individual resilience' for mentees and a community of professionals working towards a shared and common goal?

Defining well-being

Despite being regularly used, the term 'well-being' is not always clearly defined, yet its prevalence can sometimes lead to the assumption that it is easily defined and systematically understood by all who use it. As Weare (2000), in line with others, has noted, summing up well-being or mental health in a single sentence is often simplistic and inappropriate, and reducing this multifaceted and complex concept to a simple definition is impossible. It has also been argued that in trying to do so, our own 'values, preconceptions and assumptions' are side-lined (Weare, 2000), despite the fact that concepts such as mental health and well-being are influenced by our own personal views of what is usual or desirable, what behaviours are 'normal' and so on. Carr (2000, in Gott, 2003) asserts that concepts such as well-being are not 'value neutral' but are always influenced by a range of factors and contexts; as a result, any definitions provided are usually influenced by the contexts and communities that devise them. This means that definitions of well-being used in other contexts might not automatically transfer to schools, and what constitutes a definition of well-being or mental health for one group, might not be the same for another.

Research shows that the concept of well-being is difficult to define as it is often considered complex (Ortega-Alcázar and Dyck, 2012; Pollard and Lee, 2003; Dodge et al., 2012; Masters, 2004). As a term, well-being has been suggested to lack a shared understanding despite its frequent use in a systemic review of the literature (Pollard and Lee, 2003). Mental health more broadly too has also shifted and changed from medical and deficit models where it was once considered as the absence of a mental illness, to a state or condition in its own right – a *strength perspective* (Spratt et al., 2006). It would be naïve to suggest that mental health or well-being can be simply or easily defined or, indeed, that they are a fixed state. One of the key hurdles in explicitly defining the *elusive* (Ortega-Alcázar and Dyck, 2012) concept of well-being is that it is not a discrete entity, but rather multi-factorial and multi-dimensional (Dodge et al., 2012; Masters, 2004). In line with this, in our own research on well-being for ITE students as a team, we felt that well-being 'implies a sense of balance and ease with the myriad dimensions of life'. Psychological well-being can be considered as tackling challenges and engaging in personal development (Eldeleklioğlu et al., 2010). In attempting to reflect some of the complexity of the concept, whilst providing our own research participants with a meaningful task, the working definition of well-being we are using in this chapter is the same as in our research and builds on that of Dodge et al. (2012): well-being is maintaining the balance between resources and challenges; these factors may be internal or external and operate in a dynamic flux over time.

The definition of well-being chosen reflects our own experiences; becoming a teacher involves finding a balance between resources and challenges, as well as the personal and professional (Pillen et al., 2013). Resources are anything we have to support us: relationships, experiences, traits, materials, technology and so on. Challenges are anything that we need to overcome – for example assessments, health issues, financial problems – but they do not necessarily entail a negative or bad thing; challenges can be very positive, for example a weekly placement target can be a challenge and a motivator to develop. This definition is represented as a *balance* by Dodge et al. (2012), with resources at one end and challenges at the other, and became known to us as 'the see-saw' (p. 230).

In our empirical research (Thompson et al., 2020) we have found the see-saw very helpful to provide a framework for participants – beginning teachers, including trainees – to think about the breadth of challenges and resources they have and to consider the balance between them. Pillen et al. (2013, p. 241) highlighted how:

> the period of transition from student to teacher is often a struggle for a great number of beginning teachers which usually remains invisible to their teacher educators and mentors or colleagues in schools.

The see-saw provides an opportunity for trainees to make some of their challenges visible, both to themselves and to others, and we have used the same format working with a number of trainee teachers in England, as well as throughout other parts of Europe (Germany, Denmark, the Netherlands and Finland). What has struck us most vividly is that, despite the very different range of teacher education in these countries (for example, Finland comprises a five-year-long, Master's-level training course which is frequently oversubscribed, whilst in England teacher education can take a little as ten months), many of the resources and challenges trainees experience are similar or even the same (Thompson et al., 2020).

Resources and challenges

Using the data collected from our research which explored the well-being of trainee teachers in England (Thompson et al., 2020; Quickfall et al., 2021), a range of common themes emerged when asking participants to list the resources and challenges which impact them; these are summarised in Figure 15.1.

One of the research methods within our study involved participants taking photographs to represent their well-being each week (examples shown in Figure 15.2). We supported participants to analyse these using thematic analysis and a similar range of themes emerged, including seeking comfort, being with others, workload, and maintaining relationships.

In addition to the see-saws and the photographic data, we also interviewed our participants. Again, a theme reiterated was that of relationships, with one of the participants telling us 'The times my well-being was the lowest were the times I felt most alone'. The theme of relationships occurred throughout all of the sources of data as both a resource and a challenge.

The findings of our research are inline with wider studies which also suggest that social support has been found to promote psychological well-being, as well as to buffer the effects of stress (Dwyer and Cummings, 2001). This would suggest that when supporting beginning teachers (and indeed any teacher new to a school), developing and maintaining supportive professional relationships is a key factor in developing well-being – and one in which mentors can play a direct role:

> while national policies and constraints at school level may make powerful and empowering forms of Professional Learning Communities difficult to realise, it can… make a major contribution to teachers' well-being.
>
> (Webb et al., 2009, p. 406)

It is also now recognised that professional learning communities may be increasingly virtual, with online social spaces impacting geography teachers' subject identity and

Resources:
- Teachers on placement
- Family
- Mentors (school and university)
- Group tutors
- Friends
- Sharing experiences
- Downtime
- Knowledge and experience
- Literature/research

Challenges:
- Well-being/coping
- Building relationships
- Work/life balance
- Assignments
- Motivation
- Confidence
- Knowing when to seek help
- Developing a routine
- No 'one size fits all'

Figure 15.1 Research findings using the 'see-saw'
Source: Dodge et al., 2012, p. 230

Figure 15.2 Photographs depicting ITE trainee well-being

230 Emma Clarke et al.

professional practice (e.g. Brooks, 2021). Whilst Bergviken et al. (2018) recognise the value of social support provided by teacher social media groups, such as the one they examine (a Swedish teacher Facebook group of over 13,000 members), they argue that these benefits can sit in tension with engagement that is 'disadvantaging, exploitative and/or disempowering' (p. 230)

Task 15.2 Mentor reflection activity: preparing for fieldtrips and undertaking fieldwork

While beginning geography teachers are likely to be vulnerable to the same causes of poor mental health and well-being, Tucker and Horton (2019) suggest that fieldwork can be an additional focal site of distress, anxiety and ordeal for geographers, particularly for those with existing mental health conditions. Although speaking from a higher-education perspective, they argue that ideologically colonialist, masculinist and ableist approaches to field work can 'reproduce "heroic" expeditionary exploration (Rose, 1993)… and senses of "failure" and "burden" for participants unable to "keep up" (Maguire, 1998) ' (p. 86). Birnie and Grant (2001) suggest a range of factors which may contribute to this anxiety, including being away from home, being away from supportive friends and family, living communally, and being in challenging physical and social environments. Nairn (2003) adds that residential fieldtrips in particular can also cause anxieties because of communal-based living, eating and sleeping arrangements and a lack of privacy. In a context where there can be an expectation for geographers to enjoy (if not love) fieldwork, it is perhaps important for mentors to recognise the additional impact this may have on trainee well-being.

- Reflect on your own experience of fieldwork: how did this contribute to your own well-being as a beginning teacher? Is this different now as an experienced teacher and mentor?
- How might undertaking a residential fieldtrip with school students lead to a change in the resources and challenges for your mentee?
- As a mentor, how can you support your trainees to draw on their resources while preparing for undertaking a fieldtrip?

The importance of supporting relationships for beginning teacher well-being

The social resources of trainee teachers have been linked to their ability to proactively deploy coping strategies (Väisänen et al., 2018); as teacher educators ourselves, we were keen to use ideas of community to support trainee teachers. Isolation and community were themes that emerged from our anecdotal experiences of supporting trainee teachers with academic work, school experience placements, finding employment and preparing for their role in school. The idea of developing collaborative working as a group follows the *community of practice* model, with a community of practice being defined as:

> a group of individuals, who through the pursuit of joint enterprise, have developed shared practices, historical and social resources and common perspectives.
> (Coburn and Stein, 2006, p. 28)

Communities of practice are often applied to school contexts, which provide a shared domain of interest, shared activities and a shared repertoire of practice (Shields and Murray, 2017). Recent research also suggests that communities of practice have beneficial effects, particularly in terms of belonging, self-efficacy and a sense of professional identity (Kirkby et al., 2019; Vann, 2019) – issues which are also supportive factors in developing well-being.

The idea of communities of practice comes from wider social learning theory (Wenger, 1991) which considers three key aspects for the function of an effective community:

- shared goals;
- relationship formation; and
- collaborative learning.

Wenger-Trayner and Wenger-Trayner (2011), whose work dominates the field of communities of practice, elaborate on these further, suggesting the role the 'domain', the 'community' and the 'practice' play. Here they define these as:

> The domain: members are brought together by a learning need they share. The community: their collective learning becomes a bond among them over time. The practice: their interactions produce resources that affect their practice.
> (p. 1)

In terms of communities of practice, beginning teachers can be theorised as being inducted into a large community (for example, university-led partnership, SCITT (School-Centred Initial Teacher Training), subject association community, and so on) as 'legitimate peripheral participants' (Wenger, 1991, p. 64), alongside academic staff and lecturers. Their goals are shared: to successfully complete academic work and placements, and achieve Qualified Teacher Status. Whilst, in theory, the community of practice model would appear to reflect the basic realities of school experience (as communities of practice can present challenges, as well as support and resources), as a newcomer the beginning teacher may lack the competence required to engage in practice in school, and if attempts to integrate are not welcomed by the community, 'learning becomes difficult' (Johnston, 2016, p. 534). This again highlights the key role of the mentor in facilitating entry into this new community of practice when they are in school, either on teaching practice within the context of ITE, or at the start of their career as a newly or recently qualified teacher.

Task 15.3 Mentor reflection activity: developing relationships

From a *community of practice* perspective, shared goals and relationships are a key factor. Reflect on the process of working with geography beginning teachers in your own context.

- What goals do geography mentors and beginning teacher mentees share?
- How are relationships between them developed?
- What challenges are there to developing these professional relationships?
  - For the mentor?
  - For the beginning teacher?

When ITE trainees go on their school experience placements, their temporary community of practice can be considered to have shrunk down from their often-large cohort of peers to the size of a secondary school, or a single department within that school (Yandell and Turvey, 2007). These communities are temporary (Backhouse, 2018) and do not offer the same opportunity to become a legitimate peripheral participant, as trainees have 'guest-like status' (Johnston, 2016, p. 544). Most postgraduate ITE students in England, with often just ten months to qualify, spend most of their course on school placements, and must have significant teaching experience in at least two schools (DfE, 2019). Undergraduate and part-time ITE trainees usually have longer periods between school placements, so it could be argued that the postgraduate student (which most beginning geography teachers are in England) is at a disadvantage in terms of access and participation in communities of practice that provide meaningful opportunities to build relationships, and are supportive and understanding of their challenges. Emotional support provided by mentors which moves beyond a master-apprentice relationship can improve chances of a successful school placement (Shields and Murray, 2017) and it is clear that professional integration and intra-personal relationships are key to successful completion of the programme. This allies with a coaching style of mentoring which may be more time-intensive, as opposed to the mimesis or replication of practice which sometimes occurs due to a lack of time.

What might this mean in practice for beginning geography teachers?

The findings from our study on the well-being of trainee teachers begins to address the lack of research in this area and reveals some key areas that schools can address. The national and international findings from our investigation (Thompson et al., 2020) highlighted for all participating trainees, regardless of the route they took or even the country they trained in, the importance of relationships and the challenges that existed in developing these. Some of the challenges that were identified from our study around building professional relationships included:

- **Transience**: this was particularly pertinent for trainees. Here relationship difficulties were compounded by an understanding that the interactions were time-limited and temporary. This made it difficult for our participants to feel part of the school community and develop a sense of belonging.
- **Time**: trainees were often acutely aware of the time pressures on their mentors (as well as on themselves) and this made some trainees concerned about approaching busy mentors. Mentors also noted that they found interactions with trainees were, at times,

more rushed than they would have liked. This is also likely to be a significant issue for those mentoring early-career teachers.
- **Workload**: this final challenge is underpinned by the previous two. Trainee (and early-career) teachers found that their workload was often very high and their overwhelming concern was ensuring they were prepared to teach. This meant that they sometimes found it difficult to create the space to develop relationships with mentors who were also usually under a great deal of pressure.

Despite the many challenges in developing professional relationships with mentors, they were seen by our participants as essential. These relationships encouraged a sense of community, developed learning and made receiving feedback and acting on it a much more active and positive experience. Pillen et al. (2013, p. 246), in their research, cited not only the 'complexity' of learning to teach, but also the fact it is a 'very personal process'. This *personal* nature of teaching, where it is at times difficult to separate the feedback on the teaching from the feedback on the person, highlights the importance of strong professional relationships between mentors and those they are mentoring; further, it brings into focus the tension between the need for mentors to play both a developmental and evaluative role, and the impact this tension may have on their relationship with mentees (Healy and Walshe, 2022). Roffey (2012, p. 10), too, noted the role 'relational' aspects and 'social capital' play in resilience and well-being;

> Social capital in the context of school life is more about the quality of connections – the ways in which people relate to each other, as both individuals and groups.

Following on from this, it might be helpful to consider how social capital and relationships can be maximised and developed for beginning geography teachers, as well as mentors, to develop well-being. Whilst the social capital within a school context is important, Kinder (2022) has highlighted that there is also value in mentors supporting beginning teachers to navigate and productively engage with the networks and communities that make up the wider geography-subject community. As a mentor, you can model how engagement with the geography-subject community contributes to your own resources or can mitigate some of the challenges you face. This support for beginning geography teachers has the potential not just to develop well-being in the present, but also to have a long-term impact on how beginning geography teachers can maintain their well-being throughout their teaching career. Furthermore, having a subject-community approach to supporting and developing beginning teachers is likely to mitigate isolation they may be more likely to feel if they are in smaller geography departments as it extends their professional learning community (e.g. Webb et al., 2009; Kinder, 2022) beyond their immediate context.

Whole-school considerations may include: relationships need time to develop; much research highlights the link between positive relationships and well-being. *Scheduled* time needs to be provided for mentors to meet with those they are mentoring and support the development of positive, professional relationships. *Personal* time is also required to reflect on the mentoring role and its purpose. Opportunities for formal and informal networking of beginning geography teachers to exchange ideas and provide mutual support may also be a cheap and effective way of building relationships with peers. Trainees in our research reported feeling *lonely* in schools and struggling to understand basics such as school routines, key staff members and so on, as they were so focussed on the actual aspect of teaching. Schools may be able to produce a (very brief) booklet that trainees and early-career teachers can access with this sort of routine information in; this can be used to complement any in-depth induction programme.

Individual mentor actions may be generated from reflecting on the following questions:

- How could you utilise the see-saw model discussed earlier to understand the challenges and resources specific to your mentee and use this (as well as the career entry profile) to develop an individualised training support plan?
- Reflecting on the challenges and resources drawn out from our research, can you use these as discussion points with your mentee?
- Puttick (2018, p. 34) suggests 'coffee and kettle-space time' as an important time for interaction between teachers in the department. Can you share with your mentee the best times to talk formally? Can you encourage informal discussions too, to begin to develop professional relationships?
- Reflect on your support for previous trainees and/or early-career geography teachers. Using the findings from our research, what has worked well previously? Is there anything you need to adapt to support the development of professional relationships?

Conclusion

This chapter has highlighted the difficulties in defining well-being due to its complex, context-dependent and multifaceted make up. It has also drawn attention to the need to support beginning geography teachers in developing and maintaining their well-being. Using a resources and challenges model is one way of being able to do this, with a particular need for considering what challenges beginning geography teachers are specifically likely to face

This chapter has identified some of the key challenges and resources that face beginning geography teachers. These include issues relating to developing their knowledge and experience base, dealing with finding an appropriate life/work balance, and importantly developing professional relationships. It was this final factor which was identified as both a resource and challenge in our research. This suggests that relationships between mentors and mentees can be both a source of support and challenge, and as a result this chapter has focussed on developing the positive aspects of this important relationship and ensuring that as much as possible the resources are developed for both the mentor and mentee.

Links between personal and professional relationships, workload and well-being, when connected through the timelines and photo-elicitation interviews, suggested that the way the period of ITE and early-career teacher development is experienced is made of rhythmic patterns of demand and activity; this is in the same way that experienced teachers' workload has also been theorised (Wood, 2019). The challenges and resources of beginning geography teachers are dynamic, the see-saw of well-being pivots up and down rapidly, and without relationships inside and outside the programme it is difficult to move out of the 'troughs' of the experience.

For discussion

- What are your main challenges and resources as a *geography* mentor? How might these shape the mentorship you give to beginning teacher mentees?
- After examining the challenges and resources you and your mentee share, can you develop an action plan (this may include departmental/whole-school actions) to enhance the mentoring culture within your department?
- How will you address the actions that fall within your mentor/mentee relationship in the action plan developed (in the previous point) and which actions need support from the wider department/school leadership team?

Further reading and resources

1. Thompson, S., Clarke, E., Quickfall, A., and Glazzard, J., 2020. Averting the crisis in trainee teacher well-being-learning lessons across European contexts: A comparative study. *Journal of Comparative & International Higher Education*, 12, 38–56.

This paper provides an overview of our small-scale international comparative study examining the well-being of those undertaking ITE. We draw out from the findings the common thread across the participating countries of the importance of developing positive mentor/student relationships. The research was conducted across universities in Finland and Denmark and implications for best practice to support trainee teacher well-being are suggested.

2. Department for Education [DfE], 2019. *Reducing Workload: Supporting Teachers in the Early Stages of their Career Advice for School Leaders, Induction Tutors, Mentors and Appropriate Bodies*. London: DfE.

This document contains advice and guidance for mentors in supporting beginning teachers with a focus on reducing unnecessary workload. It expands on a range of common themes for early-career teachers which affect their workload and has a range of key questions for mentors and school leaders to engage with.

3. Quickfall, A., Clarke, E., and Thompson, S., 2020. The PGCE journey: Wellbeing and workload. BERA blog. Available at: www.bera.ac.uk/blog/the-pgce-journey-wellbeing-and-workload [accessed 25 January 21].

This blog summarises some of the issues affecting trainee teachers and their experiences of well-being whilst in training. It reflects on the implications of these challenges for trainees, mentors and those working more widely in ITE provision. The BERA mental health, well-being and education special interest group (SIG), which this blog is part of, contains a range of up-to-date papers and resources. Available at: www.bera.ac.uk/community/mental-health-wellbeing-and-education.

References

Backhouse, A., 2018. The PGCE (Primary) student experience. In Association for Teacher Education in Europe, 7–9 June 2018, Bialystok, Poland. Available at: http://eprints.lincoln.ac.uk/id/eprint/35991/1/The%20PGCE%20%28Primary%29%20Experience.pdf [accessed 7 May 2021].

Bates, E. A., Kaye, L. K., and McCann, J. J., 2017. A snapshot of the student experience: Exploring student satisfaction through the use of photographic elicitation. *Journal of Further and Higher Education*, 9486, 1-14.

Bergviken Rensfeldt, A., Hillman, T., and Selwyn, N., 2018. Teachers 'liking' their work? Exploring the realities of teacher Facebook groups. *British Educational Research Journal*, 44(2), 230-250.

Birchinall, L., Spendlove, D., and Buck, R., 2019. In the moment: Does mindfulness hold the key to improving the resilience and wellbeing of pre-service teachers? *Teaching and Teacher Education*, 86, 102919.

Birnie, J., and Grant, A., 2001. Providing learning support for students with mental health difficulties undertaking fieldwork and related activities. Geography Discipline Network, University of Gloucester. Available at: http://gdn.glos.ac.uk/disabil/mental/index.htm. https://doi.org/10.1111/area.12437 [accessed 21 December 2020].

Bonell, C. Humphrey, N., Fletcher, A., Moore, L., Anderson, R., and Campbell, R., 2014. Why schools should promote students' health and wellbeing. *BMJ (Online)*, 348(g3078).

Brooks, C., 2021. Teacher identity, professional practice and online social spaces. In N. Walshe and G. Healy (eds), *Geography Education in the Digital World*. London: Routledge, 7-16.

Carr, D., 2000. Emotional intelligence, PSE & self-esteem: A cautionary note. *Pastoral Care*, 18(3), 27-33.

Coburn, C., and Stein, M. 2006. Communities of practice theory and the role of teacher professional community in policy implementation. In M. Honig (ed), *New Directions In Education Policy Implementation: Confronting Complexity*. Albany: State University of New York Press, 25-47.

Collie, R., Shapka, J., Perry, N., and Martin, A., 2015. Teacher well-being. *Journal of Psychoeducational Assessment*, 33(8), 744-756.

Danilewitz, J. R., and Rodger, S., 2017. Quality of life and sources of stress in teachers: A Canadian perspective. Available at: https://ir.lib.uwo.ca/etdhttps://ir.lib.uwo.ca/etd/4469 [accessed 11 April 2019].

Danish Institute for Human Rights, 2012. Mapping of human rights education in Danish schools. Available at: https://menneskeret.dk/files/media/dokumenter/udgivelser/skole_pixi_uk_samlet.pdf [accessed 8 March 2021].

Department for Education, 2012. *Teachers' Standards*. London: DfE.

Department for Education, 2014. *Mental Health and Behaviour in Schools: Departmental Advice*. London: DfE.

Department for Education, 2016. *Teacher Workload Survey 2016*. London: DfE.

Department for Education, 2017. *School Workforce in England November 2017*. London: DfE.

Department for Education and Brown, R., 2018. *Mental Health and Wellbeing Provision in Schools*. London: DfE.

Department for Education, 2019. *Initial Teacher Training (ITT): Core Content Framework*. London: DfE.

Department for Education, 2020. *Early Career Framework Reforms*. London: DfE.

Dodge, R., Daly, A., Huyton, J., and Sanders, L., 2012. The challenge of defining wellbeing. *International Journal of Wellbeing*, 2(3), 222-235.

Dwyer, A., and Cummings, A., 2001. Stress, self-efficacy, social support, and coping strategies in university students. *Canadian Journal of Counselling and Psychotherapy/Revue canadienne de counseling et de psychothérapie*, 35(3), 208-220.

Eldeleklioğlu, J., Yilmaz, A., and Gültekin, F., 2010. Investigation of teacher trainees' psychological well-being in terms of time management. *Procedia Social and Behavioral Sciences* 2, 342-348.

Finnish National Board of Education [FNBE], 2016. *National Core Curriculum for Basic Education*. Helsinki: FNBE.

Froese-Germain, B., 2014. Work-life balance and the Canadian teaching profession. Available at: www.ctf-fce.ca/Research-Library/Work-LifeBalanceandtheCanadianTeachingProfession.pdf [accessed 11 April 2019].

Gallant, A., and Riley, P., 2017. Early career teacher attrition in Australia: Inconvenient truths about new public management. *Teachers and Teaching: Theory and Practice*, 23(8), 896–913.

Gott, J., 2003. The school: The front line of mental health development? *Pastoral Care in Education*, 21(4), 5–13.

Healy, G., and Walshe, N., 2022. Navigating the policy landscape: conceptualising subject-specialist mentoring within and beyond policy. In G. Healy, L. Hammond, S. Puttick and N. Walshe (eds), *Mentoring Geography Teachers in the Secondary School*. Abingdon: Routledge, 13–30.

Houghton, A., and Anderson, J., 2017. *Embedding Mental Wellbeing in the Curriculum: Maximising Success in Higher Education*. York: Higher Education Academy.

Johnson, S., Cooper, C., Cartwright, S., Donald, I., Taylor, P., and Millet, C., 2005. The experience of work-related stress across occupations. *Journal of Managerial Psychology*, 20(2), 178–187.

Johnston, D., 2016. "Sitting alone in the staffroom contemplating my future": Communities of practice, legitimate peripheral participation and student teachers' experiences of problematic school placements as guests. *Cambridge Journal of Education*, 46(4), 533–551.

Kinder, A., 2022. Mentoring within the geography subject community. In G. Healy, L. Hammond, S. Puttick and N. Walshe (eds), *Mentoring Geography Teachers in the Secondary School*. Abingdon: Routledge, 102–118.

Kirkby, J., Walsh, L., and Keary, A., 2019. A case study of the generation and benefits of a community of practice and its impact on the professional identity of early childhood teachers. *Professional Development in Education*, 45(2), 264–275.

Maguire, S., 1998. Gender differences in attitudes to undergraduate fieldwork. *Area*, 30, 207–214.

Margolis, J., Hodge, A., and Alexandrou, A., 2014 The teacher educator's role in promoting institutional versus individual teacher well-being. *Journal of Education for Teaching*, 40(4), 391–408.

Masters, G., 2004. Conceptualising and researching student wellbeing. In *Australian Council for Educational Research*. Adelaide: ACEReSearch, 1–6. Available at: http://research.acer.edu.au/research_conference_2004 [accessed 8 March 2021].

Nairn, K., 2003. What has the geography of sleeping arrangements got to do with the geography of our teaching spaces? *Gender, Place and Culture: A Journal of Feminist Geography*, 10, 67–81.

Ofsted, 2019. *Summary and Recommendations: Teacher Well-being Research Report*. London: Ofsted.

Ortega-Alcázar, I., and Dyck, I., 2012. Migrant narratives of health and well-being: Challenging "othering" processes through photo-elicitation interviews. *Critical Social Policy*, 32(1), 106–125.

Perryman, J., and Calvert, G., 2020. What motivated people to teach, and why do they leave? *British Journal of Educational Studies*, 68(1), 3–23.

Pillen, M., Beijaard, D., and den Brok, P. 2013. Tensions in beginning teachers' professional identity development, accompanying feelings and coping strategies. *European Journal of Teacher Education*, 36(3), 240–260.

Pollard, E., and Lee, P., 2003. Child well-being: A systematic review of the literature. *Social Indicators Research*, 61(1), 59–78.

Public Health England, 2015. *Promoting Children and Young People's Emotional Health and Wellbeing*. London: PHE.

Puttick, S., 2018. Student teachers' positionalities as knowers in school subject departments. *British Educational Research Journal*, 44(1), 25-42.

Quickfall, A., Clarke, E., and Thompson, S., 2021. The PGCE journey Wellbeing & workload. In M. Jayman, J. Glazzard and A. Rose (eds), *Researching Education & Mental Health: From 'Where Are We Now?' to 'What Next?'* (BERA Bites Issue 6). London: British Educational Research Association, 16-17. Available at: www.bera.ac.uk/publication/bera-bites-issue-6-researchingeducation-mental-health.

Roffey, S., 2012. Pupil wellbeing—Teacher wellbeing: Two sides of the same coin?, *Educational and Child Psychology*, 29(4), 8-17.

Rose, G., 1993. *Feminism and Geography: The Limits of Geographical Knowledge*. Cambridge: Polity.

Rumschlag, K. E., 2017. Teacher burnout: A quantitative analysis of emotional exhaustion, personal accomplishment, and depersonalization. *International Management Review*, 13(1), 22-36.

Seldon, A., and Martin, A., 2017. The positive and mindful university. Available at: www.hepi.ac.uk/2017/09/21/positive-mindful-university/ [accessed 7 May 2021].

Shields, S., and Murray, M., 2017. Beginning teachers' perceptions of mentors and access to communities of practice. *International Journal of Mentoring and Coaching in Education*, 6(4), 317-331.

Skaalvik, E., and Skaalvik, S., 2010. Teacher self-efficacy and teacher burnout: A study of relations. *Teaching and Teacher Education*, 26, 1059-1069.

Spilt, J., Koomen, H., and Thijs, J., 2011. Teacher wellbeing: The importance of teacher-student relationships. *Educational Psychology Review*, 23, 457-477.

Spratt, J., Shucksmith, J., Philip, K., and Watson, C., 2006. "Part of who we are as a school should include responsibility for well-being": Links between the school environment, mental health and behaviour. *Pastoral Care in Education*, 24(3), 14-21.

Thompson, S., Clarke, E., Quickfall, A., and Glazzard, J., 2020. Averting the crisis in trainee teacher well-being-learning lessons across European contexts: A comparative study. *Journal of Comparative & International Higher Education*, 12, 38-56.

Tucker, F., and Horton, J., 2019. "The show must go on!" Fieldwork, mental health and wellbeing in Geography, Earth and Environmental Sciences. *Area*, 53, 84-93.

Universities UK, 2015. Student mental wellbeing in higher education. Available at: www.universitiesuk.ac.uk/policy-and-analysis/reports/Documents/2015/student-mental-wellbeing-in-he.pdf [Accessed 7 May 2021].

Väisänen, S., Pietarinen, J., Pyhältö, K., Toom, A., and Soini, T., 2018. Student teachers' proactive strategies for avoiding study-related burnout during teacher education. *European Journal of Teacher Education*, 41(3), 301-317.

Vann, L., 2019. Creating an environment to support effective learning strategies for early career teachers – The Early Career Hub, Chartered College of Teaching: Early Career Hub. Available at: https://earlycareer.chartered.college/creating-an-environment-to-support-effective-learning-strategies-for-early-career-teachers/ [accessed 8 March 2021].

Weare, K., 2000. *Promoting Mental, Emotional and Social Health*. London: Routledge.

Webb, R., Vulliamy, G., Sarja, A., Hämäläinan, S., and Poikonen, P.-L., 2009. Professional learning communities and teacher well-being? A comparative analysis of primary schools in England and Finland. *Oxford Review of Education*, 35(3), 405-422. doi: 10.1080/03054980902935008.

Wenger, E., 1991. *Situated Learning: Legitimate Peripheral Participation, Learning in Doing*. In J. S. Pea and R. Brown (eds). Cambridge: Cambridge University Press (Learning in doing), 63-82.

Wenger-Trayner, E., and Wenger-Trayner, B., 2011. What is a community of practice? Available at: https://wenger-trayner.com/resources/what-is-a-community-of-practice/ [accessed 8 March 2021].

Wood, P., 2019. Rethinking time in the workload debate. Management in Education, 33(2), 86–90.

Yandell, J., and Turvey, A., 2007. Standards or communities of practice? Competing models of workplace learning and development. *British Educational Research Journal*, 33(4), 533–550.

SECTION 4
Conclusion

16 Mentoring matters
Contributing to a more just tomorrow in geography education

Lauren Hammond, Steve Puttick, Nicola Walshe and Grace Healy

Introduction

Throughout this edited collection authors have stressed, from a range of different perspectives, the importance of mentoring; they have also highlighted the distinctively geographical nature of mentoring in geography education. Mentoring matters because of the ways in which it shapes educational practice, teachers' experiences, the kinds of geographies children and young people engage with in schools, and the futures this makes possible. Morgan's (2022, p. 42) question – 'what sort of mentoring for what sort of geography education?' – highlights the idea of *agency* and the potential for mentors and mentoring to make a real difference to beginning teachers and geography education more broadly. So, as you read this chapter, and in your mentoring, we ask you to critically engage with the question *what kinds of futures do you hope your mentoring will produce?*

Justice, agency and voice in mentoring

As a collective, state-funded service, education has often been shaped by what hooks (2003, p. 1) terms 'conservative political underpinnings', which has, at times, resulted in the institutionalisation and (re)production of 'systems of domination' related to class, race, gender and nationalist imperialism. For example, Norcup (2015) describes her attempts to challenge the reproduction of injustices related to gender and race in geography education in London in the early 2000s, and the dismissal she faced from eminent academics and textbook publishers and in her day-to-day interactions with colleagues. She tells of being made to feel like a problem for raising concerns, and how 'through the microaggressions of everyday living, that it was not for me to put my head above the parapet' (p. 4). At the time of writing – almost 20 years after the context Norcup describes – in both academic and everyday discourse, concerns shared about injustices in society and schooling highlight the systemic and day-to-day oppression and racism that still often pervades educational systems and praxis in England (Tomlinson, 2019; Puttick and Murrey, 2020; Hammond, 2021).

The examples of Norcup's reflections and injustices in the current context raise questions of justice, agency and voice, and in this conclusion to *Mentoring Geography Teachers in the Secondary School* we reflect on how, and why, mentoring matters in and for geography education. In particular, we examine how the themes of *justice*, *agency* and *voice* have been

Justice

At the time of writing, global injustices have been brutally highlighted through multiple intersecting crises:

> As communities struggled to deal with variegated climate-related events, the arrival of the pandemic compounded crises, wreaking havoc, suffering, and deaths across countries and communities. The connections between climate breakdown and the COVID-19 pandemic expose underbellies of structural inequities and systemic marginalizations across scales and sites.
>
> (Sultana, 2021, p. 447)

Geography education has a vital role to play in understanding and addressing injustices and working towards more just futures.

Justice is a significant idea in, and underpinning of, educational debates across the spaces of policy-making, academic research and educational practice. However, Arthur et al. (2021, p. 102) argue that within these discourses the 'underlying social-moral ideal' of justice is often 'fragmented, underdeveloped and badly articulated'. Their focus is on social justice, considering *social justice in education* and *education for social justice*. As Hopkins (2020, p. 382) sets out, 'social justice is about addressing the unfair outcomes that result from both social processes and institutional decision-making'. Hopkins explains that social justice considers fairness 'the distribution of society's benefits and burdens', and 'intersects and overlaps with debates and issues relating to equality and diversity and so is a key dimension of anti-discriminatory practice' (2020, p. 382). Ideas and ideals of justice go beyond the social, to include the digital, political, economic, environmental and ecological. Interdisciplinary thinking between geography and education can contribute to a more developed ideal of *justice in geography education* and *geography education for justice*.

We begin by considering *justice in geography education*, and specifically *justice for geography teachers*. We examine three dimensions of *justice* for geography teachers that have been raised through this book: teacher well-being, teacher development, and inclusive and anti-discriminatory policies and workplaces. Following this, we engage with the idea of *geography education for justice*, examining how through mentoring you might contribute to the co-construction of a more just geography education. Here, we focus specifically on critically considering how people and places are represented in geography education.

In their chapter, Clarke et al. (2022) highlight that high teacher workloads directly impact upon teacher well-being, the development of meaningful relationships between colleagues, and teachers' decisions as to whether to remain in the profession. As the first point of contact (and more!) for beginning geography teachers, mentors have a vital role in co-constructing working practices that support teacher well-being. Mentors also have important roles in assisting beginning teachers in navigating and addressing a range of professional issues that may arise. As such, it can be seen as a matter of *justice* that mentors actively engage with well-being in their mentoring to co-construct with beginning teachers, and the school more broadly, an environment in which beginning teachers can thrive.

Teacher development is another key facet of *justice in geography education* as it impacts on teaching practice, the geography education children and young people engage with, and teachers' professional futures. Healy (2022) sets out the value of geography teachers' scholarship in developing their subject expertise, and supporting curriculum thinking in mentors and beginning teachers. Yet, if we situate Healy's argument in the context of teacher education in England – where Initial Teacher Education (ITE) can be as short as a ten-month Post Graduate Certificate in Education (PGCE), and where much in-school professional development is generic (Castree et al., 2007; Cordingley et al., 2018) – engaging with scholarship in education and geography, including with subject communities (Kinder, 2022), is neither guaranteed nor inevitable. The limited funding available to support teachers' professional development also affects the options available. As the Institute of Physics' (2020, p. 10) recent analysis of the importance of subjects in schools argues, despite investment in teachers' professional development being 'a common feature of the world's best education systems… investment in teachers' professional learning is a comparative weakness in the UK'. The financial costs of further education – including further postgraduate study, some professional development (for example, the price of membership of subject associations and conference attendance) and paywalls to journal articles – mean that opportunities for scholarship are not equally available to all beginning teachers and mentors.

In considering *justice for geography teachers*, it is also of critical importance to create and foster an inclusive approach to supporting mentors and beginning teachers to be able to access the *communities of practice* (Lave and Wegner, 1991; Kinder, 2022) within which they operate. Here, we must consider both systemic and everyday injustices in educational policies, and educational spaces and places of work. For example, Bhopal (2015) describes the racism experienced by Black beginning teachers, just as previous research has highlighted the persistent racism experienced by Black trainees on placements and its impact on their performance (e.g. Basit and Roberts, 2006; Carrington and Tomlin, 2000). Further, Henderson (2017) suggests that where institutional cultures are widely recognised as heteronormative, they can discriminate against individuals who fail to conform to *gender norms*, which can mean that LGBTQ+-identifying teachers face additional hurdles that their heterosexual counterparts may not experience (Benson et al., 2014). As a final example, Murtagh (2019) describes the *othering* experienced by parent beginning teachers (not a homogeneous group themselves) leading to marginalisation, exclusion and decreased opportunities (Moreau and Kerner, 2015). These three examples highlight why, as a mentor, you might have to reach beyond your own personal experience or identities and reflect on the unique challenges a beginning teacher might face, being mindful of the intersectionality of identities, including – among many others – race, gender, sexuality, (dis)ability and age.

Thinking across *justice in geography education* and *geography education for justice*, geography education is critical to helping children and young people to develop geographical knowledge and skills, and to make decisions about how to act in the world. Through the process of planning, Ahmed et al. (2022) highlight how geography teachers make some ideas, people and places visible and others invisible. The decisions geography teachers make are significant as they represent the world and the people who call it home, and the discipline of geography to children. For example, Brown and Browne (2016) explain how the Demographic Transition Model can be seen to represent 'heterosexual coupledom, parenthood and family arrangements' (p. 1). Failing to engage critically with the model would fail to examine with children and young people how (normative) ideas of sexuality vary between people, places and time-spaces (Brown and Browne, 2016), and how inequalities have been (re)produced in, and through, society. Mentors play an important role in supporting beginning teachers to engage critically with geographical data and representations, considering how they might inform and impact on children's geographical ideas, imaginations and futures (Palombo and Daly, 2022).

Agency

The constraints of assessment procedures associated with beginning teachers' professional accreditation creates tensions with teachers' agency and autonomy, including teachers' freedom to act on, and in, situations to work towards the kinds of just futures discussed above. Many of the chapters in this collection give explicit attention to the active ways in which mentors might seek to create space for action and to *reclaim* the capacity to act amid bureaucratic, performative systems and institutions that may value standardisation and conformity over individuals' agency. Creating opportunities for acting and taking responsibility for geography curricula is explored through the very practical ways in which mentoring conversations (Rawlings Smith, 2022), lesson observations (Puttick, 2022), and planning (Ahmed et al., 2022) might all support what Palombo and Daly (2022), following Hodkinson (2009), refer to as *expansive environments*, which:

> support teachers' development of enquiry approaches that enable them to question existing beliefs about how geography is taught and how pupils are experiencing it. In other words, educative mentoring can be unsettling. Indeed it should be, because it supports the possibility of transformational professional learning, by which individual beliefs can shift and inform continually evolving practice.
>
> (p. 211)

Ethnographic research on beginning teachers' experiences of school subject departments has highlighted the importance of their subject expertise in establishing their place within departments and providing the basis on which increasing levels of agency might be exerted (Puttick, 2018). Throughout these chapters the role and complexity of subject knowledge are emphasised, and there are important connections between *agency* and *subject expertise*. Benefiting from support offered by professional associations and subject communities (Kinder, 2022) and continuing to nurture relationships with academic disciplines (Healy, 2022) are all framed as offering an important basis on which beginning teachers' professional identities and agency might offer support in resisting the negative effects of performative accountability and making space for transformative change.

Healy's (2022) analysis of the ways in which geography and geography education scholarship might function as a mechanism for sustaining mentors' and beginning teachers' subject knowledge and curriculum thinking foregrounds the relationship between subject expertise and agency. She also argues for a social understanding: it is not with individuals holding strong subject knowledge that potential for transformative futures lies, but rather with critical, ongoing and collective engagement. Again, there are obvious tensions between this understanding of subject knowledge and the ways in which assessment may function to constrain and judge subject knowledge in binary terms as strong/weak and gaps/achieved. Navigating the powerful discourses currently surrounding knowledge (Bustin, 2022) adds to the complexity of mentors' task. Yet it is our argument that against generic uses of the idea of *knowledge*, 'engaging with geography and geography education scholarship can contribute to the collective agency of geography teachers, through which beginning geography teachers can be empowered…' (Healy, 2022, p. 202).

Discussions about the particular situations and time-spaces within which mentoring relationships are formed are developed against a background of the performative nature of (most) mentor/beginning teacher relationships. That is, in most of these situations there are ultimately some external criteria against which the beginning teacher will be judged. There are long-standing debates about the impact of assessment on learners at all stages of education, the negatives of which are captured well by Reay and Wiliam's (1999) summary of year-six students' responses to (what were then) their Key Stage 2 National Curriculum tests: 'although children's responses are varied, what most share is a sense of an event which reveals something intrinsic about them as individuals' (p. 343). There are risks that the performative assessment processes beginning teachers undergo impact on their sense of themselves and their agency – negatively. In many of these chapters the Teachers' Standards (DfE, 2013) in England are given as an example of this external criteria. Some see positive aspects of the ways in which these kinds of standards might be used to facilitate professional development (of mentor and mentee), such as Bustin (2022), whereas others are more critical; for example, Healy and Walshe (2022) discuss the tensions between judgements and support through the concept of *judgementoring* (Hobson and Malderez, 2013). Formal accreditation for mentors, including through Masters-level work looking exclusively at teacher education (Childs, 2022), has an important role to play in building capacity across the system to support this challenging work.

Voice

Agency and voice are closely related concepts; agency might be demonstrated or enacted through voice. Being able to voice something is one example of the practice of agency. The discussion of agency above explored some of the tensions that mentors and beginning teachers need to navigate, arguing that increasing beginning teachers' sense and exercise of agency is an important aim of mentoring. The ways in which the chapters in this volume consider ideas about voice crosscut ideas of agency and justice, raising an important and enduring question to reflect on: *whose voices are shared, represented, spotlighted and engaged with in geography education?* The roles and spaces given to, and shaped by, the individual and collective voices of children, beginning teachers, mentors, subject communities, teacher educators, researchers and those of academic disciplines more broadly will have significant implications for the futures made possible through mentoring relationships, pedagogy and curriculum-making. In our brief reflection, we critically consider the range of voices given space in the chapters in this collection, and the need for geography education research and mentoring to foster inclusive, decolonial futures that actively encourage and attentively listen to a wide range of people.

This book includes beginning teachers' voices, including through Collins's (2022) examination of the value of beginning teachers' agency. Collins shows that by 'actively involving them in dialogue about their progress we can hear, in their own words, what they need from their mentors' (p. 88). When justice, agency and voice are considered together, mentors and teacher education more broadly can gain richer understandings of beginning teachers' experiences of, and perspectives on, teacher education. As Ahmed et al. (2022) explore, *who* is taught is vital to making decisions about curriculum, pedagogy and purpose. More broadly they argue that bringing colleagues (including those working in different spaces) together offers the potential to: 'develop shared values in education, to challenge one another's thinking, and to stimulate discussion as to how systems and praxis might be improved' (Ahmed et al., 2022, p. 159).

Within the discipline of geography, the range of voices that have been encouraged and allowed has been relatively limited, dominated by White (Esson, 2020) Anglo-American (Muller, 2021) perspectives. There have been increasing calls for the necessity of the debate that is academic geography to 'include voices, ideas, scholarship, and places in the world that have been under-represented in geography's publication venues over the years' (Daley et al. 2017, p. 3). Such calls for a more expansive conversation involve 'collecting and unpacking the full range of stories, voice, and experiences necessary for operationalizing anti-racist geography education' (Alderman et al., 2019, p. 2). This critique of academic geography adds further complexity to the calls made throughout this collection (Bustin, 2022; Healy, 2022) for mentors and beginning teachers to be engaged with the subject knowledge of geography. This is also complex because critiques of the discipline (Esson, 2020) show there are important figures that are now more widely questioned: names that may already have been taken down from lecture theatres and other places of honour and authority. For example, in his critical evaluation of the legacy of Halford Mackinder, Kearns (2021) argues that 'by the standards of his time, Mackinder was an enthusiastic imperialist and a resolute racist' (p. 4). The discipline is dynamic, and so only going back to a geography you once knew is – on its own – not enough (Healy, 2022). Decolonising the imperial, racist foundations of aspects of the discipline is an urgent task for all teachers to engage with, replacing colonial domination with more just, sustainable and, in Dorling's (2019) words, *kinder*, futures. Dorling – whose words bring particular symbolic power in this context as the current holder of the Halford Mackinder chair in Human Geography – has argued for *kindness* as a new kind of rigour for geography:

> Turning the lens back on yourself, on ourselves, and arguing for geography to become the kind discipline of the future is not a sign of weakness. We should always apologise; it shows we are still learning and that we know we still have so much to learn. The planet is now quickly warming; its people are hugely divided; Geography should be the academic subject of the kinder future to come. What was once the core of imperial domination can and should be turned inside-out and upside-down.
>
> (p. 7)

In conclusion...

This book has demonstrated that mentoring matters in and for geography education. It matters to beginning teachers' experiences and imaginations of teacher education, schooling, school geography and leadership. It matters to beginning teachers' well-being, workload and induction into *communities of practice* at a variety of scales. Mentoring also matters to mentors in their professional development and growth, and to schools' success and flourishing. Ultimately, mentoring beginning geography teachers matters to the children and young people who are taught, to their families and to society. This is important work!

In concluding this book, we have argued that *justice, agency* and *voice* are central ideas that we – as a geography education community – should engage with. Informed by ongoing engagement with research in geography and education, these ideas can support and inform active consideration of our question: *what kinds of futures do you hope your mentoring will produce?* As you put down this book and step back into the classroom, field, lab, staff room or geography office, we hope that you will draw on the ideas put forward in the chapters, and engage with the suggested *further reading* and *for discussion* questions to support the ongoing development of your *agency* and *voice* for more *just* tomorrows.

References

Ahmed, F., Hammond, L., Nichols, S., Puttick, S., and Searle, A., 2022. Planning in geography education: A conversation between university-based tutors and school-based mentors in Initial Teacher Education. In G. Healy, L. Hammond, S. Puttick and N. Walshe (eds), *Mentoring Geography Teachers in the Secondary School*. Abingdon: Routledge, 156-172.

Alderman, D., Perez, R. N., Eaves, L. E., Klein, P., and Muñoz, S., 2019. Reflections on operationalizing an anti-racism pedagogy: Teaching as regional storytelling. *Journal of Geography in Higher Education*, 45(2), 186-200.

Arthur, J., Kristjánsson, K., and Vogler, C., 2021. Seeking the common good in education through a positive conception of social justice. *British Journal of Educational Studies*, 69(1), 101-117.

Basit, T., and Roberts, L., 2006. *Tackling Racism in school Placements: Final Report to Multiverse*. London: Multiverse.

Benson, F. J., Grant Smith, N., and Flanagan, T., 2014. Easing the transition for queer student teachers from program to field: Implications for teacher education. *Journal of Homosexuality*, 61(3), 382-398.

Bhopal, K., 2015. Race, identity and support in initial teacher training. *British Journal of Educational Studies*, 63(2), 197-211.

Brown, G., and Browne, K., 2016. *The Routledge Companion to Geographies of Sex and Sexuality*. London: Routledge.

Bustin, R., 2022. Mentoring as a professional development opportunity. In G. Healy, L. Hammond, S. Puttick and N. Walshe (eds), *Mentoring Geography Teachers in the Secondary School*. Abingdon: Routledge, 75-87.

Carrington, B., and Tomlin, R., 2000. Towards a more inclusive profession: Teacher recruitment and ethnicity. *European Journal of Teacher Education*, 23(2), 139-157.

Castree, N., Fuller, D., and Lambert, D., 2007. Geography without borders. *Transactions of the Institute of British Geographers*, 32(2), 129-132.

Childs, A., 2022. Supporting the development of geography mentors – the potential of professional learning at Masters level. In G. Healy, L. Hammond, S. Puttick and N. Walshe (eds), *Mentoring Geography Teachers in the Secondary School*. Abingdon: Routledge, 119-134.

Clarke, E., Quickfall, A., and Thompson, S., 2022. Well-being: Theory and practice for beginning geography teachers. In G. Healy, L. Hammond, S. Puttick and N. Walshe (eds), *Mentoring Geography Teachers in the Secondary School*. Abingdon: Routledge, 224-240.

Collins, G., 2022. Mentoring that makes a difference: Perspectives from beginning teachers. In G. Healy, L. Hammond, S. Puttick and N. Walshe (eds), *Mentoring Geography Teachers in the Secondary School*. Abingdon: Routledge, 88-101.

Cordingley, P., Greany, T., Crisp, B., Seleznyov, S., Bradbury, M., and Perry, T., 2018. Developing great subject teaching: Rapid evidence review of subject-specific continuing professional development in the UK. Wellcome Trust. Available at: www.wellcome.ac.uk/sites/default/files/developing-great-subject-teaching.pdf [accessed 28 April 2021].

Daley, P., McCann, E., Mountz, A., and Painter, J., 2017. Re-imagining politics & space: Why here, why now? *Environment and Planning C: Politics and Space*, 35(1), 3-5.

Department for Education [DfE], 2013. Teachers' Standards Guidance for school leaders, school staff and governing bodies (Updated 2013). Available at: https://assets.publishing.service.gov.uk/government/uploads/system/uploads/attachment_data/file/665520/Teachers__Standards.pdf [accessed 15 April 2021].

Dorling, D., 2019. Kindness: A new kind of rigour for British geographers. *Emotion, Space and Society*, 33, 1-7. https://doi.org/10.1016/j.emospa.2019.100630.

Esson, J., 2020. "The why and the white": Racism and curriculum reform in British geography. *Area*, 52(4), 708-715.

Hammond, L., 2021. London, race and territories: Young people's stories of a divided city. *London Review of Education*, 19(1), 1-14. https://doi.org/10.14324/LRE.19.1.14.

Healy, G., 2022. Geography and geography education scholarship as a mechanism for developing and sustaining mentors' and beginning teachers' subject knowledge and curriculum thinking. In G. Healy, L. Hammond, S. Puttick and N. Walshe (eds), *Mentoring Geography Teachers in the Secondary School*. Abingdon: Routledge, 187-207.

Healy, G., and Walshe, N., 2022. Navigating the policy landscape: Conceptualising subject-specialist mentoring within and beyond policy. In G. Healy, L. Hammond, S. Puttick and N. Walshe (eds), *Mentoring Geography Teachers in the Secondary School*. Abingdon: Routledge, 13-30.

Henderson, H., 2017. Gender disproportionality in K-12 school superintendent positions. Doctoral dissertation, City University of Seattle.

Hobson, A. J., and Malderez, A., 2013. Judgementoring and other threats to realizing the potential of school-based mentoring in teacher education. *International Journal of Mentoring and Coaching in Education*, 2(2), 89-108.

Hodkinson, H., 2009. Improving schoolteachers' workplace learning. In S. Gewirtz, P. Mahony, I. Hextall and A. Cribb (eds), *Changing Teacher Professionalism: international Trends, Challenges and Ways Forward*. Abingdon: Routledge, 157-169.

hooks, b., 2003. *Teaching Community: A Pedagogy of Hope*. Abingdon: Routledge.

Hopkins, P., 2020. Social Justice III: Committing to social justice. *Progress in Human Geography*, 45(2), 382-393.

Institute of Physics, 2020. Subjects matter: a report from the Institute of Physics. Available at: www.iop.org/sites/default/files/2020-12/Subjects-Matter-IOP-December-2020.pdf [accessed 15 April 2021].

Jones, M., and Lambert, D., 2018. Introduction: The significance of continuing debates. In M. Jones and D. Lambert (eds), *Debates in Geography Education*. 2nd edn. Abingdon: Routledge, 1-14.

Kearns, G., 2021. Topple the Racists II: decolonising the space and institutional memory of geography. *Geography*, 106(1), 4-15.

Kinder, A., 2022. Mentoring within the geography subject community. In G. Healy, L. Hammond, S. Puttick and N. Walshe (eds), *Mentoring Geography Teachers in the Secondary School*. Abingdon: Routledge, 102-118.

Lave, J., and Wenger, E., 1991. *Situated Learning: Legitimate Peripheral Participation*. New York: Cambridge University Press.

Moreau, M. P., and Kerner, C., 2015. Care in academia: An exploration of student parents' experiences. *British Journal of Sociology of Education*, 36(2), 215-233.

Morgan, J., 2022. What sort of mentoring for what sort of geography education? In G. Healy, L. Hammond, S. Puttick and N. Walshe (eds), *Mentoring Geography Teachers in the Secondary School*. Abingdon: Routledge, 42-56.

Murtagh, L., 2019. Others and othering: The lived experiences of trainee teachers with parental responsibilities. *Journal of Further and Higher Education*, 43(6), 788-800.

Norcup, J., 2015. Awkward geographies? An historical and cultural geography of the journal Contemporary Issues in Geography and Education (CIGE) (1983-1991). PhD thesis, University of Glasgow.

Muller, M., 2021. Worlding geography: From linguistic privilege to decolonial anywheres. *Progress in Human Geography*, 1-27. DOI: 10.1177/0309132520979356.

Palombo, M., and Daly, C., 2022. Educative mentoring: A key to professional learning for geography teachers and mentors. In G. Healy, L. Hammond, S. Puttick and N. Walshe (eds), *Mentoring Geography Teachers in the Secondary School*. Abingdon: Routledge, 208-223.

Puttick, S., 2018. Student teachers' positionalities as knowers in school subject departments. *British Educational Research Journal*, 44(1), 25-42.

Puttick, S., and Murrey, A., 2020. Confronting the deafening silence on race in geography education in England: Learning from Anti-racist, decolonial and black geographies. *Geography*, 105(3), 126-134.

Puttick, S., 2022. Geography lesson observations at the interface between research and practice. In G. Healy, L. Hammond, S. Puttick and N. Walshe (eds), *Mentoring Geography Teachers in the Secondary School*. Abingdon: Routledge, 173-186.

Rawlings Smith, E., 2022. Mentoring meetings and conversations supporting beginning teachers in their development as geography teachers. In G. Healy, L. Hammond, S. Puttick and N. Walshe (eds), *Mentoring Geography Teachers in the Secondary School*. Abingdon: Routledge, 137-155.

Reay, D., and Wiliam, D., 1999. 'I'll be a nothing': Structure, agency and the construction of identity through assessment. *British Educational Research Journal*, 25(3), 343-354.

Sultana, F., 2021. Climate change, COVID-19, and the co-production of injustices: A feminist reading of overlapping crises. *Social & Cultural Geography*, 22(4), 447-460.

Tomlinson, S., 2019. *Education and Race: From Empire to Brexit*. Bristol: Policy Press.

INDEX

Note: Page numbers in **bold** indicate tables; those in *italics* indicate figures.

active listening 140, *140*, 146-147
activist mentor 47
adaptive teacher education expertise (model of ITE practice) *37*, *38*, *39*, 211-213
Adichie, C. N. 164
affective qualities, effective mentors 139
agency 7, 243-244, 246-249; geography and geography education scholarship 202; geography subject community 113, 114; mentees' perspectives 88, 90; spatial practice 38
Ahmed, F. 245, 248
Alderman, D. 248
Aldridge, D. 175
Alexander, R. 114, 153
Ali, R. 201
Allen, G. 72
Allsop, T. 132-133
Ambition Institute 21
Anthropocene 43, 44, 82
apprenticeship model of mentoring 1
approachability, effective mentors 139
Arthur, J. 244
assemblage theory 200
assessing beginning teachers: agency 247; policy landscape 15, 16
attrition rates in teaching 59; and well-being 225, 226
autonomy 48; planning 166, 168; spatial practice 38

Balderstone, D. 195
Ball, S. J. 13-14
Barnett, E. 215

Barnett, J. 122
Barthes, R. 13
behaviour management 62, 65
Bell, J. 137
Benko, G. 44
Benson, A. 132-133
Bergviken Rensfeldt, A. 230
Bernstein, B. 4, 104, 144, 159, **199**
Bhopal, K. 245
Biddulph, M. 92, 157, 188, 195
Biesta, G. 36, 202
Birnie, J. 230
Black Lives Matter 43, 44, 212
blogs: geography subject community 106; as liminal space 89
Bonnett, A. 45
Bowe, R. 13
Boyd, P. 184
Braun, A. 14
Brookfield, S. 142-143, 146-147, 148, 153
Brooks, C. 3-4, 16, 24, 40, 75, 81, 99, 104, 130, 187, 189, 200, 203
Brown, G. 246
Browne, K. 246
Bull, B. 188
Burn, K. 4, 19, 23, 26, 165, 187, 191-192, 195
Burnett, C. 60
burnout 226
Bustin, R. 82, 137, 247
Butt, G. 45, 78

Cajkler, W. 68-69, 72, 84
career development 61, 78

Carr, D. 226
Carson, R. 44
Carter review of Initial Teacher Training 17, 18-19, 137
case for subject mentoring 2-3
Catling, S. 203
causal assumptions 147
certainty, and observation 174-175
Chabris, C. 178
challenges: and resources, relationship to well-being 228-230, *228-229*; and support, balancing 139-140, *139*, 152
change, capacity to (model of ITE practice) *37*, 38, 39
Childs, A. 3
Chizhik, A. W. 157
Chizhik, E. W. 157
Clarke, E. 235, 244
Claxton, G. 138
climate change 82, 244
coaching: instructional 21, **21**; meetings 145-146; and mentoring, distinction between 1; professional practice and development 63; well-being 232
Coburn, C. 113, 231
Cochran, K. F. 122
Cochran-Smith, M. 122, 124, 129, 209
cognitive maps 49, *50*
cognitive qualities, effective mentors 139
Coldwell, M. 60
collaboration: educative mentoring 208-216, 219-220; effective mentors 139; geography subject community 102, 106, 107, 111-112; professional development of mentors 76, 77-78; well-being 231
Colley, H. 1
Collins, G. 78, 248
colonialism: development 212-214; experiences of geography education 180-181
communities of practice: geography subject community 107, 112, 113; justice 245; networked teacher mentor 47; planning 159; professional development of mentors 77; well-being 231-232
competency model of mentoring 1
Connell, R. 36
content knowledge 188, **189**
continuing professional development *see* professional practice and development

Corbridge, A. **193-194**
Core Content Framework 145-146
Counsell, C. 188
counselling 62-63
Cousin, G. 88-89, 96, 99
COVID-19 pandemic 52; economic crisis 43, 44; justice 244; Ofsted Initial Teacher Education Inspection Framework 22; school experience suspended 94; spatial practice 34
Creswell, T. 196
crises 43-45
Croel-Perrien, A. 221-222
cultivation stage of mentoring 60
cultural crises 43-45
curricular theorising 198, **199**
curriculum artefacts 167
curriculum leadership 188-189
curriculum making: educative mentoring 213-214; geography and geography education scholarship 188, 189-191, 197, 202
curriculum map 168
curriculum policy context 196-197
curriculum thinking: educative mentoring 211; geography and geography education scholarship 188-189, 195; planning 163, 167-169

Daley, P. 180, 248
Daly, C. 3, 35, 195, 208, 246
Dawes, L. 20
debriefing *see* feedback
decolonising geography: teachers' work 248
Decolonising Geography Educators Group 201
decolonising the curriculum: educative mentoring 212-214; geography and geography education scholarship 200-201, 202; observation 180-181
decolonising geography: teachers' work 248
Deleuze, G. 200
Deng, Z. 149
Department for Education (DfE): attrition rates in teaching 59; case for subject mentoring 3; COVID-19 pandemic 94; curriculum policy context 197; Early Career Framework 35, 59; Initial Teacher Training Core Content Framework 35; policy landscape 18-19, 20, 21, 26n2; well-being 224, 225, 235
development: collaborative planning 212-216; professional *see* professional practice and development

Dewey, J. 76, 141, 216
dialogue: attention to 140, *140*, 148-152, **149**; educative mentoring 210-211, 214, 216-219, 220; effective mentors 139
Dinkelman, T. 125, 129
directive feedback **145**
diversity: geography and geography education scholarship 191; lesson planning 163
Dodge, R. 227
Dorling, D. 156, 248
Drabble, M. 43
Drew, T. 178-179
dropout rates *see* attrition rates in teaching
Dudley, R. 107
Dunphy, A. 185

Early Career Framework (ECF) 17, 20-22, **21**; case for subject mentoring 2-3; geography subject community 105; instructional coaching 145-146; professional practice and development 59, 64, 68; spatial practice 35; well-being 225
economic crises 43, 44, 45
Education Development Trust 21
Education Endowment Foundation 60
educative mentoring 6-7, 208, 221-222; agency 246; collaborative marking 219-220, *219*; collaborative planning 212-216; Early Career Framework **21**, 22; expansive learning environment 211-212, 246; geography and geography education scholarship 195; observations and post-lesson dialogue 216-217; principles and characteristics *209*, 209-211; professional development of mentors 76, 83; spatial practice 35
Ellis, V. 198
Ellsworth, E. 89
Enser, M. 82
environmental crises 43, 44
epistemic identity 138
Eraut, M. 143
Esson, J. 201, 203
ethical issues: Masters in Teacher Education 128; observation 177
evaluating beginning teachers *see* assessing beginning teachers
Evans, M. D. 72
evidence-based learning 46

expansive learning environment **211**, 211-212, 216, 246
expectations of mentor relationships 60
extended mentoring 24-25

Farver, S. 221-222
Feagin, J. 44
feedback: approaches **145**; dialogue, attention to 149; educative mentoring 216-217; meetings 145, 151, 152; mentees' perspective 91-97; mentor reflection 81; observation 173-185; planning 158-159, 166; well-being 233
Feiman-Nemser, S. 76, 208, 216-217
Field Studies Council 91
field trips and fieldwork: mentees' perspective 90-92; planning 163; professional practice and development 61-62; well-being 230
Finn, M. 200-201
Firth, R. 179, 190
Fordham, M. 24, 188
Freire, P. 47
Friedrichsen, P. 215
Fuller, A. 211
Furlong, J. 1, 2
future, facing the 49-52

Gargani, J. 176
GeoCapabilities 83, 84, 161, 190, **193**, **194**
Geoghegen, H. 195
Geographical Association (GA) 45; curriculum policy context 197; *Geography* journal **193-194**; geography subject community 103-104, 107, **108**, **109**, **110**, 112, 113; Geography Teacher Educator e-newsletter 113; *Handbook for Secondary Geography* 45; issues and challenges in geography teacher education 120; knowledge development **193**; planning 167-168; policy landscape 19, 22; racism 45; Subject Audit tool 167-168; *Teaching Geography* 113, 198
geographical imaginations 214
geographical information systems (GIS) 79
geography and geography education scholarship 6, 187, 202-203; disciplinary dimension of geography rendered visible by 198-199; engagement within curriculum policy context 196-197; situating beginning teachers' practice

and illuminating other teachers' curricular theorising and problem-solving 198, **199**; subject expertise and curriculum making 189–190, **190**; subject knowledge and curriculum thinking 188–189, **189**; sustaining subject expertise 191–196, **193–194**

geography subject community 5–6, 102–103, 114–115; connecting mentees with their 111–113; development of subject knowledge 105–11, **108–109, 110**; significance of subject knowledge 103–105; well-being 233

Geography Teacher Educator 107, **108**

Gibbs, G. 142

Glazzard, J. 235

Global Education Reform Movement 35

global financial crisis (2008) 43, 44

globalisation 43

goals *see* targets

Grant, A. 230

Gregory, D. 50

groupthink 113

Gu, Q. 221

Guatarri, F. 200

Guenther, A. 221–222

guiding feedback **145**

Hagger, H. 24

Hall, S. 49

Hammond, L. 88, 90, 91, 133, **199**

Hand, M. 180

Harpaz, Y. 168

Harvey, D. 3, 33, 40, 42, 45, 49, 50–52, 53

Hattie, J. 46

Hawley, D. **194**

Hayward, G. 123, 124

Healy, G. 16, 22, 24, 112, 180, 185, 195, 198–200, **199**, 202, 245, 246–247

Henderson, H. 245

Heraclitus 64

Heron, M. 89

higher education institutions (HEIs): geography subject community 102, 107; knowledge development **193**; Masters in Teacher Education 119–133; policy landscape 19; professional development of mentors 77–78; well-being 225

Hoadley, U. 190–191

Hobson, A. J. 15, 16, 21, 216

Hodkinson, H. 211, 216, 246

Hodson, D. 122

honesty 94

hooks, b. 157, 159, 170, 243

Hope, J. 200

Hopkins, P. 244

Hordern, J. 190–191, 196

Horton, J. 230

Hoyle, E. 48

Huckle, J. 42, 45

Hudson, P. 75, 76, 77, 79, 81, 84, 177, 181

Huling, L. 75, 76, 78, 81

humour 94

ideologies 82

imitation 62

Independent Teacher Review Groups 225

Ingvarson, L. 35

Initial Teacher Training Core Content Framework 35, 225

initiation stage of mentoring 60

inquiry-as-stance 210

inquiry community 125–126, 128, 129, 131

Institute of Physics 25, 245

instructional coaching 21, **21**

John, P. D. 48, 158, 160

Johnston, D. 231, 232

Jones, M. 123

judgementoring 15, 16, 216, 247

justice 7, 243–249

Kagan, D. M. 93

Kaplan, D. 138, 139

Kearns, G. 248

Kemmis, S. 1, 34

Kennedy, C. **199**

Kinder, A. 20, 22, 23, 114, 233

Klein, N. 42, 146, 148

knowledge-focussed mentor 47

knowledge-for-practice 210

knowledge-in-practice 210

knowledge-of-practice 209–210, 214, 215, 217, 220, 221

Kolb, D. A. 141–142

Kram, K. E. 60–61

Lacey, C. 108
Lambert, D. 80, 161, 179, 188, 190, 191, 195, 200, 212
Land, R. 89, 95
Langdon, F. 16, 24-25, 208, 221
Last, A. 201, 203
Lave, J. 142, 198
leadership 78
learning: conversations 149-152; cycle *140*, 142; educative mentoring 209-210; expansive environment **211**, 211-212, 216, 246; processual model 67; restrictive environment **211**, 211; situated 142; teacher educators 123-125, 128-129; through enquiry 149-151, *150*
learning walks 94-95
Lefebvre, H. 33
Leshem, S. 88
lesson observation *see* observation
Lesson Study 84; observation 183; professional development of mentors 77; professional practice and development 66, 68-69
Levinson, M. 43
LGBTQ+-identifying teachers 245
liminal space 88-89, 93
listening, attention to 140, *140*, 146-147
local authorities: geography subject community 107; policy enactment 14
location within space 32, 33-34, 37
Lock, R. 181-182
Lofthouse, R. M. 16, 68
Lortie, D. C. 36
Loughran, J. J. 122, 125, 128, 129
Lytle, S. 209

Mackinder, H. 248
Malderez, A. 15, 16, 216
Male, T. 122-123, 126
Margolis, J. 226
marking, collaborative 219-220, *219*
Marsden, B. 80-82
Martin, S. 139
Marxism 33, 49
Masters in Teacher Education 6, 77, 119, 132-133; aims 125; history and development 121; issues and challenges in geography teacher education 120-121; knowledge base of teacher educators 121-123; learning process 123-125; potential to development mentors' practice 129-132; Reflection and Activity portfolios (RAPs) 126-127, 128, 130; structure and rationale 125-129
Matthews, A. 198
Mayer, D. 35
Maynard, T. 1, 2
McEwan, H. 188
McIntyre, D. 14, 24
McIntyre, J. 3-4
Mcnally, P. 139
meetings 6, 137-138, 152-153; aspects of 140-153; effective mentors, qualities of 138-140, *138*, *139*; mentees' perspective 93; planning 168; structuring 151-152; well-being 233
mental health *see* well-being
mentees' perspectives 5, 88-99; threshold concepts and liminal space 88-89
Menter, I. 26
mentor meetings *see* meetings
Merriam, T. 42, 43
Merrifield, A. 48, 49, 53
Meyer, J. H. F. 89, 95
Mills, M. 35
Milner, C. 198, **199**, 202
Milton, E. 208
Mitchell, D. 133, 191, 197
modelling: educative mentoring 210, 215; geography subject community 112, 113; mentees' perspective 92; planning 166; professional development of mentors 76; professional practice and development 62; well-being 233
Morgan, J. 3, 49, 161, 179, 188, 190-191, 200, 212, 243
Muis, K. R. 178
Muller, J. 81, 190
Murray, J. 122-123, 126
Murrey, A. 197, 200, 201
Murtagh, L. 20, 245
Mutton, T. 4, 19, 26, 165
Myatt, M. 160, 168

Nairn, K. 230
National Curriculum: geographical information systems (GIS) 79; geography and geography education scholarship 196

National Standards for school-based initial teacher training mentors 17, 19-20; effective mentors, qualities of 138; geography subject community 104, 105, 112
National Strategies: observation 177; professional practice and development 59
Nayak, A. 45
neoliberalism 19, 44, 48, 52
networked teacher mentor 47-48
non-directive feedback 145, **145**
Norcup, J. 243
Norman, P. J. 208, 216-217
Norton, J. 84
noticing, attention to 140, *140*, 143-146
Noxolo, P. 201

observation 6, 173, 183-185; educative mentoring 215, 216-218; effective mentors 139; Masters in Teacher Education 128; mentees' perspective 93, 94-95, 97; noticing, attention to 140, *140*, 143-146; planning 164-166; power and knowledge 173-176, *174*; pro formas 181-183, **182**
Odell, S. J. 208
Office for Standards in Education, Children's Services and Skills *see* Ofsted
Ofqual 197
Ofsted: Education Inspection Framework 105; geography subject community 105; Initial Teacher Education Inspect Framework 17, 22-23, 24; observation 177; policy enactment 14; professional practice and development 64; well-being 225
ONSIDE mentoring 21, **21**
Opfer, D. 141
Orchard, J. 144
Oxford Internship Scheme (OIS) 123
Oxford University, Masters in Teacher Education 121-132
Ozga, J. 14

Palombo, M. 3, 4, 35, 76, 80, 105, 120-1, 133, 195, 246
paradigmatic assumptions 147
pedagogic literacy 60, 68-69, *70*
Pedder, D. 84, 141
Peiser, G. 20
personal benefits of mentoring 78

personal qualities, effective mentors 139
Piaget, J. 142
Pillen, M. 227, 233
planning 6, 156-159, 169-170; collaborative 212-216; conversation between tutors and mentors 159-169; curriculum thinking 163, 167-169; for 'delivery' and connecting with children's geographies 161-164, *162*; educative mentoring 212-216; observation and structure 164-166; pro formas 161; questioning the purposes and (mis)uses of 160-161
platform capitalism 48
policy 5, 13, 25; complexity of mentoring 23-25; curriculum 196-197; enactment 13-14; geography subject community 104-105; key English policies (2015-2020) 17-23, *17*; professional development context 14-17; spatial practice 35, 38
political economy 44
positivism 49
post-lesson dialogue 216-218; *see also* feedback
practical theorising 123, 124, 127-128, 129, 131
practice: and policy, relationship between 13-14, 17; and research, relationship between 187; role of 3-4; and theory, connecting with 159
prescriptive assumptions 147
prescriptive feedback 145, **145**
Priestley, M. 202
process model for practice development and mentoring 66-69, *70*
process philosophy 64-65
processual complexity 64-69
professional competency: effective mentors 139; professional development of mentors 75-76
professional identity of mentors 75, 76, 81, 83
professional practice and development 5, 59-60, 71; agency 247; basic features of mentoring approaches 60-64; case studies 61-62, 63, 70-71; critique 48-49; geography subject community 111; justice 245; Masters in Teacher Education 119-133; mentoring as opportunity for 5, 75-84; observation 177, 182; planning 157; policy landscape 14-17, 23-24; process model 66-71; processual complexity 64-66; *see also* educative mentoring
professional relationships, and well-being 230-232, 234

psychosocial development 62-63
Puttick, S. 16, 66, 158, 159, 173, 174, 175, 177, 178, 179, 184-185, 191, 192, 197, **199**, 200, 201, 234
Pylman, S. 221-222

Quickfall, A. 235

race and racism 43-45; discipline of geography 180-181; educative mentoring 212; geography and geography education scholarship 197, 200-203; justice 243, 245; voice 248
radical geography 47
Rawding, C. **199**
Rawling, E. 45, 82, 196, 197, 200
Rawlings Smith, E. 77, 80, 106, 111, 153, 183
Reay, D. 247
reciprocity 48; dialogue 148, 149; effective mentors 138, **138**; geography subject community 112; reflective practice 76
recruitment 79
redefinition stage of mentoring 60-61
reflective cycle *142*, 142
reflective knowledge 46
reflective practice 1; active listening 147; educative mentoring 215, 216, 217, 220; effective mentors 138, **138**, 139, 140; geography and geography education scholarship 189, 191, 195; subject community 103, 105, 111-112, 113; instructional coaching 146; learning through enquiry 149-151, *150*; Masters in Teacher Education 125, 127, 128, 130, 131-132; meetings 140-143, *140*, *142*, **143**, 145; mentees' perspective 94; observation 174, 179, 183; planning 160; professional development of mentors 76, 81, 82; well-being 226, 230-234
relationships, and well-being 230-232, 234
relative space 32-37
representational space 32, 33, 36, 37
Rescher, N. 64
research: geography and geography education scholarship 187; Masters in Teacher Education 129, 131; meetings 151; and practice, relationship between 187; role of 4, 169
research schools 59-60
resilience, effective mentors 138, **138**, 226
resourcefulness, effective mentors 138, **138**

resources and challenges, relationship to well-being 228-230, *228-229*
respect, and observation 175
restrictive learning environment **211**, 211
Richards, C. 64
risk-taking behaviour 98
Roberts, M. 80, 138, 149, 160, 179, 180, 190
Robinson, S. 202
Rodgers, C. 141
Roffey, S. 225-226, 233
role modelling *see* modelling
Rose, G. 201
Routes: The Journal for Student Geographers 167, **193**
Rowe, J. 22
Royal Geographical Society with Institute of British Geographers (RGS-IBG): curriculum policy context 197; geography subject community 107, **108**, **109**, 113; knowledge development 192, **193**; planning 167; Race, Culture and Equality (RACE) working group 201
Royal Meteorological Society (RMetS) **193**
Royal Scottish Geographical Society (RSGS) 107, 113

Sahlberg, P. 35
Scapp, R. 157, 159
Scholten, N. 144
school benefits of mentoring 78-80
School-Centred Initial Teacher Training (SCITT) 14, 19
Scott, A. 44
Scottish Association of Geography Teachers (SAGT) 107, 113
self-efficacy 48
self-reflection *see* reflective practice
self-study 125, 128, 129, 131
separation stage of mentoring 60
sharing-exchanging relationships, geography subject community 106
Sherin, M. G. 144
Shoyer, S. 88
Shulman, L. S. 121-122, 128, 144, 188
Simons, D. 178
Sirna, K. 16
situated knowledge (model of ITE practice) 37-38, *37*, 39
Smith, N. 33

Smith, P. 83
Soares, A. 181-182
social acceptance 62
social capital: geography subject community 106-107; well-being 233
social learning theory 231
social media: geography subject community 106; networked teacher mentor 47; social support 230
sociality, effective mentors 139
spatial practice 5, 31; location within space 33-34; model of ITE practice 37-39; production of space 33; reasons for seeing mentoring through a spatial lens 31-32; relative space 34-36; representational space 36
Standish, A. 82, 212
Stanulis, R. N. 137, 217, 220, 221-222
Stein, M. 231
Straker, K. 123
Strong, M. 176-177, 179
subject community *see* geography subject community
Sultana, F. 244
support and challenge, balancing 139-140, *139*, 152
supporting relationships, and well-being 230-232, 234
supportive feedback **145**
Sustainable Development Goals (SDGs) 200

Tapsfield, A. 24, 26, 75, 76, 78-79, 112, 114-115, 120
targets: educative mentoring 217; meetings 151; mentees' perspective 96; planning 165
Taylor, L. 192, **193-194**, **199**
Teach First 21, **21**
Teachers' Standards 35, 36, 138; agency 247; vs dialogic repertoires 148; professional development of mentors 77; subject knowledge 188; well-being 225
Teaching Schools Council 20
theory: connecting with practice 159; Masters in Teacher Education 128; planning 164; role of 3-4, 49-52
Thinking Environments 146, **147**, 148
Thompson, S. 235
threshold concepts 88-89, 92, 95, 96, 97, 99
Tomlinson, S. 156

Tooth, S. 201
Trolley, S. 198, **199**
trust 94, 97, 106, 107
Tucker, F. 230
typology of mentors 5, 46; activist mentor 47; evidence-based learning 46; knowledge-focussed mentor 47; networked teacher mentor 47-48; reflective knowledge 46

University College London (UCL): Early Career Teacher Consortium 21, **21**; Institute of Education (IOE) 77
University of Reading **193**
Unwin, L. 211

van Velzen, C. 124
Vernon, E. **199**
Viles, H. A. 201
vlogs 106
voice 7, 243-244, 247-248; mentees' perspectives 88-99
Vonk, J. H. C. 123

Walshe, N. 79, 144, 185, 247
Wang, J. 208
Ward, A. 221-222
Ward, L. 221
Warren-Lee, N. 158, 159, 179, 185
Weare, K. 226
Webb, R. 228
well-being 7, 224, 234-235; defining 226-227; justice 244-246; nature of 224-227; in practice 232-234; resources and challenges 228-230, *228-229*; supporting relationships, importance of 230-232
Wenger, E. 142, 198
Wenger-Trayner, B. 231
Wenger-Trayner, E. 231
Wexler, L. J. 221-222
Wheeler, K. 44
White, K. 221-222
Whitehead, A. N. 67, 68, 69, 72
Wiliam, D. 247
Willy, T. 203
Winch, C. 144
Winter, C. 192, **193-194**, 197
Witham Bednarz, S. 120

Wood, P. 68-69, 72, 77, 84, 89, 93, 149
Woodhouse, J. 149
Wooldridge, S. W. 80
Wynn, J. 158, 174, 184-185

Young, M. 25, 47, 81, 104, 189, 190
Yusoff, K. 156

Zeichner, K. 119, 121, 123

For Product Safety Concerns and Information please contact our EU representative GPSR@taylorandfrancis.com
Taylor & Francis Verlag GmbH, Kaufingerstraße 24, 80331 München, Germany

www.ingramcontent.com/pod-product-compliance
Lightning Source LLC
Chambersburg PA
CBHW080118020526
44112CB00037B/2778